IGNATIUS OF ANTIOCH
and the
PARTING OF THE WAYS

IGNATIUS
OF ANTIOCH
and the
PARTING OF
THE WAYS

Early
Jewish-Christian
Relations

THOMAS A. ROBINSON

HENDRICKSON
PUBLISHERS

Ignatius of Antioch and the Parting of the Ways: Early Jewish-Christian Relations
© 2009 by Hendrickson Publishers Marketing, LLC
P.O. Box 3473
Peabody, Massachusetts 01961-3473

ISBN: 978-1-59856-323-8

Printed in the United States of America

First Printing — September 2009

Cover art: Romanized Christ as Good Shepherd. Fresco (1st–3rd C.E.) from the Catacombs of Saint Priscilla, Rome, Italy.
Photo Credit: Erich Lessing / Art Resource, N.Y.

Hendrickson Publishers is strongly committed to environmentally responsible printing practices. The pages of this book were printed on 30% postconsumer waste recycled stock using only soy or vegetable content inks.

Library of Congress Cataloging-in-Publication Data

Robinson, Thomas A. (Thomas Arthur), 1951–
    Ignatius of Antioch and the parting of the ways : early Jewish-Christian relations / by Thomas A. Robinson.
        p. cm.
    Includes bibliographical references and indexes.
    ISBN 978-1-59856-323-8 (alk. paper)
    1. Antioch (Turkey)—Church history. 2. Judaism (Christian theology)—History of doctrines. 3. Christianity and other religions—Judaism.
    4. Judaism—Relations—Christianity. 5. Ignatius, Saint, Bishop of Antioch, d. ca. 110. I. Title.
    BR1085.A58R63 2009
    270.1—dc22
                                2009009160

DEDICATION

for grandson David,
contagious with joy

Contents

Preface

Ignatius is a man most famous for dying. What we know about him comes almost entirely from letters he wrote as he was on his way to martyrdom, with full knowledge that he had only a few weeks left to live. Not surprising, much of his reflection turns to dying, but his thoughts turn to other matters too. From such material, scholars have tried to reconstruct the wider environment in which Ignatius lived and to determine Ignatius's religious perspective and his place within the Christian community. Nothing like a full biography of Ignatius has been written, nor could it be.

My effort here is not to provide as complete a study of Ignatius as is possible. Many questions I leave untouched. But I do wish to stir the pot a little, largely by challenging some widely held views of Ignatius and his world and by asking a few new questions or by answering old questions in a slightly different way. In doing so, a few larger issues come into focus: in particular, the make-up of early Christian assemblies and the coming to distinctive identity of the Christian movement, or what has come to be called *the parting of the ways*.

Ignatius's language against Judaism is sharp, sweeping, uncompromisingly dismissive, and perhaps even shameful. Scholars sometimes attempt to redirect this language so that it is solely against Christian Judaizing elements in Ignatius's church and not against Judaism as a whole, but such efforts obscure the historical grit and grime inherent in the turbulent conflicts out of which new religious movements come into being. Ignatius's language and attitudes reflect the intensity of a powerful change in religious perception, and it is within that world that Ignatius lived and acted and makes sense. Present efforts to build bridges between Judaism and Christianity are not helped by attempts to sanitize the past. We are not responsible for what Ignatius said nor is he responsible for how we use what he said. To quote Brent Shaw, a former colleague of mine:

> But what the sources record is, for better or for worse, what the sources record. A good part of what they record, certainly, is made up of systematic and successful repressions, but tinkering with the moral balance of the past is a disservice to the study of history and to the reform of society. The past is dead. We cannot change it. What we can change is the future; but the way to a better future requires an unsentimental and accurate understanding of what happened in the past, and why. A

more civil and humane modernity will not be achieved by tendentious misreadings of antiquity."[1]

My effort here is to understand Ignatius's world. If that helps us understand our own, so much the better. I will not be disappointed, however, if my work simply helps us understand a bit more clearly some aspects of Ignatius's distant world.

The *New Revised Standard Version* has been used for English translations of the Bible. Various translations of Ignatius's letters and the Apostolic Fathers have been used. Unless otherwise indicated, Bart Ehrman's translation of *The Apostolic Fathers* in the Loeb Classical Library is used.[2] Sometimes Kirsopp Lake's 1912 translation in the Loeb series,[3] which Ehrman's work replaces, offers the better translation, and Michael W. Holmes's revision[4] of the classic translation by J. B. Lightfoot and J. R. Harmer is always worth consulting.

---

[1] Brent Shaw, "A Groom of One's Own," *The New Republic* (July 18, 1994): 41.

[2] *The Apostolic Fathers* (ed. and trans. Bart D. Ehrman; LCL 24–25; Cambridge, Mass.: Harvard University Press, 2003).

[3] *The Apostolic Fathers* (ed. and trans. Kirsopp Lake; LCL; Cambridge, Mass: Harvard University Press, 1912).

[4] Michael W. Holmes, ed. and trans., *The Apostolic Fathers: Greek Texts and English Translations* (Grand Rapids: Baker Academic, 2007).

Abbreviations

General

B.C.E.	before the common era
C.E.	common era
ca.	circa
cf.	compare
ch(s).	chapter(s)
diss.	dissertation
e.g.	*exempli gratia,* for example
ed(s).	edition(s); editor(s)
esp.	especially
et al.	*et alii,* and others
etc.	*et cetera*
i.e.	*id est,* that is
ibid.	*ibidem,* in the same place
idem	the same
intro.	introduction
n.	note
no.	number
p(p).	page(s)
repr.	reprinted
trans.	translated by, translator(s)
vol(s).	volume(s)

Biblical Books

Dan	Daniel
Matt	Matthew
Rom	Romans
1–2 Cor	1–2 Corinthians
Gal	Galatians

Eph	Ephesians
Phil	Philippians
Col	Colossians
1–2 Thess	1–2 Thessalonians
1–2 Tim	1–2 Timothy
Phlm	Philemon
Heb	Hebrews
Jas	James
1–2 Pet	1–2 Peter
Rev	Revelation

Primary Sources

Papyri

P.Lond.	*Greek Papyri in the British Museum* (London: British Museum, 1893–)

Apostolic Fathers

Barn.	*Barnabas*
1 Clem.	*1 Clement*
Did.	*Didache*
Herm. Mand.	*Shepherd of Hermas, Mandate(s)*
Herm. Sim.	*Shepherd of Hermas, Similitude(s)*
Herm. Vis.	*Shepherd of Hermas, Vision(s)*
Ign. Eph.	Ignatius, *To the Ephesians*
Ign. Magn.	Ignatius, *To the Magnesians*
Ign. Phld.	Ignatius, *To the Philadelphians*
Ign. Pol.	Ignatius, *To Polycarp*
Ign. Rom.	Ignatius, *To the Romans*
Ign. Smyrn.	Ignatius, *To the Smyrnaeans*
Ign. Trall.	Ignatius, *To the Trallians*
Pol. Phil.	Polycarp, *To the Philippians*

Other Ancient Writings

Dio Cassius	
Hist. rom.	*Historia romana*
Eusebius	
Hist. eccl.	*Historia ecclesiastica*

Irenaeus
  Haer. *Adversus haereses*
Josephus
  Ag. Ap. *Against Apion*
  Ant. *Jewish Antiquities*
  J.W. *Jewish War*
Justin
  1–2 Apol. *1–2 Apology*
  Dial. *Dialogue with Trypho*
Origen
  Cels. *Contra Celsum*
Pausanias
  Descr. *Graeciae descriptio*
Philo
  Flaccus *Against Flaccus*
Pliny the Younger
  Ep. *Epistulae*
Strabo
  Geogr. *Geographica*
Tacitus
  Ann. *Annales*
  Hist. *Historiae*

Secondary Sources

BAR	*Biblical Archaeology Review*
BHT	Beiträge zur historischen Theologie
BJS	Brown Judaic Studies
CBQ	*Catholic Biblical Quarterly*
CRINT	Compendia rerum iudaicarum ad Novum Testamentum
HTR	*Harvard Theological Review*
JBL	*Journal of Biblical Literature*
JECS	*Journal of Early Christian Studies*
JEH	*Journal of Ecclesiastical History*
JRS	*Journal of Roman Studies*
JSNT	*Journal for the Study of the New Testament*
JSNTSup	Journal for the Study of the New Testament: Supplement Series
JTS	*Journal of Theological Studies*
NovT	*Novum Testamentum*

NTS	*New Testament Studies*
OrChrAn	Orientalia christiana analecta
SBEC	Studies in the Bible and Early Christianity
SCJ	Studies in Christianity and Judaism
SecCent	*Second Century*
SNTSMS	Society for New Testament Studies Monograph Series
SR	*Studies in Religion*
TAPA	*Transactions of the American Philological Association*
TSAJ	Texte und Studien zum antiken Judentum
VC	*Vigiliae christianae*
WUNT	Wissenschaftliche Untersuchungen zum Neuen Testament

CHAPTER 1

———⊰⊱⊰———

Antioch: The City and Its People

Ignatius

The Life and Times—a well-worn but appropriate enough title for the biography of most characters of note from the past. But not so for Ignatius of Antioch, famous bishop and early Christian martyr. We know almost nothing about Ignatius's life. We do not know when or where he was born and in what cultural context he was raised. The best guess is that he grew up in Antioch in a pagan home, but he could have been born and raised in any Greek city,[1] and it is possible, although perhaps unlikely, that he was raised as a Christian.[2] We know nothing about his family, whether he was married, and at what occupation he worked for

---

[1] Ignatius's language is Greek. Many scholars think that urbanism and the Greek language went hand in hand, with native languages having the monopoly of the countryside. But the sharp distinction between the urban and the rural has perhaps been overstated in terms of language and of culture more broadly, for the lines between city and countryside were often somewhat ambiguous. City and country were interwoven in a way that prevents definition of neat boundaries. Andrew Wallace-Hadrill calls attention to the tendencies in modern scholarship to reject older theories of stark divisions between town and country (Introduction to *City and Country in the Ancient World* [ed. John Rich and Andrew Wallace-Hadrill; Leicester-Nottingham Studies in Ancient Society 2; New York: Routledge, 1991], ix). See also Robin Lane Fox, *Pagans and Christians* (New York: Alfred A. Knopf, 1987), 40–46. Further, the effort to specify the characteristics of an ancient Greek city often depends on Pausanias's list of urban features: theater, agora, gymnasium, government buildings, fountain (*Descr.* 10.4.1), but Pausanias probably captures the ideal rather than the reality. John D. Grainger raises relevant questions about the varied use of the term *polis* (*The Cities of Seleukid Syria* [Oxford: Clarendon, 1990], 63–65).

[2] There probably were fourth-generation Christians in Antioch at the time of Ignatius. The church was established there in the first decade of the Christian movement, about seventy-five years before Ignatius. Speculation about Ignatius's childhood and religious upbringing is, however, unproductive. A story that he was the child whom Jesus blessed (Mark 9:36) circulated in the ancient period, but it looks like the stuff of legend. Most serious reconstructions of Ignatius depend almost entirely on what we can glean from the seven letters Ignatius wrote in the last weeks of his life. These provide no glimpses of childhood memories or even reflections on his conversion and Christian life. Ignatius is God's dying disciple; it is martyrdom about to be grasped that marks almost all of Ignatius's personal reflections.

most of his life.[3] Nor do we know how old he was when he died or why he died a condemned criminal of the Roman justice system. Indeed, even the most common title by which Ignatius is identified, "bishop of Antioch,"[4] raises questions about whether he was, in fact, the bishop in any meaningful sense and, if he was, how he came to that position in Antioch[5] and how long he had been a member of the Christian assembly there and held the chief office.[6] Christine Trevett captures this paucity of evidence: "Ignatius of Antioch, bishop, letter-writer and martyr, appears on the scene like Melchizedek . . . without father, mother, genealogy or beginning of days."[7] In similar vein, J. B. Lightfoot speaks of the "pitchy darkness" surrounding Ignatius's life and work.[8]

We must not despair too much because of these large gaps in our knowledge of Ignatius's life. To only a slightly lesser degree, we encounter such scarcity of information regarding most of the notable characters of the earliest Christian centuries.[9] Even about leading individuals such as Paul, whose writings are often

---

[3] Harald Riesenfeld ("Reflections on the Style and Theology of St. Ignatius of Antioch," in *Papers Presented to the Third International Conference on Patristic Studies Held at Christ Church, Oxford, 1959* [ed. F. L. Cross; 4 vols.; Studia patristica 3–6; Texte und Untersuchungen zur Geschichte der altchristlichen Literatur 78–81; Berlin: Akademie, 1961–1962], 2:317) has suggested that Ignatius perhaps had been an advocate or a politician before his conversion, on the basis of what appears to be a rhetorical education.

[4] See the discussion in ch. 3, pp. 95–99.

[5] Some scholars argue that the office of bishop was itself new, having been instituted by Ignatius himself to gain control of the church in Antioch. Walter Bauer, *Rechtgläubigkeit und Ketzerei im ältesten Christentum* (BHT 10; Tübingen: Mohr Siebeck, 1934), put the matter sharply and influentially, but his work was not translated into English for almost forty years (*Orthodoxy and Heresy in Earliest Christianity* [ed. Robert A. Kraft and Gerhard Krodel; trans. a team from the Philadelphia Seminar on Christian Origins; Philadelphia: Fortress, 1971]). I have challenged some of Bauer's main conclusions in Thomas A. Robinson, *The Bauer Thesis Examined: The Geography of Heresy in the Early Christian Church* (SBEC 11; Lewiston, N.Y.: Edwin Mellen, 1988), 163–205.

[6] It is perhaps a safe guess that Ignatius had lived in Antioch for some time, for he had come to hold the chief position in the church there, or could credibly present himself as head of the church there, even against some in Antioch who may have resented or challenged his claim. Some scholars have suggested that Ignatius rose to high office in the church shortly after his conversion, mainly as a consequence of his rank in the larger secular society before he converted (Theodor Zahn, *Ignatius von Antiochien* [Gotha: F. A. Perthes, 1873], 403). There were cases where pagans of status, such as Cyprian and Ambrose, quickly gained high church office after their conversion to Christianity, but we know nothing of Ignatius's background that would permit us to say that such was the case with him.

[7] Christine Trevett, *A Study of Ignatius of Antioch in Syria and Asia* (SBEC 29; Lewiston, N.Y.: Edwin Mellen, 1992), 1.

[8] J. B. Lightfoot, *S. Ignatius, S. Polycarp* (2 vols. in 3; part 2 of *The Apostolic Fathers*; 2d ed.; London: Macmillan, 1889–1890), 2.1.31.

[9] "Our information with respect to these early ages of the Church is singularly defective and capricious" (Lightfoot, ibid., 2.1.15). Lightfoot's reconstruction of the period

quite autobiographical, little is known, and even the details that appear in his writings and associated literature are often the subject of considerable debate.[10]

That said, we do need to be a little more careful in reconstructing our portrait of Ignatius than that of most other characters from Christian antiquity. We have an unusually narrow window on Ignatius's life—a few days at most and under extreme conditions: difficult travel, with hungry beasts and martyrdom at the end of the trip; far from home and without the usual resources of friends, colleagues, and family that normally would have supported him.[11] Further, although seven of Ignatius's letters have survived[12]—a fairly rich body of literature from any person of that time—they represent only one glimpse, not several, into his life, for all the letters were written within days of each other (perhaps four of them on the same day) and they address the same concerns.[13] Also, the letters may provide a

---

is carefully guided by this recognition; not all historians after him have read the silences as cautiously.

[10] Paul explicitly states that he was raised as a strict Pharisee (Phil 3:5) and that he persecuted the church (1 Cor 15:9; Gal 1:13; Phil 3:6). In various passages, he outlines his involvement in the Christian community (Rom 15:14–16:23; 1 Cor 1:14–17; 2:1–5; 4:14–21; 9:1–7; 16:1–11; 2 Cor 1:8–10, 15–16; 2:12–13; 7:5–6; 9:1–5; 11:21–12:10; 13:1–3; Gal 1:13–2:14; Phil 1:7, 12; 2:19–24; 4:10–18; 1 Thess 2:1–2, 18; 3:1–6). Other biographical hints can be culled from these letters or from the more disputed Pauline writings.

[11] This mention of family is not intended to suggest that we know that Ignatius had close living relatives in Antioch, although it is more likely than not that he did. But whether he had close relatives there or not, there would have been individuals in Antioch with whom Ignatius had intimate ties. My primary point is that Ignatius was torn from all such associations and our only glimpse of him is some weeks after that painful separation. Granted, Ignatius has a remarkable ability to identify quickly with, and draw strength from, new acquaintances along the way (Ign. *Eph.* 2.1; 5.1; Ign. *Magn.* 2.1; Ign. *Trall.* 12.1; Ign. *Rom.* 10.1; Ign. *Phld.* 1.1–2; Ign. *Smyrn.* 12.1; 13.1–2; Ign. *Pol.* 8.2). Yet he must have felt the loss of those who had been his daily associates and supporters for many years. When we meet Ignatius, he is removed from that warm, familiar, and supportive circle, however much he was able to create new circles of support along the way.

[12] We do not know whether Ignatius wrote other letters on his fateful journey. He intended to write others (Ign. *Eph.* 20.1; Ign. *Pol.* 8.1). Later, a number of letters and versions of letters claimed his authorship. The work of Theodor Zahn and J. B. Lightfoot established the authenticity of what is called the "middle recension," and few have challenged their conclusions. For a review of the debate regarding the authenticity of the Ignatian letters and a discussion of recent challenges to the middle recension, see Trevett, *A Study of Ignatius,* 9–15; C. P. Hammond Bammel, "Ignatian Problems," *JTS* 33 (1982): 62–70; William R. Schoedel, *Ignatius of Antioch: A Commentary on the Letters of Ignatius of Antioch* (Hermeneia; Philadelphia: Fortress, 1985), 3–7.

[13] Four letters (to the Ephesians, the Trallians, the Magnesians, and the Romans) were written in Smyrna while Ignatius awaited boat passage to Rome. Three letters were written from Troas, where his journey experienced a short delay. Except for that to the Romans, the letters address similar concerns: the unity of the church behind its bishop,

distorted portrait of Ignatius, for they were written during an extremely difficult situation, under armed guard and on his way to execution. Even the concerns that Ignatius so keenly addressed in these letters may not illuminate much of his environment: some scholars argue that these letters deal more with the concerns and themes of the recipients in Asia Minor than with the Antioch-centered interests of Ignatius himself.[14] Whatever the case, the letters are rarely explicit about the situation in Antioch. In general, only by reading between the lines will we learn about the beliefs and practices of the Christian community in Antioch[15] and the relationship Christians had with the Jewish community there[16] and with the larger pagan society. Further, except for a few comments about Ignatius by Polycarp, everything that has come down to us about Ignatius is either legendary

---

heresy and schism, Ignatius's approaching martyrdom, and the validation of suffering and the Christian sufferer. Virginia Corwin contends that failure to note the closeness in time of the writing of these letters has sometimes created a caricature of Ignatius's concerns (*St. Ignatius and Christianity in Antioch* [New Haven: Yale University Press, 1960], 20–21).

[14] An unresolved debate in the field of Ignatian studies is whether Ignatius's letters reflect the situation in Antioch (Ignatius's hometown) or that in the province of Asia (the area to which his letters were addressed). It is obvious to me that the letters reflect both environments. The question is, Which situation is reflected in specific comments? Even this question, although often puzzling enough, should not be exaggerated. Whether a particular comment applied specifically to either Ignatius's situation in Antioch or his readers' situation in Asia Minor, both parties would have mainly understood what was being said. Most of Ignatius's responses suggest developed reflection on the matter, and indeed, some of his counterarguments—his status as prisoner and his quest for martyrdom—are tied to a situation that originated in Antioch. Although Ignatius addresses the crises in the Asian churches in a specific and informed way, he can do so only because he has ready-made arguments at hand. C. K. Barrett reads the matter differently. He thinks that Ignatius encountered a group of heretics in Asia and that Ignatius was caught off guard by their arguments and stumbled in his reply to them (in Philadelphia), which suggests that their views were not something he had encountered in Antioch ("Jews and Judaizers in the Epistles of Ignatius," in *Jews, Greeks, and Christians: Studies in Honour of W. D. Davies* [ed. R. Hamerton-Kelly and R. Scroggs; Leiden: E. J. Brill, 1976], 240). Ignatius may have been caught off guard by one of their arguments. This, however, would indicate only that Ignatius was unfamiliar with that particular spin, not that he was unfamiliar with the overall beliefs of the group.

[15] Ignatius does go into some detail on how the church hierarchy should be structured: one bishop at the head of a subordinate council of elders, assisted by a number of deacons. Some scholars have argued that Ignatius's portrait is, at best, ideal and obscures the opposition to monarchical bishops, a position that I have argued against in Robinson, *The Bauer Thesis Examined*, 163–205.

[16] This study will examine at various places the relationships between Jews and Christians in Antioch in the time of Ignatius. Ignatius leaves tantalizing clues, but nothing as specific as we would like. Presumably, a range of relationships existed, from sympathetic to hostile. Ignatius's relationship with Judaism and with Judaizers is heated and hostile. What his relationship was with individual Jews is another matter, as is the attitude of other Christians in Antioch to Jews and Judaism.

or clearly dependent on Ignatius's letters.[17] We know little, then, about Ignatius's life except for a brief glimpse of the man under the most trying circumstances.[18]

Why, then, dedicate a full monograph to Ignatius? There are two reasons. First, Ignatius's writings speak forcefully to almost every issue in our contemporary debates about the early Christian movement, from the shaping of Christian self-understanding and its perception of the "parting of the ways" from Judaism to the question of the diversity of early Christian assemblies, to the numerous developments that came to characterize the Christian movement by the mid-second century. Unfortunately, Ignatius's relevance to these matters sometimes has been unfairly compromised by unattractive portraits of Ignatius promoted by modern scholarship, from suggestions that Ignatius had become insane from the pressures of his approaching martyrdom[19] to suggestions that Ignatius had been shamed and discredited by his failure as leader to maintain peace in his church in Antioch.[20] Such negative portraits, which misrepresent a leader well respected in his own time, have worked to make Ignatius seem a more peripheral or abnormal player than he was.

In particular, recent scholars have become convinced that they have resolved one central matter related to Ignatius: the cause of Ignatius's plight as a convict of the Roman justice system on his way to execution in Rome. The near-consensus opinion is that the Roman authorities were bit players; the principal controversy was an internal church conflict that Ignatius could not control and for which he

---

[17]We learn from Polycarp that Ignatius stopped in Philippi (or, more likely, its port at Neapolis), and that he had assistance from the church there (Pol. *Phil.* 1.1; 9.1–2). We learn, too, that his letters were preserved by the church in Smyrna and copied and circulated from there (13.2).

[18]Trevett reviews some of the speculative attempts to fill in the gaps of Ignatius's life (*A Study of Ignatius*, 1–2).

[19]For many scholars, Ignatius's detailed reflection on his death and on Christian martyrdom can help little to understand either Ignatius himself or his times. According to this perspective, Ignatius's reflection on these themes developed late, under the gravity of his recent trial and death sentence. If this is so, it is argued, the theme of martyrdom does not portray Ignatius's thinking under normal conditions. Some have even suggested that Ignatius had cracked under the strain and that this accounted for what appeared to be bizarre statements he made about his approaching martyrdom (P. N. Harrison, *Polycarp's Two Epistles to the Philippians* [Cambridge: Cambridge University Press, 1936], 102). Lightfoot, with his characteristic balance, dismisses such assessments as "cheap wisdom" (*S. Ignatius, S. Polycarp*, 2.1.38). Lightfoot notes that much of the language used in later reflection on martyrdom has its first parallel in the letters of Ignatius, although he recognizes that it is quite possible that Ignatius "adopted language already familiar when he wrote" (ibid.).

[20]Trevett, for example, calls Ignatius "a man who was profoundly dissatisfied with himself," and says that his self-depreciatory language "is less suggestive of modesty than it is of guilt" (*A Study of Ignatius*, 59–60). See ch. 5 for a discussion of Ignatius's sense of unworthiness.

held himself accountable. Either Ignatius offered himself up willingly to execution to take the heat off the rest of the assembly or his opponents in the church fingered him as the culprit when the authorities came to investigate an internal dissension that had come to public notice and complaint. This study will attempt to show that this much-repeated view of Ignatius's final days is a distortion of Ignatius's predicament and of the wider world in which he lived.[21]

The second issue of focus in this monograph is the shaping of the distinctive identity of the Christian movement as separate from Judaism. Ignatius's sense of the matter will be addressed in detail. It is my contention that the distinction between Judaism and Christianity is sharper than the trends in the current debate have admitted, and that Ignatius's pointed assessment of Judaism is much more dismissive and uncompromising. Further, I contend that Ignatius represents a mainstream position; he is neither a lone nor a novel voice.

This study will not address every aspect of Ignatius's theology and ecclesiology, which are quite validly the foci of some studies on Ignatius. Such matters concern this investigation only insofar as they illuminate Ignatius's church situation and the relation of Christianity to Judaism in the period. The primary concern here is to show where treatments of Ignatius need to be disregarded or refined, and thereby to add to our understanding of the development of the early church.

The City of Antioch

We are hardly in a more data-rich environment when we turn from Ignatius's life to his times. Ignatius differs considerably from other characters in early Christian history, whose cities of residence usually have rich extant data, both literary and archaeological. The only locale of any significance we have for Ignatius is Antioch itself, and we know almost nothing of Antioch in this period, let alone of Ignatius and the Christian assembly within it.[22] Frederick Norris cautions:

> Antioch on the Orontes was no less than the fourth largest city of the Mediterranean world behind Rome, Alexandria, and Seleucia on the Tigris. Yet information about its entire history is sorely lacking. Theodor Mommsen indicated that inscrip-

---

[21] See ch. 5.

[22] Ignatius would have passed through several cities in western Asia Minor. He visited churches along the way (Philadelphia, Smyrna, and Philippi) and met with delegates from some cities off the main route (Tralles, Magnesia, and Ephesus). We know, too, that he died in Rome—a conclusion based on Ignatius's own writings, which indicate that he was on his way to martyrdom in Rome. There is little of credible comment in the tradition that refutes this, although one late tradition, from the Byzantine historian John Malalas, does have Ignatius martyred in Antioch rather than in Rome. For a discussion of the evidence, see Lightfoot, *S. Ignatius, S. Polycarp*, 2.2.436–48.

tions from greater Antioch were worthy of a small North African town. . . . The great Hellenistic histories of the city are lost. Most of our written sources deal only obliquely with Antioch as they tell of other things.[23]

Scholars have tried to fill some of the gaps. For example, in situations involving the Jewish community, the tendency is to use the experiences of Jews in other cities of the empire, where the information is richer. Historians often use this technique to help make sense of specific situations. But some caution should be exercised. The warning of John D. Grainger deserves attention both because the general caution needs to be repeated frequently in historical work and because Grainger's concerns stem specifically from treatments of Syria:

> It is one of the temptations, and one of the problems, of Hellenistic history, to make up for the paucity of evidence in certain areas (of which Syria is emphatically one) by referring to other places and drawing parallels. In the case of cities, the practice exists of referring to old Greece for information on subjects for which Syrian sources are lacking. It is my contention that this procedure is wrong, that it is bad historical practice, and that it should not be indulged in. . . . The urban development of Syria took place in a Syrian context above all, and references to the history of Egypt or Asia Minor or old Greece can only mislead and distort, as well as discounting the individuality of all these areas.[24]

For the current study, such caution is particularly necessary. Since our focus is on Ignatius, we are dealing with a time when Christianity was young and its relationship with Judaism and the larger society was still uncertain. Further, the Jews of Antioch may have been in a unique situation for a Diaspora community, a matter that will become clearer in the discussion that follows. Thus appeal to other Jewish communities or even to a later, more Christianized Antioch might be misleading and so will be kept to a minimum.

This chapter now examines Antioch itself and the peculiar features of this city that inform us of Ignatius's religious and political environment. We will not examine every feature of life in Antioch; that would be neither possible here nor necessary for understanding the world of Ignatius. Rather, we will look at events affecting the city around Ignatius's time and affecting Ignatius as a resident there. Some broader introductory material regarding Antioch is necessary, however, to set the stage. We will thus begin with the founding of the city about four hundred years before Ignatius. The relevance of this earlier history will become clearer

---

[23] Frederick W. Norris, "Artifacts from Antioch," in *Social History of the Matthean Community* (ed. David L. Balch; Minneapolis: Fortress, 1991), 248. Strabo, writing a century before Ignatius, lists these four cities (*Geogr.* 16.2.5). Fergus Millar attributes some of the loss of materials from Antioch to the silting of the Orontes River (*The Roman Near East, 31 B.C.–A.D. 337* [Cambridge: Harvard University Press, 1993], 259).

[24] Grainger, *The Cities of Seleukid Syria*, 3.

when we consider the Jewish presence in the city and the rights claimed and tensions aggravated by the Jewish community in Antioch about the time of Ignatius.

The Founding of Seleucid Antioch

Antioch on the Orontes was founded during the politically charged situation that developed after the death of Alexander the Great and the breakup of his empire.[25] For a few years, the dynasty of Alexander survived, but more in name than in substance. Neither of Alexander's heirs was fit or ready to govern, thus prominent generals from Alexander's army acted as regents and governors.[26] Some of these men had ambitions of their own. Rather than promoting the survival of the grand empire of Alexander the Great under his unimpressive or "half-Greek" heirs, they saw themselves, tested and proven in battle, as more deserving heads of a grand empire. In the long struggle for control, Perdiccas, one of Alexander's generals and the appointed guardian of Alexander's heirs, was

---

[25] Antioch on the Orontes, sometimes called Antioch by Daphne, is often identified simply as Antioch, since it was the most prominent of the cities bearing that name. Seleucus built fifteen other Antiochs, so naming them to honor his father, the otherwise little-known Antiochus. Seleucus's firstborn son and successor, a half-Iranian prince from Seleucus's marriage to a Bactrian princess from the far northeastern part of his empire, also bore the name Antiochus, as did nine others in that dynasty. The major study addressing Antioch during our period of interest is the sweeping work of Glanville Downey, *A History of Antioch in Syria from Seleucus to the Arab Conquests* (Princeton: Princeton University Press, 1961). Parts of other books are useful: Markus N. A. Bockmuehl, *Jewish Law in Gentile Churches: Halakhah and the Beginning of Christian Public Ethics* (Edinburgh: T&T Clark, 2000), 49–83; Irina Levinskaya, *The Book of Acts in Its Diaspora Setting* (vol. 5 of *The Book of Acts in Its First-Century Setting;* ed. Bruce W. Winter; Grand Rapids: Eerdmans, 1996), 127–35; Frank Kolb, "Antiochia in der frühen Kaiserzeit," in *Geschichte-Tradition-Reflexion: Festschrift für Martin Hengel* (ed. H. Cancik, H. Lichtenberger, and P. Schäfer; 3 vols.; Tübingen: J. C. B. Mohr [Paul Siebeck], 1996), 2:97–118; Robert R. Hann, "Judaism and Jewish Christianity in Antioch: Charisma and Conflict in the First Century," *Journal of Religious History* 14 (1987): 341–60; John M. G. Barclay, *Jews in the Mediterranean Diaspora: From Alexander to Trajan (323 BCE–117 CE)* (Hellenistic Culture and Society 33; Berkeley: University of California Press, 1999), 242–45, 249–58; Carl H. Kraeling, "The Jewish Community in Antioch," *JBL* 51 (1932): 130–60; E. Mary Smallwood, *The Jews under Roman Rule: From Pompey to Diocletian* (Leiden: E. J. Brill, 1976), 358–64; and Aryeh Kasher, *The Jews in Hellenistic and Roman Egypt: The Struggle for Equal Rights* (TSAJ 7; Tübingen: J. C. B. Mohr [Paul Siebeck], 1985), 297–309. J. H. W. G. Liebeschuetz, *Antioch: City and Imperial Administration in the Later Roman Empire* (Oxford: Clarendon, 1972), covers the later period.

[26] Alexander's illegitimate half-brother, Philip, was mentally handicapped and epileptic; Alexander's child by Roxane, a Bactrian princess, was yet unborn. Even though Roxane's pregnancy was to produce a son and thus a proper heir, opposition to this half-barbarian claimant could have been expected from elements of the Macedonian army. The two heirs briefly shared a dual kingship under the names Philip III and Alexander IV.

assassinated, a fate that later befell Alexander's heirs themselves.[27] The generals who had been assigned the care of parts of the empire now felt little restraint on their own imperial ambitions.

These generals were called the Diadochi ("successors"). Various alliances and power struggles followed, with a final settlement recognizing the Seleucid, Ptolemaic, Antigonid, and Macedonian kingdoms as the primary realms, with Greece becoming a less important player. Seleucus,[28] one of the Diadochi, had been assigned the charge of the most eastern part of Alexander's conquests, but by the time of Seleucus's death, he had come to control the largest territory—a vast sweep of lands from the borders of India to the coast of the Aegean Sea.[29]

Some of Seleucus's territory had come from the partition of the territory of Antigonus, the strongest of the Diadochi. The other Diadochi had formed an alliance against and defeated Antigonus and divided the captured lands among themselves.[30] The territory along the eastern Mediterranean coast, called Coele-Syria,[31] which included Palestine, fell by default to Seleucus, since it was contiguous with Seleucus's other holdings. It had been originally assigned to Ptolemy

---

[27] Perdiccas was assassinated in 321 B.C.E., two years after the death of Alexander. Philip III was killed in 317; Alexander IV was killed in 309.

[28] Seleucus is often referred to as Nicator ("conqueror"). Arrian, who wrote nearly a half millennium after Alexander, refers to Seleucus as the greatest king to have succeeded Alexander (*Anabasis* 7.22.5).

[29] Seleucus's success had come only after considerable reverses and losses. In 316 B.C.E., five years after Alexander's death, Seleucus was ousted from all his holdings by another of the Diadochi, Antigonus, whose primary holdings had been in Anatolia and the eastern coast of the Mediterranean (Coele-Syria). Seleucus had to flee to Egypt for safety under Ptolemy, another of the Diadochi. Because of the aggressive maneuvers of Antigonus and what appeared to be a plan to bring all of Alexander's vast conquests under his control, the other members of the Diadochi formed a successful coalition against Antigonus. By 312 B.C.E., Seleucus had regained Babylonia, and the coalition had driven Antigonus back to his original borders. However, suspicions about the ambitions of Antigonus continued, and a series of battles marked the next decade. Finally, in 301 B.C.E., Antigonus was killed during the defining battle against a second coalition at Ipsus.

[30] This was not the end of the matter. Seleucus then attacked Lysimachus, who had received a large part of Asia Minor as his reward in the victory over Antigonus. Seleucus captured most of Lysimachus's land, reaching to the shores of the Aegean by the time of Lysimachus's death in 281 B.C.E. Now that he had reached the Aegean Sea, Macedon itself stood as Seleucus's next and final goal—a reasonable ambition with Lysimachus, the master of Thrace, now dead. But it was a fatal goal, for Seleucus was assassinated within the year by a son of Ptolemy I (Ceraunus), who, cut off from the succession in Egypt, had ambitions of his own regarding Macedon.

[31] The etymology of the name Coele-Syria is uncertain; a common explanation is that it means "hollow Syria," so named for the prominent valley in Lebanon called al Biqaʾ, or the Biqaʾ Valley. As a label to identify a specific political or geographical area, the term displays some elasticity among its ancient users, and so the etymology of the term is of little use for determining the precise area an author intended by the term.

before the battle with Antigonus.[32] Ptolemy had "missed" that crucial battle, and his colleagues felt justified in cutting him off from the booty. Ptolemy, however, simply disregarded the terms of settlement and seized Coele-Syria as rightfully his.

From this point on, the Seleucid and Ptolemaic kingdoms viewed each other with distrust. The disputed territory held by Ptolemy reached as far north as the Eleutherus River, near Tripolis, two-thirds of the way up the eastern Mediterranean coast, almost like a spear pointed at Seleucus's realm. Further, Ptolemy already had control of Cyprus and some cities on the south coast of Asia Minor, and these were threats to Seleucus's new holdings and his increasing western ambitions.

Seleucus immediately undertook a massive building program designed to guarantee his hold on the newly acquired territories. He had already established a capital on the Tigris River in 305 B.C.E., which he named Seleucia, and in 300 B.C.E., within months of his conquest of Syria and Armenia, he founded several cities in Syria,[33] including a capital at Antioch.[34]

The founding of Antioch is to be understood in light of the highly charged political reality that had just unfolded. On the speedy founding of a series of cities in Syria, of which Antioch was central, Grainger comments,

> These city foundations did not occur as an act of generosity on Seleukos' part, nor were they a mere whim. They were, rather, a coolly calculated political device, designed to establish his political authority firmly in his new territory, and to provide a firm foundation for further expansion.[35]

One crucial consideration in the choice of location for the new city of Antioch must have been its closeness to the disputed Coele-Syria territory, which the Ptolemies held but Seleucus claimed.[36] The timing and the location of the founding of Antioch could not have been simply coincidental. And as argued later

---

[32] Ptolemy, a Macedonian general under Alexander the Great, became the master of Egypt after the death of Alexander. He declared himself king in 304 B.C.E. His dynasty was to last until the death of Cleopatra (30 B.C.E.). See Walter M. Ellis, *Ptolemy of Egypt* (New York: Routledge, 1994). For a quirky and novelistic, but still useful, recent popular account of the Ptolemies, see Duncan Sprott, *The Ptolemies* (New York: Alfred A. Knopf, 2004).

[33] Grainger, *The Cities of Seleukid Syria,* discusses in minute detail Seleucus's founding of cities in Syria.

[34] There is some debate about which term best describes Antioch's status. The term "capital" must be seen against a structure where multiple capitals were possible and where a roving capital was likely, shifting locations with the king as the occasion demanded. Grainger argues that Antioch was not capital until 188 B.C.E. (ibid., 122, 124–50).

[35] Ibid., 54; see also 58.

[36] Ibid., 58–60. Grainger views Apamea as a first line of defense for Antioch, and he describes Antioch as the "lynch-pin of the whole structure" (60), ideally located as the key communications center.

in this study, the crisis environment provided an ideal setting for considerable rights to be extended to Jews at the time of the founding of the city.

As the Seleucid Empire expanded westward by wrestling Anatolian land from Lysimachus, Antioch found itself at a most central location in the empire, and the juncture of major east-west and north-south trade routes there heightened the importance of its location. This enhanced Antioch's prestige and increased the city's importance in the Seleucid Empire.

The Booms and Busts of Antioch

Almost from Antioch's first days, the empire of which Antioch was a featured part began to crumble. Rarely at peace after its dramatic thirty-year expansion from India and the Persian Gulf to the Aegean Sea, the Seleucid Empire steadily shrank. From the outset, Seleucid control of its westernmost territories in Anatolia was challenged. The Gauls were a frequent problem, settling in the central area of Asia Minor (Galatia) by 275 B.C.E. The kingdom of Pergamum expanded considerably, defeating the Gauls and seizing all of the Seleucid lands in Asia Minor in 230 B.C.E., although some of this territory was regained by 223 B.C.E.[37] As Seleucid land was being lost in Asia Minor, a similar threat to the Seleucid possessions in the east was developing. By 247 B.C.E., the Parthians had begun to take land from the Seleucids there.

Military crises near the center of the empire hindered adequate response to these matters on its periphery. Wars against the Ptolemies to capture the disputed lands of Coele-Syria marked much of the Seleucid Empire's first century.[38] Ptolemy III captured Seleucia and Antioch in 246 B.C.E. He held Antioch only for a few months—long enough to clean up a political mess there, but he retained Seleucia, Antioch's port fifteen miles to the west on the Mediterranean coast. The loss of Seleucia worked to the advantage of Antioch: with close-by Seleucia now in the hands of the Ptolemies, Antioch had to be strengthened, and this new political development assured that Antioch would quickly become the key

---

[37] A. H. M. Jones, *The Cities of the Eastern Roman Provinces* (2d ed.; Oxford: Clarendon, 1971), 40–41.

[38] Five main wars mark the first century of the Seleucid-Ptolemaic conflicts: (1) In 275 B.C.E., Ptolemy II invaded Seleucid lands. In 261, Antiochus II invaded Ptolemaic lands. (2) In 252, a peace treaty was sealed by the marriage of Antiochus II and Berenice, the daughter of Ptolemy II. But Antiochus II and Berenice were murdered in 246 by partisans of Antiochus's first wife, Laodice, and her son Seleucus. (3) This provoked Ptolemy III to invade Syria to avenge the death of his sister. (4) In 218–217, Antiochus III (the Great) invaded Ptolemaic territories but was defeated. Matters then deteriorated in Egypt, particularly under Ptolemy V, a mere boy when he came to the throne. (5) Civil war broke out in Upper Egypt, and Antiochus III invaded again—this time with better success, finally gaining the long-disputed Coele-Syria territories.

city for the Seleucids. According to Strabo, Antioch underwent expansion after coming back into Seleucid hands—a reasonable conjecture even without Strabo's witness.[39]

The first and only substantial expansion of the otherwise shrinking Seleucid territory came when the Seleucids, under Antiochus III (223–187 B.C.E.), were finally able to make good their hundred-year-old claim to the Coele-Syria territory in 200 B.C.E. But almost immediately the Seleucid fortunes suffered further reverses elsewhere as Rome began to expand eastward and as revolts broke out in various areas of the far-stretching empire.[40] The problems on the periphery of the empire would not necessarily have affected the fortunes of Antioch initially. As the borders of the empire weakened, the center of the empire had to be strengthened. Whatever decline Antioch may have experienced, it is unlikely to have been nearly as serious as the decline of the empire itself.

More destabilizing for the Seleucids than the troubles on the periphery of the empire were the struggles by rival claimants for the Seleucid throne. Civil war became a mark of Seleucid politics from about the middle of the third century B.C.E., weakening the empire to such a degree that various native powers, of whom the Maccabees in Palestine were but one, were able to wrest their homelands from Seleucid control. Groups seeking independence could play off one rival Seleucid claimant against another to obtain the best possible deal for their homeland, as the Maccabees, for example, did.[41] Each successful revolt damaged the shrinking Seleucid Empire until, by the end of the second century B.C.E., the empire boasted little more than the immediate territory around Antioch. Even then, Antioch retained a measure of prestige, for, as Grainger points out, the legitimacy of the rival claimants to the Seleucid throne was enhanced if they held Antioch.[42]

Antioch could not escape forever the decline that devastated the empire, and its inhabitants came to identify more with their city than with the evaporating empire of which they had been the prominent part. In one instance, at the time of the Maccabean crisis, the residents of Antioch showed displeasure with

---

[39] Strabo, *Geogr.* 16.2.4; see also Grainger, *The Cities of Seleukid Syria*, 123–24.

[40] In the eastern part of the Seleucid territory, the Arsacid (Parthian) dynasty established itself ca. 251 B.C.E. This power was to last for five hundred years, and was a frequent thorn in the side of the Seleucids and of their successors, the Romans. By 126 B.C.E., the Parthians had taken Babylonia. In the western areas of the Seleucid territories, Pergamum, Pontus, and Cappadocia established independent states in the early 200s B.C.E. soon after the battles among the Diadochi. Rome then came on the scene. As early as 189 B.C.E., long before the Roman conquest of Syria, Rome had started its subjugation of Seleucid territory in Anatolia, defeating Antiochus III at Magnesia and taking as hostage the future Antiochus IV. The kingdom of Pergamum was willed to Rome by its last leader, Attalus III, in 133 B.C.E. The territory became the Roman province of Asia in 129 B.C.E.

[41] Josephus, *Ant.* 13.35–42.

[42] Grainger, *The Cities of Seleukid Syria*, 125.

both claimants to the Seleucid throne, and even proclaimed the Ptolemaic king, Philometer, as their own king.[43]

The residents of Antioch came to feel isolated, surrounded by a hostile native Syrian population whom they once had dominated. Matters had deteriorated so gravely as a result of Seleucid infighting that Seleucid cities often lacked the services and defense that cities had come to expect from the national government. In order to safeguard their city, the residents of Antioch invited the Armenian king to become their protector in 83 B.C.E. Twenty years later, the Romans were on the scene, and Antioch became part of the Roman world.[44]

Roman Antioch

Antioch had declined considerably before the arrival of Rome, and Rome was unable to give the city its immediate attention. Civil war among the Roman generals kept the focus on military matters.[45] As the situation stabilized, Rome had to decide on a center for the administration of the Seleucid territories. Initially, areas other than Antioch may have been of interest to the Romans. Rome established a colony at Berytus (modern Beirut), and there is some ambiguity in the evidence regarding the status of Antioch in the early Roman period.[46]

Whatever the case during the initial years of Roman rule, Antioch soon came to play a significant role in the Roman system, especially as Rome clashed with Parthia, whose border lay nearby. Parthia had presented an obstacle to Rome's eastern ambitions from the time of Rome's first presence in the area, when some Jews in Palestine aligned with the Parthian-supported Hasmonean claimant against Rome's Hasmonean ally. Rome's victory in that showdown resulted in the rise of the Herods, a puppet dynasty of the Romans. The threat from Parthia continued, however, although a measure of quiet had been negotiated by 37 or 38 C.E., with Armenia serving as somewhat of a buffer.[47] But suspicion lay close to the surface. Finally, in the second decade of the second century C.E., politics gave way

---

[43] Josephus, *Ant.* 13.113–115. Josephus explains that Philometer declined the honor out of concern that this might offend the Romans.

[44] "Syria had broken up into a medley of warring cities and principalities long before Pompey formally abolished the shadow of Seleucid rule" (Jones, *The Greek City from Alexander to Justinian*, 26).

[45] From 53 to 31 B.C.E., Rome endured the Wars of the First Triumvirate and the Wars of the Second Triumvirate until Octavian, as Augustus, became the sole emperor of the Roman Empire.

[46] Fergus Millar speaks of the "slowly emerging role of Antioch as a secondary Imperial 'capital'" (*The Roman Near East*, 105).

[47] Tacitus, *Ann.* 2.58; 13.7; Josephus, *Ant.* 18.96–98. According to Josephus, the pact happened under Tiberius rather than the more likely Gaius (see Millar, *The Roman Near East*, 58, n. 7; 66).

to conflict. Rome annexed Armenia, and Parthia and Rome were immediately at war. The emperor Trajan seized Mesopotamian lands, but the victory was a hollow one. Jews and others revolted in wide areas of Rome's eastern holdings (Cyrene, Egypt, Cyprus, and Mesopotamia), and Trajan died shortly afterwards, in 117 C.E. The new emperor, Hadrian, withdrew from the newly acquired lands to a more secure border near Antioch.[48] Such activity on the eastern front made Antioch the imperial residence for extended periods on several occasions about the time of Ignatius, establishing it as a crucial city in the Roman machinery of government in the east.

This is only a brief sketch of the fortunes of Antioch during its first four centuries, up to the time of Ignatius. It is not the concern in this study to determine every nuance of the status of Antioch in the Roman world or the various shifts in imperial favor that affected the fortunes of the city. These matters have had their debates in the scholarly literature, and many issues remain unsettled.[49] It is enough to establish that the city was a dominant one in the eastern Mediterranean, and whatever its technical status as capital of the Roman province of Syria, it was possible for informed people writing at the time of Ignatius to speak of Antioch as the capital, without their having to defend that use of the term, and to describe Antioch as one of the greatest cities of the empire.[50] Whatever Antioch had lost in its last days under the Seleucids, it soon regained under the Romans.[51]

The Population and Cultural Mix of Antioch

Determining the size of the population of the Roman world, of cities within the empire, or of ethnic groups within these cities is fraught with difficulties. The population estimates for Antioch at its height range from a low of 100,000 to a

---

[48] Millar, *The Roman Near East*, 100.

[49] For a summary, see Robyn Tracy, "Syria," in *The Book of Acts in Its Graeco-Roman Setting* (ed. David W. J. Gill and Conrad Gempf; vol. 2 of *The Book of Acts in Its First-Century Setting*; ed. Bruce W. Winter; Grand Rapids: Eerdmans, 1994), 236–39.

[50] Josephus describes Antioch as the third-ranking city in the Roman Empire in extent and wealth at the time of Vespasian (*J. W.* 3.29).

[51] Shortly after the Roman capture of Antioch, Herod the Great, Rome's puppet king, began a series of building projects both inside and outside Palestine, including the temple in Jerusalem. One of Herod's projects directly benefited Antioch—a major renovation of its central thoroughfare, a striking feature around which the renewal of Antioch blossomed. It was six times longer than the later, better-known Arcadian Way in Ephesus. Although Josephus attributes the project solely to Herod (*J. W.* 1.425), both Herod and Emperor Tiberius contributed (see Glanville Downey, "Imperial Building Records in Malalas," *Byzantinische Zeitschrift* 38 [1938]: 299–311; Corwin, *St. Ignatius*, 37, n. 24).

high of about 800,000. J. H. W. G. Liebeschuetz, a modern authority on Antioch, opts for a range from 200,000 to 390,000,[52] although he notes other ways of determining population, some of which give different results.[53] Downey, another authority on Antioch, puts the population of free inhabitants at 300,000. He thinks it impossible to determine the number of slaves and residents who did not have citizenship.[54]

Whatever number we accept, the population of Antioch at the time of Ignatius may have been near its peak, although we cannot be certain.[55] Antioch certainly was the significant center of the northeastern area of the Roman Empire at the time of Ignatius, and it was becoming increasingly important as tensions heated up on the borders with Parthia, a mere hundred miles to the east. According to Josephus, writing around this time, Antioch was the metropolis of Syria, and "without dispute" it deserved "the place of the third city in the habitable earth that was under the Roman empire, both in magnitude, and other marks of prosperity" (*J. W.* 3.29). There is no reason to disagree with this description, but to say anything beyond this about the size of Antioch at the time of Ignatius is to engage in unproductive and unnecessary speculation.

The ethnic mix of the city is probably more important for our purposes than questions about the size of the population, but equally difficult to determine. As one of the major cities of the Mediterranean world, lying at the crossroads of trade routes, founded by diverse peoples in the midst of a foreign population, Antioch became a destination for peoples from far and wide. Its population was probably almost as diverse as most large cities in the twenty-first century and certainly as diverse as any city in the Roman Empire. As Libanius, a leading citizen of Antioch in the fourth century, noted:

> Indeed, if a man had the idea of travelling all over the earth, not to see how cities looked, but to learn their ways, our city would fulfill his purpose and save him his journeying. If he sits in our market place he will sample every city, there will be so many people from each place with whom he can talk . . . the city loves the virtues

---

[52] Liebeschuetz, *Antioch*, 93.

[53] Ibid., 92–100.

[54] Glanville Downey, "The Size of the Population of Antioch," *TAPA* 89 (1958): 86.

[55] Frequently numbers are offered without any comment regarding the period for which they are relevant. Populations, however, fluctuate. If the size of the population is important in our consideration of an issue, it is crucial to determine not the population of a city at its height but at the time of the events we are examining. But it is almost impossible to specify the size of any ancient city at any time, let alone to chart the size during the various booms and busts in population over time. Indeed, the main tool by which urban populations are determined—the city walls—tells us little regarding how crowded or deserted areas of the city were at any given time. The wall was a fixed feature; the population within it changed with the fortunes of the time. See Downey, "The Size of the Population of Antioch," which attempts to trace the population of Antioch over its history.

of those who come to it exactly as it does the virtues of its children, imitating the Athenians in this also.[56]

Antioch's location on a key trade route, with a Mediterranean port, Seleucia, on the coast about fifteen miles away, made the city a key commercial center. Its strategic location, at the center of the Seleucid Empire and later at the eastern edge of the Roman Empire, made it an important military base also. At times, Antioch served as the functioning capital of the Roman Empire, when emperors made it their home, often for years, while they dealt with matters in the eastern empire.[57] Its pleasant climate made it a holiday destination as well, and its "Olympian" Games became famous, enduring well into the period of the Christian empire.[58]

Antioch's intellectual tradition was equally rich. Cicero spoke of the city as "the seat of learned men and of liberal sciences."[59] According to Justin, Samaritan gnostic teachers made the city their home and gained a considerable following there.[60] In the various Christian debates, Antioch developed such a rich theological tradition that modern scholars often speak of Antioch and Alexandria as the two great centers of Christian learning, although the contrast between the theological traditions of the two cities, once routinely assumed, is now judged to have been too sharply drawn.[61]

The Religious Milieu of Antioch

Given Libanius's depiction of the city, Antioch was probably as religiously diverse as any city in the empire. It formed a crossroads for ethnic and cultural

---

[56]Libanius, *Orationes* 11. This oration, in praise of Antioch, provides a rich description of major aspects of life in the city. Although Libanius's assessment was made about two and a half centuries after Ignatius's time, nothing suggests that Antioch's makeup differed much from the earlier time.

[57] Warwick Ball offers a brief survey of imperial residence in Antioch (*Rome in the East: The Transformation of an Empire* [New York: Routledge, 2000], 155–56).

[58] An endowment from Augustus established the games. At first they were regional, but they grew in popularity. When Emperor Theodosius outlawed the original Olympic Games in 393 c.e., the games at Antioch continued, matching the games once held at Olympia. They ended in the early 500s after riots between rival parties, the "blues" and the "greens." See Glanville Downey, "The Olympic Games of Antioch in the Fourth Century A. D." *TAPA* 70 (1939): 428–38; Liebeschuetz, *Antioch*, 136–44.

[59] Cicero, *Pro Archia* 3; Pausanias, *Descr.* 8.33.3.

[60] Justin, *1 Apol.* 26.

[61] See, for example, Mary Cunningham, "The Orthodox Church in Byzantium," in *A World History of Christianity* (ed. Adrian Hastings; London: Cassell; Grand Rapids: Eerdmans, 1999), 70. For a more cautious assessment of the "two schools" idea, see Rowan Williams, *Arius: Heresy and Tradition* (2d ed.; Grand Rapids: Eerdmans, 2002), 158–59.

interchange: a Macedonian/Greek city in origin, established in the midst of a Syrian countryside, under Roman rule, and with various immigrant populations, including Jews and Samaritans, who would have congregated in substantial numbers.

Like any Greek city, Antioch had its patron god—Apollo, the patron god of the Seleucids.[62] Other Greek gods and goddesses were also associated with the city; Tyche, for example, was honored prominently.[63] In addition, the gods of the various elements of the mixed population would have had their abode there too. As immigrants made the city their home, so would have their gods. This is how gods traveled—in the suitcases of devotees who left their native land but not their native world, taking with them their beliefs, cultural behaviors, and gods, and settling in neighborhoods composed of fellow countrymen.[64]

The ancient world, even at its skeptical best, was largely religious, and we can assume that most of the inhabitants of Antioch had some religious sensibilities. In this population, Jewish and Samaritan religion would have been represented, perhaps in their considerable diversity. Unlike the early Christian apologists who were soon to appear after Ignatius and confront Greco-Roman religion head on, it is Judaism against which Ignatius distinguishes and defines Christianity. Yet the larger religious world could not have escaped Ignatius or members of the early Christian community in Antioch. Indeed, perhaps most members of Ignatius's assembly converted to Christianity from paganism—perhaps even Ignatius himself.[65]

---

[62] Myths grew up associating Apollo in a special way with the area. A temple of Apollo stood in Daphne, a rich suburb of Antioch. According to Greek mythology, Apollo fell in love with Daphne, a beautiful river nymph, after he was struck by Cupid's arrow. But Daphne spurned his advances, for she had been hit by an arrow from Cupid that caused her to find Apollo's interest repulsive, a situation created to frustrate Apollo for his mockery of Cupid. Apollo's continued pursuit forced Daphne to plead to the gods for escape. Just as Apollo was about to reach her, she was turned into a laurel tree. The laurel leaf, then, became a symbol of Apollo, and Daphne was thick with laurel trees.

[63] Downey, *A History of Antioch*, 216–17.

[64] Ramsay MacMullen offers evidence of this kind of religious dispersion, where gods traveled in the company of immigrant people and took up their abode wherever their devotees settled in sufficient numbers to support a temple (*Paganism in the Roman Empire* [New Haven and London: Yale University Press, 1981], 112–30). He argues against reconstructions that read evidence of religious *dispersion* as proof of the *conversion* of native populations to recently introduced gods. Given the ancient expectation that people would be loyal to their native gods and traditions, MacMullen interprets religious dispersion as evidence simply of the movement of peoples with their native gods rather than of a movement of people from their old gods to new ones.

[65] Chapter 2 argues that proselytes and God-fearers are unlikely to have been a significant component of Ignatius's assembly. One might wonder whether Ignatius had any affiliation with Judaism before joining the Christian movement. He certainly does not strike one as somebody steeped in Judaism.

Religion shaped Ignatius's life and death. Membership in one religion over against another was a matter of concern for him. The definition of the boundaries separating one religion from another was a pressing and necessary business for him. His reflection on these issues is perhaps his most important contribution to the development of the Christian movement.

The Jews of Antioch

The primary evidence for the Jewish situation in Antioch about the time of Ignatius comes from the writings of Josephus. Whatever we make of Josephus as a historian and however difficult it is to determine his sources at times, he is a near-contemporary witness to the time of Ignatius, and he comments on the Jewish situation in Antioch as a relatively informed observer. Josephus has no hesitation in describing Antioch as the significant city in Syria and indeed as one of the most significant cities in the Roman Empire (*J. W.* 3.29). He describes it, too, as a major center for Jews.[66] Neither point is disputed. But when he describes Jewish-Gentile relationships in Antioch, some scholars think that he is spinning the story somewhat.[67] And when he contends that Jews had citizenship in Antioch, most think that his information was wrong, perhaps intentionally.[68]

As noted earlier, it is difficult to be precise about the size of the population of Antioch at its height or at any other point in its history. Determining the size of a particular ethnic element in Antioch is equally difficult, yet attempts have been made, particularly regarding the Jewish component of the city. Beloch, who performed much of the early work on population figures, places the number of Jews in Antioch during the time of Augustus at forty-five thousand,[69] and Kraeling accepts that number.[70] Some scholars reduce the number by half, but even the lower number makes for a sizeable Jewish community.[71]

---

[66] Josephus says that although Jewish populations are found throughout the world, Jews are particularly numerous in Syria and especially in Antioch (*J. W.* 7.43).

[67] Chapter 4, below, deals at length with the matter of Jewish-Gentile tensions.

[68] Josephus wants to make a solid case for Jewish rights in Greek cities. This chapter will discuss the matter in detail.

[69] J. Beloch, *Die Bevölkerung der griechisch-römischen Welt* (Leipzig: Duncker & Humblot, 1886). For a detailed critique of Beloch's work, see Elio Lo Cascio, "The Size of the Roman Population: Beloch and the Meaning of the Augustan Census Figures," *JRS* 84 (1994): 23–40. For a review and critique of older and newer methods to determine ancient population statistics, see Tim G. Parkin, *Demography and Roman Society* (Baltimore and London: Johns Hopkins University Press, 1992).

[70] Kraeling, "The Jewish Community at Antioch," 130–60.

[71] Wayne A. Meeks and Robert L. Wilken settle for twenty-two thousand (*Jews and Christians in Antioch in the First Four Centuries of the Common Era* [Society of Biblical Literature Sources for Biblical Study 13; Missoula, Mont.: Scholars Press, 1978], 8).

The attempt to be specific about population statistics for the ancient world is risky and often little better than guesswork, even when ancient texts themselves provide precise numbers.[72] No such precise numbers exist for Antioch, although Josephus noted and tried to explain the considerable size of the Jewish population there. If Josephus felt compelled to address the size of the Jewish community there, it is likely that it was noticeably large, and it is equally likely that the size of the Jewish community in Antioch had not escaped the notice of the non-Jews there.

Perhaps the safest method for determining the size of the Jewish population in Antioch is an impressionistic approach. No one disputes that Antioch was one of the largest centers of Diaspora Judaism. We can safely say that Antioch and its surrounding area had a Jewish population larger than that found in most other Diaspora cities, Alexandria probably being the only exception. More precision than this is probably impossible and, for most questions, unnecessary.

Proximity to Palestine and Mesopotamia (the second center of Judaism in the ancient world) may help explain the size of the Jewish community in Antioch. Indeed, this is what comes to mind for Josephus when he attempts to account for the number of Jews in Antioch (*J. W.* 7.43). Other factors have been proposed, but Josephus's simple explanation of the proximity of Antioch to Palestine and Mesopotamia has perhaps the most merit.[73] As a booming city on the route between the two primary areas of Jewish concentration, Antioch would have been an attractive and convenient home for Jewish immigrants from both lands.

Given the difficulty of determining with any accuracy either the size of the city or the size of the Jewish component within the city, an attempt to establish the precise proportion of the Jewish element in Antioch would be equally futile. Fortunately, these are not issues important for our concern to understand Jewish-Gentile relationships in Antioch. More important is the recognition that the *proportion* of Jews to Gentiles would have shifted from time to time, sometimes quite dramatically. Such shifts in the complexion of Antioch's population could have upset the equilibrium (or appeared to do so, which would have had the same impact). These changes may have created tensions because of either real or perceived losses and gains. The key to understanding the nature of Jewish-Gentile relationships in Antioch, then, is not the mere presence of a Jewish community in Antioch, or even the size of the community; rather, the shifts in the ratio of the populations or perceived changes in privileges or power are probably most important.

---

[72] Even when ancient texts offer numbers, we generally should consider the numbers as impressionistic, rhetorical, or propagandistic. This does not mean, however, that we should discard all such information as unreliable. Although impressions may be mistaken and rhetoric and propaganda may often mislead, they can have some roots in reality. Nevertheless, ancient population numbers generally do not provide any more precision than we would have without them.

[73] See the discussion below on the question of Jewish family size and the impact of abortion and exposure of the newborn as factors in family size.

In the modern world, immigrant communities often settle in their own ethnic enclaves, where they have the comfort and support of a familiar community. The same was true for at least some immigrant communities in the ancient world. Jews lived primarily in two sectors of Alexandria, although they were also scattered throughout the remainder of the city.[74] The same clustering of families appears to have been the case for Jews in at least some of the other settlements in Egypt.[75] Rome, too, seems to have had one area where Jews were known to dwell in large numbers.[76] It is more difficult to determine the situation of Jews in the area of Antioch. There appears to have been one grouping of Jews within the city walls close to the gate leading to the suburb of Daphne, and some Jewish settlement in Daphne, but Jews made their residence in other areas also.[77]

The other sources regarding the Jewish presence in Antioch at the time of Ignatius are Christian. Ignatius's letters are primary, but the book of Acts may offer useful material. Many scholars argue that other Christian documents, particularly the Gospel of Matthew[78] and the *Didache,* reflect the situation in Antioch

---

[74] Philo, *Flaccus* 55.

[75] Louis H. Feldman, *Jew and Gentile in the Ancient World: Attitudes and Interactions from Alexander to Justinian* (Princeton: Princeton University Press, 1993), 63–65.

[76] Philo, *On the Embassy to Gaius,* 23.155.

[77] Downey, *A History of Antioch,* 206. Kraeling locates Jews in three areas: a southern Jewish quarter within the walls, the suburb of Daphne, and perhaps to the north of the city ("The Jewish Community at Antioch," 140–43). John Malalas mentions a synagogue in Daphne (*Chronographia* 10.45; Johannes Thurn, ed., *Ioannis Malalae Chronographia,* Corpus Fontium Historiae Byzantinae 35 [Berlin: Walter de Gruyter, 2000]). John Chrysostom speaks of synagogues in Daphne and Antioch (*Adversus Judaeos* 1.6; 6.12). Although such evidence is late, these communities may well have remained in the area of their founding.

[78] The Gospel of Matthew, in particular, has been assigned an Antiochene, or at least a Syrian, milieu. Matthew's connection to the area is strong. It appears that Ignatius either used Matthew's Gospel or drew from the same oral tradition; see Charles Thomas Brown, *The Gospel and Ignatius of Antioch* (Studies in Biblical Literature 12; New York: Peter Lang, 2000), 1–6; Christine Trevett, "Approaching Matthew from the Second Century: The Under-Used Ignatian Correspondence," *JSNT* 20 (1984): 59–67; Raymond E. Brown and John P. Meier, *Antioch and Rome: New Testament Cradles of Catholic Christianity* (New York and Ramsey, N.J.: Paulist, 1983), 45–72; Éduard Massaux, *The First Ecclesiastical Writers* (vol. 1 of *The Influence of the Gospel of Saint Matthew on Christian Literature before Saint Irenaeus;* trans. N. J. Belval and S. Hecht; New Gospel Studies 5.1; Macon, Ga.: Mercer University Press, 1990); Michelle Slee, *The Church in Antioch in the First Century CE: Communion and Conflict* (JSNTSup 244; London: Sheffield University Press, 2003), 118–55. No examination of the parallels between Ignatius's writings and the Gospel of Matthew should be attempted without first reading Robert M. Grant, "Scripture and Tradition in Ignatius of Antioch," in *After the New Testament* (Minneapolis: Fortress: 1967), 37–54. An even stronger case for Matthew's Syrian or Antiochene origins can perhaps be made if Ignatius did not use a copy of Matthew's Gospel but each author drew independently from the same oral traditions. Such sharing would suggest a common locale in

or Syria.[79] They contend that a weighty enough case can be made for these documents' Syrian or Antiochene milieu that they should not be excluded from reconstructions of early Christianity in the area. A few scholars have argued that other documents also may be from Antioch.[80] Examination reveals that every Christian document associated with Antioch puts the Jewish factor into prominent focus and suggests a tension between the Christian community and Judaism (although we perhaps can say this of most early Christian literature).

Christians would certainly have lived somewhat in the shadow of Judaism during Ignatius's time, and it is unlikely that we can understand Ignatius without understanding something of the relations between Christians and Jews in Antioch. Few Ignatian scholars, however, have addressed the matter directly; most have simply investigated Jewish Christians or Judaizing Christians in that city. Even these investigations frequently have muted the force of Ignatius's comments about Judaism and Judaizers, finding in other opponents, such as Gentile Judaizers and particularly the Docetists, Ignatius's more serious and irreconcilable enemy.[81]

But Ignatius's writings present a much starker view of the matter. Christianity and Judaism stand in sharp tension. Ignatius saw no remedy for this other than on completely Christian terms. There could be no reconciliation or fellowship, and those on the Christian side who encouraged such alliances were dangerous and perhaps damned. The two movements were fundamentally different, and Ignatius uses the terms "Christianity" and "Christian" to signify and secure the

---

which certain stories were prominent in the oral tradition. The assumption here is that, at least in part, the memory of the church (where the oral tradition had its life) would have featured a range of material best suited for its particular needs and that different locales would have reflected somewhat different needs and interests. Regarding the Jewish factor in Matthew, it is clear that Jews feature prominently in all the Gospels, but Matthew's Gospel is particularly sensitive to the matter. What this sensitivity implies is debated: some scholars think that the Matthean community is still associated with the synagogue; others argue that the community is in the process of breaking away; still others, that the break is in the past and reconciliation is not possible. The debate is addressed at a number of levels in David L. Balch, ed., *Social History of the Matthean Community* (Minneapolis: Fortress, 1991). Of the articles there, Robert H. Gundry, "A Responsive Evaluation of the Social History of the Matthean Community in Roman Syria," 62–67, makes the most compelling case. See also K. W. Clark, "The Gentile Bias in Matthew," *JBL* 66 (1947): 165–72.

[79] The *Didache* is sometimes assigned to Syria, and it shows Jewish influence. It, too, draws many of its traditions from the same pool as Matthew and Ignatius, and it likewise has a particular sensitivity to Judaism. See Slee, *The Church in Antioch, CE,* 54–116.

[80] Reginald Fuller, *A Critical Introduction to the New Testament* (London: Duckworth, 1966) 107, places the Gospel of Mark in Antioch. Some scholars place the *Acts of Peter* there (Harry O. Maier, *The Social Setting of the Ministry as Reflected in the Writings of Hermas, Clement, and Ignatius* [Dissertations SR 1; Waterloo, Ont.: Wilfrid Laurier University Press, 1991],151).

[81] See the section "Ignatius's Opponents" in ch. 3, pp. 113–26.

new self-understanding of the Christian movement against identification with, or absorption into, Judaism.

Ignatius's hostility toward Judaism[82] and his intentional differentiation of Christianity from Judaism demand that any attempt to understand Ignatius take into consideration the Jewish factor in Antioch.[83] The need for such attention is heightened when we note that every mention of Antioch in the Christian literature prior to Ignatius either highlights or implies a tension between Jewish and Christian belief and practice.[84] Thus Ignatius is not eccentric, standing alone in his critique of Judaism; he reflects a tension that goes back, it seems, to the first days of the church there.

The Status of Jews in Greek Cities

Too often scholars of the early church assume that most Jews of the Diaspora were urban.[85] Sometimes related to this assumption is the belief that Jews were to some degree prosperous. For example, Trevett thinks that the Jews in Antioch "fared well" and had "opportunities for commerce."[86] Zetterholm implies a similar situation, where the Jewish synagogue was able to supply for the needs of its own community but also had sufficient surplus to aid non-Jewish newcomers to the city who required assistance.[87] The reality, however, was probably quite different. Even if urban life presented opportunities for prosperity, most Jews would have

---

[82] The language that Ignatius uses against Judaism is undeniably harsh (see esp. ch. 3, pp. 102–4). As with most matters related to Ignatius, a range of hypotheses vie for attention, from seeing an ugly anti-Semitism in Ignatius's words to contending that Ignatius had no gripe with "orthodox" Judaism at all but only with docetic Gentile schismatics who misused the Jewish tradition. These matters will be addressed below in several places.

[83] A still standard treatment is Kraeling, "The Jewish Community in Antioch," 130–60.

[84] See the section "Jewish-Christian Relations in Antioch" in ch. 4, pp. 141–53.

[85] W. H. C. Frend, *The Rise of Christianity* (Philadelphia: Fortress, 1984), 30–43; Wayne A. Meeks, *The First Urban Christians* (New Haven and London: Yale University Press, 1983), 34; Meeks and Wilken, *Jews and Christians in Antioch*, 1; Rodney Stark, *The Rise of Christianity* (Princeton: Princeton University Press, 1996), 57; S. W. Baron, *A Social and Religious History of the Jews* (2d ed.; New York: Columbia University Press, 1952–), 1:170.

[86] Trevett, *A Study of Ignatius*, 38; see also Colin J. Hemer, *The Letters to the Seven Churches of Asia in Their Local Setting* (JSNTSup 11; Sheffield: JSOT Press, 1986), 160. Meeks and Wilken speak of the Jews of Antioch as being "more affluent" than rural Jews (*Jews and Christians in Antioch*, 10), suggesting some degree of economic success. They also mention, however, that Jews were of all social levels and, "for the most part, they were poor" (p. 12).

[87] Magnus Zetterholm, *The Formation of Christianity in Antioch: A Social-Scientific Approach to the Separation between Judaism and Christianity* (New York: Routledge, 2003), 125–27.

been unable to take advantage of such situations.[88] Many would have been slaves; many, agriculturalists; many, day laborers; many, poor; and perhaps most, rural.[89]

---

[88] See Mikael Tellbe, "The Temple Tax as a Pre-70 CE Identity Marker," in *The Formation of the Early Church* (ed. Jostein Ådna; WUNT 183; Tübingen: Mohr Siebeck, 2005): 32, n. 55. Tellbe points to works by G. LaPiana, H. J. Leon, Leonard Victor Rutgers, and M. H. Williams and cites Williams's comment that "not a single rich or even moderately prosperous Jew is found in all the literature of the late Republic and the early empire" (M. H. Williams, "The Expulsion of the Jews from Rome in A. D. 19," *Latomus* 48 [1989]: 781–82).

[89] The rural element of Diaspora Judaism has gained some recognition. Frend admits that "there may have been something that could be termed a rural Dispersion" ("Town and Countryside in Early Christianity," in *The Church in Town and Countryside* [ed. Deker Baker; *Studies in Church History* 16; Oxford: Blackwell, 1979], 35). A few other writers are less equivocal. Martin Hengel argues that for the early Hellenistic period in Egypt, Jews were "predominantly a peasant people" (*Jews, Greeks, and Barbarians: Aspects of the Hellenization of Judaism in the pre-Christian Period* [trans. John Bowden; Philadelphia: Fortress, 1980], 87], and he provides a brief discussion of the character of Diaspora Judaism in his chapter titled "Jews in a Greek-Speaking Environment: Mercenaries, Slaves, Peasants, Craftsmen, and Merchants." This is a far more nuanced and adequate treatment of the Jewish Diaspora than is reflected in the sweeping statements, often confidently made, about the urban character of the Jewish Diaspora. Hengel (p. 91) further points to Josephus's comment that Jews were not merchants but peasants (Josephus, *Ag. Ap.* 1.60). Jacob Neusner contends that rabbinic literature arose in the town and village, not the city, and that most Jews were rural in Palestine and Mesopotamia at least ("The Experience of the City in Late Antique Judaism," in *Studies in Judaism and Its Greco-Roman Context* [vol. 5 of *Approaches to Ancient Judaism*; ed. William Scott Green; BJS 32; Atlanta: Scholars Press, 1985], 37–52). Neusner dismisses the city/country dialectic as not of much significance (pp. 44, 46). Tessa Rajak recognizes that although we "cannot say much about rural settlements," it is clear that there were rural Jews, though all numbers are "highly speculative" ("The Jewish Community and Its Boundaries," in *The Jews among Pagans and Christians in the Roman Empire* [ed. Judith Lieu, John North, and Tessa Rajak; New York: Routledge, 1992], 10). Victor Tcherikover believes that Jews were spread throughout Egypt, and he offers evidence for Jews in villages there (*Hellenistic Civilization and the Jews* [trans. S. Applebaum; Philadelphia: Jewish Publication Society of America, 1959], 285–86). S. Applebaum thinks that for Pamphylia the evidence suggests that "a considerable part of the Jewish population of the region was rural, and unattached to city communities" ("The Organization of the Jewish Communities in the Diaspora," *in The Jewish People in the First Century: Historical Geography, Political History, Social, Cultural, and Religious Life and Institutions* [ed. S. Safrai and M. Stern; 2 vols.; CRINT 1; Assen, Neth.: Van Gorcum; Philadelphia: Fortress, 1974–1976]: 1:486). For almost every other area of the empire, Applebaum's conclusion is the same: Diaspora Jews had a considerable rural contingent (S. Applebaum, "The Social and Economic Status of Jews in the Diaspora," ibid., 2:701–27). Smallwood comments that most of the Jews of Palestine were agricultural rather than commercial in the first century, although she does not carry this observation over to the Diaspora (*The Jews under Roman Rule*, 122). Most recently, Stephen Mitchell, who, in his detailed study of Anatolia, questions the supposed urban character of Diaspora Judaism, comments, "The conventional picture of diaspora Jews as a distinct urban minority group, which earned a living from crafts and trade, has never

More important than the economic condition of Jews has been the question of the status of Jews as citizens. Although the nature of Jewish rights in Hellenistic cities is debated,[90] this much is agreed upon: Jews had long been residents of some of the cities, where they constituted a significant and identifiable segment of the population. Further, they claimed and possessed special rights. These rights were begrudged enough for enemies of the Jews to seek to curtail them and valued enough for the Jews to defend them.

Much of the modern debate over the status of Jews has focused on the nature of the Greek city *(polis)*. This focus may be somewhat misdirected. Grainger warns that we should not be thinking in terms of the Greek *polis* in our discussion of citizenship. He points out that the cities of Seleucid Syria were not *Greek* cities, but *Macedonian,* and he questions efforts to define the Seleucid cities in terms of the *polis.* These cities were framed to suit the needs of Seleucus and the Seleucid state; none fit exactly the definition of *polis,* a term that itself was not fixed.[91] This recognition removes some of the barriers that had restricted the debate over the nature of the status of Jews in cities such as Antioch.

Some scholars have argued that part of the reason for the confusion about Jewish rights is that different sets of rights may need to be distinguished.[92] There is the right of citizenship in a Greek city (the *polis*), but there are also rights specifically assigned to particular groups within a city by powers superior to the local city authorities—that is, by the Macedonian rulers who succeeded Alexander's empire and by the Romans who replaced these dynasties. Although these rights would not technically have been rights of citizenship in the local *polis,* they could have been substantial.

Regarding the question of citizenship, two main lines of argument have been relied on to establish that Jews, as a group, did not have such privileges.[93] The first argument asserts that the religious scruples of the Jews and the civic obligations

---

carried much conviction" (*Anatolia: Land, Men, and Gods in Asia Minor* [2 vols.; Oxford: Clarendon, 1993], 2:35). He reminds us that the Jewish settlers under Antiochus III were "first and foremost farmers" (p. 35) and offers a range of evidence for rural Jewish presence in Asia Minor (35–37).

[90] For a brief summary of some of the issues, see Zetterholm, *The Formation of Christianity in Antioch,* 32–37. See also Aryeh Kasher, *The Jews in Hellenistic and Roman Egypt;* and idem, "The Rights of the Jews of Antioch on the Orontes," *Proceedings of the American Academy for Jewish Research* 49 (1982): 69–85.

[91] Grainger, *The Cities of Seleukid Syria,* 54–55. Downey made a similar point earlier (*A History of Antioch,* 114–15). Zetterholm, however, thinks that the organization of Antioch reflected the traditional structure of the polis (*The Formation of Christianity in Antioch,* 44, n. 27). Grainger's position was worked out earlier by a number of scholars. For an overview of the evidence, see Kasher, "The Rights of the Jews."

[92] Kasher, "The Rights of the Jews."

[93] For a brief review of the matter, see Zetterholm, *The Formation of Christianity in Antioch,* 32–37.

of citizens would have clashed. The typical Jew, considered to be pious and observant, would have been unable to shoulder the responsibilities of citizenship in Hellenistic cities, which presumably would have included at least token recognition of the pagan gods.[94] Those who so argue usually admit that certain Jews (most probably apostate) could have gained full citizenship, and typically a number of examples are pointed out.[95] The second line of argument puts forward the *politeuma* (πολίτευμα) as the formal association of Jews in Greek cities. This structure supposedly allowed particular ethnic groups who were resident in a city but not entitled to citizenship to live in the city mainly according to their ancestral traditions.

Both assertions contain elements of weakness. Given that the status of Jews in the Diaspora is, admittedly, complicated and sometimes frustratingly ambiguous, the precise status of the Jews in Hellenistic cities is likely to remain a topic of debate for years to come.[96] There is enough evidence, however, to raise questions about the common assumptions just mentioned.

Jewish Religious Scruples

The clash between Jewish religious scruples and the obligations of citizenship in Hellenistic cities probably has been drawn too starkly by those who dismiss the likelihood of full citizenship rights for Jews.[97] Indeed, the possibility of a collision

---

[94] Smallwood (*The Jews under Roman Rule,* 359–60), following closely the view of Downey (*A History of Antioch,* 79–80), cautions against the conclusion that the original Jewish settlers of Antioch had full rights as citizens. She argues that the obligations of such citizenship would have entailed religious duties that could not be performed by observant Jews. Smallwood therefore expects that if full citizenship was extended to the original Jewish settlers, few would have accepted it. She thinks it more probable that Seleucus simply extended the right of citizenship to Jews who individually requested it, rather than making a blanket inclusion of the entire Jewish community. Smallwood sees the clash of obligations occurring for Jews not just in Antioch but in any Hellenistic city. See also Lester L. Grabbe, *Judaism from Cyrus to Hadrian* (Minneapolis: Fortress, 1992), 2:405–9.

[95] These examples include Antiochus of Antioch (Josephus, *J. W.* 7.47) and Tiberius Julius Alexander, a nephew of Philo, who was Roman governor of Palestine and Egypt (Josephus, *Ant.* 20.100). Surely there were countless more. See Feldman, *Jew and Gentile in the Ancient World,* 79–83.

[96] Applebaum comments that the "problem of Jewish status in the cities of the Hellenistic kingdoms is perhaps one of the most complicated in Jewish history" ("The Legal Status of the Jewish Communities in the Diaspora," in *The Jewish People in the First Century: Historical Geography, Political History, Social, Cultural, and Religious Life and Institutions* [ed. S. Safrai and M. Stern; 2 vols.; CRINT 1; Assen, Neth.: Van Gorcum; Philadelphia: Fortress, 1974–1976], 1:434).

[97] For recent scholarship on the subject of the status of Jews in Hellenistic cities, see Erich S. Gruen, *Diaspora: Jews amidst Greeks and Romans* (Cambridge and London: Harvard University Press, 2002), 126–31. In ch. 2, Gruen discusses in detail the

between Jews' religious and civic obligations does not seem to have occurred to observant Jews of the period.[98] Josephus argues that Jews had full citizenship rights in cities such as Antioch and Alexandria, and he assumes it for Jews in many other Hellenistic cities.[99] For our purposes here, it does not matter whether Josephus was correct or mistaken about the status and rights of Jews. The telling point is that a Jewish author—and, we assume, his readers—were able to think in terms of Jewish citizenship in Hellenistic communities without any sense of the supposedly impossible religious predicament that modern scholarship contends must have confronted these Jews.[100] Consider, too, the comment in Acts

---

situation of Jews in Alexandria (pp. 54–83). See also Applebaum, "Legal Status of the Jewish Communities," 420–63; idem, "The Organization of the Jewish Communities in the Diaspora," 464–503; Tessa Rajak, "Was There a Roman Charter for the Jews?" *JRS* 74 (1984): 107–23.

[98] What it meant to be an observant Jew in antiquity is a matter of debate. See p. 61, n. 60.

[99] Josephus is the main source for information about the citizenship claims of Jews. Although Philo's comments are less clear, it appears that Philo's family had citizenship in Alexandria and that he experienced no clash between religious sensibilities and civic duties (see Lester L. Grabbe, "The Hellenistic City of Jerusalem," in *Jews in the Hellenistic and Roman Cities* [ed. John R. Bartlett; New York: Routledge, 2002], 18).

[100] A passage frequently cited to demonstrate that citizenship in Greek cities entailed activities in which the pious Jew could not participate is 3 Macc 2:30. Given that the context is Ptolemy IV Philopator's exceptional hostility and resentment of the Jews, stemming from Jewish attempts to bar him access to the Jerusalem temple, we must be careful not to take the conditions of citizenship expressed here for Alexandria as definitive for all Greek cities or even for Alexandria when relations between Jews and Greeks were less strained. A more detailed description of how Jews might accommodate the demands of citizenship within the obligations of Judaism appears in 2 Macc 4:7–22. This passage recounts Jason's gaining the high priesthood and enrolling the people of Jerusalem as citizens of Antioch in the early years of the reign of Antiochus IV Epiphanes (see Grabbe, "The Hellenistic City of Jerusalem," 6–21, for a full discussion). What is most telling about the description of activities under the new status is that there is no significant change in the religious activities: pagan rites do not replace the rites of Judaism. Although it is true that the author is offended by the diversion of the attention of some priests from their temple duties to the entertainment of the gymnasium, it is not a change in religion that has occurred; it is, rather, a change in the *careful* performance of the rites. The author of 1 Maccabees reports a starker departure from the practices of Judaism. He notes that some removed the marks of circumcision (1 Macc 1:15). His other comments are of a general nature: Jews "abandoned the holy covenant" and "sold themselves to do evil." Such comments may reveal more about the author's perception of the situation than the concrete changes in practice. Had such radical departure from Jewish rites followed from the enrollment of Jews as citizens of Antioch, the author of 2 Maccabees would have made this a significant point of his critique. Indeed, the author notes how Jews handled one situation of potential conflict so as to keep their Judaism intact (2 Macc 2:18–20). Later, under Antiochus, Judaism was outlawed, but this had nothing to do with the question of citizenship and its obligations (1 Macc 1:41–50; 2 Macc 6:1–11).

about Paul's citizenship in Tarsus (Acts 21:39). Again, it does not matter whether the author had his facts right about Paul's status. The point is that a writer, well acquainted with Judaism and the world of the Diaspora, could speak naturally of a pious Jew's citizenship in a Greek city.[101]

Our perceptions about what constituted the duties of citizenship do not seem to mesh with what the ancient Jews themselves understood citizenship to entail. Some ancient Jews, at least, seem to have understood the loyalties demanded by citizenship in Greek cities and faithfulness to Judaism as generally compatible, not competitive. It appears not to have been an issue for Jews generally and thus not a matter of focus in Jewish literature of the period. In light of this, arguments that build on the supposed clash of Jewish scruples with obligations of Greek citizenship must be set aside or more carefully qualified.

What is perhaps most significant about the supposed clash of Jewish piety and civic responsibilities is that, according to Josephus, generally neither Greek citizens nor Jews themselves raise the matter. Rather, it is raised by groups who are themselves seeking citizenship or Greeks who appear to be attempting to curtail rights that Jews already possess.[102] At least, that is the situation in the passage to which appeal is most often made. Despite Josephus's apologetic spin here, the details of his account deserve consideration. In Alexandria, Egyptians, some of whom did not have citizenship in Alexandria but were trying to make their case for inclusion, were the ones who brought into the debate the incompatibility of Jewish obligations. Thus these opponents of Jewish citizenship are better viewed as advocates for their own claim for citizenship than as perceptive commentators on Jewish rights and obligations. It appears that these Egyptians attempted to strengthen their case by disputing the qualifications of a group already having citizenship rights, the Jews. By raising the issue of religious obligations, they introduced a matter that might be problematic for Jews but not for Egyptians. Granted, this suggests that some saw the issue of obligations as having potential to sway the debate; it does not indicate, however, that it was the decisive factor or that such a matter complicated Jewish citizenship before this incident. Indeed, Josephus implies that a clash of Jewish loyalties had never been an issue with the Greeks and Macedonians. That is not to say that issue could

---

[101] For a brief comment on Jewish participation in the larger society without a clash of loyalties, see Paula Fredriksen, "What 'Parting of the Ways'? Jews, Gentiles, and the Ancient Mediterranean City," in *The Ways That Never Parted: Jews and Christians in Late Antiquity and the Early Middle Ages* (eds. Adam H. Becker and Annette Yoshiko Reed; Texte und Studien zum antiken Judentum 95; Tübingen: Mohr Siebeck, 2003), 44–46; see also John C. Lentz Jr., *Luke's Portrait of Paul* (SNTSMS 77; Cambridge: Cambridge University Press, 1993), 34–43.

[102] Josephus, *Ag. Ap.* 2.69–72. Philo also points to the "Egyptian" character of the opposition to Jews in Alexandria (*Flaccus* 4.17).

not be raised by Greek citizens themselves, and such appears to have happened in an incident in Ionia.[103]

When Josephus discusses Jewish citizenship, he never hints at a clash of obligations. This would be puzzling if such an issue were the barrier that long had restricted Jews from access to citizenship. It appears, then, that a clash of religious obligations may not have been a primary issue in the debate over citizenship.

Politeuma

The *politeuma* theory proposes that Jews (and other ethnic groups) were recognized as self-governing communities, or *politeumata*, within Hellenistic cities. It was in such a structure that Jews had their status defined and their rights maintained.[104]

Not everyone accepts this popular hypothesis. Constantine Zuckerman offers a forceful critique of this theory and discusses some of the literature in his review of *The Jews in Hellenistic and Roman Egypt* by Aryeh Kasher.[105] Furthermore, Gert Lüderitz, who has provided a detailed analysis of the use of the term *politeuma,* concludes that the term had a variety of meanings and that the meaning that attached itself to the discussion of Jewish status in Hellenistic cities is, at best, forced.[106] If these objections to the *politeuma* theory should gain wide acceptance, the older theory of Jewish citizenship in Hellenistic cities is likely to receive new life, although other reconstructions certainly may be possible, given the ambiguity of much of the evidence.

The attractiveness of the *politeuma* thesis is that it provides a category of enough ambiguity to help explain why there could have been a debate over the rights of Jews. If the status of Jews was clear-cut, one wonders how there could have been a debate at all: either Jews were citizens or they were not. If, however, the status of Jews was connected to the *politeuma,* then there may have been

---

[103] Josephus, *Ant.* 12.125–26.

[104] Applebaum tries to refocus the debate, suggesting that scholars have rejected the likelihood of Jewish citizenship in Greek cities because of "too exclusive a preoccupation with the issue in relation to Alexandria," which in turn has led to a dismissal of Josephus's witness regarding these rights in other cities ("Legal Status of the Jewish Communities," 434).

[105] Constantine Zuckerman, "Hellenistic *politeumata* and the Jews: A Reconsideration," *Scripta classica israelica* 8–9 (1985–1989): 171–84. Feldman comments that Zuckerman "has pointed out the rather astounding fact that there is no mention of a *politeuma* of this nature in Philo, Josephus, or the *Corpus Papyrorum Judaicarum*, or, for that matter, in any of the statements of the anti-Jewish bigots, who supposedly fought to abolish these Jewish organizations" (*Jew and Gentile in the Ancient World,* 92.).

[106] Gert Lüderitz, "What Is the Politeuma?" in *Studies in Early Jewish Epigraphy* (ed. Jan Willem van Henten and Pieter Willem van der Horst; Leiden and New York: E. J. Brill, 1994), 182–225.

debate over what rights within the *politeuma* corresponded to the rights of citizenship. Before we could build much on the *politeuma* thesis, however, we would need more convincing evidence that the *politeuma,* as understood in modern scholarship for defining the status of Jews, ever really existed.

The Status of Jews in Antioch

Whatever the case regarding the status of Jews in many Greek cities, Jews in Antioch may have had a particularly strong case for status as full citizens. Seleucus had founded Antioch with Athenian and Macedonian soldiers.[107] Josephus adds a third founding people, Jewish mercenary troops, and he is explicit about the status of Jews in Antioch: (1) they represented one group in the population of the original city when Seleucus I founded it in 300 B.C.E., and (2) Jews had full rights as citizens.[108] The value of Josephus's statement is debated, given the apologetic nature of many of his comments.[109] But this in itself is not sufficient grounds to dismiss his statement outright.

The situation Josephus describes, in which Jews received full rights as citizens in Antioch, fits well the historical situation for the founding of that city. The objection usually raised against this possibility is that Jewish religious sensibilities would not have permitted Jews to participate in the cultic obligations of a citizen, but this argument is not compelling for the period of the founding of Antioch, whatever the case may be for the later period.[110] For one thing, it is unlikely that all Jews were equally "observant"—if this term has any meaning for the period about 300 B.C.E., when so much of the character of a "common Judaism" had

---

[107] Antiochus III added settlers from Aetolia, Euboea, and Crete in 189 B.C.E. (Jones, *The Cities of the Eastern Roman Provinces,* 242). The Macedonian component could not have been large. Jones notes that Alexander had only fifteen thousand Macedonian troops with him, and these had to be shared among the successors. Strabo speaks of a "multitude of settlers" in Antioch (*Geogr.* 16.2.4); only a few of these could have been Macedonian.

[108] Josephus, *Ant.* 12.119; *Ag. Ap.* 2.39.

[109] Although Josephus is explicit that Jews constituted part of the original population of Antioch, many studies of Antioch's foundation pass over this comment in silence. Grainger, for example, does not mention Jews at all in the founding of Antioch, nor does he mention the service of Jews as mercenaries in Seleucus's army (*The Cities of Seleukid Syria*). Cummins reviews the debate (*Paul and the Crucified Christ in Antioch,* 141–42). Kasher has attempted to make a case in support of Josephus's statement (*The Jews in Hellenistic and Roman Egypt,* 298–99).

[110] Josephus, *Ant.* 12.125–126; *Ag. Ap.* 2.39. It is possible to accept Josephus's comment that Jewish settlers were part of the original inhabitants of Antioch and at the same time not be convinced that they had been granted full rights. R. Marcus, for example, does not think Jews in Antioch gained special rights until the time of Antiochus Epiphanes; see appendix C in Josephus, *Antiquities of the Jews* (LCL; Cambridge: Harvard University Press, 1943), 7:739.

yet to be worked out. Even if Jewish mercenaries were generally observant, it is improbable that Seleucus would have been aware of the scruples connected to observant Judaism or that the Jewish mercenaries would have understood every obligation of citizenship. For that matter, we cannot be sure that these issues had yet been fully worked out in the minds of the new Macedonian masters. The establishment of new Hellenistic communities, made up of quite diverse groups, was a new phenomenon, unexplored and, in its initial stages, probably provisional. Boundaries may yet have had to be fully drawn, sensibilities may yet have had to shape themselves to the new situation. Grainger's reminder is important: the cities of Seleucus were more Macedonian than Greek, and the structure was tailored specifically to the needs of the Seleucid regime.[111] It is not at all certain, then, that Jews would have encountered a clash of loyalties in accepting citizenship in Antioch.

At the same time, we cannot merely take Josephus's word on the Jewish component of the city's founding population. He was himself an apologist for Jewish rights in Antioch, and early rights for Jews going back to the establishment of the city would have helped his case. Is there reason to believe that Jews were, as Josephus says, part of the original settlers in Antioch? Were conditions such that Seleucus would have wanted to include Jews as an essential element of his new city and grant them full privileges?

As noted above, Antioch was founded within months of Ptolemy's seizure of land that had been assigned to Seleucus. As a result, Ptolemy's new borders came threateningly close to the major routes by which Seleucus's territory was held together. Antioch was one of four cities strategically founded north of the new borders, serving as a center from which Seleucus could resist further expansion from Ptolemy and protect the new territories he now held in Asia Minor and Syria.[112] Given the charged political situation during which the site was chosen and the city built, is there reason to think that an element of Jewish mercenaries would have been an attractive component, in Seleucus's mind, for his new city? There is.

The value of Jewish settlers is particularly enhanced by the taint on almost every other group that was incorporated into the new city. Grainger points out that not just the threat from Ptolemy's new borders would have concerned Seleucus; internal tensions also would have jeopardized the general security of Seleucus's new state.[113] But Grainger does not consider how this could have made Jewish mercenary troops an attractive addition to Antioch's founding core.

First, there was the hostility of the native Syrian population to the Macedonians and Greeks, regardless of which of Alexander's generals sought or claimed

---

[111] Grainger, *The Cities of Seleukid Syria*, 67–87.

[112] Ibid., 57–61.

[113] Rather than discuss all of Grainger's points, I will address only those that seem directly relevant to the status of the original Jewish settlers in Antioch (ibid., 54).

their territory and loyalty. If the natives resented Alexander the Great, they would hardly have welcomed his generals.[114] A second problem for Seleucus was that certain Greek communities had already been established as trading posts in the area before the invasion of Alexander, and there is reason to think that they were not particularly keen on the new Macedonian power and that they harbored a resentment that appears not to have escaped Seleucus's notice.[115] It is important to remember that Philip of Macedon had defeated Greek city-states and that Greek cities frequently revolted under Alexander and his successor Macedonian generals. Indeed, some Greeks even had served as mercenaries in the Persian forces that opposed Alexander. A third source of insecurity for Seleucus came from the Macedonian and Greek troops of Antigonus, whom Seleucus and members of the alliance had just defeated. Some of these troops had been in this area for thirty years or more, settled by Alexander or Antigonus to protect this newly-captured territory; others had been active soldiers in the forces of Antigonus. These troops had owed loyalty to Antigonus, and even with Antigonus dead, there was some suspicion that the loyalty of these soldiers now might lie with Antigonus's still-active son Demetrius rather than with Seleucus, who had just defeated them.[116] Problems were made graver by the fact that most of Seleucus's loyal Macedonian troops were engaged in holding the recently conquered lands of Mesopotamia and the east. Seleucus was also, for the most part, cut off from further recruitment in Macedonia and Greece, and—amplifying these matters—he had had the smallest army at Ipsus, where the coalition had defeated Antigonus. Thus Seleucus had a critical manpower shortage at a time when he needed increased troop strength to secure his hold on his newly acquired lands in Syria and when the ambitions of Ptolemy had robbed him of what he perceived as his rightful lands of Coele-Syria.[117]

The original Macedonian and Greek settlers of Antioch were, at best, doubtful supporters of Seleucus, however much Seleucus was able to win their loyalty later in his reign. A body of Jewish mercenaries, owing allegiance to no one other than the highest bidder and already having a record of service in Seleucus's army, may have been among Seleucus's choice settlers. Insofar as these Jewish troops had a sense of loyalty, it would have been to Seleucus. Under such conditions,

---

[114] Ibid., 31–33.

[115] Ibid., 32–47, 51. As evidence that Seleucus viewed the earlier Greek settlers with some suspicion, Grainger points out that one of Seleucus's first acts after gaining the Syrian territory was to destroy Antigonia, the only Greek city in the land (p. 47). Grainger speaks of this destruction as "in part an exorcism of Antigonos" (55). Seleucus did, however, raise the status of some smaller Greek settlements (53).

[116] Ibid., 54–55. Demetrius was able to control the Mediterranean Sea and the cities of Tyre and Sidon.

[117] Grainger comments on the problem of manpower (ibid., 60–61). Specific problems are mentioned in scattered comments throughout Grainger's work.

we cannot assume that a body of Jewish troops would have appeared inferior or less valuable to Seleucus in his new city than the other groups from which he had to choose, all of whom were somewhat tainted. If Josephus is correct that Jews constituted part of the original settlers of Antioch (a reasonable enough conclusion), it is certainly within reason to assume that Jews were not considered an inferior component by Seleucus or denied the full rights extended to the other founding groups.

Aside from Josephus's comment that Jewish mercenaries were part of the original city, almost nothing is known about Jews in Antioch in the first one hundred years of the city's existence. This should not be read as evidence, however, against a Jewish presence in Antioch in its earliest years. Any evidence for the area of Antioch during this period is scarce, whether about Jews, Macedonians, Greeks, or native Syrians.

Even if Josephus is mistaken about Jews constituting an original element in the city's foundation, they must have begun to immigrate to Antioch shortly after the city's founding. The nexus between Syria and Mesopotamia was strong. Both were prominent areas of the Seleucid kingdom and were linked by important trade routes. With a considerable Jewish population in Mesopotamia and with Antioch as a midway point between Mesopotamia and Jerusalem, it is unlikely that Antioch was long without a Jewish element. Further, not only did Jews become residents of Antioch; they must have done so in considerable numbers, for they were later afforded special rights.

Population Shifts and Immigrants in Antioch

General Considerations

Antioch would have experienced various booms and busts during its history. The population at times would have declined quite dramatically, for earthquakes and epidemics were recurring realities, and the chaotic period of the breakup of the Seleucid Empire before the conquest by Rome would have further weakened the city.[118] Such events, however, are unlikely to have altered the ethnic mix.[119] But,

---

[118] Stark has made much of earthquakes and epidemics in population decline and social instability (*The Rise of Christianity*, 73–94, 158–61). Zetterholm, basically following Stark, argues that Antioch's size was such that it experienced an increased risk of epidemics (*The Formation of Christianity in Antioch*, 28–30). Stark's and Zetterholm's views of city life, however, maybe too bleak.

[119] Stark's argument that the ratio of Christians noticeably increased as a result of Christian care during epidemics is not convincing. Even if he is correct on the Christian/pagan population shifts, Stark does not address how the Jewish proportion would have been altered, which is our concern here (*The Rise of Christianity*, 73–94). His arguments

as suggested above, it is the shift in the proportion of ethnic groups in Antioch and, more important, the resulting shift in perceptions of privilege and power that are likely to have caused the most strain on relationships between Jews and the other groups in Antioch.

Significant shifts in the ratio of the various populations could occur when an ethnic group was expelled from a city, but we have no evidence of such actions related to the Jews of Antioch. This is not to say that such events did not occur, for such action was *attempted* against the Jews in Antioch and was *successful* elsewhere.[120]

Some scholars have argued that the ratio of the Jewish population could have risen as a result of the Jewish prohibition against abortion and infanticide, two practices that would have tended to make the size of Jewish families somewhat larger than Gentile families, who had fewer reservations about these practices.[121] Others, however, have dismissed such circumstances as irrelevant for explaining the size of the Jewish population.[122] At any rate, these practices would not have produced as dramatic and immediately noticeable shifts in the ethnic mix of the

---

often seem to have a way of coming full circle, gathering enough counterevidence in the process to require a heavy qualification of the primary assertion. If, for example, the Christian community had a better survival rate during epidemics because of the care they gave their sick, then surely the Jewish community would have reflected a similar success, and the sense that the Christian God was the best protector would have been less obvious than Stark asserts.

[120] See the section "The Request to Expel the Jews" in ch. 4, pp. 137–38. Note, however, Gruen's caution that even where edicts of expulsion survived, they may not have been carried out (*Diaspora*, 38–42).

[121] Hecataeus of Abdera (late 300s B.C.E.) mentions that the Jews were always rich in manpower because they did not expose their children (cited by Diodorus Siculus, *Bibliotheca historica* 40). Tacitus, too, points to this prohibition on exposure in order to explain the size of the Jewish population (*Ann.* 5.5.3). Josephus mentions the Jewish prohibition against the exposure of infants, but he does not associate it with the size of the Jewish population, although this does not mean that he would have denied such an association (*Ag. Ap.* 2.25). See Patrick Gray, "Abortion, Infanticide, and the Social Rhetoric of the *Apocalypse of Peter,*" *JECS* 9 (2001): 313–37; Martin Goodman, *Mission and Conversion: Prozelytizing in the Religious History of the Roman Empire* (Oxford: Clarendon, 1994), 84. The significance and frequency of abortion and exposure in the Greco-Roman world are themselves matters of debate. Bruce W. Frier offers a careful evaluation of the phenomena of abortion and exposure in "Natural Fertility and Family Limitations in Roman Marriage," *CP* 89 (1994): 318–33. See also Donald Engels, "The Problem of Female Infanticide in the Greco-Roman World," *Classical Philology* 75 (1980): 112–20; and William V. Harris, "Child-Exposure in the Roman Empire," *JRS* 48 (1994): 1–22; idem, "The Theoretical Possibility of Extensive Infanticide in the Graeco-Roman World," *Classical Quarterly* 32 (1982): 114–16.

[122] Feldman accepts that the Jewish prohibition against infanticide and abortion would account for some increase in population, but he argues that these are insufficient factors to account for the sizeable Jewish population in the Greco-Roman period, which,

population as other factors might have, such as large-scale immigration or resettlement. For our purposes, therefore, it is important to determine when there may have been significant pressures from immigration (for both Jews and non-Jews) and what tensions may have arisen from a change in the proportion of the various ethnic groups in Antioch by the introduction of a new element into the city.

Jewish Immigration

Population shifts, immigration, and the presence of distinctive ethnic groups would not have gone unnoticed by the population of Antioch, or of any city.[123] Indeed, it appears that Jews were often able to distinguish even within their own community between the older Jewish residents of Antioch and the newly-arrived Jews, or perhaps between Jews with a formal membership in the community and those still judged as foreigners—a term that even Josephus used to distinguish some Jews in Antioch from other Jews there (*J. W.* 7.47).[124] It is unclear in what contexts it was important for the permanent Jewish residents of Antioch to make a distinction between themselves and "foreign" Jews.[125] If there was a formal procedure controlling who gained membership in the Jewish community in

---

for Feldman, makes proselytism a necessary condition of Jewish growth (*Jew and Gentile in the Ancient World*, 293).

[123]We have a variety of evidence particularly related to Judaism. At Rome, Jews were expelled on occasion (Leonard Victor Rutgers, "Roman Policy toward the Jews: Expulsions from the City of Rome during the First Century C.E.," in *Judaism and Christianity in First-Century Rome* [ed. Karl P. Donfried and Peter Richardson; Grand Rapids: Eerdmans, 1998], 93–116). At Alexandria the Jewish community was identifiable, and action could be directed against them (see pp. 133–34). The Roman edicts that required that Greco-Roman cities provide an adequate supply of kosher meat for Jewish residents suggest some measure of clear identification of Jews, as does the Esther story. The point is that the Greco-Roman cities seem to have been able to identify the Jewish community and, at times, to take action to repress it.

[124]Who these "foreigners" (ξένους) in Josephus were is not clear. Kasher thinks they may have been Jewish zealots from Palestine (*The Jews in Hellenistic and Roman Egypt*, 305). Smallwood speculates that they may have been Christians (*The Jews under Roman Rule*, 362); see later in this chapter. The label "foreigner" is usually negative. Note that Flaccus refers to Jews of Alexandria as "foreigners" and "immigrants" (Philo, *Flaccus* 54).

[125]Cummins (*Paul and the Crucified Christ in Antioch*, 140, n. 7), following Kasher, claims that Antiochus, the son of the Jewish *archōn* of Antioch, differentiated between Jewish residents and Jewish foreigners in Antioch and that Antiochus fingered the Jewish foreigners as those who were behind a plot to burn the city. But Josephus gives no indication that Antiochus distinguished between two groups of Jews. In Josephus, the foreign Jews seem to have been no more to be blamed for the plot than were resident Jews; indeed, Antiochus accuses his own father, the *archōn* of the Jews in Antioch, as well as other Jewish residents of Antioch, and he seems to have taken action against the practice of Judaism (*J. W.* 7.47–53), which would have affected all observant Jews.

Antioch,[126] this could have resulted in a situation of some disadvantage to Christian Jews who moved to Antioch, particularly if tensions and suspicions were forming regarding the Christian group. Further, if Jewish immigrants needed formal admission into the Jewish community, some Jews could have failed that process and been expelled from the community as well. Again, such a situation could create some jeopardy for Christians.

Although evidence for Antioch is lacking, the situation in Alexandria may be relevant. Gideon Bohak points to evidence that increased immigration of Jews to Egypt was linked to difficulties in Palestine during wartime.[127] Although one must be cautious in comparing evidence from one city with that from another, Bohak's observations are what we might expect for Antioch also: war in Palestine would have created mobile groups of Jews (slaves and refugees), and nearby great cities of the empire, Alexandria and Antioch, would have been natural destinations. For refugees, the large Jewish population already established in these cities may have provided vital family connections to which Jews of Palestine could appeal in times of crises. It is a reasonable conclusion that population shifts similar to those in Alexandria were experienced in Antioch, a city as close and easy to reach as Alexandria and with a countryside much more Semitic and familiar.

The devastating famine of the 40s c.e.[128] and crises such as the brutal Jewish War[129] of 66–73 c.e. would have driven some Jews to seek refuge elsewhere, and these immigrants would have included Christian Jews who had been affected by the same calamities. Nearby Antioch, already containing a sizeable Jewish

---

[126] Most scholarly discussion has focused on the citizenship status of Jews in Greek cities. An equally important but largely neglected question is how a newly-arrived Jewish immigrant established his or her identity as a Jew and to what degree the local Jewish community controlled admission into its circle.

[127] Gideon Bohak, "Ethnic Continuity in the Jewish Diaspora in Antiquity," in *Jews in the Hellenistic and Roman Cities* (ed. John R. Bartlett; New York: Routledge, 2002), 187.

[128] Nicholas H. Taylor, "Palestinian Christianity and the Caligula Crisis, Part II: The Markan Eschatological Discourse," *JSNT* 62 (1996): 13–41; Gerd Theissen, *The Gospels in Context: Social and Political History in the Synoptic Tradition* (Minneapolis: Fortress, 1991), 125–65.

[129] There is a tradition that Christian Jews fled to Pella at the outbreak of the Jewish War. For a review of the evidence and a challenge to the traditional view, see Gerd Lüdemann, "The Successors of Pre-70 Jerusalem Christianity: A Critical Review of the Pella-Tradition," in *The Shaping of Christianity in the Second and Third Centuries* (vol. 1 of *Jewish and Christian Self-Definition*; ed. E. P. Sanders; Philadelphia: Fortress, 1980), 161–73. Also see Craig Koester, "The Origin and Significance of the Flight to Pella Tradition," *CBQ* 51 (1989): 90–106; Marcel Simon, "La migration à Pella: Légende ou réalité?" *Recherches de science religieuse* 60 (1972): 40–52; B. E. Gray, "The Movements of the Jerusalem Church during the First Jewish War," *JEH* 24 (1973): 1–7. Eusebius knew of traditions linking apostles and other first-century Christian notables to Asia Minor and elsewhere; this suggests some immigration of Christians from Palestine (*Hist. eccl.* 3.5, 18, 31).

population, would have had its attraction. Many Palestinian Jews must have had family connections with members of the Jewish community there and with Jews in other large centers of Jewish immigration in the eastern empire. But such an influx is likely to have sparked concern. A decree relayed to Alexandria about three decades before the war expressly forbade resident Jews from "bringing or inviting" Jews to Alexandria.[130] Although the decree is addressed to Alexandria, it is unlikely that the concern expressed in it related only to that city. Jews in Antioch also likely would not have operated freely, without restrictions on how many immigrants their community could absorb.[131] If the Jewish community was under some pressure regarding immigration and residency in the city, it is likely that they would have been forced to take a careful look at Jews who were hoping to find a home in the city. Some discrimination may have occurred, and if Christians were becoming a matter of concern, the discrimination may have had a greater impact on immigrants linked to the troublesome Christian movement.

Such an influx of foreign Jews may have created a new and more complex situation for the Jewish community in Antioch. If a group of Jews had been part

---

[130] The decree was from Emperor Claudius, who attempted to calm the tensions in Alexandria after the disturbances of 38–41. Two forms of the decree are extant: one is preserved in Josephus (*Ant.* 19.278–85); the other can be found in Victor Tcherikover, ed., *Corpus papyrorum judaicarum* (3 vols.; Cambridge: Published for Magnes Press, Hebrew University, by Harvard University Press, 1957–1964), 2:36–55. Only the latter contains the prohibition against Jewish immigration. Most scholars think that Josephus's version was modified in the interest of Jewish apologetic either by Josephus or by someone before him. The prohibition in the decree suggests that Jews had attempted to increase their numbers through immigration (or at least could be suspected or accused of this) and that non-Jewish residents regarded the practice as threatening in some way.

[131] The matter is not clear-cut. Cities tended to treat residency as a matter of privilege. Under Roman rule, the power of the city elders to deal with immigrants probably was more restricted, although local conditions may have varied considerably. Examples from both Alexandria and Antioch seem to indicate that these cities did not have the power to exclude undesirable immigrants or to expel elements of their population who were already resident but who had become undesirable. In the case of Alexandria, Jews were accused of bringing in immigrants, and the city itself seems to have been unable to prevent such influx without the authorization of Rome. In the case of Antioch, the citizens twice petitioned Titus to expel the Jewish residents after the Jewish War, but he refused (Josephus, *J. W.* 7.100–103, 109). Both cases suggest that under Roman rule Greek cities lost some of their power to control residency, and this could have aggravated tensions and increased senses of privilege and loss. The evidence also suggests, however, that cities continued to maintain an interest in controlling residency, even though their power may have been somewhat restricted. The Romans seem not to have been completely unsympathetic to the desire of the cities to control their populations, and the authorities probably tended to side with the local governments on the matter, perhaps mainly because of the Roman interest in maintaining the status quo. Rome is another matter; various peoples were expelled from time to time.

of the founding population in Antioch, we cannot expect that the rights granted to them would have been automatically extended to all later Jewish immigrants. Most likely, rights given to the original Jewish families in a city would have been inherited only by their descendants and would not have been extended to any and every Jew who happened to choose Antioch as home at a later time. This would create classes of Jews and of privilege in Antioch.[132]

Whatever the case, any mass movement of Jews into the area of Antioch would not have gone unnoticed by the city leaders, by the larger populace, or by the Jewish community itself. Indeed, we cannot assume that the older Antiochene Jewish community welcomed every wave of Jewish immigration from Palestine or elsewhere. Antiochene Jews may have offered a cool reception to any flood—or even trickle—of immigrants, particularly when elements in the larger society were pressing to have all Jews expelled from the city, as was the case toward the end of the Jewish War. Indeed, it is possible that the influx of Jewish refugees into Antioch during the Jewish War is what prompted elements in the larger society to press for the removal of all Jews. At least it is likely that to a certain extent the issue of refugees figured in the crisis confronting the Jewish community in Antioch during the Jewish War. Jews as a group would have been very much on the minds of the residents of Antioch in the late 60s of the first century, since Antioch served as the main base of Roman military operations for the attack on Palestine and Jerusalem, with troops moving out of and returning to the city.[133] Further, during the initial stages of the Jewish War, Jews had slain the Gentile populations in many of the towns and villages of Syria, and Jews met similar fates as the Gentile populations retaliated. Josephus recounts the widespread incidents of slaughter in grim detail. In such an environment, many motivations spark conflict. Josephus offers three reasons for the attacks on the Jews: hatred, fear, and greed.[134]

Some citizens in Antioch took a particularly harsh stance against Jewish residents, even hoping to have them expelled from the city or, failing that, to

---

[132] The situation would have been different for Jewish immigrants had the original Jews been granted rights as a *politeuma*. New immigrants would have been more easily incorporated into the Jewish community and would have received the protection afforded to members of that community; this would not have been available to them had they lived in the city merely as resident aliens. But perhaps even then a Jew moving to Antioch would not have had immediate or unconditional membership in the recognized Jewish community.

[133] See Millar, *The Roman Near East*, 71–72.

[134] Josephus, *J. W.* 2.457–510. Jews in Antioch, Sidon, and Apamia did not suffer slaughter, slavery, or imprisonment, which was the common experience of Jews in the other cities of Syria and Palestine. Josephus does not mention such exceptions to the slaughter to prove a point or aid a particular agenda. He simply states that these cities were exceptions, and it is clear that he is puzzled as to why this was the case (*J. W.* 2.479).

terminate the specifically prescribed and guaranteed rights of the Jews there.[135] In such an environment, the Jewish leadership may have had an interest in silencing any disputes in the Jewish community that could bring further unwanted attention on the community from already hostile inhabitants.

Without probing the issues in depth here, the examination above points to the possibility of tension developing within the larger populace and within the Jewish community itself from an influx of Jewish immigrants or immigrants of any kind in significant numbers. Although we may not be able to determine the scope of the tension created by the pressures of immigration, the issue is not irrelevant for understanding aspects of the conflict between Jews and Christians. Such tension is, for the most part, unaddressed in the scholarly literature that examines the early Christian church in Antioch. Granted, answers are elusive for many of the questions related to such an environment of tension. For example, we cannot determine whether sufficient numbers of Jewish Christians fled to Antioch after the first organized persecution of Christians in Jerusalem for that influx to have come to the notice of the local Jewish or Roman administrators, although the influx need not have been massive to have caught their attention. Even a small number of Christian immigrants might have come to the attention of the Jewish leadership, for the network linking Jerusalem and Antioch would have kept the Jewish authorities in Antioch aware of crises and concerns in Jerusalem. Even the fledgling Christian community seems to have had an effective network between the two cities.[136] It is highly unlikely that the organized and well-established Jewish communities in these cities had no such effective network.

Non-Jewish Immigration

Non-Jewish immigration to Antioch would have had its high points and resulting pressures also. During the first twenty years of the city's existence, immigration from either Macedon or Greece would have been made difficult by the state of war in the intervening territory. After Seleucus's final victory, his territory bordered Greece and Macedon, but it is not certain that even then Greek and Macedonian immigrants would have chosen distant Antioch over the much nearer and long-established Greek cities on the Aegean coast of Asia Minor, assuming that such people desired to move at all and had a choice about where to reside.[137]

---

[135] As we have seen, however, not all Jewish residents could have been included in this sweeping proposal, since some Jews betrayed others and may have used underlying native suspicion against their own people.

[136] The treatment of the Jerusalem Council in Acts and its relations with Christians in Antioch—whatever the historicity of the accounts—indicates that the author considered such networks and communications natural.

[137] Jones notes how little interest Greeks generally had in settling in the east (*The Greek City from Alexander to Justinian*, 23–25).

Some immigration of Greeks and Macedonians to Antioch occurred in the second century B.C.E. Grainger argues that the Roman expansion into western Asia Minor at the expense of the Seleucid kingdom increased immigration east-ward.[138] This would have added to the Macedonian and Greek elements in An-tioch, but it is not known whether this population shift was a matter of concern to the Jewish residents or brought them any disadvantage.[139]

It is possible, too, that the proportion of the Greek population increased without immigration, simply by a mass movement of a non-Greek group *from* the city. We do not know whether Palestine became an attractive center for Jew-ish emigration from Antioch as the Maccabees expanded their territories.[140] This is possible, however, particularly given that Antioch experienced difficult times in the latter part of the second century and early part of the first century B.C.E. and that perhaps the Jews in Antioch were somewhat tainted by the Maccabean revolt. Any decline in the size of the Jewish community in Antioch probably was reversed, however, as Antioch became a key city under Roman rule. As already mentioned, when Josephus wrote at the end of the first century C.E., the size of the Jewish population in Antioch was large enough for him to comment and to offer some explanation.

Although details are not known, it is clear that Antioch would have experi-enced various population shifts. And it is possible, though not provable, that the Jewish population swelled so dramatically on occasion that other groups noticed the change with concern and placed the situation under a watchful eye. At other times, an influx of non-Jews into the city may have put pressure on living condi-tions, brought some disadvantage to the Jewish community, and provoked ethnic tensions.

---

[138] Grainger, *The Cities of Seleukid Syria*, 141; Jones thinks that the last group of Greek immigrants to Antioch were Euboeans and Aetolians, settled there under Antiochus the Great (*The Greek City from Alexander to Justinian*, 16).

[139] Jones maintains that the total number of Greek immigrants would have made little impact on the proportion of the ethnic mix (*The Greek City from Alexander to Justinian*, 24–25).

[140] Some of the Maccabean expansion in Galilee resulted in the forced conversion of conquered people. Certain native-born Jews may have moved to Galilee when the area came under Hasmonean control, although initially Jews already in Galilee had to be evacuated to Jerusalem for their safety. It is unclear whether Diaspora Jews came in any numbers to settle the area. For recent debate on the Jewish character of Galilee, see Mark A. Chancey, *The Myth of a Gentile Galilee* (SNTSMS 118; Cambridge: Cambridge University Press, 2002).

CHAPTER 2

Christian Conversion in Antioch

Jews, Nouveau Jews, and Near Jews

To understand Christianity in Antioch, one must determine the nature of the pool of religious seekers from which Christianity could draw its members. The most immediate circle, Jews, is complicated by the existence of proselytes and "God-fearers," two subspecies of associates of Judaism.[1] In the strictest traditional sense, a proselyte (προσήλυτος) was a full convert to Judaism who submitted to the prescriptions of Torah, including food laws, Sabbath observance, and, if male, circumcision—all matters possessing a social stigma or provoking comment in the ancient Mediterranean world.[2] The term "God-fearer" (ὁ φοβούμενος [τὸν θεόν]) and the associated term "God-worshiper" (ὁ σεβομένος [τὸν θεόν] or θεοσεβής), in their strictest sense, identified Gentiles who had not assumed the full obligations of Torah observance, but each of these terms could have a more elastic use, even identifying native-born Jews. All these expressions appear in early Christian literature, and to understand the relationships between Jews and Christians, some clarity must be gained about the status and significance of these groups within the Jewish and Christian communities.[3] Were proselytes and

---

[1] Martin Goodman, *Mission and Conversion*, 60–90.

[2] For a collection of ancient comments on Judaism, see Molly Whittaker, *Jews and Christians: Graeco-Roman Views* (Cambridge Commentaries on Writings of the Jewish and Christian World, 200 BC to AD 200, no. 6; Cambridge: Cambridge University Press, 1984), 3–130. For a detailed analysis of the matter, see Hans Conzelmann, *Gentiles, Jews, Christians: Polemics and Apologetics in the Greco-Roman Era* (trans. M. Eugene Boring; Minneapolis: Fortress, 1992), 45–233.

[3] The references to proselytes and God-fearers in the early Christian literature are not nearly as extensive as we might be led to believe from the attention given to these groups in many modern reconstructions of the early stages of the Christian movement. Proselytes are mentioned only in Acts (2:11; 6:5; 13:43) and Matthew (23:15); there are no references in the Apostolic Fathers. "God-fearers" are mentioned slightly more often (Acts 10:2, 22, 35; 13:16, 26), as are "God-worshipers" or "God-reverers" (Acts 13:43, 50; 16:14; 17:4, 17; 18:7). In early Christian literature, only the author of Acts uses a phrase that can be translated "God-fearer" in a way that seems to identify a group of pious

"God-fearers"/"God-worshipers" rare or numerous? Was their inclusion in the Jewish community generally welcomed, or was it a matter of controversy?[4] Was the degree of their commitment to Jewish life and law marginal or meticulous? Would Christianity really have offered a compelling option for them, as is often assumed? These questions are related, and the resolution of each has implications for any reconstruction of the early Christian movement.

Regarding Antioch and a Gentile interest in Judaism, Josephus states that Jews were "constantly attracting to their religious ceremonies multitudes of Greeks, and these they had in some measure incorporated with themselves."[5] Within a decade or two of this assessment, Ignatius offers evidence for the same kind of attraction, although he treats it as dangerous rather than as desirable.[6] Unfortunately, neither author uses the term "proselytes" or "God-fearers" for the situation in Antioch; this complicates the matter further, particularly when some modern reconstructions make proselytes or God-fearers the primary opposition to Ignatius and many theories make these groups the primary pool from which the Christian movement initially drew a substantial number of members.[7]

Gentiles somewhat attached to Judaism but distinguishable from Jews (10:22; 13:43, 50; 16:14; 17:4, 17; 18:7), and some modern scholars have disputed even these references. For a recent treatment of God-fearers in Acts, see chs. 3 and 4 in Shelly Matthews, *First Converts: Rich Pagan Women and the Rhetoric of Mission in Early Judaism and Christianity* (Stanford, Calif.: Stanford University Press, 2001), 51–95; and Irina Levinskaya, *The Book of Acts in Its Diaspora Setting*.

[4] Goodman notes that it was rare for ancient communities to let outsiders join and that Judaism was an exception, as it permitted non-Jews to join the Jewish community (*Mission and Conversion*, 61). Many Jews had a negative view of any effort to convert Gentiles, Goodman argues, and even those who had a more positive attitude did not engage in proselytizing until the end of the first century, in response to Christian proselytizing.

[5] ἀεί τε προσαγόμενοι ταῖς θρησκείαις πολὺ πλῆθος Ἑλλήνων, κἀκείνους τρόπῳ τινὶ μοῖραν αὑτῶν πεποίηντο (Josephus, *J. W.* 7.45). English translation: *Josephus* (trans. Ralph Marcus; LCL 281 [Cambridge, Mass: Harvard University Press, 1934]). The language is somewhat ambiguous, but there is a general impression that a noteworthy number of Gentiles in Antioch had developed a positive religious association with the Jewish community there. Such language does not help in determining what this number may have been or how these people were incorporated into the Jewish community. From Josephus's comment it need not follow that there were thousands.

[6] Ignatius warns, "But if anyone should interpret Judaism to you, do not hear him. For it is better to hear Christianity from a man who is circumcised than Judaism from one who is uncircumcised" (Ign. *Phld.* 6.1). It is not always clear in specific passages whether Ignatius is speaking of Jews, proselytes, God-fearers, or Gentiles who had no prior relationship to, or interest in, Judaism before becoming converts to the Christian movement. Ignatius's comment, for example, that "it is outlandish to proclaim Jesus Christ and practice Judaism" (Ign. *Magn.* 10.3) provides too little information for confident identification of the group, although it is clear that the passage is of interest to a discussion of adherents to Judaism.

[7] See the section "Ignatius's Opponents" in ch. 3, pp. 113–26.

Proselytes (Nouveau Jews)

There has been considerable recent debate about whether Judaism was pro-pelled by a missionary interest during the early period of Christian expansion.[8] The older view was that Jews were zealous proselytizers. Some scholars sense that a new and opposite consensus is taking shape: Jews were not driven by mission-ary zeal.[9] It is an exaggeration, however, to say, with Paula Fredriksen, that the theory about Jewish mission to non-Jews in the ancient world was "one of the biggest historiographical mistakes of the past century."[10]

Some Gentiles were certainly attracted to Judaism, and some in Antioch were attracted to such a degree that they became full converts, undergoing cir-cumcision and accepting the obligations of Torah.[11] This much is indicated by a

---

[8] For a collection of ancient comments on proselytes, see Whittaker, *Jews and Christians*, 85–91. Modern scholarship is divided on the question of Jewish interest in, or suc-cess at, proselytizing. The traditional view is restated in Dieter Georgi, *The Opponents of Paul in Second Corinthians* (Philadelphia: Fortress, 1986): 83–151; Louis D. Feldman, *Jew and Gentile in the Ancient World;* Thomas M. Finn, "The God-Fearers Reconsidered," *CBQ* 47 (1985): 75–84; John G. Gager, "Jews, Gentiles, and Synagogues in the Book of Acts," *HTR* 79 (1986): 91–99; Paul R. Trebilco, *Jewish Communities in Asia Minor* (SNTSMS 69; Cambridge: Cambridge University Press, 1991), 145–66; Matthews, *First Converts*, 1–9. Goodman challenges this view, arguing that Jews had little interest in proselytizing in the first century, although he admits that there is evidence that such interest developed in later centuries (*Mission and Conversion*, 60–90, 129–53). Chapter 4 of Goodman's book appeared in an earlier form as Martin Goodman, "Jewish Proselytizing in the First Cen-tury," in *The Jews among Pagans and Christians in the Roman Empire* (ed. Judith Lieu, John North, and Tessa Rajak; New York: Routledge, 1992), 53–78. See also Scot McKnight, *A Light among the Gentiles: Jewish Missionary Activity in the Second Temple Period* (Min-neapolis: Fortress, 1991). For a short summary of the debate, see Paul W. Barnett, "Jewish Mission in the Era of the New Testament and the Apostle Paul," in *The Gospel to the Na-tions: Perspectives on Paul's Mission* (ed. Peter Bolt and Mark Thompson; Downers Grove, Ill: InterVarsity; Leicester, U. K.: Apollos, 2000), 263–83. For some probing questions, see Brian McGing, "Population and Proselytism: How Many Jews Were There in the Ancient World?" in *Jews in the Hellenistic and Roman Cities* (ed. John R. Bartlett; New York: Routledge, 2002), 100–118.

[9] Shaye J. D. Cohen, "Adolf Harnack's 'The Mission and Expansion of Judaism': Chris-tianity Succeeds Where Judaism Fails," in *The Future of Early Christianity: Essays in Honor of Helmut Koester* (ed. Birger Pearson; Minneapolis: Fortress, 1991), 163–69.

[10] "What 'Parting of the Ways'?" 43, 48–56. Scholarship is crowded with historio-graphical mistakes as the discipline of history has sought to refine itself. Indeed, all disci-plines are relatively new; all are crowded with their methodological blind spots and dead ends. It is hardly likely, however, that the mistake about Jewish proselytizing (if indeed it is a mistake) rises to the exceptional level of blunder that Paula Fredriksen claims.

[11] The question of whether Gentiles became full converts has become a matter of debate. Against the traditional view, Shaye J. D. Cohen has argued that the idea of the proselyte becoming a Jew is a Gentile comment, not one that Jews made—at least there is

comment about Nicolaus, the first Christian identified with Antioch.[12] The characteristic by which the author of Acts chose to identify Nicolaus was his status as a Jewish proselyte. He is introduced as one of seven deacons, a group selected by the Hellenists at the behest of the apostles. These deacons were to supervise the distribution of food to the widows in the church in Jerusalem. Nicolaus alone is identified as a proselyte. The other six apparently were Jews, although they too, along with Nicolaus, were considered Hellenists.

It is not clear why the author notes Nicolaus's status as proselyte. The comment appears in a story where labels are important and where questions of status and advantage seem to lie close to the surface; thus the label "proselyte" may have been a characteristic that the author particularly wished to highlight here. On the other hand, Nicolaus may have been simply known as Nicolaus the proselyte and referred to in this way regardless of the story in which he might have been featured. Even in the latter case, the very fact that someone was identified routinely by such a label suggests that questions of status and identity were perhaps never far removed from the religious and social world of a proselyte.[13]

---

no record of Jews having made such a comment ("Crossing the Boundary and Becoming a Jew," *HTR* 82 [1989]: 14, 29). Jews would have viewed proselytes not as Jews but as a special kind of Gentile, according to Cohen. See also Goodman, *Mission and Conversion*, 86. But the Greco-Roman world appears to have judged proselytes as Jews, and the apparent expectation that proselytes would undergo circumcision would have reinforced that perception. Whatever, then, the nuanced ways with which Jews may have viewed proselytes, the reality is that both Jews and proselytes would have understood proselytes to be more closely associated with God's salvation than they had been in their prior state as Gentiles, and in the larger society such people would have been viewed as having moved into the world of Judaism.

[12] At the point in the story where Nicolaus appears, he is a resident of Jerusalem, but he is presented as a foreigner from Antioch (Acts 6:5). The story raises unanswered questions: Was Nicolaus one of many from Antioch who had made Jerusalem his home? Why had he moved there—for commercial or religious reasons or for something else? What kinds of contacts did he maintain with his previous community?

[13] The mention of Nicolaus as a proselyte does not help determine how many other proselytes were in either the Christian or the Jewish communities of Jerusalem and Antioch. Perhaps Nicolaus was a rarity and was chosen for this reason. On the other hand, he may have been chosen because some of the Hellenists in Jerusalem were proselytes and one of their own may have been seen as a necessary choice, especially since the matter to be resolved included questions of fairness within a community with subgroups. It is difficult to determine if Jerusalem had a sizeable population of proselytes. Whether Judaism had attracted a large number of proselytes in the Diaspora is an unresolved issue. As converts to Judaism, proselytes could have been attracted to Jerusalem in much the same way as Greek-speaking Jews of the Diaspora (this is suggested by the comment in Acts 2:10), and some proselytes may have made Jerusalem their home. The presence of Greek-speaking synagogues in Jerusalem suggests that some Jews (and probably proselytes) moved from the Diaspora to Jerusalem (see Martin Hengel, "The Pre-Christian

Most scholars have accepted that Nicolaus converted to Judaism in Antioch and later became a Christian either in Antioch or in Jerusalem, on the assumption that proselytes were always first interested in Judaism and that some later became interested in Christianity.[14] But during the turbulent and somewhat experimental period of the definition of early Christian membership, there is another possibility: that there were Gentiles who wished to convert directly to Christianity but the church, before working out a direct path into Christianity, simply guided the individuals through Jewish proselyte conversion into Christianity.

In addition, this assumption that Christianity gained its first considerable body of non-Jews from Gentile proselytes, such as Nicolaus, who had earlier converted to Judaism, is tenuous in several points.[15] First, Acts has routinely been misread as presenting a case for the success of Christian mission among proselytes. But Acts does not offer such a portrait. Proselytes are mentioned only three times. Once, as we have seen, the term is associated with Nicolaus, an early convert to the Christian movement. On the other two occasions, proselytes are linked with Jews in the phrase "Jews and proselytes" (Acts 2:10; 13:43 [NRSV "converts"]). Nothing in either passage suggests that proselytes had a keener interest in the Christian message or responded in greater numbers than did Jews, nor does either passage present proselytes as a middle ground between Jews and Christians. Some Jews and Jewish proselytes were receptive to the Christian message; most, however, were not, and according to Acts, Paul quickly turned to Gentiles after his message was rejected by most Jews (and, it would seem, by most Jewish proselytes as well). The story of Acts does not present proselytes in a more positive light than anyone else. Second, the only other reference to proselytes in early Christian literature is in the Gospel of Matthew, a document often associated with Antioch or Syria and perhaps familiar to Ignatius's own community. In one passage, Jesus offers his most stinging criticism of the Pharisees, using

---

Paul," in *The Jews among Pagans and Christians in the Roman Empire* [ed. Judith Lieu, John North, and Tessa Rajak; New York: Routledge, 1992], 41–43).

[14] See, for example, the popular work of Karen Armstrong, *A History of God: The 4000-Year Quest of Judaism, Christianity, and Islam* (New York: Alfred A. Knopf, 1993), 90. A more cautious assessment is expressed by Fearghus Ó Fearghail, who points out that the view in Acts is not that God-fearers converted to Christianity in greater numbers than did Jews ("The Jews in the Hellenistic Cities of Acts," in *Jews in the Hellenistic and Roman Cities* [ed. John R. Bartlett; New York: Routledge, 2002], 50).

[15] The contention here is that such an assumption is tenuous, not that it cannot be defended. However, the limited evidence available for Jewish proselytization and Jewish proselytes makes such a defense difficult. Christian literature, which should be rich with material relevant to the question of proselytes (assuming that great numbers of Jewish proselytes flocked into the Christian movement), relegates the issue to a largely obscure and irrelevant corner. Even Acts, which seems to have the keenest interest in the issue, treats the matter of proselytes rather peripherally.

the phrase "child of hell" to describe them.[16] But Jesus said more: a proselyte is *twice* the child of hell that the Pharisee is. Commentators frequently pass over in silence this doubly harsh attack on proselytes.

Matthew's comment suggests a situation in which the Jewish proselyte was not seen as sympathetic to the Christian movement. In fact, quite the opposite impression is left: a striking hostility or contempt for the proselyte marks the language.[17] It seems unlikely that Matthew's comment is directed to a church filled with proselytes and still drawing most of its new members from that pool. Somewhat later, in some of the sharpest encounters between Christians and Jews, it is the Jewish proselyte who represents Judaism. Justin comments that proselytes, upon converting to Judaism, are more vitriolic in their criticism of Christianity and in their persecution of Christians.[18] Tertullian's *Adversus Judaeos* is prompted by a debate between a Christian and a Jewish proselyte (1.1).

Other questions concern the significance of proselytes to the early expansion of the Christian movement. First, there is no evidence by which to determine the total number of Jewish proselytes in the ancient world—let alone the number of Jewish proselytes who might have been attracted to Christianity.[19] Jewish

---

[16] Matt 23:15. The Greek reads, υἱὸν γεέννης.

[17] Goodman reads the passage in a different way: the term "proselyte" does not refer to a Gentile convert to Judaism but to a Jew converted to the increased halakic observance of the Pharisees (*Mission and Conversion*, 70–73). Levinskaya follows Goodman (*The Book of Acts in Its Diaspora Setting*, 38–39). The Septuagint's use of the word "proselyte" almost always indicates a Gentile convert, however, as Goodman himself admits (*Mission and Conversion*, 72–73). Although Goodman's reading is possible, the Septuagint's evidence suggests that the traditional interpretation of Matthew's comment is perhaps more probable. Even were we to grant Goodman's interpretation, such an identification of the proselyte in Matthew's gospel would have had almost no impact on Christian thinking about the matter. By the time of the writing of Matthew's gospel, and certainly by the regular use of that gospel in a Christian community, the identification of the proselyte would have shifted from a Jewish convert to stricter halakic practice to a Gentile convert to Judaism, and this would have certainly been the case in Ignatius's church.

[18] Justin, *Dial.* 122–123.

[19] Some scholars have argued that Judaism must have included large numbers of proselytes, for the birth rate of native-born Jews could not, in itself, account for the large number of Jews in the Roman Empire (Feldman, *Jew and Gentile in the Ancient World*, 293). But there are no reliable numbers for the Jewish population in the Roman era, and so it is not possible to determine whether other than native-born Jews were a necessary component in the Jewish complexion of the empire. The common contention that there were six or seven million Jews in the empire has come under recent challenge. Judith Lieu, John North, and Tessa Rajak, eds., *The Jews among Pagans and Christians in the Roman Empire* (New York: Routledge, 1992), 5, speak of the "high (if not inflated) estimates of the Jewish population of the Diaspora" that scholars have accepted. Much earlier, Tcherikover questioned the bases upon which the high numbers rest (*Hellenistic Civilization and the Jews*, 292–95). Keith Hopkins expresses similar concerns ("Christian Number

proselytes need not have numbered more than a few thousand in the Mediterranean for the group to have become a matter of debate in the Jewish and Christian communities and a matter of comment in the larger society. If proselytes
were relatively rare,[20] then they probably are largely irrelevant to the question
of the complexion or success of early Christianity. Second, even if there was a
considerable number of proselytes, it is not clear that proselytes were generally
discontented with their new religious situation in Judaism or that they were still
seeking a yet more congenial option. Granted, proselytes may have, in some ways,
felt themselves somewhat strangers within Judaism, and not all Jews would have

---

and Its Implications," *JECS* 6 [1998]: 213–14). Others, however, have argued for much
higher numbers. S. W. Baron, for example, thinks that 20 percent of the Hellenistic East
were Jews (*Social and Religious History,* 170–71). But high numbers and a largely urban
Diaspora make for an impossible reconstruction. What is most problematic about the
high numbers often offered for Jews in the empire is that the widely accepted estimate
of six to seven million Jews seems to be based entirely on a misreading of an ancient text.
The number comes from a comment made by the thirteenth-century author known as Bar
Hebraeus. Tcherikover suspected that Bar Hebraeus was confused (*Hellenistic Civilization
and the Jews,* 292), but he was unable to prove this, although he provided a number of
reasons for caution about the high numbers proposed (pp. 292–95). Further examination showed that Tcherikover was on the right track. Shortly after the publication of the
original Hebrew edition of Tcherikover's book, Judah Rosenthal pointed out that Bar Hebraeus's number is identical to the number found in Eusebius's *Chronica,* where, however,
the number specifies the total number of Roman citizens (not Jews), as determined by
a census in the reign of Claudius ("Bar Hebraeus and a Jewish Census under Claudius,"
Jewish Social Studies 16 [1951]: 267–68). Eusebius's number is one million greater than
that provided by Tacitus for this census (*Ann.* 11.25). See McGing's review of the debate
about this data in "Population and Proselytism," 93–94; and Fredriksen, "What 'Parting
of the Ways'?" 50.

[20] Some scholars, such as Goodman, argue that Jewish proselytes were rare in the
first century and that Judaism did not engage in a zealous proselytizing effort until after
Christianity began to succeed among the Gentiles. Conzelmann (*Gentiles, Jews, Christians,* 18) points out that only nine of more than seven hundred Jewish tomb inscriptions
in J. B. Frey, ed., *Corpus inscriptionum iudaicarum* (2 vols.; Rome: Pontificio Istituto di
Archeologia Cristiana, 1936–1952) are identified as proselytes, although he recognizes
problems in the data. If Goodman is correct that evidence for Jewish proselytes is largely
second-century or later, one might suggest that at least a portion of the new proselyte
movement in Judaism came from Gentiles who first joined the Christian movement and
then, as their familiarity with Judaism increased through their Christian environment,
moved from Christianity to Judaism. Further, if Jewish proselytes do not appear in great
numbers until sometime in the second century or later, then they are, for the most part,
irrelevant for explaining the Christian success. The early stages of Christian growth would
not have had a significant proselyte base to draw from; in later stages of Christianity (the
second and third centuries), interested Gentiles would have been more aware of a choice
between Judaism and Christianity, unlike earlier, when only Judaism was a conspicuous
religious option.

welcomed proselytes into Judaism.[21] This need not have mattered much, however, for Judaism was itself diverse; whatever the general attitude of Jews to proselytes, some Jewish groups were receptive, and it is likely that proselytes would have associated with such groups and found a meaningful community in such circles.

There is also the question of the social status of proselytes and, by extension, of God-fearers. We are perhaps more accustomed to think of such people as from among the more wealthy classes because much of the surviving evidence appears on inscriptions that list people who had contributed in some way to the support of the local Jewish community.[22] Some scholars have suggested, however, that God-fearers were predominantly from among the poor and that the disadvantaged, in particular, turned to Judaism to benefit from the charitable resources available to those in the Jewish community. Feldman mentions this as one of the reasons for the growth of Judaism,[23] and as we will see, Zetterholm builds on the theories of Rodney Stark regarding the loss of social networks that many immigrants to the city would have experienced. The resources of the synagogue and the apparent stability of the Jewish community would have been an attractive source of relief to such newly arrived, resourceless Gentiles, according to Zetterholm. He points to the "purely social and pragmatic motivation" that drew many to "the social network of decisive importance" that Judaism provided.[24] Both Feldman and Zetterholm, however, must assume that the Jewish community would have welcomed such people. Such receptiveness is a matter of debate, as Zetterholm recognizes in his quotation of Tacitus, who comments that "the Jews are extremely loyal toward one another, and always ready to show compassion, but toward every other people they feel only hate and enmity" (*Hist.* 5.5). Zetterholm maintains that, in spite of Tacitus's comment, "it is reasonable to assume that some Gentiles were also embraced by the charitable activities in the synagogue."[25] A better conclusion to be drawn from Tacitus's comment is that the number of people admitted into Judaism on the basis of their lack of resources was too small to alter the character of Judaism or to provide an ample stock of people from which Christianity might draw converts.

Even if there were a sufficient number of converts to form a consequential block of proselytes in the Jewish community, it is not certain that these people

---

[21] The evidence is conflicting about how welcoming the Jewish community was to proselytes. Goodman notes the generally negative attitude to foreigners in the Jewish literature of the time (*Mission and Conversion*, 38–59).

[22] The primary evidence for God-fearers is the inscription from Aphrodisias, which lists benefactors (Joyce Renolds and Robert Tannenbaum, *Jews and Godfearers at Aphrodisias* [Supplementary Volume 12; Cambridge, U. K.: Cambridge Philological Society, 1987]).

[23] Feldman, *Jew and Gentile in the Ancient World*, 171–72.

[24] Magnus Zetterholm, *The Formation of Christianity in Antioch*, 126–27.

[25] Ibid., 127.

would have been ripe candidates for a further move into Christianity. According to Stark's theory, which is followed by Zetterholm, generally converts are individuals whose social networks have been lost and who find in their new religion adequate networks to substitute for their previous loss and to stabilize their present situation. It must be noted, against Stark and Zetterholm's theories, that proselytes were not people *without* social networks; they were people who found satisfying networks within the community of Judaism. They cease, then, to be ideal candidates for conversion to the Christian group.

Supposing the unlikely—that proselytes generally were not content with their new status within Judaism[26]—it is not clear that Christianity would have offered Jewish proselytes the religious world they sought, although this is an all-too-common assumption in scholarship, which sometimes presents Judaism almost as a way station for pious Gentiles on their way to Christianity. It is unlikely that Christianity would have been able to present itself as a reliable supplier of networks of stability and support in the way that the synagogue could.[27] For proselytes, Christianity must have appeared as a mainly leaderless, obscure, and suspect movement, condemned alike by the Jewish leadership and the Roman authorities. Further, it is unlikely that the prominent features of the Christian message were more appealing to proselytes than what Judaism had to offer, for Judaism had various flavors of apocalyptic thought similar to what marked the early Christian message. Even the more flexible attitudes toward circumcision, food laws, and the Sabbath that could be found within elements of the Christian movement would not necessarily have been particularly appealing to proselytes.[28]

---

[26] Josephus notes that not every Gentile who joined Judaism remained faithful to his or her original commitment (*Ag. Ap.* 2.124). It is not clear whether he means proselytes or God-fearers. Probably Josephus would not have found it necessary to discriminate between the two groups here, for it is unimportant to his point. Although proselytes gained membership in the Jewish community, they may have enjoyed less than full equality and so become disenchanted. See Cohen, "Crossing the Boundary and Becoming a Jew"; Martin Goodman, "Proselytizing in Rabbinic Judaism," *JTS* 40 (1989): 176–85.

[27] Zetterholm and others do not distinguish between the synagogue and the church, for they consider the *ekklēsia* to have been just another synagogue among many, albeit composed of Jesus-believers, both Jews and Gentiles (*The Formation of Christianity in Antioch*, 194).

[28] Josephus claims that a large part of the female population of Damascus had attachments to Judaism (*J. W.* 2.559–560). Matthews notes that circumcision was not an important issue because the majority of proselytes appear to have been women (*First Converts*, 69–70), but she misses a key point: most Jewish proselytes may have been women precisely because circumcision was indeed a considerable issue and the revulsion that circumcision usually provoked made fewer males ready to convert. Early Christian literature reveals that circumcision was very much an issue for the Christian movement, although the rejection of circumcision in the Christian movement seems to have been prompted more explicitly by theological issues than by the mere discomfort of the physi-

The proselytes had already dealt with these issues, opting in favor of the Jewish position and making a major religious realignment in joining Judaism. Conversion of such magnitude likely would have come about only after long and careful consideration, given the serious consequence of such conversion and the social stigma attached. Whatever obstacles circumcision and other matters of Torah observance may have presented to interested Gentiles, for the proselyte these were no longer deterrents. The issues had already been encountered and resolved in favor of the Jewish position.

We probably should not expect, then, a higher proportion of proselytes than of native-born Jews to have joined the Christian movement. Indeed, it might be argued that insofar as Christian converts came from the body of the religiously disillusioned or unsatisfied, a higher proportion of native-born Jews than of proselytes is likely to have joined the Christian movement. Christianity would have been an option for consideration to the religiously discontented Jew, but it was Judaism itself that had become the satisfying option for the religiously discontented non-Jew, the proselyte. The religious restlessness of the proselyte had already found its relief in Judaism.[29]

What of the situation in Antioch? It is not surprising to find proselytes there, for Jews had resided in the area for about four centuries by the time of Ignatius, making their religion familiar at some level to non-Jewish residents. Some of the Gentile residents would have developed a curiosity and interest. Although Josephus provides some evidence of tension and antagonism in Antioch, he generally paints a picture of Jews and Gentiles living together harmoniously.[30] Probably the truth lies somewhere in between. Whatever the rancor of some of the citizens of Antioch against their Jewish neighbors, the environment had been sufficiently amicable to attract multitudes of Jewish immigrants, making the city one of the largest centers of Judaism in the Mediterranean world. Further, Judaism was not so odious to the Gentiles of Antioch that attraction or conversion to Judaism was either rare or enigmatic, at least according to Josephus's witness (*J. W.* 7:44–45). Still, Jews in Antioch would have faced the same general suspicion and comment that Jews throughout the Roman world faced on a routine basis, and perhaps just before Ignatius's time, the relationship between Jews and the larger society

---

cal act itself. Still, a certain stigma was associated with circumcision (Whittaker, *Jews and Christians*, 80–85). See also Judith Lieu, "The 'Attraction of Women' in/to Early Judaism and Christianity: Gender and the Politics of Conversion," *JSNT* 72 (1998): 8–22; idem, "Circumcision, Women and Salvation," *NTS* 40 (1994): 358–70.

[29] We have already noted how little is made of proselytes in early Christian literature. If proselytes had been a primary source for members for the new Christian movement, it is surprising to find so little positive comment on the matter in early Christian literature. Even Jewish literature does not heavily feature proselytes, which may suggest that this group was far less important to either Christians or Jews than is often proposed.

[30] See the section on "Jewish-Gentile Tensions," pp. 128–41.

of Antioch may have become particularly strained, given the recent Jewish War and its aftermath.[31] Under such conditions, some Gentiles would nevertheless have become converts to the sober world of Jewish monotheism and ethics, just as some Jews would have moved away from Judaism under the glitter and sophistication of cosmopolitan Antioch.[32]

Ignatius does not mention proselytes. It could be that he judged the group irrelevant to his concerns, even though they were present in his communities. More likely, proselytes were so rare in the churches with which Ignatius had contact that they did not create a situation needing attention. For whatever the importance of proselytes to early Christian growth, they probably would have ceased to be an element of any real significance by the time of Ignatius. The initial wave (or ripple) of proselytes into the Christian movement in Antioch very likely would have been over by the time of Ignatius—a factor routinely overlooked in scholarship.

At the beginning of the Christian movement, some proselytes may have been drawn to Christianity in much the same way as native-born Jews were. Christianity would have presented itself as a new option. Within a few decades of the beginning of the Christian movement, non-Jews interested in some form of Judaism increasingly would have been confronted with the Christian option *before* becoming Jewish proselytes. Indeed, if they became proselytes to Judaism, it becomes increasingly likely that they had already considered the Christian option and had rejected it. Had the Christian option been attractive, such individuals would have joined Christianity directly without even a brief engagement with Judaism as proselytes. Judaism was not a stepping-stone to Christianity; Judaism and Christianity offered paths to different destinations. The attraction of Jewish proselytes to Christianity must have been a brief moment in the history of the relationship between Judaism and Christianity. Those who argue that the Judaizing opponents of Ignatius were Jewish proselytes fail to recognize that proselytes, as a group within Christianity, probably were largely an obsolete category and a distant memory—if even that—by the time of Ignatius.

Within a few decades of the beginning of the Christian movement, proselytes should not be counted as the most receptive audience for the Christian message (if they should be considered such for any period). Indeed, proselytes were probably the *least* receptive audience, for increasingly they would have already decided

---

[31] See chs. 2 and 4 for more detailed discussions of the Jewish experience in Antioch.

[32] Zetterholm (*The Formation of Christianity in Antioch*, 55–61) explores some of the recent studies of immigrant populations in Europe and their sense of identity. We must be careful not to assume that Jewish participation in the larger Greco-Roman social world always entailed a denial of Judaism. Jews had had many hundreds of years in the Diaspora to come to terms with the larger culture and to accommodate themselves to the social and political realities about them, and they had been able to do so while maintaining their identity as Jews.

against Christianity in the process of converting to Judaism. If Ignatius's church encountered proselytes, such people were probably the church's enemies rather than its most likely converts.

The "God-Fearers" (Near Jews)

The accommodation that Jews already had forged with the "God-fearers" may be enlightening for understanding the Christian experiment of incorporating Gentiles fully into the Christian movement without the requirements of Torah. For our purposes, two questions are important. First, who exactly were God-fearers? Second, how significant was the God-fearer group in the expansion of Christianity?

First, who were the God-fearers? Indeed, did God-fearers ever really exist? The traditional view is that God-fearers were Gentiles who had some interest in Judaism and some association with the synagogue but who had not committed themselves to the full observance of Torah—a semiproselyte of sorts.[33] A. T. Kraabel provoked controversy when he contended that the category "God-fearer" was nothing more than a literary invention of Luke, with no connection to the ancient historical reality.[34] Kraabel's position now has been generally judged untenable because of the discovery of inscriptions in which a term of apparent parity appears, "God-worshiper" (θεοσεβής).[35] The term seems to have been employed

---

[33] The terms "God-fearer" and "God-worshiper" were less defined than was "proselyte." For a brief summary of these matters, see Lester L. Grabbe, *Judaism from Cyrus to Hadrian*, 2:533–37. For a more detailed treatment, see Levinskaya, *The Book of Acts in Its Diaspora Setting*, 109–135; Matthews, *First Converts*, 55–62, 66–71. Goodman does not think that God-fearers were a "formally recognized group" until the third century C.E. ("Jewish Proselytizing in the First Century," 74). For a review of the evidence about God-fearers and related issues, see John J. Collins, *Between Athens and Jerusalem: Jewish Identity in the Hellenistic Diaspora* (Grand Rapids: Eerdmans, 1999): 264–70; Louis H. Feldman, *Jew and Gentile in the Ancient World*, 342–82; and idem, "The Omnipresence of the God-Fearers," *BAR* 12 (1986): 58–69. Sometimes the terms are confused in modern literature. Feldman (*Jew and Gentile in the Ancient World*, 357), for example, seems to think that Justin is referring to "God-fearers" or "half-Jews" in his *Dialogue with Trypho* (10.2), but this group seems more likely to have been full converts—proselytes—since they are circumcised. It is difficult to imagine a Gentile undergoing Jewish circumcision but refusing to observe other elements of Jewish practice. Circumcision seems to have been the point at which the adoption of Jewish practices was most likely to encounter resistance from the interested Gentile. (However, see p. 56, n. 50 below).

[34] Thomas Kraabel, "The Disappearance of the 'God-Fearers,'" *Numen* 28 (1981): 113–26; Robert S. MacLennan and Thomas Kraabel, "The God-Fearers—a Literary and Theological Invention," *BAR* 12 (1986): 47–53.

[35] Irina Levinskaya, "The Inscription from Aphrodisias and the Problem of God-Fearers," *Tyndale Bulletin* 41 (1990): 312–18; P. W. van der Horst, "'De waarachtige

at times in a sort of technical way to identify pious pagans with some kind of interest in Judaism, although the term could apply in a descriptive, nontechnical way to a pious Jew as well, as Kirsopp Lake observed many years ago.[36] Acts uses the phrases ὁ σεβόμενος τὸν θεόν and ὁ φοβούμενος τὸν θεόν apparently as synonyms. They refer, at least at times, to what we mean by "God-fearer" in the strictest sense.[37] The near consensus now is that such a group, however loosely defined, did exist by the beginning of the Christian movement.[38] The following discussion uses the term "God-fearer" in its narrowest and most traditional use—an interested observer of Judaism, or half-proselyte, so to speak. Even with

---

en niet met handen gemaakte God," *Nederlands theologisch tijdschrift* 45 (1991): 177–82; idem, "Das Neue Testament und die jüdischen Grabinschriften aus hellenistisch-römischer Zeit," *Biblische Zeitschrift* 36 (1992): 161–78; J. Murphy-O'Connor, "Lots of God-Fearers? *Theosebeis* in the Aphrodisias Inscription," *Revue biblique* 99 (1992): 418–24; Judith Lieu, "The Race of the God-Fearers," *JTS* 46 (1995): 483–501.

[36] Kirsopp Lake, "Proselytes and God-Fearers," in *The Acts of the Apostles* (5 vols.; part 1 of *The Beginnings of Christianity*; ed. F. J. Foakes-Jackson and Kirsopp Lake; London: Macmillan, 1920–1933), 5:74–96.

[37] Lieu ("The Race of the God-Fearers," 483) points out the "enigmatic" switch in the use of these phrases halfway through Acts. The phrase "God-fearer" is used in Acts 10:2, 22, 35; 13:16, 26, but the phrase "God-worshiper" appears after that point in Acts (13:43, 50; 16:14; 17:4, 17; 18:7). There may be nothing problematic, however, in the switch of phrases. Either phrase may have worked for the author, and once he used the second phrase, it is this phrase that may have come to the author's mind in the next few references to the idea. The phrases occur only eleven times in Acts. What especially diminishes the importance Lieu's concern is that four of these occurrences appear *in the same passage*—in the account of Paul and Barnabas at Antioch of Pisidia—and there they are used as equivalents. The last locus in Acts to use the phrase "God-fearer" (13:16, 26) and the first locus in Acts to use the phrase "God-worshiper" (13:43, 50) appear in the same passage, and the phrases clearly refer there to the same group. (A cluster of other terms is also used to express piety [cognates of σεβ-, in particular θεοσεβ- and εὐσεβ-].)

[38] In the broadest use of the term, a God-fearer is any religiously observant person, regardless of the particular religion of his or her loyalty (Jewish or pagan). As a narrower label, used by Jews and Christians, it identifies individuals who have some level of religious discomfort with aspects of paganism and some level of interest or religious curiosity about something other than paganism—in other words, about Judaism or Christianity, broadly considered. See Bernd Wander, *Gottesfürchtige und Sympathisanten: Studien zum heidnischen Umfeld von Diasporasynagogen* (WUNT 104; Tübingen: Mohr-Siebeck, 1998); Conrad H. Gempf, "The 'God-Fearers,'" in Colin J. Hemer, *The Book of Acts in the Setting of Hellenistic History* (ed. Conrad H. Gempf; Winona Lake, Ind.: Eisenbrauns, 1990), 444–47; Martinus C. de Boer, "God-Fearers in Luke-Acts," in *Luke's Literary Achievement: Collected Essays* (ed. C. M. Tuckett; JSNTSup 116; Sheffield: Sheffield Academic, 1995), 50–71; Lieu, "The Race of the God-Fearers"; J. A. Overman and R. S. MacLennan, eds., *Diaspora Jews and Judaism: Essays in Honor of, and in Dialogue with, A. Thomas Kraabel* (South Florida Studies in the History of Judaism 41; Atlanta: Scholars Press, 1992); Matthews, *First Converts*, 55–62, 66–71; Feldman, *Jew and Gentile in the Ancient World*, 342–82.

this restricted definition, we should recognize that such God-fearers would not have been a uniform group but would have consisted of individuals reflecting a range of interest in Judaism, with primary motivations perhaps sometimes more political than religious.

The second issue of concern here is the significance of the God-fearer group to the expansion of Christianity. It is commonly assumed that some Christians redefined membership in their community so as to permit the inclusion of God-fearers without the observance of Torah and that this change brought large numbers of interested Gentiles into the church.[39] This flood of converts supposedly gave the Christian movement the initial mass necessary for its survival and future growth.[40] A number of considerations, however, challenge the neatness of this reconstruction.

First, we do not know if God-fearers were ever of adequate numerical strength to make more than a ripple in the membership of the new Christian movement, even with a scenario where all God-fearers left Judaism for Christianity—which we know is not the case.[41] Second, we do not know whether the Acts portrait of the God-fearers should be taken as anything more than a literary stepping stone (although not a literary fiction) in the presentation of the expansion

---

[39] The evidence for God-fearer conversion to Christianity is surprisingly scarce, but the evidence for the counter position—that such conversions did not take place in large numbers—is equally scarce. Matthews, who provides a useful review of the debate (*First Converts*, 55–61), comments, "The argument that 'God-fearers' became Christians in droves finds its way into several New Testament introductory textbooks," and lists those by Perrin and Duling, Bruce, and Conzelmann (p. 130, n. 60). It is also a frequent enough position outside textbooks. Jürgen Becker's comment is typical: "It is known that especially the God-fearers were a special target group of the early Christian mission, and among them Christianity attracted many 'fringe participants' from the synagogue" (*Paul: Apostle to the Gentiles* [trans. O. C. Dean Jr.; Louisville: Westminster John Knox, 1993], 149). See also Martin Hengel, "Early Christianity as a Jewish-Messianic, Universalistic Movement," in *Conflicts and Challenges in Early Christianity*, by Martin Hengel and C. K. Barrett (ed. Donald A. Hagner; Harrisburg, Pa.: Trinity Press International, 1999), 29–30; Philip F. Esler, *Community and Gospel in Luke-Acts: The Social and Political Motivations of Lucan Theology* (SNTSMS 57; Cambridge: Cambridge University Press, 1987); and Oskar Skarsaune, *In the Shadow of the Temple: Jewish Influences on Early Christianity* (Downers Grove, Ill.: InterVarsity, 2002), 174–75.

[40] Zetterholm builds his reconstruction of Christianity in Antioch almost entirely upon his belief that multitudes of Gentiles were attracted to Judaism as God-fearers (*The Formation of Christianity in Antioch*, 121–29).

[41] Hemer, looking at the inscriptional evidence from Aphrodisias, concludes that God-fearers were numerous (*The Book of Acts in the Setting of Hellenistic History*, 447). If, however, the label "God-fearer" was primarily applied specifically to donors, then perhaps the inscription includes the full contingent of the God-fearers of Aphrodisias. If that is the case, perhaps we should not assume that a large company of Aphrodisian God-fearers existed beyond that.

of Christianity in Acts.[42] Third, even if there were large numbers of God-fearers and the early Christian mission was intentionally directed in an early stage at that group, we cannot conclude that large numbers of God-fearers found the Christian option more appealing than other options within Judaism.

Regarding the attractiveness of Christianity to God-fearers, we cannot assume, as some do, that masses of Gentiles hung around the borders of the synagogues, keenly waiting for some way to attain full membership in Judaism without the circumcision knife or the restrictive dietary laws—finally finding that long-sought option in the new, more flexible Christian experiment.[43] The degree to which the liberal Christian option would have been attractive to God-fearers is not without its ambiguities.[44] That some God-fearers joined is clear from early Christian literature, as we have seen. That all or even most of the God-fearers joined the Christian movement, however, is not clear. Indeed, it is improbable that they did. Many God-fearers must have been quite content with the ambigu-

---

[42] The pattern in Acts is that Paul and company enter a new city and immediately visit the local synagogue (although their preaching usually stirs up opposition from the Jews and often from the townspeople as well). It is clear that the author of Acts intends to portray Paul and his company as customarily following this procedure. Eight cities are named where Paul is said to have first visited the synagogue: Salamis (Acts 13:5); Antioch in Pisidia (13:14, 42–44); Iconium (14:1); Thessalonica (17:1–2); Beroea (17:10); Athens (17:16–17); Corinth (18:4); Ephesus (18:19; 19:8); and Apollos in Ephesus (18:26). In 17:2 the author states that this was Paul's custom, and so we can assume that the author thinks that a visit to the synagogue probably occurred in other cities, both named and unnamed. Acts is also clear about the opposition that Paul's presence provoked (13:6–12, 45, 50; 14:2, 19; 17:5; 18:1–17). In only one passage does the author report that a significant number of God-fearers became believers (17:4), although some success is implied in the story in 13:43–50. Even here, however, opposition from God-fearers is reported. The question is whether the portrait in Acts (mainly centered around Paul) is in line with Paul's missionary procedure as reflected in his letters, where there is little to suggest a crucial role of God-fearers or an initial visit to the synagogue. A more telling question, however, is whether God-fearers have a prominent role in the portrait of the Christian movement even in Acts—the only place where the matter is raised. Judith Lieu speaks of "tendentious elements" in the Acts presentation of God-fearers ("Do God-Fearers Make Good Christians?" in *Crossing the Boundaries: Essays in Biblical Interpretation in Honour of Michael D. Goulder* [ed. S. E. Porter, P. Joyce, and D. E. Orton; Leiden: E. J. Brill, 1994], 329–45; repr. in *Neither Jew nor Greek? Constructing Early Christianity* [New York: T&T Clark, 2002], 31–47, here 34).

[43] Goodman notes that many societies practiced circumcision. He comments that it is "naive" to think that dropping the requirement of circumcision could bring "a flood of proselytes in the Jewish fold" ("Jewish Proselytizing in the First Century," 68; *Mission and Conversion*, 81–82).

[44] Lieu raises a similar point, stating that "it is hardly obvious that [God-fearers] would have become Christian at all, or at least not with any regularity or uniformity" ("Do God-Fearers Make Good Christians?" 45). See also Matthews, *First Converts,* 67–70.

ous position they had with Judaism.[45] And those who were not content would not necessarily have found the Christian movement attractive. Judaism contained many appealing features unavailable to the Christian movement. It had antiquity—a feature cherished in the culture and religion of the time.[46] It had impressive synagogues, in some cases at the very center of urban life.[47] And it had liturgy and structure and text. It is not a foregone conclusion that Christianity, which was novel, with borrowed texts, and without temple or tradition, would have been viewed as a credible religious option for the pious pagan attracted to Judaism. Some God-fearers, and perhaps even most, would have remained sympathetic to Judaism, unmoved and perhaps even repulsed by the new Christian option, as most Jews themselves seem to have been.

Granted, one might attempt to argue that initially the Christian movement may have appeared as a part of Judaism to interested Gentiles and therefore not starkly different from Judaism or necessarily less attractive. But there is one crucial difference. From all the available evidence, the more liberal branch of Christianity (to which, supposedly, God-fearers were more readily attracted) was discredited from the outset and viewed by Judaism as a whole as an invalid interpretation of Judaism.

In spite of this negative environment, some God-fearers did find in the Christian option the right fit for their religious aspirations and their sense of religious and communal identity, although we cannot determine their number or significance.[48] The radical Christian option did offer a somewhat intriguing vision: a

---

[45] Indeed, as Lieu points out, God-fearers may have had no religious interest in Judaism. Many of the God-fearers in Aphrodisias may have been merely benefactors having social and political associations with Judaism ("Do God-Fearers Make Good Christians?" 38).

[46] On the importance of antiquity in providing status to ancient religions, see Ramsay MacMullen, *Paganism in the Roman Empire*, 1–5.

[47] The synagogue at Sardis is the most impressive, located in the very center of the city. The late-fourth-century synagogue of Apamea in Syria (about sixty miles south of Antioch) is also near the city center (Fergus Millar, "The Jews of the Graeco-Roman Diaspora between Paganism and Christianity, AD 312–438," in *The Jews among Pagans and Christians in the Roman Empire* [ed. Judith Lieu, John North, and Tessa Rajak; New York: Routledge, 1992], 100).

[48] Jewish opponents of the Christian innovation doubtless believed that Jews would become more Gentile-like, deserting the traditions of Judaism that had made Jews distinctive in the larger world. There is, however, no evidence that the early Christian innovators saw the matter in this way. From the Christian perspective, both Jew and Gentile needed to desert their old ways and enter into the newness brought by Christ (Gal 3:18; Ign. *Smyrn.* 1.2). Christian missionaries had an equally colorful range of polemics against paganism and Judaism. Indeed, they borrowed heavily from the Jewish stock of objections to paganism for their own attack on paganism. There is no clear favoring of paganism over Judaism in the new Christian experiment. Indeed, Christian opposition to paganism may have been sharper than Jewish opposition had been (Goodman, *Mission and Conversion*, 96–97).

community where Jews and Gentiles had membership on equal footing, drawn together not by the Gentile becoming more Jewish[49] but rather by the irrelevance of the distinction between Jew and Gentile within the community's common identity as followers of Christ. This seems to have been an entirely new approach. If some Jewish group before the rise of the Christian movement experimented with a community in which Jew and Gentile had equal standing, we know nothing of it.[50] What is clear is that the Christ factor central to the Christian innovation gave the experiment the foundation it needed to make the effort succeed. But it is also clear that most within Judaism would have judged such accommodation as so starkly contrary to the inner essence of Judaism that they would have demanded its rejection and suppression. Indeed, this became the Jewish attitude to

---

[49] Granted, Gentiles would have appeared in many ways to have become more Jewish because Christianity was so endued with elements of Judaism. Even so, by becoming Christians, Gentiles did not become Jews.

[50] Shaye J. D. Cohen argues that there is no evidence for the existence of any community where Jews and Gentiles had equal footing (*The Beginnings of Jewishness* [Berkeley: University of California Press, 1999], 219–21). Gary Gilbert attempts to argue the counter position in "The Making of a Jew: 'God-Fearer' or Convert in the Story of Izates," *Union Seminary Quarterly Review* 44 (1991): 299–313. Michelle Slee argues the same case, but she makes too much of a rabbinic debate regarding whether one became a Jew at baptism or with circumcision. The rabbinic debate is not over which rite should be performed but at what point one was counted as part of the community. The assumption from both sides in the debate is that all male converts would become circumcised. This debate is not evidence that "it was possible for a male to convert to Judaism without undergoing the rite of circumcision," as Slee contends (*The Church in Antioch*, 27). Goodman challenges the view that Gentile proselytes were not required to undergo circumcision (*Mission and Conversion*, 81–82). From a somewhat opposite slant, Jacob Neusner argues that in the early Christian period, Judaism was not ethnic, that the concept of Israel was similar to the concept of the church—universalistic and without ethnic boundaries. He finds Paul responsible for the defining of Israel in ethnic terms ("Was Rabbinic Judaism Really 'Ethnic'?" *CBQ* 57 [1995]: 281–305). Neusner goes to great effort to show that Israel constituted a "religious community," with Jews and Gentiles on equal footing as "the people of Israel." Although he is critical of scholars who have confused a theological understanding of "Israel" with a historical one, it is precisely on the matter of history that Neusner's own analysis fails. Regardless of how broadly Jews may have been willing to define "Judaism" or "Israelite" in the first century, the reality was that most people in the first-century world thought of Judaism as primarily, though not exclusively, ethnic. Neusner also misses the novelty of the Christian position as expressed by Paul: both Jew and Gentile become something that they had not been. For Judaism, no matter how open it was to proselytes or how fully and quickly it incorporated proselytes, the perception would have been that the proselyte had become something that the Jew already was. But the crux of the Christian innovation was that Christians can claim that Jews and Gentiles are truly equal and, by basing the new status on Christ rather than Torah, they can see the implications of this theological position become part of the historical reality. For Judaism, this theological inclusivity failed to work itself out historically. Why this was the case can be debated, but its reality cannot be denied.

the Christian effort, at least in the portrait presented by early Christian literature, a matter that is discussed later.

Even if there were numerous God-fearers, and a successful Christian mission targeted them, the question remains whether God-fearers need to be considered at all after the first generation or two of the Christian movement. Does the issue of God-fearers have any place in the discussion of Ignatius's situation? That some God-fearers joined Christianity is indisputable. But as with the proselytes, so with the God-fearers: their significance to the growth and definition of Christianity declined rapidly after the first point of contact between the new Christian option and the established Jewish community with which the God-fearers were in some way associated. In the first two or three generations of the Christian movement, the body of God-fearers would have been confronted with the new option, and individuals within that group would have decided, probably within a few months or less, either to remain loosely attached to Judaism or to move from their loose association with Judaism into full membership in the new Christian experiment, where the circumcised and the uncircumcised had equal status. After this initial period of contact and decision, however, the flow of the remaining God-fearers into the Christian movement would have dried up or been significantly reduced.[51] The matter of the Christian option would have been settled for most God-fearers in one way or another very quickly. Within a few decades of the beginning of the Christian movement, Christianity would have begun to compete with Judaism as an option of first choice for the religiously restless Gentile, and Judaism would have ceased to be the usual environment out of which Gentile converts came into Christianity.

The presentation of the book of Acts confirms, rather than challenges, this view of the limited window of God-fearers' association with the Christian movement. Granted, we should not rush to take the Acts portrait at face value, but since it is only in Acts that we learn anything of the association of God-fearers with Christianity, we cannot ignore the details that portrait provides. The clearest element of the portrait in Acts is that the Christian contact with the synagogue, where God-fearers would have been encountered and won, was over with by the author's time. Indeed, even in the stories recorded in Acts, the encounter between Christian missionaries and God-fearers associated with the synagogue is generally brief and not always positive. God-fearers sometimes present serious opposition to the Christian movement, although some did become Christian converts.[52] Opposition from Jews is a consistent element in the reports for each

---

[51] Not everyone accepts this view. Paul J. Donahue argues that God-fearers remained an important source of converts to Christianity at least until the mid-second century ("Jewish-Christian Controversy in the Second Century: A Study in the Dialogue of Justin Martyr" [PhD diss., Yale University, 1973]).

[52] See p. 51, n. 33 above.

city that Acts offers, and Christians are expelled from the synagogues on their first visit or within a few weeks of initial contact.[53] This leaves limited room for contact with the synagogue community, where Christians would have had their most likely contact with Jews and God-fearers.[54]

One further matter is that the Acts portrait of God-fearers does not seem to have been inserted into the larger story in order to attract God-fearers of the author's own time to the Christian movement. According to the author, church and synagogue had long parted ways after bitter hostility from both Jews and God-fearers. The narratives of Acts cannot have offered an attractive portrait of Christianity to God-fearers still associated with the synagogue. Indeed, it seems highly unlikely that the author of Acts, who makes much of the break between church and synagogue in his story, expected his work to have any audience with the God-fearers associated with the synagogues of his day. The most that we gain from the portrait of God-fearers in Acts is an ambiguous and narrow window of movement into the church in the earliest days.

In Ignatius's situation, removed by about seventy years from the initial contact of Christianity with Judaism in Antioch, the God-fearers are unlikely candidates for the main body of members in the church or for the Judaizing party of Ignatius's letters, despite some modern reconstructions that make them central. By Ignatius's time, God-fearers would have become considerably less relevant to the Christian movement, and perhaps for Ignatius not an issue at all.[55]

Paul Donahue suggests that the Judaizers of the Ignatian letters were God-fearers who had converted to Christianity but who, having been nurtured in Judaism, "shared with Jewish Christians both a reverence for the Law and the conviction that it remained binding."[56] But Donahue's conclusion does not hold up to examination. Since the God-fearers were not circumcised, it does not seem that they would have understood the Law as still binding, as Donahue maintains,

---

[53] The consistent reporting of this opposition should not be taken as merely the author's inventive story telling. Many early Christian documents have a common concern about Jewish opposition although they express a wide range of attitudes to Judaism. It is hardly likely that Paul, one of the most radical voices in the Christian movement, encountered no opposition.

[54] The portrait of the church in Acts does not associate the church in substantial ways with the synagogue. Although the author has Paul consistently going to the synagogue on his first visit to a city, he just as consistently reports that the contact failed and Paul was forced to find another setting for his preaching. It would be strange if the author of Acts presented this portrait in an environment where such separation was not the experience of any Christian group and, particularly, not the experience of his own group.

[55] The Cornelius story in Acts shows some Christian interest in God-fearers. But even at the time of the composition of the Gospel of Luke, God-fearers appear as a thing of the past.

[56] Paul J. Donahue, "Jewish Christianity in the Letters of Ignatius of Antioch," VC 32 (1978): 89.

for they had removed a key element of Torah observance—circumcision—from the scope of Torah obligations.

The more important matter is not how many ideas Christian God-fearers shared with Jewish Christians but whether they shared in the same community with the strict Jewish Christians. It appears that they did not; rather, they were welcomed by, and received into, a community that did not force Torah observance. It is unlikely the Christian God-fearers, welcomed by the more tolerant wing of the church reflective of Ignatius's tradition but rejected by the Jewish-Christian group, would have been promoters of a vision closer to that of the community that refused them admission. Donahue also argues that the separate eucharists that Ignatius condemned stood in line with the separation of Peter from table fellowship with Paul and the Gentiles in Antioch many years earlier.[57] But if so, is it not likely that the God-fearers would have been Ignatius's supporters rather than his opponents, for they would have been excluded from table fellowship by the other group?

Further, Donahue assumes that God-fearers would have represented a signifi-cant group in churches within Ignatius's orbit. But as argued above, neither God-fearers nor proselytes are likely to have been an element of any real significance in Antioch at the time of Ignatius. The initial movement of God-fearers into the Christian movement in Antioch would have been long over by that time, and most of the God-fearers who had made the transfer to Christianity would have been long since dead. Further, if such God-fearers had pressed for greater obser-vance of Torah, separating themselves from Ignatius's church for matters such as the eucharist,[58] it is difficult to explain Ignatius's considerable concern about the matter, for such separate eucharists must have been the routine practice of this Judaizing group for the better part of the previous seventy years.[59] There seems to be something novel and recent in the separate eucharists of Ignatius's concern, and this demands an explanation as to why the issue of separate eucharists had only recently risen. There is nothing to suggest that a new wave of God-fearers had, for whatever reason, suddenly decided to join the Christian movement at

---

[57] Ibid., 89–91.

[58] It is possible that the issue of separate eucharists was related to the Sabbath/Sunday dispute. If the issue of Sunday observance came into focus only in the first decade of the second century, then the separation may have occurred closer to Ignatius's time. Some scholars have suggested another potential concern: the connection of the eucharist with the *agapē*, where questions of food taboos might arise or cause offense but that would have been a problem of long standing, not one recently arising in the church context in Antioch, as seems to have been the object of Ignatius's concern.

[59] Even if Donahue changed his thesis to feature proselytes instead of God-fearers, my observations and cautions would be applicable in a similar way. And if the Judaizers were simply Jewish Christians, as Donahue sometimes says ("Jewish Christianity," 84, 87, 91), the problem remains in that the separation of the two communities would be many decades old by this time.

the time of Ignatius, provoking a crisis for Ignatius because they insisted on a strict Torah observance (if indeed God-fearers, as uncircumcised, would have ever insisted on strict Torah observance).

Judith Lieu, one of the minority of scholars to argue that God-fearers would likely have had little interest in the Christian option, does not believe that the few God-fearers who opted for Christianity made good Christians.[60] But it seems, on the contrary, that they would have made at least as good Christians as Jews or pagans who joined the movement. It is certainly not obvious that God-fearers in the Christian movement would have been the most insistent promoters of aspects of Judaism, as Lieu concludes. They had already considered Judaism and had stopped short of full acceptance. Their turning to Christianity, in most cases, must have represented an even more pronounced refusal to proceed fully into Torah observance, for the only Christian movement that was open to them as full members was one that had already set aside major aspects of Judaism and had thereby come under the censure of "official" Judaism and under suspicion by the more Jewish wing of the Christian movement. A few God-fearers may have opted for the more Jewish wing of the Christian movement, retaining an ambiguous, semi-attached relationship with Judaism but altered now somewhat by their belief in Jesus. It is unclear what aspects of Judaism such God-fearers might have been interested in promoting. Sabbath observance and some food laws are possibilities,[61] although these are likely to have been attractions primarily for God-fearers who were already under the influence of the synagogue community, which followed

---

[60] Judith Lieu, "Do God-Fearers Make Good Christians?"

[61] The comments in ancient literature are few and sometimes ambiguous. Josephus mentions that, in imitation of Jewish practices, "there is not one city where our practice of the seventh day on which we abstain from work, and the fasts and the lighting of lamps and many of our prohibitions regarding food have not spread" (*Ag. Ap.* 2.280–83). Lieu points out that such imitation "could well be independent of any relationship with the Jewish community" ("Do God-Fearers Make Good Christians?" 43). But Josephus is obviously exaggerating if he is suggesting a significant imitation of the Jewish lifestyle by non-Jews, for the distinctive practices that Josephus mentions were the primary marks by which the larger world was able to identify Jews in the ancient world. Such markers would have been useless if large numbers of non-Jews were also performing them. Recent debate has raised the issue whether there was a standard set of behaviors that identified a Jew in the ancient world—what has come to be called "common Judaism." E. P. Sanders describes this Judaism in detail (*Judaism: Practice and Belief, 63 BCE – 66 CE* [London: SCM; Philadelphia: Trinity Press International, 1992]). For a reconsideration of the issue, see the essays in D. A. Carson, Peter T. O'Brien, and Mark A. Seifrid, *Justification and Variegated Nomism* (2 vols.; Grand Rapids: Baker Academic, 2001–2004); Judith Lieu, *Christian Identity in the Jewish and Graeco-Roman World* (Oxford: Oxford University Press, 2004), 108–26; Tessa Rajak, "The Jewish Community and Its Boundaries," in *The Jews among Pagans and Christians in the Roman Empire* (ed. Judith Lieu, John North, and Tessa Rajak; New York: Routledge, 1992), 9–21.

such practices. God-fearers who became part of Ignatius's Christian community were different. They would have had synagogue and Judaizing influences reduced rather than intensified in an environment of Christian preaching and practice that rejected such aspects of Judaism.

Indeed, Judaizing tendencies are more likely to have arisen among pagans who joined the Christian movement directly or from Jews who joined than from God-fearers. Pagans would have been exposed, perhaps for the first time, to aspects of Judaism from within their new Christian environment, and some would have become attracted to features of Judaism beyond what the Christian community had retained. Native-born Jews in the Christian movement could have exhibited Judaizing traits if they resisted some of the developments within Christianity as it set aside more aspects of Jewish tradition.[62] In both cases, that of the pagan convert and that of the Jewish convert, the term "Judaizer" might be appropriately applied, and it is more likely that they were the target of the label than the few God-fearers who identified with the Christian movement.[63]

Finally, God-fearers should not be viewed as the middle ground between Judaism and Christianity, as many suggest, or even the middle ground between Christianity and paganism.[64] But it may be proper to view God-fearers as the middle ground between paganism and Judaism. Some comments in the ancient literature could be loosely taken to imply this.[65] Whatever the case, the middle ground between Judaism and paganism perhaps held by God-fearers does not transfer automatically to a middle ground between Christianity and paganism—and even less to a middle ground between Judaism and Christianity. If we want to speak of a middle ground, *both* Christianity and the God-fearers should be considered such between paganism and Judaism, providing for some pagans a pathway into Judaism. But these are "middles" of a different kind, largely unrelated and linking the two worlds of Judaism and paganism from different directions. Both God-fearers and the Christian movement provide open doors into Judaism; that God-fearers provided an open door into the Christian movement is a much less likely scenario.

---

[62] Some Jewish converts to Christianity must have become Judaizers by default. As the Christian movement became less Jewish, Christian Jews who resisted such changes soon would appear to have become Judaizers, although their position had remained unchanged—an Old Believers scenario of sorts.

[63] Some scholars have argued that Jews could not be called Judaizers: Jews were Jews; only Gentiles could be Judaizers. But such precision of language probably has no place in the context of polemics. People and groups are tagged with specific labels not because of the accuracy of the label but because of the power of the term to damage and dismiss.

[64] Lieu, "Do God-Fearers Make Good Christians?" 46.

[65] From the few pagan comments we have on the matter, God-fearers might as well be Jews, for the middle ground was only a slippery slope into Judaism (Whittaker, *Jews and Christians*, 85–91).

Antioch, Anxiety, and Religious Conversion

As we have seen, in discussions of Christianity in Antioch, it is customary to talk about proselytes and God-fearers as potential converts to the Christian movement. But some scholars think there is another group of potential converts—the never-ending procession of newly arrived residents to Antioch. These individuals presumably experienced a disruption in interpersonal attachments and a loss of a sense of security and well-being as a result of their move to the strangeness of a new city. Although this group does not appear explicitly in the ancient evidence, as do proselytes and God-fearers, they come into focus from sociological theories that base the success of new religious movements on the physical density but personal distance characteristic of urban areas. Newcomers to such an environment, who have lost or left the network of interpersonal support that once maintained them, find themselves very much alone in the crowded city, ripe for the picking, so to speak, of any group that can offer an adequate replacement for the lost network of support. This reconstruction is particularly important to the analyses of Rodney Stark and Magnus Zetterholm regarding Christianity's success in Antioch.[66]

Such reconstructions tend to offer an excessively bleak depiction of life in Antioch. We must be careful, however, not to measure the past by our standards. The ancients cried and laughed, groaned and hoped, despaired and dreamed, labored and rested, mourned the death of friends and family and sang soft lullabies to their children. Stark and Zetterholm depend on far too grim a view of the life of most people at most times. It is not widescreen televisions, Disney, and the Big Mac that have finally made life bearable for the human family.[67]

---

[66] The theory bears many similarities to the older "age of anxiety" thesis, popularized by E. R. Dodds, *Pagan and Christian in an Age of Anxiety: Some Aspects of Religious Experience from Marcus Aurelius to Constantine* (Cambridge: Cambridge University Press, 1965). Dodds believes that the crises of the Roman Empire in the third century produced an upheaval of sufficient dimensions to cause substantial religious change, particularly to the advantage of the Christian movement. Rodney Stark's description of life in Antioch uses much the same language as Dodds in describing the empire: misery, fear, despair, and cataclysmic catastrophes (*The Rise of Christianity*, 160–61). But such a view of the empire has been challenged by MacMullen, *Paganism in the Roman Empire*, to which Zetterholm makes no reference. MacMullen mocks the idea of an "age": "What sense does it make to assign a single character to so long an era?—as if one were to say, 'in Italy, Switzerland, the Low Countries, Britain, France, and Spain between 1400 and 1600, people were tense and worried'" (p. 123). Others have challenged Dodds also. See Robert C. Smith and John Lounibos, eds., *Pagan and Christian Anxiety: A Response to E. R. Dodds* (Lanham, Md.: University Press of America, 1984); Fox, *Pagans and Christians*, 64–66.

[67] Zetterholm does seem to distance himself from this bleak focus later in his book (*The Formation of Christianity in Antioch*, 181).

Stark and Zetterholm's analysis cannot, however, be dismissed entirely, although it likely depends too much on this supposed bleakness of life in ancient cities. They are correct in pointing to the fact that in the Roman Empire, where various factors (from epidemics to infanticide) kept urban population in deficit, cities could remedy their population crises only by an influx of people from the countryside or from other cities. This would have provided a continuous stream of potential converts whose patterns of social support and engagement had been disrupted. It is another matter entirely, however, whether Christianity would have grown substantially in such a context.

These newcomers would have been mainly from the countryside, since that is where most people lived: 85 to 90 percent of the empire's population was rural. But this fact is overlooked by the current and near unanimous view among scholars that the early church was mostly urban in its character and membership.[68] Even if all members of the Christian church were drawn from city dwellers, many of these individuals would be rural in their sensibilities and recently rural in terms of their residence, having moved into the city only a short time earlier.[69]

Stark and Zetterholm run into problems at this point. Both describe cities populated, in part, with newcomers,[70] and it is the dislocation that such

---

[68] Wayne A. Meeks champions the case for the urban character of early Christianity in *The First Urban Christians,* his prize-winning work, and it is almost impossible to find any voice of dissent. Yet the theory faces profound difficulties. On the basis of numbers alone, it needs substantial revision. It is widely accepted, for example, that the empire was about 15 percent urban and the population about 10 percent Christian at the time of the Constantine's conversion (Hopkins, "Christian Number and Its Implications," 192). Since a very large majority of Christians resided in the eastern half of the empire, the numbers above would require that almost all urban dwellers in the east be Christian by the time of Constantine—something that no one would find credible. Add to this number the Jews of the Diaspora, who are mostly eastern and, according to most theories, mainly urban as well. If we substantially increase the proportion of the empire that we consider urban, all the cities of the eastern empire would still be populated almost solely with Jews and Christians—again, a credible reconstruction in no one's mind. How to resolve this difficulty is unclear. Were there fewer Jews and Christians? Were Jews and Christians more rural? Further research into this problem is needed.

[69] It is not clear that all newcomers from the countryside would have lost their links to their rural families or that all newcomers would have remained permanently as city dwellers. Indeed, it may well be that the constant influx of rural people into the cities and the departure of some back to life in the country established a network for Christian expansion into the rural empire. The story of the Prodigal Son suggests that some movement from the countryside to the city and even back again was part of the listeners' world of experience. This matter deserves substantial attention, but for the purposes here, it need only be shown how some reconstructions of the membership of the early church in Antioch might be challenged by the rural element of city life.

[70] Zetterholm states that "Antioch was populated largely with newcomers" (*The Formation of Christianity in Antioch,* 42; see also 30–31), but we have no way of knowing that this

newcomers experience that supposedly accounts for the particularly successful Christian mission among this group.[71] Yet both authors link the Christian success to another group situation also: the presence of Jewish proselytes and God-fearers around the synagogues.[72] Neither admits to dealing with two profoundly different social realities. Zetterholm, in fact, fuses the two groups (God-fearers and the recent immigrants) into one.[73] But the two groups are not the same, nor is there a convincing way to associate them.

Proselytes and God-fearers are not likely to have been the most recent arrivals to the city. In fact, they appear to have been among the more permanent residents of Antioch, for they had time to become aware of the Jewish presence, to investigate the Jewish community and satisfy whatever curiosity the Jewish presence provoked, and to ally in some way with the Jewish community there. Further, proselytes and God-fearers do not fit well the description of people without social networks. Indeed, it might be argued that proselytes and God-fearers were among the most religiously comfortable, socially stable, and financially secure members of society.[74] As we have seen, if proselytes and God-fearers had become attached to the synagogue because of a religious quest, this restlessness would have been calmed by their association with Judaism, and this would hardly have made them ideal candidates for Christian conversion. On the other hand, if proselytes and God-fearers were attached to Judaism mainly because of political motivations rather than religious reasons, they were not ideal candidates for either Jewish or Christian conversion.

Newcomers, particularly from the countryside, may well have been at the opposite end of the social order from God-fearers. Indeed, perhaps the only parallel between God-fearers and the newly arriving immigrants is that neither would

---

was the case. We can assume, on the other hand, that there was a certain degree of stability in the populations within the city. Jews had lived there perhaps for four hundred years by the time of Ignatius, as had Macedonians and Greeks. If such groups were able to maintain their presence over such a period, one expects that they were not the only groups able to do so. No one argues, not even Zetterholm, that, for example, the Jewish community was mostly made up of newcomers. Perhaps a more cautious portrait of the newcomers in Antioch is that they represented a sizeable minority but hardly the dominant presence.

[71] Ibid., 195.

[72] Ibid., 194; Stark, *The Rise of Christianity*, 137. In other places, Stark passes over God-fearers, turning to Hellenized Jews as the more likely converts to Christianity (pp. 57–64). I think Stark is correct on this point, though I disagree with him about how long the Christian movement remained attractive to Hellenized Jews.

[73] Zetterholm, *The Formation of Christianity in Antioch*, 42.

[74] At least the inscriptions from Aphrodisias suggest such status, and this material is the clearest evidence available about God-fearers (Renolds and Tannenbaum, *Jews and Godfearers at Aphrodisias*). Admittedly, such inscriptions may provide an imbalanced view, for the evidence is of individuals who are wealthy enough to be benefactors and thus be memorialized in dedicatory inscriptions. It is possible that there was a mass of poor God-fearers whose existence would never have been carved into lasting memorials.

have been ideal candidates for Christian conversion. The newcomers would not have had significant prior contact with Judaism, particularly if the thesis of the urban character of the Jewish Diaspora is maintained. It is not clear that rural newcomers, upon arriving, would have been attracted to the synagogues or that the synagogues would have been particularly receptive to them. The primary reason Zetterholm links the newcomers to the synagogue is that he needs to posit a contingent of Gentiles who could more easily pass as Jews and thus avoid the religious obligations of the polis. From these individuals Zetterholm wants to draw heavily for the members of the Gentile side of early Christianity in Antioch.[75]

The character of Judaism in Antioch cannot, however, be so neatly determined. That Judaism was diverse in this city is likely. But it is less certain that Judaism had a large Gentile element there, and still less likely that this Gentile element was drawn mainly from newcomers to the city. Most unlikely, as argued earlier, is that this Gentile element in Judaism was the primary source from which the Christian movement drew substantial numbers.

Competition for Converts

The traditional view—that Christianity rapidly expanded by attracting various sorts of adherents to Judaism, particularly proselytes and God-fearers—needs to be more cautiously stated. For one thing, it has not been established that Judaism had a great pool of proselytes and God-fearers from which Christianity could draw its first Gentile members. For another, even if there were large numbers of proselytes and God-fearers, we cannot assume that the Christian option would have been irresistible—or even minimally attractive—to most of them.

Further, regarding the movement of proselytes and God-fearers between Judaism and Christianity, we must be careful not to assume that Christianity was the numerical beneficiary overall. In the initial years after the founding of the Christian movement, Christianity is likely to have been the beneficiary, for it presented an option that native-born Jews, proselytes, and God-fearers were discovering for the first time, and in this encounter some would have found their religious aspirations stirred and satisfied by Christianity. But as Christianity began to win converts directly from a Gentile population that had no previous attachment to or interest in Judaism, the situation changes. Christianity would then introduce important aspects of Judaism's heritage to these Gentiles for the first time. In some cases, converts to Christianity are likely to have found their curiosity about Judaism sparked, especially when, in the first three centuries, Judaism stood out impressively against the ragtag Christian movement. Indeed, two of the most famous Jews of the second century, the translator Aquila and the rabbi

---

[75] Zetterholm, *The Formation of Christianity in Antioch*, 124–27.

Tarphon (or Tarfon), were proselytes; Aquila moved from paganism to Christianity but finally converted to Judaism about the time of Ignatius.[76]

If either religion served as a stepping-stone to the other for pious Gentiles moving away from paganism, perhaps a better case can be made for Christianity serving such a role, with pagans moving through Christianity to end up finally in Judaism. The synagogue was attractive to members of the church for many centuries, presenting such a problem that church leaders often had to warn about the dangers of such association. Such was the case even after the emperor became Christian and Christianity gained favored status.[77] Indeed, in Antioch itself, well after the initial alliance between the state and the church, John Chrysostom frequently preached against the dangers of association with Judaism 350 years after the beginning of the Christian movement.[78] This is an understandable situation, since many Gentiles had their first substantial contact with Judaism as a result of joining the Christian movement. If competing allegiances between Judaism and Christianity had to be confronted as late as the period of the Constantinian dynasty and later, one can imagine the difficulty the earliest Gentile converts to Christianity must have experienced in maintaining their distance from Judaism, particularly as the church retained some elements of Judaism and rejected others—and not always consistently or uniformly.[79] This must have led some, at least, to continue their journey from paganism *through* Christianity into Judaism—proselytes-in-the-making, so to speak, during their period of membership in the Christian community.

---

[76] Lieu mentions that some Gentiles in the Christian community might have developed an interest in a "more full-blooded synagogue version" of religion, and she notes some of Justin's observations on the matter ("Do God-Fearers Make Good Christians?" 46). There are additional reports about such an interest in, and transfer to, Judaism. Aquila of Pontus, who produced a new translation of the Hebrew scriptures (ca. 128 C.E.), had earlier been a member of the Christian church and then became a Jewish proselyte; Irenaeus mentions his status as proselyte (*Haer.* 3. 21. 1). Two other revisions of the Septuagint appear to have been done by proselytes; see Carmel McCarthy, "Texts and Versions: The Old Testament," in *The Biblical World* (ed. John Barton; 2 vols.; New York: Routledge, 2002), 1:215–16. Rabbi Akiba, the most famous of the Tannaim, was the son of a proselyte.

[77] A mass of new converts from paganism swelled the church's membership in the 300s, largely attributable, it is thought, to the Constantinian dynasty's favoritism of the church. We do not know how these new conditions affected Judaism, but if there was a rush of pagans into the church because of the new attitude of the state, there could have been some increased movement of Jews into the church also, particularly since Judaism's status as a religion fell below that of Christianity for the first time.

[78] John Chrysostom, *Discourses against Judaizing Christians* (trans. Paul W. Harkins; Fathers of the Church 68; Washington, D. C.: Catholic University of America Press, 1979); Robert L. Wilken, *John Chrysostom and the Jews: Rhetoric and Reality in the Late Fourth Century* (Berkeley: University of California Press, 1983).

[79] The Quartodeciman controversy is the best-known case, where churches in Asia Minor celebrated Easter at the time of the Jewish Passover but Christians in Rome and elsewhere did not (Eusebius, *Hist. eccl.* 5.24.14–17).

Although the level of members' movement between Judaism and Christianity cannot be determined with any certainty, such movement is undeniable. For the present study, what is important is the sense of loss and gain that such transfer of allegiance might have sparked, with each group viewing the other as a competitor worthy of monitoring.[80] Further, if Judaism became more missionary-driven in the second and third centuries, as Martin Goodman argues, the sense of competition would have become more pronounced as both groups sought members from the same pool.

Whatever attraction Christianity may have initially held for God-fearers and proselytes—and it is important not to exaggerate it—such attraction must have declined by the second century as Christianity battled rumors about scandalous practices and as Judaism set itself more firmly against the Christian option and perhaps increased or refined its proselytizing activities. The point at which the Jewish community felt the sharpest sense of a loss of proselytes and God-fearers to the Christian movement was probably in the first few decades of the Christian movement. This would make some sense of the relative lack of interest in God-fearers and proselytes in the Christian literature of the second century and the narrow window of interest in these groups in Christian literature of the first century. It would also make some sense of the early tensions between the Christian movement and Judaism.

Jews would have been the losers in the first round, for Christians' gains of proselytes and God-fearers would have been at the expense of the Jewish community. The Christian movement would not have had a contingent of members already in its fold to whom Judaism might make its pitch. In the second round, Christians more than likely were the losers.[81] By this time, the Christian

---

[80] Christianity would have always been aware of Judaism, both as a competitor and as a combatant. The degree to which Judaism was aware of the Christian movement in Antioch is more difficult to gauge. Nothing in the self-definition of Judaism would require an awareness of Christianity, whereas it was against Judaism that Christianity defined itself. This does not mean, however, that the Jewish community in Antioch was, for the most part, unaware of the Christian movement. Competition for the same members or the movement of members from one group to the other would have brought the groups to the attention of each other. Even without this kind of competition, all the evidence points to Judaism's early awareness of, and almost always opposition to, the Christian movement. The evidence is mostly Christian, but it cannot have been completely fabricated, whatever its rhetorical context.

[81] Ignatius is himself witness to the attraction that Judaism held for Christian converts in the early days of the church. Other documents from the period provide further evidence that Christians were attracted to the Jewish synagogue and to Jewish practice. Even after Christianity gained victory over the old pagan world, assured largely by the long reign of the sympathetic Constantinian dynasty, Judaism still presented an impressive presence in many of the chief cities of the empire, and it still attracted the interest and curiosity of Christians, which church leaders of the time saw as a situation of sufficient

movement would have attracted a number of members directly from the Gentile population. This would have brought these pagan converts into their closest contact with Judaism, and the curiosity of some may have been aroused, causing them to move from Christianity into Judaism.

The letters of Ignatius fit such a situation well. The distinction that Ignatius draws between Christians and Jews is highly charged, and it suggests an explosive level of tension in Antioch.[82] For him, there are two sides—Christianity and Judaism, and paganism is not a competitor. Members of each side probably were aware of the other. Certainly those on the Christian side were aware of the Jewish group, for Ignatius's letters would make little sense unless his audience was familiar with Judaism and in some ways saw (or could be made to see) their identity in opposition to Judaism. The issue of God-fearers and proselytes in itself did not seem to be a matter of concern.[83] It was the attraction of Christians to Judaism

---

danger to compel them to preach frequently against it. See A. Lukyn Williams, *Adversus Judaeos: A Bird's Eye View of Christian Apologiae until the Renaissance* (Cambridge: Cambridge University Press, 1935).

[82] This is not to say that every Jew and Gentile in Antioch had some interest in the debate or had even heard of the new Christian group and its tension with Judaism. But neither is it likely that the tension was totally disguised. The prominent Jewish community is unlikely to have been able to hide such a conflict within its ranks, especially when the Christian dispute concerned the Gentile question at its very core. The question is how significant the Christian issue was for Jews in Antioch. The Christians' view would be that it was a crucial debate; how could they have seen it otherwise when they were at the center of it and were shaping their self-understanding in the heat of this tension? But for the larger Jewish community, the Christian problem would have been one of many with which they had to deal. This does not mean that it was an issue of little consequence or interest. Antioch seems to have been the frontline of the early Christian experiment with a more radical, less Jewish identity, and the coining of the name "Christian" to capture this new thinking reflects to some degree the difficulty of merely absorbing this perspective within Judaism's already diverse community. Furthermore, if some God-fearers joined the radical wing of the Christian movement, those within Judaism who were open to God-fearers may have reckoned such a change in loyalties as a loss for Judaism. If some of these God-fearers were prominent members of the society, the loss may have been counted as even greater. In addition, if also some proselytes, and even some full Jews themselves, left Judaism for the radical Christian option, the potential for tension over membership between Judaism and Christianity would have become very real.

[83] Some scholars have taken Ignatius's comment about the uncircumcised who teach Judaism to be a reference to God-fearers. There is no reason to conclude, however, that these were God-fearers rather than Gentile converts to Christianity who then became interested in aspects of Judaism. Indeed, if these converts were God-fearers who joined Ignatius's church but wanted to practice aspects of Judaism, we must ask what aspects of Judaism they would have been promoting. It would not have been circumcision, for as God-fearers they would have been on Ignatius's side in this issue. Nor would it have been monotheism or the ethical dimensions of Judaism, for Ignatius's church would not have differed from Judaism on most of these issues. Granted, there could have been some in

or to its practices that riled Ignatius. That these Judaizers had been proselytes or God-fearers before joining Ignatius's church is possible, but such a scenario is neither necessary nor even likely.

Ignatius's sharp comments about the Jewish complexion of his opponents and about the irrevocable deactivation of Judaism by Christianity make sense in an atmosphere of competition and if the Christian movement was feeling increasing loss as some of its members went over to Judaism or to Jewish practice.

Christians in Antioch

Although we know the names of scores of cities with Christian communities by the time of Ignatius, little information is available about the specific character of any of the churches within them. Most of the time our knowledge is limited to the mere name of a city in which a Christian church existed. In a few cases a document is addressed to a church in a particular city; more rarely, we have a document from a church in a particular city.[84] More of these documents give the perspective of an individual than of an entire community—as is the normal case for most documents from any period and of any community, Christian or other, ancient or modern. We must therefore be careful in trying to reconstruct the Christian community in any city, for such reconstructions must be, at best, provisional and mainly hypothetical. Even for Antioch, which left as rich a literary record as any early Christian city in the first century of the Christian movement,[85] caution is required.[86]

Ignatius's church who promoted aspects of Judaism that, from Ignatius's perspective, went over the line. If we make Ignatius's opposition much more Jewish in their observance, however, the question arises why they joined Ignatius's church in the first place.

[84] Ephesus leads with three (from "Paul," John [in Revelation], and Ignatius). John and Ignatius both addressed Smyrna and Philadelphia; Paul and Clement addressed the church in Corinth; Paul and Polycarp addressed the church in Philippi; and John and Paul addressed the churches in Colossae and Laodicea, although Paul's letter to Laodicea does not survive (Col 4:16).(No distinction is made here between the authentic Pauline Letters and those written in his name, for this matter is not relevant to the issue here.)

[85] Antioch fares comparatively well in the quantity and quality of evidence for reconstructing its Christian community, although even here the evidence is not such as we might like. Paul mentions the church there in his letter to the Galatians; the author of Acts features the city in part of his story; and Ignatius, a leader of the church there, writes a number of letters. Although Ignatius's letters are not addressed to the church in Antioch, it can be argued that they reflect, to some extent, matters and attitudes shaped in the environment of the Christian community there.

[86] One problem with the evidence for the church in Antioch is that a single document has been allowed to dominate the reconstructions. Adding to the problem is that this most favored piece of evidence is also the least reliable and least balanced of the evidence available for reconstructing the situation at the time of Ignatius. The document in question is Paul's letter to the Galatians. On the basis of a conflict in Antioch that this letter

The first Christian identified with Antioch is a proselyte named Nicolaus. According to Acts, he was appointed one of the original seven deacons, a group selected in the hope of resolving a dispute among "Hebrews" and "Hellenists"[87] over distribution of charity to the widows of the Christian community in Jerusalem (Acts 6:5). Shortly after, the Acts narrative describes a persecution that broke out when a Jewish mob murdered Stephen, one of the recently appointed deacons. Some Christians who had been living in Jerusalem then fled as far as Antioch (11:19).

At this point in the Acts narrative, within one paragraph, the author pulls together six incidents related to Antioch:

1. The believers who fled to Antioch from the persecution in Jerusalem preached only to the Jews there (11:19).

2. Men from Cyprus and Cyrene came to Antioch and began to preach successfully to the Gentiles (11:20–21).[88]

---

addresses, the divided character of the church in Antioch has become the prominent feature in reconstructions of the church in Antioch even three or four generations after the incident. Granted, Paul offers a firsthand account, but it is only his view, and this at one heated moment. And granted, the attention given to the Jerusalem council in the book of Acts indicates that the dispute described there was still somewhat of an issue in the later period. But unlike other documents associated with Antioch that are much closer in time, Galatians was a sixty-year-old document by Ignatius's time. To allow Paul's letter to the Galatians a privileged place in the reconstruction of the church in Antioch at the time of Ignatius seems methodologically unsound. A better reconstruction might be based on Acts, Ignatius's letters, and perhaps Matthew's Gospel and the *Didache*.

[87] There is some debate over what the terms identify. See Todd Penner, *In Praise of Christian Origins: Stephen and the Hellenists in Lukan Apologetic History* (Emory Studies in Early Christianity 10; New York: T&T Clark, 2004); Craig C. Hill, *Hellenists and Hebrews: Reappraising Division within the Earliest Church* (Minneapolis: Fortress, 1992); Todd Klutz, "Paul and the Development of Gentile Christianity," in *The Early Christian World* (ed. Philip F. Esler; 2 vols.; New York: Routledge, 2000), 1:168–97; Martin Hengel, *Between Jesus and Paul: Studies in the Earliest History of Christianity* (London: SCM, 1983); Brown and Meier, *Antioch and Rome*, 33, n. 77; 34, n.79.

[88] These areas are known to have contained large numbers of Jews, and both areas were involved in the uprisings of 115–117 c.e. Cyprus is mentioned in the New Testament only in Acts. It is one of the places disciples flee to following the death of Stephen and the persecution of Christians (or Hellenist Christians) in Jerusalem. Only one person from Cyprus is mentioned by name in Acts: Mnason, a disciple of long standing. When we meet him, he is a resident of Jerusalem and Paul is his guest (Acts 21:16–17). One might speculate that Mnason had lived in Jerusalem in the early days of the Christian movement and was one of the persecuted disciples who fled to Cyprus, his homeland, only to return to Jerusalem later. Perhaps this Mnason was part of the circle of Jews in Cyprus who went to Antioch and preached to the Gentiles there or at least supported the mission there. That Paul is his guest suggests some affinity of perspective, which may indicate a bond between some members of the Jerusalem church and those of the pro-Gentile

3. When the Jerusalem church heard, it sent Barnabas, apparently to investigate, and he concluded that the Gentile work was legitimate (11:22–24).

4. Barnabas then went to Tarsus and returned with Paul, and the two preached together in Antioch for a year (11:25–26).

5. It was in Antioch that the believers were first called Christians (11:26).

6. When he was in Antioch, Agabus, a prophet from Jerusalem, predicted a major famine, and Christians in Antioch provided relief for the church in Judea (11:27–30).[89] The author places the famine in the reign of Claudius (41–54 C.E.).[90]

Antioch is mentioned two chapters later, when Barnabas and Paul are sent on their first mission (13:1–4), returning with stories of their success among the Gentiles (14:26–27). This success is linked closely with a new radical openness to the Gentiles, demonstrated most sharply by a setting aside of the Jewish requirement of circumcision.[91] For a second time, representatives from Jerusalem traveled to Antioch to investigate and to restore traditional practice (15:22).[92]

---

perspective in Antioch. Insofar as Acts has reliable data here, the Christian situation in one city may not long have escaped the notice of Christian or Jewish authorities in the other, for the pro-Gentile element of the Christian movement would have had members in both Jerusalem and Antioch. We know that the Christian movement became a matter of some concern to the Jewish authorities in Jerusalem from the early period, given that Paul himself was engaged in the suppression of Christians within perhaps months of the beginning of the movement. That no rumor of such action made its way to Jews in Antioch is unlikely.

The opening of the door to Gentiles is perhaps the most intriguing, pivotal, and puzzling development in the history of early Christianity. However idealized the story in Acts may be, the author recognizes that the move to include Gentiles had significant ramifications for the Christian community and that the approval of such an innovation was not without controversy.

[89] See Kenneth S. Gapp, "The Universal Famine under Claudius," *HTR* 28 (1935): 258–65.

[90] Acts 11:28. Josephus reports a drought in Palestine between 45 and 48 (*Ant.* 20.51–53).

[91] Both Paul (Gal 2:2–9; 5:2–6; 6:12–15) and the author of Acts (15:1–5) make circumcision a key point, although it clearly has implications for a wider range of behavior, perhaps particularly related to table fellowship (Acts 15:19–20, 28–29; Gal 2:11–14). On table fellowship, see Jerome H. Neyrey, "Ceremonies in Luke-Acts: The Case of Meals and Table Fellowship," in *The Social World of Luke-Acts: Models of Interpretation* (ed. Jerome H. Neyrey; Peabody, Mass.: Hendrickson, 1991), 361–87. Zetterholm makes the issue a key to understanding the situation in Antioch at the time of Ignatius (*The Formation of Christianity in Antioch*, 149–64).

[92] Whether the reports of these trips are strictly historically accurate or not, they fit into a larger picture of what is likely to have happened. There would have been countless trips between these two communities in the first century, some more official than others.

Barnabas and Paul, along with others from Antioch, resisted and went to Jerusalem in an attempt to resolve the matter (15:1–3). This resulted in a settlement in favor of the Gentiles, and a letter from the apostles in Jerusalem was sent with a delegation to Antioch (15:22–35). Antioch is not mentioned again in Acts until a report of Paul briefly stopping there (18:22).

Antioch is featured, then, only in the later part of Acts 11 and, in a less direct way, in the dispute about the Gentile mission (Acts 15). Antioch is even less prominently featured in the other documents of the New Testament. Outside Acts, it is mentioned explicitly only in Galatians 2:11, where Paul and Peter clash over proper association with Gentile Christians. This seems to parallel the incident that sparked the events highlighted in Acts 15.

One problem with the New Testament evidence for Antioch is that almost all of it comes from Acts, and scholars have wrestled with the historical value of these traditions.[93] Did the author of Acts, writing perhaps in the last decade of the first century, have reliable sources? Did he care about sources at all, being primarily interested in providing an idealized or theological portrait of the primitive period? We should not exaggerate the problem, however, for it is difficult to imagine that the church's tension regarding its Jewish heritage is without some foundation. An examination of the few other references to Antioch in other early Christian literature confirms this tension. Paul's mention of Antioch reflects it (Gal 2:11–14), as do the Gospel of Matthew, thought by many scholars to be from Antioch or Syria,[94] and the *Didache*, which also may have been written in the area. Ignatius's comments about conflicts with Judaizers in Antioch and his dismissal of Judaism are, then, not surprising or out of character with the trends of the times.

Non-Christian literature from this period does not explicitly mention Christians in Antioch, whether this displays hostile or neutral intent. Some scholars argue that a number of recorded incidents may feature situations involving Christians even though Christians are not explicitly mentioned—matters that will be examined in chapter 4.

Was the Christian Church a Jewish Synagogue?

It is widely recognized that the earliest Christians functioned within Judaism, particularly by attending synagogues and submitting to synagogue discipline.[95]

---

[93] See Daniel Marguerat, *The First Christian Historian: Writing the "Acts of the Apostles"* (trans. Ken McKinney, Gregory J. Laughery, and Richard Bauckham; SNTSMS 121; Cambridge: Cambridge University Press, 2002).

[94] Douglas R. A. Hare, *The Theme of Jewish Persecution of Christians in the Gospel according to St Matthew* (SNTSMS 6; Cambridge: Cambridge University Press, 1967).

[95] Evidence of synagogue discipline is found in 2 Cor 11:24. The primary point of disagreement regarding Christian participation in synagogues relates to the practice of Paul and his followers (see n. 42 above for a discussion of Paul's practice). It generally is

Some scholars think that the Christian communities existed as distinctly *Christian* synagogues within Judaism, on the assumption that Jewish synagogues were arranged somewhat as "denominational" units, each reflecting a particular theological perspective, religious practice, or social class.

Zetterholm attempts to reconstruct early Christianity in Antioch, but his reconstruction depends precariously on this assumption of denominational diversity among synagogue congregations.[96] If Zetterholm were to show that individual synagogues could be formed around a common group ideology that contrasted with other synagogues in a particular area, then it would follow that Christians might have assembled together as Christians in their own synagogue, to the exclusion of others, while still functioning under the umbrella of Judaism.[97] This situation would allow Gentile Christians protected status, for they would be regarded as Jews under the arrangement.[98]

Zetterholm tries to make his case for Christian synagogues in a number of ways, but none can carry the weight he puts on it. For example, he points out that Ignatius refers to Christian meetings as "synagogues."[99] Zetterholm maintains that Ignatius's use of the term indicates that the Christian church must have functioned as a synagogue in its strictest Jewish sense.

But surely the depiction of the Christian assembly as a synagogue within Judaism would have been the last thing Ignatius intended by his use of the term. Everything that Ignatius says about Judaism shows that he sees himself and the Christian community as separate from Judaism—not merely separate from this or that synagogue. Further, other Christian writers besides Ignatius used the term "synagogue" for the church without any hint that connections to Judaism were implied.[100] Even Jews did not use this word as the exclusive (or even the favorite) term for their assembly.[101] Zetterholm is demanding a much narrower definition of the term "synagogue" than the realities of the period would allow.

---

assumed that the more conservative Jewish Christians would have been associated with the synagogue. Some Christians would have found the temple important also. Acts mentions a number of incidents concerning Christians and the temple (Acts 2:46; 3:1–4:3; 5:20–26, 42; 21:26–30; 22:17; 24: 6, 12, 18; 25:8; 26:21), but some Christians may not have had much interest in either the synagogue or the temple (see below, p. 133, n. 19).

[96] Zetterholm, *The Formation of Christianity in Antioch*, 91–95.

[97] Goodman views Christian communities as separate and distinct from synagogues (*Mission and Conversion*, 100–101).

[98] Zetterholm, *The Formation of Christianity in Antioch*, 198.

[99] Ibid., 94.

[100] Justin, *Dial.* 63; *Herm. Mand.* 11.14. The reference in Jas 2:2 may be narrower. See Rainer Riesner, "Synagogues in Jerusalem," in *The Book of Acts in Its Palestinian Setting* (ed. Richard Bauckham; vol. 4 of *The Book of Acts in Its First-Century Setting*; ed. Bruce W. Winter; Grand Rapids: Eerdmans, 1995), 207–8.

[101] For a discussion of matters related to the synagogue, see Tessa Rajak, "Synagogue and Community in the Graeco-Roman Diaspora," in *Jews in the Hellenistic and Roman*

Zetterholm points, further, to the various names by which some synagogues were identified, hoping to establish cases in which synagogues represent individuals of a common perspective, from which he can argue for distinctive *Christian* synagogues. But the names of many of the synagogues he considers seem more likely to reflect the names of patrons or of honored individuals. Where there is a possibility that a synagogue served a specialized community, the evidence is at best ambiguous. For example, Zetterholm mentions the synagogue of the Freedmen in Jerusalem. This term, however, does not necessarily indicate the "common origin of the individuals who belonged to it."[102] The only reference to this synagogue in ancient literature is in Acts 6:8–9. According to the brief note there, the synagogue included Cyrenians, Alexandrians, and people from Cilicia and Asia. Zetterholm speculates that these were the descendants of Jews who had been captured by Pompey a hundred years earlier. It seems unlikely, however, that the descendants of people scattered as slaves would maintain a sense of shared origins and destiny strong enough to draw them together into the same synagogue community back in Jerusalem, especially when a number of generations had passed during which contact most probably was not maintained. It is at least as reasonable to understand the "Freedmen" label to indicate the patrons or benefactors, as is often the case with the names of other synagogues.

Nor is it likely that synagogues were organized along craft or occupational lines, although some scholars have so argued. References are few and generally unsupportive of the hypothesis. In one case we learn that workers were seated together as distinct trade groups *within* the synagogue, but the telling point is that the various trades all had congregated in the same synagogue community.[103] In another case, an important inscription from Aphrodisias records donations for the support of a synagogue there. Although the inscription has become prominent in current scholarship primarily for the discussion of God-fearers, its list of the occupations of many of the donors makes it important to our question here. In this case at least, a wide range of trades joined together in support of a common synagogue.[104] Much the same seems to have been the case for Rome. According to Harry Leon, it was not the custom of Jewish trade groups to form their own synagogue, and he offers a more likely explanation for the one Roman synagogue that some have thought indicates a trade identity:

Cities (ed. John R. Bartlett; New York: Routledge, 2002), 22–38; and Anne Fitzpatrick-McKinley, "Synagogue Communities in the Graeco-Roman Cities," ibid., 55–87. Jews in the Diaspora seem to have preferred the term προσευχή for what we now commonly refer to as a synagogue.

[102] Zetterholm, *The Formation of Christianity in Antioch*, 92.

[103] See Jerusalem Talmud, *Sukkah* 5.1, 55, A–B.

[104] Renolds and Tannenbaum, *Jews and Godfearers at Aphrodisias*, 116–23.

that the term probably reflects merely the name of the street or city section where the synagogue was located.[105]

There is further evidence against the likelihood that Jews segregated into "denominational" synagogues. Only the largest cities of the empire would have had multiple synagogues. Most Jews, then, probably experienced Judaism in a synagogue that encompassed diversity as a matter of course. Furthermore, according to early Christian writings, Christians were expelled from the synagogues or were at risk within them;[106] this would not be the case if Christians had their own synagogues. The options for Christians seem to have been either to be part of the synagogue or not to be part; there is no suggestion that the options were framed in terms of being part of this synagogue rather than that synagogue, as Zetterholm requires.

Lieu offers balanced, but unfortunately often disregarded, guidance: "Advocates of 'multiple Judaisms' in the Second Temple period have tended to assume that divergent interpretations—which can be objectively mapped in the texts of the period—create (or presuppose) divergent communities or identities."[107] She asks, "How far should we posit differentiated social identities on the basis of differentiated interpretations?"[108] The danger is to hypothesize multiple distinctive communities of Jews (or Judaisms) on the basis of nuanced differences in documents, when in reality groups were able to function with a range of options within single communities. As we will see, this was the case also with the churches with which Ignatius was acquainted.

Zetterholm tries to strengthen his case for denominational synagogues by appealing to Tacitus's comment that Christians had a "hatred of the human race" and to his use of other derogatory terms about Christians that Gentiles routinely used to slander Jews.[109] But Zetterholm attempts to draw too much out of the use of these

---

[105] Harry J. Leon, *The Jews of Ancient Rome* (Philadelphia: Jewish Publication Society, 1960), 143. In ch. 7, "The Synagogues of Ancient Rome," Leon gives a summary of the main issues for each of eleven synagogues and other buildings thought by some to be synagogues (pp. 135–66). See also Peter Richardson, "Augustan-Era Synagogues in Rome," in *Judaism and Christianity in First-Century Rome* (ed. Karl P. Donfried and Peter Richardson; Grand Rapids: Eerdmans, 1998), 17–29. Richardson, *Building Jewish in the Roman East* (Waco, Tex.: Baylor University Press, 2004), addresses a wider range of issues, but there is much that touches on our question here. It is possible that there were cases where members of a particular trade were prominent in a synagogue simply because trades were often concentrated in a particular area of a city and people probably attended a synagogue near where they lived and worked (Henrik Mouritsen, *Plebs and Politics in the Later Roman Republic* [Cambridge: Cambridge University Press, 2004], 83).

[106] Mark 13: 9 (Matt 23:34; Luke 21:12); Matt 10:17; Luke 12:11; John 9:22; 12:42; 16:2; Acts 6:9; 9:2; 22:19; 26:11; Justin, *Dial.* 16; 47; 96; 137.

[107] Lieu, *Christian Identity*, 154.

[108] Ibid., 164.

[109] Zetterholm, *The Formation of Christianity in Antioch*, 95–96. Tacitus mentions Christians in the context of the fire in Rome under Nero (*Ann.* 15.44.2–4).

terms when he concludes that "The Christians in Tacitus's account are thus geo-graphically as well as ideologically connected to Judaism rather than to a separate cult."[110] All the passage in Tacitus shows is that Tacitus uses dismissive language in his description of Christians and that ancient writers applied this language also to Judaism. Whether Tacitus intended to link Christianity and Judaism must be deter-mined not by an occasional phrase but by more explicit evidence. Although Tacitus knew that the Christian movement began in Judea (who did not know that?), there is no evidence that Tacitus connected Christians ideologically to Judaism.[111] He simply made no comment on the matter, not mentioning Jews or Judaism at all.

The more significant question is not whether Tacitus connected Christian-ity geographically and ideologically to Judaism; rather, it is whether Tacitus saw Christianity as a separate cult from Judaism or as a group clearly identifiable within Judaism in such a way that it could be distinguished from other Jewish groups and held accountable for actions for which other Jews were not judged responsible. It seems that Tacitus did treat Christianity as distinct from Judaism, no matter how ideologically connected the two groups were. No one truly denied this connection in the ancient world except the peripheral Marcion. Zetterholm, in the end, seems to weaken his argument by contending that Tacitus, writing fifty years after the persecution of Christians under Nero, "incorporates anachronistic concepts from his own time, when Christianity certainly had begun to emerge as a non-Jewish, separate religion."[112]

Were There Separate Christian Assemblies in Antioch?

Many reconstructions of Christianity in Antioch offer a portrait of Christian-ity as multiform, with numerous theological expressions each operating in their own independent and often isolated religious communities.[113] Virginia Corwin

---

[110]Zetterholm, *The Formation of Christianity in Antioch*, 96.

[111] Since the Gospels are set in Palestine and the story of the death of Jesus was linked to a Roman governor of Judea, anyone familiar with Christianity would have noted the Judean connection.

[112]Zetterholm, *The Formation of Christianity in Antioch*, 96. Zetterholm comments further, "Tacitus may have thought that the 'Christians' of the 60s in the city of Rome were the same 'Christians' as those in the beginning of the second century with whom Tacitus himself may have been in contact" (p. 96). This is very likely, as everyone in Taci-tus's world, including Christians, would have made this association.

[113]For a more sober analysis of early Christian diversity, see the articles in Richard Bauckham, ed., *The Gospels for All Christians: Rethinking the Gospel Audiences* (Grand Rapids: Eerdmans, 1998). See also Paul R. Trebilco, *The Early Christians in Ephesus from Paul to Ignatius* (WUNT 166; Tübingen: Mohr Siebeck, 2004). As Trebilco points out, certain "litmus tests" may have allowed diverse groups to enjoy fellowship while exclud-ing the groups' opponents (p. 593).

speculates that several Christian churches "of different religious and perhaps so-cial backgrounds" existed in Antioch at the time of Ignatius. These churches were "exposed to diverse influences," and "their theological tendencies continued at variance because they rarely met together."[114] Donahue offers a similar portrait: early Christianity was "an extremely varied movement"; the middle ground (be-tween "extreme Jewish Christianity" and Marcionism) "was occupied at every point"; "congregations developed theologically to some extent independent of one another."[115] This view has become dominant.[116]

It is difficult, however, for the portrait of multiple early Christian commu-nities to account for the ethereal and ephemeral histories of such diverse and independent churches. If early Christianity encompassed so many distinctive theological communities at the beginning of the second century, why did these distinctive communities so soon evaporate, leaving no trace of their existence? The existence of distinctive theological documents is insufficient evidence for the existence of distinctive and independent theological communities. Indeed, the very question at issue is whether scholars are justified in positing distinct com-munities on the basis of documents that express points of theological difference, whether real or imagined. By the middle of the second century, much of this supposed diversity had evaporated.

We do not have at this time a Johannine church (or several Johannine churches), a Pauline church (or several), a Petrine circle, a network of Asia Minor churches under the influence of the book of Revelation, a Q tradition, a "Di-otrephite" church,[117] a docetic church (or several), several churches with various degrees of Judaizing, and a supposed host of other distinctive communities re-flecting the shades of emphasis found in the Synoptic traditions. Rather, what we have primarily is the "Great Church."[118] It is true that there were distinctive Jewish Christian churches whose precise status remains a matter of dispute.[119] A number

---

[114] Virginia Corwin, *St. Ignatius*, 49.

[115] Donahue, "Jewish Christianity," 92.

[116] Trevett, *A Study of Ignatius*, 42. For a recent collection of articles on Jewish Chris-tianity, see Matt Jackson-McCabe, ed., *Jewish Christianity Reconsidered: Rethinking Ancient Groups and Texts* (Minneapolis: Fortress, 2007).

[117] There is clear evidence of a developing schism between the elder and Diotrephes in 3 John 9. However, this division alone, found in a document where schism is the defin-ing issue, does not warrant that we posit the existence of an entire distinctive Christian community.

[118] By the time of Celsus (ca. 175), outsiders appear able to distinguish a "Great Church" from a few other Christian groups, primarily gnostic (Origen, *Cels.* 5.61–62). This portrait of the church is likely to be somewhat older than Celsus, since it comes to mind for him as the most natural way to view Christianity.

[119] Irenaeus, *Haer.* 1.26.22; Tertullian, *De praescriptione haereticorum* 33; *De carne Christi* 14.18; Origen, *Cels.* 2.2; *De principiis (Peri archōn)* 4.2.21; Epiphanius, *Panarion (Adversus haereses)* 30. Justin does not use the term "Ebionite," but he speaks of two

of other groups also existed—for example, the Marcionite church or the slightly later Montanist church. Yet most of these had links to the Great Church and origins rooted in the Great Church. There were gnostic communities, some tied closely to the Great Church, others more loosely associated, and some perhaps not at all.[120] The attachment of gnostic groups to the Great Church is surprising, for we would expect gnostic roots to lie in the separated docetic group of a half century earlier—if there ever was a docetic *group* substantial enough to deserve a label and a history of its own. All considered, with the exception of the Jewish Christian assemblies, the churches that we encounter in the latter half of the second century are mainly churches that clearly grew out of the Great Church (e.g., Marcionism and Montanism) or that had roots in churches within Ignatius's orbit (docetic/gnostic). We are hard pressed to find substantial Christian communities whose roots lie in one of the traditions that supposedly had distinct communities in the early part of the second century.[121] Those who contend that there were numerous theologically distinctive Christian communities in the year 100 must rest their argument on communities mostly without histories or futures.[122]

One cannot get around this problem by contending that alternative forms of Christianity were suppressed and thus disappeared. From the available evidence, the primary targets of suppression by what was to become the dominant church were groups with Judaizing and docetic tendencies, and these survived far beyond the period we are considering. Nor is the argument persuasive that there were multiple forms of Christianity at the beginning of the second century that by the middle of the century had congealed into the Great Church. Why would these diverse tendencies have come to see their destinies in a common tradition rather than in the distinctive groups in which they had successfully functioned

---

groups of Jewish Christians (and only two): both of whom keep Torah, though one does not see Torah observance as universally necessary for all Christians (*Dial.* 47). Justin's work is dated ca. 140.

[120] See Michael A. Williams, *Rethinking "Gnosticism": An Argument for Dismantling a Dubious Category* (Princeton: Princeton University Press, 1996).

[121] The second century offers a rich diversity of Christian literature, as illustrated in the New Testament Apocrypha. The concrete evidence for distinctive Christian communities corresponding to each of these documents is even sparser than it is for first-century documents. For a recent presentation of these documents, see Bart D. Ehrman, *Lost Christianities: The Battles for Scripture and the Faiths We Never Knew* (New York: Oxford University Press, 2003); and idem, *Lost Scriptures: Books That Did Not Make It into the New Testament* (New York: Oxford University Press, 2003).

[122] One can only guess the number of distinctive and independent Essene or Qumran communities that would have been proposed had the Dead Sea Scrolls not been found together but scattered from Egypt to Asia Minor, Syria, and the banks of the Dead Sea. Each scroll could easily have served as the basis for a new distinctive Qumran community in much the same way the early Christian documents have been used to serve as evidence of distinctive Christian communities.

for several decades prior? Bauer's claim that Rome had a major role in it was challenged when he made it more than seventy years ago, and it has not become more compelling since for the period we are examining here.[123]

It seems, then, that the existence of such numerous, diverse, and competing Christian communities is largely unsupported by the evidence.[124] To obtain a picture of the typical Christian church in the early second century, we should look at the churches in Ignatius's orbit. However innovative and idealistic Ignatius may have been in his presentation of the Christian church, certain observations about Ignatius's Christian community cannot be denied: Ignatius's community draws from a broad range of Christian literature and reflects a diverse rather than a monochromatic theological idiom.[125] As Meier points out:

> Both Matthew and Ignatius depict one Christian community made up of Jews and Gentiles, defined over against the Jewish synagogue and various dissident Christians (e.g., false prophets in Matthew, docetists and Judaizers in Ignatius). One does not get the impression from either Matthew or Ignatius that there are a number of different organized churches existing side by side in the same place.... Indeed, even at the time of Ignatius, we do not hear of any rival bishop *(episkopos)* or council of elders *(presbyterion)* among the dissidents or "heretics."[126]

The view of a multiform Christianity has become the near-consensus position in scholarship, yet it does not seem to reflect the understanding of the early Christian movement itself, where schism or a separate assembly is always judged abnormal.[127] Ignatius's treatment of schism is without nuance: there is but one

---

[123] Walter Bauer, *Orthodoxy and Heresy,* 111–29. See the various reviews of Bauer's work in Appendix 2 of the English translation.

[124] This is not to deny that schism occurred within the Christian community, only that it was *characteristic* of early Christianity. There would have been clashes over belief and practice, some of which resulted in separate communities. Paul's letters offer evidence of the competitive character of some of the early Christian mission, and opposition to Paul continued well into the second century. Other evidence of schism comes from the Johannine literature (1 John 2:19; 3 John 9). Ignatius himself speaks frequently of separate assemblies or eucharists. My objection is to the practice of creating hypothetical communities on the basis of perceived or real theological differences between documents.

[125] Meier, who likewise holds that the one church in Antioch used considerably diverse material (Brown and Meier, *Antioch and Rome,* 51–86), calls Matthew's Gospel, which he locates in Antioch, a work of "inclusive synthesis" (p. 57). James E. Goehring has shown, for example, that Egyptian monasticism worked with diverse texts and traditions ("Monastic Diversity and Ideological Boundaries in Fourth-Century Christian Egypt," *JECS* 5 [1997]: 61–84).

[126] Meier in Brown and Meier, *Antioch and Rome,* 40.

[127] It is clear from early Christian literature that the church was viewed as one body and that conflict and schism were abhorrent to early Christians, although it is difficult to determine the extent or consequence of the divisive tendencies that are identified (John 10:16; Rom 12:4–5; 1 Cor 1:10–13; 3:3–9; 10:17; 12:12–27; 2 Cor 11:13–23;

bishop; there is but one eucharist; there is but one assembly; a different eucharist is not a valid eucharist; a separate assembly is not a valid assembly; only what is done under the bishop's authority qualifies as valid.[128] Nothing in Ignatius's letters shows an awareness of numerous, considerably diverse, and independent local Christian groups, each with a long history and distinctive texts. For Ignatius, schism seems recent and at odds with accepted standards of Christian structure and conduct. The numerous monolithic and isolated assemblies that scholars have proposed based on the various documents of the period do not fit the character of what Ignatius and other writers reflect regarding the churches of the period.

It might seem at first glance that Ignatius's comments about separate eucharists and assemblies support the theory of a diverse collection of competitive Christian options at least in major urban areas such as Antioch or the large cities of western Asia Minor. By Ignatius's own witness, there were separate and diverse assemblies.[129] But an important detail is often overlooked: Ignatius also clearly points out that the schisms or separate assemblies were *recent*. If Christianity had been characterized from its earliest days by numerous independent assemblies, it would have made little sense for Ignatius to speak with such shock about schism or separation, for a new schism would constitute merely another independent group in the midst of many. If they had been long-standing, separate *assemblies* would be nothing unusual for the Christian movement—the normal situation rather than the abnormal and objectionable.

Further, the more diverse the Christian movement was in an area, the less likely it is that a schism would have produced a new separate assembly, for a range of other separate Christian options would have been available for the disillusioned schismatics to join.[130] Also, it would be difficult to account for the presence

---

Gal 3:26–28; Col 3:15; Eph 2:14–16; 4:3–6, 13–16; 2 Pet 2:1; 1 John 1:9–10). Schism is a prominent theme, too, in the letters of Ignatius and *1 Clement*.

[128] Ign. *Magn.* 7.1; Ign. *Trall.* 2.2; 3.1; 7.2; Ign. *Smyrn.* 8.1–9.1; Ign. *Pol.* 4.1.

[129] A number of passages suggest or explicitly charge that separate meetings were sometimes held (Ign. *Eph.* 5.2–3; 20.2; Ign. *Magn.* 4.1; 6.2–7.2; Ign. *Phld.* 2.1; 3.1–3; 4.1; 7.2; 8.1–2; Ign. *Smyrn.* 6.2; 8.1–2). It is difficult to determine some key aspects of these separate meetings. We do not know how routine they were in any of the churches where they occurred and whether such meetings would have appeared as "separate" to those who participated in them or to members of the community from which they had withdrawn for part of their religious life. Indeed, it appears that in some cases the supposedly separate assembly still considered itself part of the bishop's church and still met for some of its activities under the authority of the bishop (Ign. *Magn.* 4.1; Ign. *Phld.* 7.1–2). As other scholars have noted, it may even be that Ignatius saw a danger in such separate assemblies that others did not see and that he brought the matter somewhat to a head.

[130] Scholars debate the character of the church in Antioch and whether we should be speaking of churches rather than church, given the variety of Christian perspectives that some think are represented in Antioch: James and the Jerusalem church faction, a variety of Petrine, Pauline, Matthean, and Johannine perspectives, and whatever Jewish or Juda-

of a single docetic group or individual in Ignatius's assembly if other groups with docetic leanings existed and were ready to receive new members of like belief. If, on the other hand, there were no separate docetic or Judaizing assemblies until the recent schisms in Antioch or western Asia Minor, as Ignatius portrays the situation,[131] we must ask what separate Christian assemblies would have existed in Antioch. Judaizers and Docetists are considered at the extreme ends of early Christian diversity. If they were able to fit for years in Ignatius's church, surely the less radical elements could fit there even more easily.

Scholars have accounted in different ways for the schisms reflected in Ignatius's letters. Separate assemblies and eucharists of the Judaizers may have become necessary because these individuals preferred to meet on the Sabbath rather than on Sunday, the day on which the bishop's eucharist was celebrated.[132] The Docetists' view of the passion may have clashed with the bishop's eucharist, which was so profoundly tied to the death of Jesus that Docetists may not have been able to participate in the eucharist as other Christians observed it. The docetic Christians may have had only two options: either remove themselves from the bishop's eucharist or repudiate their own beliefs about the nature of Jesus and so cease being Docetists.[133] It should be noted, however, that

---

izing Christians are not represented by the previous labels (such as Essene and perhaps proto-Ebionite; Docetists and proto-Gnostics (if they are not the same group); and Ignatius himself, who has been associated in modern scholarship with almost every group just listed. Hammond Bammel thinks that the Ignatian group was a mixture of Johannine and Matthean traditions, with secondary Pauline influence ("Ignatian Problems," 84–87), or a Johanno-Pauline alliance (p. 89). She thinks that the Docetists were a splinter from the Johannine group. After reviewing the various theological perspectives with which Ignatius has been associated, Trevett concludes that Ignatius cannot be identified with any one movement (*A Study of Ignatius*, 164). In such a diverse world, it would be difficult to determine who, if anyone, controlled the majority. Trebilco, who challenges a similar view with respect to Ephesus—a matter he studies in some detail—claims that Ignatius writes to all the Christians in the city, not to a subgroup (*The Early Christians in Ephesus*, 645–47).

[131] Ignatius's portrait of the churches cannot easily be dismissed as idealized—that is, so blatantly false that the portrait of diverse independent and autonomous communities is more accurate. Ignatius does have a view of what the ideal is—all Christians in subjection to the bishop—but he makes little effort to present such an ideal as the actual situation.

[132] Hans-Werner Bartsch, *Gnostisches Gut und Gemeindetradition bei Ignatius von Antiochien* (Gütersloh: Bertelsmann, 1940), 39–42. C. K. Barrett is of the opinion that Ignatius had stronger feelings about the inadequacies of the schismatics' eucharist ("Jews and Judaizers", 226). Schoedel, however, thinks that the schismatics may not have been observing the Sabbath, but that Ignatius found that "over-emphasizing" Sabbath observance provided "a convenient point of departure for illustrating the unacceptability of 'Judaism'" (*Ignatius of Antioch*, 123).

[133] Ignatius attempts to explain why the schismatics abstain from the bishop's eucharist: they do not believe that the eucharist is the flesh of Christ (Ign. *Smyrn.* 7.1). He

the Docetists did not reject the eucharist altogether, although some have given this interpretation to Ignatius's comment about those who "abstain" from the eucharist (Ign. *Smyrn.* 7.1). Shortly after commenting about those who abstain from the eucharist, Ignatius condemns separate eucharists (8.1), suggesting that the schismatics do have a eucharist.[134] Ignatius more likely means simply that they departed from the bishop's eucharist—not that they did not celebrate some eucharist of their own.

For any explanation of the situation, the problem is much the same. If the separation of assemblies and eucharists was long-standing, why is Ignatius raising the matter so sharply and prominently at this point?[135] If, on the other hand, the separation was recent (as seems more likely), how is it that such diverse perspectives met together in Ignatius's church, given the multitude of early Christian groups commonly assumed in modern scholarship to have existed in each city? If the differences between these schismatic groups of Ignatius's assemblies had been minor, it is conceivable that the groups might have existed together for some time, later becoming separate on some matter of greater or lesser principle. We are not speaking, however, of closely similar groups but, rather, of the far ends of the Christian spectrum (Docetists and Judaizers), groups that according to most modern reconstructions of early Christianity would not have had fellowship with one another. Yet these groups seem to have had their home in Ignatius's church circle until shortly before Ignatius wrote.

The belief that the Christian movement in Antioch must have been marked by various distinct Christian communities stems not from the evidence of Ignatius's own time but from the much earlier and near-legendary clash between Peter and Paul in that city (Gal 2:11–14). Paul had called attention to this incident in a letter written in the 50s, apparently because his opponents in Galatia were trying to give a different interpretation to the resolution of the conflict, to the disadvantage of Paul. Apparently the story had some staying power, for the matter was important enough for the author of Acts to feature it as pivotal in his story, written in the 80s or 90s, many decades after the encounter (Acts 15).

---

makes no reference to the Sabbath to explain separate eucharists. Although Ignatius's explanation seems to apply more naturally to Docetists, the comment could be appropriate to Judaizers also—not because it is pointedly accurate but because it is broadly negative. The explanation that the schismatics do not believe that the eucharist is the flesh of Christ is in a highly charged, polemical passage. Ignatius's church believes that the eucharist is the flesh of Christ; those who do not participate in the bishop's eucharist must believe that it is not. The accusation need not have a more specific target.

[134] Schoedel, *Ignatius of Antioch*, 240.

[135] The standard explanation is that Ignatius is attempting to impose a monepiscopate in Antioch, requiring that all Christians submit to the authority of the one bishop. Burnett Hillman Streeter, *The Primitive Church* (New York: Macmillan, 1929), 168–83, featured such an explanation, followed by Bauer a few years later (*Orthodoxy and Heresy*, 61–69).

The question is not so much whether Paul and the Pauline tradition encountered opposition. This can be settled in the affirmative.[136] The more debatable question is whether Paul lost in the debate in Antioch. It is becoming routine in scholarship to contend that he did lose.[137] Yet given what appears to be the state of affairs at the time of Ignatius and the Pauline coloring of much of his thought, few would have concluded that Paul lost the dispute in Antioch if neither Paul nor the author of Acts had mentioned it.[138]

We must be cautious not to make Paul's supporters and his opponents in Antioch into permanently hostile competitors. Ignatius links Paul and Peter together in a comment that would suggest that these leaders are not the heroes of rival groups in Antioch and Asia Minor (Ign. *Rom.* 4.3). Ignatius refers to Peter elsewhere without any sense of divided party loyalty (Ign. *Smyrn.* 3.2). Further, he routinely mentions apostles as foundational in the structure of the church—which would be puzzling if his opponents' church had primary claim to such traditions.[139] And Matthew's Gospel, whose provenance is often thought to have been Antioch or Syria and which some have called "un-Pauline," clearly draws

---

[136] Paul speaks of considerable opposition from individuals he disdainfully calls "super-apostles" and "false apostles" (2 Cor 11:5, 13), suggesting that Paul faced, and perhaps provoked, opposition to his preaching from among fellow Christians. An anti-Paul sentiment continued into the second century, although this evidence may point more clearly to the victory of Pauline thought than to its failure, a point rarely recognized. For a general survey, see Dennis R. MacDonald, *The Legend and the Apostle: The Battle for Paul in Story and Canon* (Philadelphia: Westminster, 1983).

[137] Some scholars argue that the dispute was not resolved, and they offer as evidence the dual tradition of Peter and Paul appointing bishops in Antioch. The *Apostolic Constitutions* (7.46) names Euodius as the appointee of Peter and Ignatius as the appointee of Paul; see Trevett, *A Study of Ignatius*, 41–42; Hammond Bammel, "Ignatian Problems," *JTS* 33 (1982): 77. Zetterholm speaks of the *"ideological defeat"* that Paul suffered (*The Formation of Christianity in Antioch*, 162). Henry Chadwick expresses the reservation that "it is unlikely that the apostle of the Gentiles emerged victorious" (*The Church in Ancient Society: From Galilee to Gregory the Great* [Oxford: Oxford University Press, 2003], 68). Hammond Bammel states that perhaps the Pauline group was in the minority at the time of Ignatius ("Ignatian Problems," 88–89), a case argued earlier by Bauer (*Orthodoxy and Heresy*, 83–85). Whereas Bauer believes that a group of Gnostics represented the majority tradition, Hammond Bammel thinks that Jewish Christians, holding a position like that of Peter years earlier, were the majority against a Johanno-Pauline minority that would have included Ignatius ("Ignatian Problems," 89). Some scholars have qualified the matter of Paul's supposed loss in Antioch: Trevett is aware that "Paul's heritage" was not lost there (*A Study of Ignatius*, 42).

[138] 2 Cor 11:13; 12:11. See Dieter Georgi, *The Opponents of Paul*.

[139] Ign. *Magn.* 6.1; 7.1; 13.1–2; Ign. *Trall.* 2.2; 3.1; 7.1; 12.2; Ign. *Phld.* 5.1; 9.1; Ign. *Smyrn.* 8.1. Note that Matthew's gospel refers to the twelve as apostles (10:2), and ends with the commissioning of the eleven disciples—after the loss of Judas (28:16–20). This places the early Christian apostles within the orbit of Matthew's church.

from the same body of oral traditions that Ignatius, a Paulinist in may respects, comfortably uses—if, indeed, Ignatius is not using the Gospel of Matthew itself.

The situation in Antioch is probably more nuanced than is indicated by the language of "winners" and "losers" that marks much of the discussion. As argued above, one problem in scholarship is that it often treats differences in beliefs and behaviors found in *documents* as evidence of separate *assemblies.*[140] But the boundaries of groups must be more carefully examined. Not all diversity consti- tutes grounds for exclusion. We must attempt first to determine the boundary by which a group understands its identity and beyond which its essence is dan- gerously compromised. It is perhaps unfair, for example, to describe Matthew's Gospel as un-Pauline when we attempt to determine its primary boundaries and distinctiveness. In Matthew the boundaries of identity are drawn between the church and the synagogue,[141] not between one church and another, whether Pauline or something else. So, too, with the *Didache.*[142] In a similar way, Ignatius draws primary lines between Christianity and Judaism. These are the kinds of clear boundaries that defined early Christian identity. Yet often these much more significant, definitive boundaries are overlooked in favor of nuanced, often hypo- thetical boundaries of separation within the Christian community itself.

We should therefore be careful not to make too much of the schism in Ig- natius's churches. His comments about schism and separate assemblies are not evidence of long-standing, isolated, and distinctive Christian communities. In- deed, it is difficult to determine how significant the schism was in the minds of the participants themselves, for the relationship with the bishop's church seems to have been maintained at some level and the schisms, being recent, might well still have been open to resolution.[143] Certainly the evidence of schism so promi- nent in the Ignatian letters can provide *no* support for the popular hypothesis of multiple and isolated Christian communities dotting the landscape of each

---

[140] Other scholars have dealt with these differences by providing chronological dis- tance instead of conflicting conceptual distance between what they perceive to be the two distinct perspectives reflected by Matthew and Ignatius. Matthew is placed prior to Ignatius, but in a developing tradition of which both Matthew and Ignatius are members (cf. Meier in Brown and Meier, *Antioch and Rome,* 13).

[141] The usual way to speak of the Jewish place of assembly in the Synoptic tradi- tion and other early Christian literature is simply to say "the synagogue(s)" (Mark [nine times]; Luke [fifteen]; John [five]; Acts [twenty-two]). In contrast, Matthew uses the phrase "the synagogue" only three times (6:2, 5; 23:6). Matthew prefers to speak of "their" synagogue (4:23; 9:35; 10:17; 12:9; 13:54) and has Jesus directly addressing the Jews by referring "your synagogues" (23:34). Mark uses the phrase "their synagogue(s)" twice (1:23, 39); Luke once (4:15). In light of how the other Synoptic writers use the expres- sion, Matthew's use of "*their* synagogue" seems highly charged.

[142] See below, p. 161, n. 116.

[143] For a review of the situation, see the section, "So Many Christianities, So Few Opponents," on pp. 123–24.

city. Indeed, the Ignatian letters speak strongly against such a hypothesis, as do recent focused studies of early Christianity in Antioch, such as those of Meier and Zetterholm, who see the Christian community there mainly in terms of Matthean and Ignatian perspectives (Meier sees Ignatian Christianity as a later stage of Matthean Christianity, and Zetterholm sees it as part of Matthean Christianity until a rupture late in the first century).

What are our choices? Was Ignatius's church but one of many, all more or less equal and with their own histories, or was his church the primary church of the city, with perhaps small pockets of disgruntled members meeting separately for at least some of their religious life and with perhaps a separate Jewish Christian assembly of similar size and character? The latter seems more in line with the presentation in the Ignatian letters and with recent focused studies of Christianity in Antioch.

House-Church Units

It has become customary to speak of the gathered assembly of Christians as a house church. In a city of any size, one could expect to find several and perhaps scores of such units.[144] Most researchers have found in the voluntary associations (collegia) of the Greco-Roman world an adequate parallel to the house-church unit, and it is common now to think of patrons and clients as an appropriate image by which we might understand the relationship between the owner of a residence and the house-church unit that regularly met there.[145]

Some questions have been raised, however, about the adequacy of the comparison of the house church to other voluntary associations.[146] For one thing, the

---

[144] Bruce Chilton, in his somewhat popularized depiction of Antioch, presents the Gentile side of Christianity during Paul's time as having a dozen or so house-church units, made up of no more than forty members each (*Rabbi Paul: An Intellectual Biography* [New York: Doubleday, 2004], 109). If one were to add to this the Jewish branch of Christianity in Antioch, we would have about a thousand Christians in Antioch in the mid-50s. On the Jewish side, Zetterholm thinks that Antioch had twenty to thirty synagogues in the first century (*The Formation of Christianity in Antioch*, 38). There is no way, however, of knowing what the numbers were.

[145] Ancient literature uses various terms for what could be broadly called "voluntary societies." See R. S. Ascough, *What Are They Saying about the Formation of Pauline Churches?* (New York: Paulist, 1998); Philip A. Harland, *Associations, Synagogues, and Congregations: Claiming a Place in Ancient Mediterranean Society* (Minneapolis: Fortress, 2003); and John S. Kloppenborg and Stephen G. Wilson, eds., *Voluntary Associations in the Graeco-Roman World* (New York: Routledge, 1996).

[146] Related to this reexamination of the *collegia* is the sense that the Jewish synagogue, to which the Christian church is often compared, was not strictly a *collegium*. See L. I. Levine, "The First-Century Synagogue: New Perspectives," *Svensk teologisk*

Christian groups seem to have had a sense of participating in a large, "translocal" movement that the typical voluntary association in Roman society would not have had, although some scholars have tried to dismiss the significance of the translocal sense of early Christian communities. Richard S. Ascough, for example, seeks to qualify the early church's sense of itself as "universal." However, his argument does not adequately address Ignatius's unambiguous perception of the church. Ascough mentions Ignatius only once and mostly dismisses the value of his evidence by saying that Ignatius's "idea of the primacy of the bishop of Rome is not entirely clear."[147] But at this point in the development of a translocal consciousness of the church, the primacy of Rome is simply not relevant to the discussion. It is clear from Ignatius' writings that he and the churches within his orbit had a clear sense, both in word and in action, of the translocal nature of the church.[148] The examples of a translocal consciousness are numerous: various interplays of visits and letters between Ignatius and the leaders and congregations of the churches in Asia Minor and elsewhere, including Rome, and Ignatius's requests for prayer and then for delegates to go to Antioch.[149] Further, Ignatius stands in line with an older sensibility within Christianity of "being a single body," as Lieu points out.[150]

We see the translocal consciousness of the early Christians, not only in the contacts between churches of different cities, but within the cities themselves. In at least some of the cities mentioned by Ignatius, more than one house-church unit would have existed. The churches in Ephesus, Smyrna, and Philadelphia had been established for some time (assuming a connection between the

---

kvartalskrift 77 (2001): 27–28; and S. Walker-Ramisch, "Graeco-Roman Voluntary Associations and the Damascus Document: A Sociological Analysis," in *Voluntary Associations in the Greco-Roman World* (ed. John S. Kloppenborg and Stephen G. Wilson; New York: Routledge, 1996), 131. For the case for synagogues as *collegia*, see Peter Richardson, "Early Synagogues as Collegia in the Diaspora and Palestine," ibid., 90–109. Richardson admits some differences between the synagogues and *collegia* in "Augustan-Era Synagogues in Rome," 17–18. Much earlier than all of these discussions is Wayne Meeks's contention that the Pauline communities were unique structures (*The First Urban Christians*, 75–84).

[147] R. S. Ascough, "Translocal Relationships among Voluntary Associations and Early Christianity," *JECS* 5 (1997): 239. For the opposite view, see Trevett, *A Study of Ignatius,* 154–55.

[148] See esp. Ign. *Phld.* 9.1; Ign. *Smyrn.* 1.2; 8.2; Ign. *Pol.* 5.1; see also Ign. *Eph.* 5.1; 17.1; Ign. *Trall.* 2.3; Ign. *Phld.* 3.1; 5.1; Ign. *Smyrn.* 5.1; 9). The author of Acts has this same sense, with an important Jerusalem-Antioch connection (Acts 11:22–24, 27–30; ch. 15)

[149] This translocal sense is further strengthened by the exchange of letters between Polycarp and the church at Philippi (Pol. *Phil.* intro.; 13.1–2; 14:1).

[150] Judith Lieu, " 'The Parting of the Ways': Theological Construct or Historical Reality," *JSNT* 56 (1994): 101–19; repr. in *Neither Jew nor Greek? Constructing Early Christianity* (New York: T&T Clark, 2002), 11–30, here 19.

communities Ignatius addressed and those of the book of Revelation or those associated with Paul's activities),[151] and these cities are likely to have had a number of house churches.[152] Consider the impression left by Ignatius's comments to Polycarp, which offer advice on everything from widows, virgins, and slaves (both male and female) to the married and the celibate (Ign. *Pol.* 4–5). The collected church was diverse and large enough that the bishop needed to be encouraged to know everyone by name. This suggests that we are dealing with more members than what might be expected in a typical *collegium,* where a few dozen at most, rather than hundreds, would have met and where everyone would have known each other's name.[153] In Ephesus the church is able to send five delegates to visit Ignatius, which suggests at least a few house-church units in the city, if not many. These separate house-church units have a sense of identity, however, that is translocal even within the city. The collection of a number of house-church units under an umbrella of common identity makes the typical local *collegium* not an ideal parallel for the early Christian communities. For lack of a better parallel, *collegia* no doubt will continue to be used to illuminate aspects of the early Christian gatherings, but such parallels should not be allowed to obscure the more important fact that Christian gatherings marked their identity and circle of *koinōnia* in profoundly abstract and universal ways unavailable and unintelligible to the typical *collegium.*

---

[151] Trebilco analyzes the Christian groups in Ephesus in considerable detail. He sees at least five groups: the Pastor's group (Pauline), the opponents of the Pastor, the Johannine group, Johannine secessionists, and probably Nicolaitans (*The Early Christians in Ephesus,* 589, n. 1). But then he significantly qualifies this diversity by asserting that the Pastor's group and the Johannine group, though distinct, had friendly, or at least "non-hostile," contact and that the author of Revelation saw the Christian community as unified enough to address "a range of Christians," not a specific group (pp. 589–90). I would go farther and assert that we must be careful not simply to assume that the "secessionists" had a substantial membership or an enduring history. They may well have had both, but this needs to be determined on other bases. While modern scholarship endeavors not to mute the voices of groups who "lost," we must be equally cautious not to give a voice and center stage to those who never had such a stage in their own times.

[152] It is not possible to determine the size of the churches in Magnesia or Tralles. Ignatius's letters are the first to mention these churches.

[153] A detail sometimes raised in the discussion of Antioch and Asia Minor is whether an entire body of Christians was small enough to meet together in one assembly. Harry O. Maier, for example, is convinced that the church met in a large assembly for at least some of its regular corporate worship (*Social Setting,* 147–56). Although this was possible in the earliest days, the likelihood of such a meeting would have become more and more remote as the church grew. For Ignatius, the issue is not that the church should meet in one physical location but that it should meet in one metaphysical location, under the authority of the bishop. Most passages in Ignatius that refer to a common assembly or the like can be read in this way.

Use of the Term "Christian"

Antioch is associated with the coining of the term by which the Christian movement would come to identify itself. "It was in Antioch that the disciples were first called Christians," writes the author of Acts (11:26).[154] The comment comes at the end of a passage recounting a critical change in the Christian mission. Until that time, according to Acts, the disciples had spoken to no one except the Jews. Now they had turned to the Greeks.[155]

Within a few years of the writing of this story, the terms "Christian" and "Christianity" were rolling easily off the lips of Ignatius. He uses the terms seventeen times, usually in contrast to Judaism.[156] The use of such terms reflects a monumental shift in the perceptions of the religious realities and relationships between Jews and Christians in Antioch at the beginning of the second century. For Ignatius, the Christian movement stands separate from Judaism and at parity with it as a distinct religion.

The coining of the term "Christian" and the development of the concept of "Christianity" suggests that from early on the primary Christian identity in Antioch could not be easily accommodated within Judaism. The term "Christian," particularly if it is a Roman or Greek invention, likely indicates that some informed outsiders viewed the Christian movement not as a sect within Judaism but as something quite distinct. The early sharp tensions within the Christian community of Antioch lend further support to the view that innovations by the Christians of Antioch were judged to have challenged the core self-understanding of the Christian community and probably of the Jewish community also. By Ignatius's time, Christianity was viewed, at least in the way Ignatius used the word, as neither a sect within Judaism nor even as a child of Judaism. Although we see the struggle only as it is worked out within the Christian movement, it is difficult to imagine this development occurring without provoking some responses from within the Jewish community in Antioch. The next chapter discusses Jewish-Christian relationships in Ignatius's city. Ignatius's sharp and uncompromising language hints that all was not well.

---

[154] For a helpful review of the evidence, see Trebilco, *The Early Christians in Ephesus,* 554–60.

[155] Acts 11:19–20. There is a textual variant here. Some manuscripts read "Greeks"; others read "Hellenists." In context, "Greeks" seems the preferred reading, for the intended contrast is between Jews and Greeks. If "Hellenists" was intended, the striking contrast of this crucial moment would be lost, for Hellenists had not only already been included in the Christian audience, some had been given roles of leadership in the charitable activities of the church at Jerusalem (Acts 6:1–6). Further, the author had already set up the Hebrews as an appropriate contrast to the Hellenists. See p. 70, n. 87 above for more extended debate about these terms.

[156] See p. 204, n. 3.

CHAPTER 3

Ignatius in Antioch

Ignatius's Church and the Matthean Community

Almost every theological tradition reflected in early Christian literature has been posited as the source of Ignatius's church. The most recent detailed work on the church in Antioch at the time of Ignatius places the origin of the Ignatian church within the Matthean community. This viewpoint is likely to gain some influence, since it is built upon the popular sociological theories of Rodney Stark.[1]

According to Magnus Zetterholm, Ignatius's church, whom Zetterholm identifies with the Matthean community, represents a radical break of Jesus-believing Gentiles from Jesus-believing Jews.[2] This was allegedly the first significant and permanent schism within the Christian community in Antioch. According to Zetterholm, Jewish Christians and Gentile Christians in Antioch worshiped together in a Jewish synagogue that was Christian in its membership—a "denominationally" Christian synagogue, although Zetterholm does not use the term.[3] This synagogue would have been much the same as other synagogues in Antioch, with a mixture of Jews and God-fearing Gentiles. Each synagogue would have been denominationally distinct in some way.

Zetterholm maintains that the issue complicating matters for Christians in Antioch (and elsewhere) was the *fiscus judaicus,* a kind of head tax imposed on Jews at the end of the Jewish War by Vespasian.[4] At first, Zetterholm contends,

---

[1] Rodney Stark, *The Rise of Christianity.* Although some of Stark's investigations are less than convincing, his work raises issues that scholarship on the early church has overlooked.

[2] Zetterholm, *The Formation of Christianity in Antioch.* Zetterholm's terms "Jesus-believing Jews" and "Jesus-believing Gentiles" do not seem to add clarity over the more traditional terms "Jewish Christians" and "Gentile Christians," and so I will use the latter here unless it is important to Zetterholm's point to use his terms.

[3] Zetterholm's arguments for such synagogues are unconvincing. See the argument against Zetterholm's position in the section "Was the Christian Church a Jewish Synagogue" in ch. 2, pp. 72–76.

[4] It is not possible to determine whether Domitian's policy primarily affected Rome only or the whole empire. Zetterholm admits the lack of evidence for increased enforce-

Jewish Christians and Gentile Christians were able to remain in the same wor-
shiping community, for non-Jews could pass as Jews by paying the tax.[5] But when
the tax was more rigorously collected and Jewish identity more closely scruti-
nized under the reign of Domitian, the situation would have changed for Gentile
Christians. This new state of affairs becomes central to Zetterholm's thesis.[6]

The main support Zetterholm offers for his proposition is that under Domitian the collection of the *fiscus* and the question of Jewish identity began to be
enforced with more offensive vigor.[7] However, it is not clear that a Gentile who
was paying the *fiscus judaicus* would have come to notice or would have had to
prove his Jewishness in some way, as Zetterholm assumes. The more rigorously
enforced collection of the tax seems to have been intended to catch those who
were liable for the tax but who were not paying—in other words, non-paying
Jews. People who were already paying the tax, whether Jews or Gentiles, would
not have been a matter of concern. Nerva, who succeeded Domitian, almost
immediately modified Domitian's offensive policy.[8] Thus Zetterholm is correct
to think that Domitian's policy regarding the *fiscus* reflected a significant and
worrisome change in practice. This does not mean, however, that the Jewish-
Christian situation in Antioch can be explained mainly in terms of the *fiscus* policy of Domitian. Zetterholm's reconstruction hangs on a number of connected

---

ment outside Rome, but he argues that Antioch was such a center of Roman presence
that similar pressures occurred there also (*The Formation of Christianity in Antioch,* 191).

[5] Ibid., 215–16. On the *fiscus,* see L. A. Thompson, "Domitian and the Jewish Tax,"
Historia 31 (1982): 329–42; Martin Goodman, "Nerva, the fiscus *judaicus,* and Jewish
Identity," *JRS* 79 (1989): 40–44; idem, *Mission and Conversion,* 46, 121–25.

[6] Zetterholm, *The Formation of Christianity in Antioch,* 186–89. It is not clear when
Domitian, emperor from 81 to 96 C. E, intensified the collection of this tax. According to
Suetonius, it seems to have occurred after major building projects that put financial pressure on Domitian's administration. A reasonable guess is ca. 85 C.E. Zetterholm points
to several events that indicate increased financial pressures. A fire in Rome in 80 C.E.
had necessitated a massive rebuilding program from the first year of Domitian's reign.
In 85 C.E. the silver content in the denarius was reduced. This date would fit Suetonius's
description (*Domitianus* 12) of himself as a youth when he observed a ninety-year-old
man publicly humiliated by the authorities, who checked whether he was circumcised in
order to confirm his Jewishness, an incident that most, including Suetonius, associated
with Domitian's increased enforcement of the *fiscus judaicus.*

[7] It is likely that all Jews, whether observant or not, were forced to pay the tax. There
is a tradition that Domitian took action against close relatives for atheism and the practice of Jewish rites, executing Clement and exiling Flavia Domitilla (Eusebius, *Hist. eccl.*
3.18; Jerome, *Epist.* 58.7). Some think Christians were involved (cf. Paul Keresztes, "The
Jews, the Christians, and Emperor Domitian," *VC* 27 [1973]: 1–28; E. Mary Smallwood,
"Domitian's Attitude toward the Jews and Judaism," *Classical Philology* 51 [1956]: 1–13;
James S. McLaren, "Jews and the Imperial Cult: From Augustus to Domitian," *JSNT* 27
[2005]: 257–78).

[8] Dio Cassius, *Hist. rom.* 68.1.2.

conditions, and the failure of any one of these can significantly weaken the overall construction.

Zetterholm contends that the impact of the *fiscus judaicus* did not disturb the Christian community in Antioch immediately after its introduction, and that it was not until a more strict enforcement of the tax under Domitian that the Christian community was driven to schism. To account for the delay of the impact of the *fiscus* for Gentile Christians, Zetterholm posits that Gentile Christians were treated as God-fearers within the Christian synagogues. His crucial contention here is that Jews never placed God-fearers within the covenant and therefore Jews never required that their Gentile associates separate themselves from the civic polytheistic religion.[9] Had the Jews required this of God-fearers, such separation would have placed these Gentiles at risk and perhaps would have tainted the reputation of the Jewish community itself within the larger society.

Zetterholm claims that Paul changed the situation. By insisting that Gentiles were part of the covenant, Paul demanded that Gentile Christians withdraw from the religion of the polis. Normally this would have placed such individuals at risk in the larger society, but Gentile Christians supposedly were able to mute this danger by paying the temple tax and later the *fiscus judaicus*, thus blending as Jews into the social fabric of cities such as Antioch. It appears that Zetterholm sees God-fearers as having two options: either they could continue to fulfill the civic obligations as members of the polis, or, if they took the more radical approach of Paul and refused the obligations of the polis, they might blend in as Jews by paying the tax. In the latter case, the lapse in their civic obligations might go unnoticed.[10]

This explanation is suspect at four points. First, as Zetterholm himself admits, Jews did not expect, and were perhaps reluctant to accept, a temple tax from Gentiles.[11] Thus Jews may not have made available to Gentiles the mechanism whereby Gentiles might have disguised their neglect of civic duty by appearing Jewish.[12] Second, since Zetterholm contends that Jews generally wanted

---

[9] Following a similar line, Paula Fredriksen argues that Gentiles were to be included with Jews eschatologically but they were not to be converted to Judaism, which would have put them at risk in regard to their civic duties ("What 'Parting of the Ways'?" 54–56).

[10] According to this reconstruction, Gentile Christians would have paid the Jewish temple tax until the Jewish War; then they would have paid the *fiscus judaicus*, which the Romans imposed as a replacement of the temple tax, with revenues now directed to the building and support of a pagan temple rather than a Jewish one.

[11] Zetterholm, *The Formation of Christianity in Antioch*, 193–98. Zetterholm argues against M. D. Nanos, who thinks that God-fearers were permitted to pay the temple tax (*The Mystery of Romans: The Jewish Context of Paul's Letter* [Minneapolis: Fortress, 1996], 309).

[12] Mikael Tellbe argues that Gentiles were permitted to contribute to the temple tax, but his main evidence is from Josephus (*Ant.* 14.110), who comments that God-fearers occasionally contributed ("Temple Tax," 21). But Josephus's statement sounds more like evidence that God-fearers did not generally pay the tax. Tellbe also points to S. Mandell,

God-fearers to maintain their civic obligations, it is only God-fearers of the Pauline sort that would have needed to appear as Jews so that they could escape notice as being delinquent in their civic duties. Against this, however, is the unlikelihood that the Jewish authorities would try to accommodate the most problematic and nonconformist group of Jews, Paul's circle, who were already under suspicion and resentment even within Christian circles. Third, Zetterholm must assume that God-fearers, by paying the temple tax (if, indeed, they could do so), would have passed as Jews and not simply as Jewish sympathizers. If they passed simply as sympathizers, they would still be considered Gentiles and thus having civic obligations. Zetterholm tries to avoid this difficulty by populating the body of God-fearers not with local, established residents of Antioch whose prior identity as Gentiles would have been known by their neighbors, but rather with newcomers to the city, who apparently are able to be more anonymous in regard to their Gentile identity. A fourth objection that might be brought against Zetterholm's reconstruction is that many interpreters think that even the Jewish Christians in Matthew's community did not pay the temple tax.[13] Zetterholm's basic reconstruction, though possible, is therefore unconvincing.

In addition, even if there had been a body of Gentile Christians who were able to disguise themselves as Jews, as Zetterholm asserts, it is unlikely that they would have acted in the way that Zetterholm proposes. According to Zetterholm, the relative security that these God-fearers were able to gain by their association with Judaism lasted until a stricter enforcement of the *fiscus*. At that point, Gentile Christians enjoyed significantly reduced benefits in their association with the Jewish community, a connection they had maintained mainly through their connection with Jewish Christians. Before this stricter enforcement of the *fiscus*, the association with Judaism would have worked to disguise the fact that these God-fearers were not performing the religious aspect of their civic duties. This benefit would have balanced the disadvantage God-fearers experienced by not being considered full members of the covenant by the Jewish-Christians with whom they associated. After the Jewish War, the association with suspect Judaism brought suspicion on the God-fearers also, particularly after the stricter enforcement of the *fiscus*. Zetterholm contends that the Gentile Christians now judged that they could improve their situation by fashioning themselves into a distinctive *collegium* separate from Judaism.[14]

"The Jewish Christians and the Temple Tax," *SecCent* (1989): 76–84, which discusses the rabbinic prohibition against Gentiles' paying the temple tax. Mandell thinks that the position on the temple tax changed in the Tannaitic period.

[13] Tellbe, "Temple Tax," 26–29.

[14] Zetterholm, *The Formation of Christianity in Antioch*, 202. Tellbe treats the issue from a slightly different angle: it is the Jewish community that exposes Gentile Christians who had been paying the temple tax to avoid their civic obligations ("Temple Tax").

The last proposition, however, faces several difficulties. The most obvious is that the danger to the Gentile Christians would not be eased by the new arrangement, for they would have brought themselves conspicuously to the attention of the authorities when they tried to register as a *collegium*.[15] Such attention was the very thing Gentile Christians had been hoping to avoid by their association with Judaism up to this point, according to Zetterholm's reconstruction.[16] It hardly seems likely that the Gentile Christians would have thought they could convince the civic authorities that they were the true interpreters of Judaism, as Zetterholm suggests, and thus, as the "real" Jews, would be exempted from obligations to sacrifice to the gods of the polis, as Jews normally were.[17] If Judaism or Jews were discredited by the war, it is unlikely that any association with Jews or Judaism would endear a group to the larger society—particularly a group made up of poor, rural Gentile newcomers to the city.[18] Further, the main elements that the Gentile Christian group wanted to retain from Judaism were its monotheism and the exemption from civic duties of a religious kind—the very points most troubling to the mostly polytheistic society. Nothing suggests that Gentile Christians were going to gain a sympathetic ear from the authorities by dropping their association with Jewish Christians and starting their own group that would continue to refuse civic obligations.

---

[15] It is possible that Christians were able to register as *collegia* initially but that this right was taken away when their activities came under greater suspicion. The evidence most often pointed to is Trajan's prohibition of clubs or associations (Latin: *hetaeriae*; Pliny the Younger, *Ep.* 10.96). Pliny says that Christians ceased to meet (perhaps only for the common meal) when he informed them of Trajan's prohibition against clubs. But we must be careful not to read into this that Christians had already organized and registered as *collegia*. Christians had apparently been able to continue meeting even after Trajan's prohibition against associations. Further, it was not their meetings that brought them to the attention of the governor, nor was it their violation of Trajan's order that placed them in jeopardy. If, then, Christians could continue to meet, apparently unnoticed, after Trajan's prohibition of such meetings, then surely they could have met regularly before that order and gone undetected—and unregistered. Paul R. Trebilco's contention that Ignatius's frequent exhortations for the church to meet together more often must mean that "Christianity was not regarded as an illegal *collegium* at this time" (*The Early Christians in Ephesus*, 630–31) is not convincing. It is equally possible that Christianity had no status—legal or illegal—meeting without registration and without notice. Perhaps scholars have bought into the *collegia* thesis too quickly.

[16] Judith Lieu contends that if church members were joining the synagogue to escape the responsibilities to the imperial cult, Ignatius would have dealt with the matter more forcefully (*Image and Reality: The Jews in the World of the Christians in the Second Century* [Edinburgh: T&T Clark, 1996], 45, 51). Lieu notes, too, that the matter of the *fiscus* was not raised in Christian literature until Origen (p. 287). This suggests that the matter perhaps was not as serious for Christians as Zetterholm presents it, for one might expect to find some evidence of this kind of crisis in the early literature.

[17] Zetterholm, *The Formation of Christianity in Antioch*, 219–20.

[18] See pp. 62–68 for a more detailed discussion.

Another difficulty for Zetterholm's reconstruction is the short time frame in which the significant changes would have had to play themselves out. He is not dealing with a period of ten years (from Domitian's more rigorous enforcement of the *fiscus* to the reversal of these new measures under Nerva), but rather with perhaps only a year or two. Significantly, the Gospel of Matthew, written in the 80s or 90s C.E., shows no evidence that the *fiscus judaicus* created troubles for the Christian community by causing tensions to develop between Jesus-believing Jews and Jesus-believing Gentiles in the Christian assembly. There is tension in Matthew's Gospel, but it is between the church and the synagogue, not between Christians of Jewish and Gentile background.[19] Further, the Gentile group must have had a sufficient number of peaceful years in the Matthean community *after* the composition of the Gospel of Matthew for this gospel to have become as much theirs as it was the gospel of the Jewish Christians in Matthew's church. According to Zetterholm, when the community fractured, both groups retained Matthew's Gospel as a primary text. Since Nerva immediately reversed the severity of the *fiscus judaicus* on his ascension (96 C.E.), only a short time was available for Zetterholm's focal issue to play itself out. How would matters have become so serious that the Christian community, in which Jews and Gentiles had worshiped together for half a century, did not seek or could not find a solution to the new situation created by Domitian's policy? It would be puzzling if, in response to new imperial policy, the Christian group split quickly, apparently without even experimenting with less rash proposals first. It would be even more puzzling if they split into such violently hostile forces that no reconciliation was possible after the imperial policy was reversed. If Christian Jews and Gentiles lived together in peace for many decades, the change in imperial policy (which lasted only a short time) is unlikely to have driven such a permanent wedge between Jewish Christians and Gentile Christians as Zetterholm proposes.

Zetterholm's work offers much of value regarding Antioch and Ignatius. Unfortunately, the least convincing element of his work is his innovative explanation of how Ignatius's community came into existence. It is much more likely that the Matthean community stood in some kind of continuity with the Ignatian community, as an earlier stage of the Ignatian church.[20] This would explain both the hostile attitude to Judaism displayed by both groups and the considerable use of the Matthean tradition in the Ignatian community.

---

[19] Zetterholm maintains that Matthew's Gospel was used simultaneously both in the conflict between Matthew's community and formative Judaism *and* in the conflict between Matthew's community and the Ignatian community (*The Formation of Christianity in Antioch,* 216). The problem for Zetterholm's thesis is that the conflict with the Ignatian community does not leave traces in the Matthean material, although the conflict with the synagogue is pronounced and prominent in this material.

[20] Brown and Meier, *Antioch and Rome,* 11–86.

Ignatius as Bishop

Ignatius presents himself as leader of the church in Antioch and appears to be received as its leader by a host of churches along the journey to Rome and apparently by the Roman church as well.[21] Indeed, Ignatius's arrest itself may indicate that the civil authorities considered Ignatius the bishop of the church in Antioch. Some scholars, however, contend that Ignatius was not a bishop at all, except perhaps in his own mind.[22] Others claim that he was the first bishop of the area and largely responsible for the establishment of the office.[23] Some claim that his election was the issue that divided the church.[24]

Such hypotheses are far less compelling than Ignatius's own claims. Ignatius's view is that he could claim to be the bishop and that he did not need to defend this title when writing to a wide Christian audience. This suggests that Ignatius expected his claim to the title to be understood and to go unchallenged, as indeed seems to have been the case. Further, Ignatius's use of the term "bishop" to identify officers in the churches of western Asia Minor suggests that Ignatius was not freshly introducing the idea of a single bishop with subordinate presbyters and deacons into these communities, although we have no way to determine how recent its introduction may have been.[25]

---

[21] Ignatius usually identifies himself with the church in Syria or Antioch, generally without specifying his office. In four letters, he associates himself with the church in Syria (Ign. *Eph.* 21.2; Ign. *Magn.* 14.1; Ign. *Trall.* 13.1; Ign. *Rom.* 13.1); in two letters, with the church in Antioch in Syria (Ign. *Phld.* 10.1; Ign. *Smyrn.* 11.1); and in one letter, simply with the church in Antioch (Ign. *Pol.* 7.1). But he could also be quite explicit about his position as bishop (Ign. *Rom.* 2.2). Because he refers to Antioch in some letters but to Syria in others, some scholars have raised suspicions about common authorship of the letters (J. Rius-Camps, *The Four Authentic Letters of Ignatius, the Martyr* [OrChrAn 213; Rome: Pontificium Institutum Orientalium Studiorum, 1980]). But Ignatius uses both terms in some of his letters (Ign. *Phld.* 10.1; Ign. *Smyrn.* 11.1, 2; Ign. *Pol.* 7.1–2). It seems, then, that for Ignatius either term was satisfactory to locate his church, and no mystery need be made out of his use of one term rather than the other.

[22] Walter Bauer, *Orthodoxy and Heresy*.

[23] Streeter, *The Primitive Church*, 168–83.

[24] Hammond Bammel, "Ignatian Problems," *JTS* 33 (1982): 79. Trevett, *A Study of Ignatius*, 65, holds a similar view. If it were a disputed election that fractured the church and Ignatius's victory caused his opponents to create such an uproar that the authorities intervened, it would be puzzling that the opposition group in Asia Minor, which disregards the bishop in some way, seems to praise Ignatius and seek his approval (Ign. *Phld.* 7.1–2; Ign. *Smyrn.* 5.2). One should be hesitant to argue that Ignatius's election as bishop was opposed in Antioch (where we have no comment on the matter) but widely accepted in Asia Minor, even by the opponents there.

[25] Some scholars have suggested that the institution of the office of bishop had not yet made its way to Philippi, on the basis of Polycarp's exhortation to the church at Philippi to be subject to the "presbyters and deacons" (Pol. *Phil.* 5.3).

A more important question is the scope of a bishop's community and authority. As seen earlier, the popular scholarly theory is that the Christian church in each city was in fact a collection of churches, some of which may have had friendly relations with others but many of which, because of differences in conduct and belief, had guarded, if not out-and-out hostile, contact with each other. Thus it is common to speak of "Christianities" (or something of that sort) rather than "Christianity."[26] This state of affairs has largely come about because in recent years scholars of early Christian literature have become accustomed to routinely locating each document in its own distinctive theological community, creating as many distinctive communities as there are documents. Indeed, scholars have created even more distinctive communities than there are documents by analyzing supposed redactional layers within each document. The result of such handling of the literature is that early Christianity is seen as not only multiform in its beliefs but also multiform in its concrete appearance, being divided into numerous separate and often non-communicating local churches.[27]

Some scholars have argued that Ignatius was the leader of one of a multitude of Christian assemblies in Antioch, that he did not represent the majority in Antioch, and that a majority there did not support the hierarchical system of bishop, presbyters, and deacons so dear to Ignatius.[28] Even those who believe that Ignatius represented a majority often contend that his vision of church structure was more defined and that he more vigorously defended it than most people with whom he associated.[29]

However, the most natural reading of Ignatius's letters shows a church solidly behind Ignatius and supportive of his vision of leadership. Not only is Ignatius the leader of the majority group in Antioch; he also retained the support of the body of presbyters and deacons there throughout whatever crisis hit the community and placed him in jeopardy. The telling point is that Ignatius has a consistently

---

[26] See "Perspective 3: Christianities and Judaisms," on pp. 214–19.

[27] The trajectory paradigm, developed by James M. Robinson and Helmut Koester, places a number of documents in a common chronological and theological continuum (*Trajectories Through Early Christianity* [Philadelphia: Fortress, 1971]). Such reconstructions are not particularly compelling, however, when they are used to outline the history of a movement, for they simply link together a number of hypothetical communities, each created around its own distinctive document or a redactional layer within a document. The methodological error is multiplied, not corrected, by this process. See the criticism of the trajectory paradigm in Thomas A. Robinson, *The Bauer Thesis Examined,* 139–42.

[28] Bauer argues that the Gnostics were in the majority (*Orthodoxy and Heresy,* 62–63), but few now agree with him on this point. Schoedel, for example, in his detailed commentary, treats Ignatius as the leader of the majority tradition in his community (*Ignatius of Antioch,* 110).

[29] Brown and Meier, *Antioch and Rome,* 75, n. 166. It does appear that Ignatius may have drawn lines more narrowly than others generally had. See Corwin, *St. Ignatius,* 52–53; Trevett, *A Study of Ignatius,* 50.

high regard for presbyters and deacons.[30] With unqualified praise,[31] he calls on the church to respect and obey the presbyters,[32] and sometimes he explicitly mentions that presbyters are supportive of the bishop, as the whole church should be.[33]

Whatever Ignatius's rhetorical excesses, his comments make sense only if presbyters and deacons were largely on his side and his opponents lacked this kind of credible and core support.[34] Ignatius clearly views the bishop as the primary authority in each church. Further, there is no evidence in Ignatius's writings that the threat to the bishops' authority came from the other officials in the church. Had there been threat or opposition from these quarters, presbyters and deacons would have been the targets for some of Ignatius's sharpest attacks, and he certainly would not have encouraged the churches in Asia to obey presbyters and deacons without some kind of explicit warning or qualification.[35] Ignatius explicitly states in a number of passages that the threat to the bishops was from outsiders or from insiders not in positions of leadership.[36] If the threat were from within the ranks of the presbytery, such a mistake by Ignatius in the identification of the opposition would have been worse than no warning at all.[37] This weakens

---

[30] Sometimes Ignatius mentions presbyters and deacons together, but more often he focuses on the presbyters alone. Presbyters are mentioned twenty-one times in the Ignatian letters. Although deacons are mentioned almost as often (seventeen times), some of the occurrences merely indicate the office of a named individual rather than commenting about deacons generally.

[31] Ign. *Eph.* 4.1; Ign. *Magn.* 2.1; 13.1; Ign. *Phld.* 5.1; Ign. *Smyrn.* 12.2.

[32] Ign. *Eph.* 2.2; 20.2; Ign. *Magn.* 2.1; 6.1; 7.1; Ign. *Trall.* 2.2; 3.1; 7.1; 13.2; Ign. *Phld.* intro.; 7.1; Ign. *Smyrn.* 8.1; Ign. *Pol.* 6.1. On occasion, deacons are included with presbyters.

[33] Ign. *Eph.* 4.1; Ign. *Magn.* 3.1.

[34] For a recent discussion of Ignatius's rhetoric, see Harry O. Maier, "The Politics and Rhetoric of Discord and Concord in Paul and Ignatius," in *Trajectories through the New Testament and the Apostolic Fathers* (ed. Andrew F. Gregory and Christopher M. Tuckett; Oxford: Oxford University Press, 2005), 9–23.

[35] Robinson, *The Bauer Thesis Examined,* 175–82, deals at some length with the condition and conduct of the presbytery in the churches of the Ignatian letters. See also Corwin, *St. Ignatius,* 81–82.

[36] The clergy seem to be fully behind the bishops or at least sufficiently supportive that Ignatius makes no issue about it. Some of the opposition seems to be from elsewhere (Ign. *Eph.* 9.1; Ign. *Smyrn.* 4.1).

[37] Scholars debate how to read comments of praise made by a writer about the readers of a letter. Does the praised behavior reflect what the readers are doing or what the writer hopes to motivate them to do? Mikael Isacson recognizes that Ignatius "flatters" his readers and that Ignatius does not provide an "accurate description" but hopes to "persuade" his readers. But Isacson adds this qualification: "If this description of the addressees' behaviour had differed from the reality in any striking sense, this rhetorical device would have failed" ("Follow Your Bishop! Rhetorical Strategies in the Letters of Ignatius of Antioch," in *The Formation of the Early Church* [ed. Jostein Ådna; WUNT 183; Tübingen: Mohr Siebeck, 2005], 336). See also idem, *To Each Their Own Letter: Structure, Themes, and Rhetorical Strategies in the Letters of Ignatius of Antioch* (Coniectanea biblica:

any theory supposing that the schismatics were in the majority or that Ignatius left his church in Antioch at serious risk of takeover by the schismatics or by rivals from within the leadership.

Regarding schism and the call to harmony, Ignatius calls for submission not just to the bishop but to the presbytery as well and sometimes to the deacons.[38] Walter Bauer and others have argued that bishops were having their authority questioned and that the former locus of authority, the presbytery, was still the structure of choice for many Christians. However, if that were the case, we would expect Ignatius to single out the bishop particularly as the one to whom the church should submit.[39] But Ignatius calls the church to submit not simply to the authority of the bishop, but to the authority of bishop, presbyters, and deacons. Such a call is hard to understand if the presbytery and deacons are divided or if such structures, or members of them, stand in opposition to the bishops.[40] As Corwin notes, Ignatius emphasizes institutional unity "symbolized by a united ministry," a position he could not have held in the face of "widespread defections among the clergy."[41]

This does not mean that everyone in every church was happy with the bishop. The comments that fill Ignatius's letters about submitting to the bishop or doing nothing without the bishop's approval provide clear enough testimony of some tension. Unfortunately, such comments have become the basis for hypotheses

---

New Testament Series 42; Stockholm: Almqvist & Wiksell, 2004). However, we should note that Ignatius is not all compliments when addressing the churches. Trebilco reads the matter somewhat differently (*The Early Christians in Ephesus*, 634–39).

[38] Ign. *Eph.* 20.2; Ign. *Magn.* 6.1–7.1; Ign. *Trall.* 2.2; 3.1; 7.1–2; Ign. *Phld.* intro.; 3.3–4.1; 7.1; Ign. *Smyrn.* 8.1.

[39] Bauer, *Orthodoxy and Heresy*, 62–70.

[40] Only one passage in the Ignatian correspondence might appear to suggest some tension or less-than-zealous support for the bishop among the presbytery (Ign. *Trall.* 12.2–3). Bauer makes much of this passage in his effort to show that Ignatius was weak and in a minority situation (*Orthodoxy and Heresy*, 68–69). Such a negative reading of this passage is challenged, however, by Ignatius's call throughout the letter that everyone submit to and respect the presbytery (Ign. *Trall.* 2.2; 3.1; 7.2; 13.2)—comments that would be unlikely had serious opposition to the bishop existed among the presbyters in Tralles. Further, as Schoedel has suggested, Ignatius may have addressed the presbyters of Tralles in this way simply because the bishop of this church traveled alone to greet Ignatius and Ignatius then directed his exhortations regarding support for the bishop to both the assembly and the presbyters there (*Ignatius of Antioch*, 159–60, n. 3). Although Schoedel does not mention it, there is nothing particularly suspicious about the bishop of Tralles being the lone representative of his church (Ign. *Trall.* 1.1). Tralles is farther away than any other church that sent delegates to Smyrna to visit Ignatius. Such distance and the likelihood that Tralles was a young church, perhaps with limited resources, could account easily for the bishop's attending without presbyters. More people traveled from closer cities: five from Ephesus (Ign. *Eph.* 2.1) and four from Magnesia (Ign. *Magn.* 2).

[41] Corwin, *St. Ignatius*, 81.

that the office of bishop was novel and was repudiated by large elements of the church and that the leadership was fractured. But these comments in fact reveal only that there were some problems in the church and that some members were favoring options not approved by the bishop—a situation that Ignatius never tries to disguise.[42]

The evidence seems compelling that the bishops mentioned by Ignatius were supported by the majority in their churches. This means little, however, if these churches constituted only a small element of the full contingent of Christians in the area, so that Ignatius's bishops would be the big fish only because they are in a very small pond. The significant question is whether the churches in Ignatius's orbit represented the majority of Christians in the cities addressed by Ignatius and in Antioch itself.

The broad spectrum of theological reflection found within the churches points to the significant scope of the authority of the bishops in these cities. Several groups are included in these churches, including Judaizers and Docetists, both of whom Ignatius opposes but treats as members of his community, albeit members in poor standing. Little is left outside Ignatius's orbit, and certainly nothing of significance.[43] The bishop seems to be the leader of the primary church in the area rather than the leader of a small, isolated, largely uniform expression of Christianity that was but one of numerous distinctive Christian groups in the area.

Did Ignatius Establish the Office of Bishop in Antioch?

Ignatius supplies the earliest evidence of what appears to be a fairly clearly defined three-part structure of authority: a bishop, with a subordinate presbytery, assisted by a group of deacons. This structure is referred to as a "monarchical episcopate," or perhaps more precisely, the "monepiscopate," so named after the nature of its highest office.[44] Since Ignatius is the earliest witness to this structure, some scholars have suggested that he was either the creator of this ecclesiasti-

---

[42] Ignatius's comments about separate eucharists and assemblies provide the clearest evidence, pp. 81–82, n. 133.

[43] The common argument for expanding the diversity of early Christianity contends that much of early Christian literature was lost as a result of the victory of catholic Christianity. This argument has some validity. Any collection of "New Testament apocryphal" writings witnesses to the diversity of early Christian writing. We know the names of many books that were lost, and we have copies of others that became little used. However, it is one thing to recognize the prolific and diverse character of early Christian literature, and it is another matter entirely to maintain that each document had a sizeable or committed following or a religious community of its own.

[44] Trebilco, *The Early Christians in Ephesus*, 642–43, n. 63.

cal framework of authority or the primary promoter of it and the reason for its success.[45]

The problem with this thesis is that Ignatius is able to use the term "bishop" in its rather full-blown form in letters addressed to churches far removed from Antioch. Ignatius assumes that the churches in the province of Asia have a three-fold division of leadership and that the members there understand the terms of office in roughly the same way as he uses them.[46] Indeed, the terms for the offices prominently dot the pages of Ignatius's correspondence.[47] It cannot be easily argued that Ignatius simply fails to realize that the terms will not apply to the Asian churches he is addressing, as might be argued had the letters been written from Antioch to churches with which Ignatius had had no prior contact. Ignatius writes these letters to the churches of Asia with representatives of these very churches present.

That the readers understood the terms as Ignatius intended them is suggested by three observations. First, Ignatius shows no awareness of a need to explain his particular use of these terms, as he surely would have had he just pressed through these supposedly novel hierarchical reforms in Antioch and wished to establish similar structures in the churches of Asia. The terms appear to be used for offices already established, not for offices just being established or redefined. Second, it appears that Ignatius employed Burrhus, a leader of the church at Ephesus, as the amanuensis for these letters.[48] Had Ignatius's use of these terms carried a meaning out of line with how they were being used in the churches of Asia, one might expect that Burrhus would have asked for clarification. Nothing in these

---

[45] The argument goes back to Streeter, *The Primitive Church*, 168–83. Yet Streeter became overly focused on trying to analyze Ignatius's "abnormal psychology" (p. 171). For the latest presentation of this position, see Allen Brent, *Ignatius of Antioch: A Martyr Bishop and the Origin of Episcopacy* (New York: T&T Clark, 2007).

[46] Isacson argues that Ignatius is not attempting to introduce the office of bishop in the area ("Follow Your Bishop!" 336–37). Schoedel thinks that the threefold ministry was in place and the authority of the one bishop recognized in the churches of Asia, although the situation was "still somewhat in flux" (*Ignatius of Antioch*, 22). Trebilco thinks the office was "not very well established in Asia (*The Early Christians in Ephesus*, 668), but he recognizes that writers such as the author of Revelation and Ignatius himself wrote to all the churches in the area (p. 675), which suggests a sensibility about the unity of the church in an area that could easily lead into a single bishop figure.

[47] The terms are used more than one hundred times in the letters of Ignatius.

[48] Burrhus probably was the scribe for all seven of Ignatius's letters, although he is mentioned by name as the amanuensis in only two, those to Philadelphia and Smyrna (Ign. *Phld.* 11.2; Ign. *Smyrn.* 12.1). Both letters were written from Troas, which suggests the kind of work Burrhus was selected to provide for Ignatius when his services were offered earlier in Smyrna (Ign. *Eph.* 2.1). A comment in Ign. *Rom.* 10.1 notes that it is being written "by the Ephesians," a likely reference to Burrhus, who was from Ephesus. The duties and office of Crocus are less clear (Ign. *Eph.* 2.1; Ign. *Rom.* 10.1).

letters, however, suggests an awareness, at any level, of a need to clarify the terms. Third, Ignatius identifies a number of people from the churches of Asia by name and rank, as bishop, presbyter, or deacon.[49] If the churches had presbyters and deacons before the institution of a monarchical office, the lone bishop, as head of the church in the city, would not have existed. Yet Ignatius identifies someone as bishop in each of the five Asian assemblies he addresses.[50] Nothing in the language suggests that Ignatius was appointing these men to an elevated bishop's office by so naming them, although this unlikely theory has been proposed.[51] Were he doing so, more specific comments to this effect would be expected.

Also, in all five Asian churches with which Ignatius has contact, he senses that each bishop is on his side. How would this be possible if the church were fractured and the division were reflected in the presbytery as well? The situation reflected in Ignatius's letters suggests that the threefold hierarchical structure was already in place in churches of Asia by the time Ignatius passed through, with the clergy united and the laity generally supportive.

Why, then, does Ignatius speak so much about the bishop's office, defending it in a number of ways, if it is the standard structure of authority in the churches to which he writes? One should not quickly jump to the conclusion that the office must have been novel and not yet securely established for Ignatius to make it his emphasis.[52] A more natural reading of Ignatius's letters is that the office of bishop was sufficiently accepted in Asia Minor that Ignatius could use it to define the

---

[49] Bishop: Onesimus (Ign. *Eph.* 1.3; 6.1–2); Damas (Ign. *Magn.* 2.1); Polybius (Ign. *Trall.* 1.1); Polycarp (Ign. *Pol.* intro.). Presbyter: Bassus and Apollonius (Ign. *Magn.* 2.1). Deacon: Burrhus (Ign. *Eph.* 2.1); Zotion (Ign. *Magn.* 2.1). Three individuals are mentioned by name without specification of an office: Crocus (Ign. *Eph.* 2.1; Ign. *Rom.* 10.1); Euplus, and Fronto (Ign. *Eph.* 2.1).

[50] Although Ignatius does not mention the bishop by name in his letters to the Philadelphians or Smyrnaeans, he speaks of the bishop in such a way as to indicate that both he and the readers know who is meant (Ign. *Phld.* intro.; 1.1; Ign. *Smyrn.* 8.1; 12.2). His letter to Polycarp confirms this, at least for the situation in Smyrna. Indeed, any reference to a bishop in the Ignatian letters is clearly a reference to a particular individual whom the recipients of the letters would have no difficulty in identifying.

[51] Patrick Burke, "The Monarchical Episcopate at the End of the First Century," *Journal of Ecumenical Studies* 7 (1970): 499–518. Burke even argues that there were no bishops in Asia Minor until Ignatius passed through and that various individuals were raised to this position when Ignatius simply applied the label "bishop" to them. Burke assumes that Ignatius was able to bring about this transformation of the hierarchy by weight of his authority as leader of the church in Antioch, which Burke believes stood as the mother church to the Asian churches. Against his thesis are the lack of any evidence that Antioch possessed the status of a mother church and the strained reading that Burke must apply to the texts in which Ignatius refers to established bishops of particular churches in western Asia Minor.

[52] Even Meier, who thinks the three-part hierarchy is a "*fait accompli*" by the time of Ignatius, maintains that Ignatius's "incessant exhortations to be submissive to the bishop

church and discredit the schismatics, for this is how the appeal to the bishop is employed throughout the letters. Ignatius is defining the church (those submitting to the bishop and presbytery); he is not defining the bishop, nor does it seem necessary for him to do so.

Ignatius and the Jews of Antioch

There appear to have been varying degrees of association between Jews and Gentiles in Antioch. Nicolaus was a proselyte—a Gentile who had become fully Jewish. He would have been circumcised. Ignatius, on the other hand, seems to know of individuals who were attracted to Judaism but were not circumcised (Ign. *Phld.* 6.1) and Christians who were "living according to Judaism" (Ign. *Magn.* 8.1). Whatever he means by the latter, he treats such involvement as dangerous and unacceptable. He also knows of circumcised individuals (whether native Jews or proselytes) to whom he would entrust the teaching of Christian doctrine (Ign. *Phld.* 6.1).

Josephus addresses the matter of Jewish-Gentile relations in Antioch from a Jewish perspective. He qualifies, but in an ambiguous manner, the relation of interested Greeks to Judaism: they were "in some measure" incorporated into the Jewish community.[53] Neither Ignatius nor Josephus is of help, however, in determining the precise relationship of Gentiles to Judaism or the degree of observance practiced by interested Gentiles. Perhaps the ambiguity best captures a situation in which various nuanced engagements between Judaism and the Gentile population could be found.

The relationships that Jews and Gentiles already had forged in Antioch before the rise of the Christian movement may help us understand the Christian effort to accommodate Gentiles. The available literature helps reconstruct several kinds of relationships.[54] On the Jewish side, there are at least five positions of interest to this study, each of which likely has finer subdivisions:

1. Jews who rejected Gentiles of any kind;

2. Jews who accepted only full converts, or proselytes;

3. Jews who accepted, in whatever qualified way, God-fearers;

---

seem to indicate that the role of the single-bishop is relatively new" in the churches of Asia (Brown and Meier, *Antioch and Rome,* 75, n. 166).

[53] Josephus, *J. W.* 7.45. The Greek reads τινὶ μοῖραν.

[54] These categories are not intended to be comprehensive or inflexible but, rather, only suggestive. Various other groupings have been proposed.

4. Jews who were apostates;[55] and

5. Jews who had, with the rise of Christianity, become Christians.[56]

On the Gentile side, there would have been equally nuanced positions:[57]

1. Gentiles who were hostile to Judaism;

2. the God-fearers, Gentiles who, though interested in aspects of Judaism, hesitated at full conversion;

3. the proselytes, Gentiles who fully converted to Judaism;

4. Gentiles who converted to an esoteric or peripheral branch of the Jewish tradition but were nonetheless accepted by the larger Jewish community (the Judaizing side of Christianity might be one example);[58] and

5. Gentiles who converted to a suspect branch of the Jewish tradition and were rejected by the larger Jewish community (Christians of the complexion of Paul or Ignatius are primary examples).

This last group already could be distinguished from Judaism by the Antiochene-coined label "Christian" around the time of Ignatius, and the situation of separation may have been decades old by that time.[59]

Ignatius reflects a more developed but intentionally less nuanced sense of the divisions. For him, there are but two camps—Judaism and Christianity.

---

[55] From certain Jewish perspectives, Jews who had become Christians (group 5) were, in fact, apostates (group 4).

[56] Meier divides early Christianity into four groups (Brown and Meier, *Antioch and Rome*, 2–8). As is clear from the early Christian literature, Jews who became Christians had no uniform position on Gentiles. Indeed, it is probable that the range of attitudes toward proselytes and God-fearers among Christian Jews was not strikingly different from the range of attitudes toward proselytes and God-fearers that was found within Judaism itself, except perhaps for the Hellenist/Pauline option, which emphasized the inclusion of Gentiles.

[57] Shaye J. D. Cohen offers seven possible positive relationships that a Gentile might have to Judaism ("Crossing the Boundary," 13–33).

[58] It is not clear how Jews who confessed Christ but maintained Torah practice were treated. There are hints that some fellow Jews were tolerant, but it is impossible to determine how long this attitude lasted. By the middle of the second century, Justin sees Jewish Christian believers shut off from both Judaism and Christianity (*Dial.* 47). Related to this issue is the considerable debate over the relevance and occasion of the addition to the Eighteen Benedictions in the synagogue prayers and what the consequences were for Jewish Christian groups (see William Horbury, "The Benediction of the *minim* and Early Jewish-Christian Controversy," *JTS* 33 [1982]: 19–61).

[59] It is unclear what groups were included in the first use of the term "Christian." Were all believers in Jesus tagged with the term or only those who had distanced themselves more starkly from Judaism by allowing Gentiles to join without the obligations of Torah?

Whatever the nuances within these camps, they are irrelevant to his main distinction. Where he finds subgroups within Christianity, he opposes and dismisses them.[60] That he would have had a keener interest in the subgroups of Judaism is unlikely. Indeed, for Ignatius, the variations within Judaism would be simply "deadly poisons" of different kinds.[61] None would have been mild or safe enough to recommend itself for consideration or consumption. All are "tombstones and sepulchers."[62] Only one division concerns Ignatius—that between Christianity and Judaism. Ignatius will not take the bait in the discussions about the circumcised teaching Christianity or the uncircumcised teaching Judaism; the issue for Ignatius is that *Christ* be taught.[63] Those who argue that Ignatius is concerned only with Christians who Judaize have missed the sweep of Ignatius's perspective on the matter. He is not fishing with a hook for only a certain species. Ignatius's net catches in it all things Jewish.

Glimpses of Ignatius's Church Life

Ignatius's letters were not intended to provide a description of life in early Christian churches. Although Ignatius mentions a few primary Christian practices (baptism, eucharist, and Sunday assembly), he mentions them only by way of saying that all Christian activity, of which these seem central, must be done under the bishop's authority. He offers no instructions on how these or other aspects of Christian life should be conducted. Some scholars have tried to wrest more from Ignatius's various comments, but the results provide little of major significance. Probably the most significant item we learn is that some schismatics appear to have been meeting on the Sabbath for their separate eucharists whereas Ignatius's church appears to have conducted its corporate religious life primarily on Sunday.[64] Even the oft-repeated mention of bishops, presbyters, and deacons tells us little about the duties of the clergy. We learn mainly that

---

[60] See Ignatius's comments about separate assemblies and eucharists (see pp. 80–82).

[61] Ign. *Tral.* 6.2. "Deadly poison" is from Lake's translation; Ehrman opts for "deadly drug." Such language is sharp, sweeping, and uncompromisingly dismissive. It may even be shameful, but it is exactly the kind of language that we might expect in the turbulence of the birth of a new religious movement. See further discussion regarding such language in the conclusion to ch. 6, p. 241.

[62] Ign. *Phld.* 6.1 (Lake's translation); Ehrman translates it as "monuments and tombs of the dead."

[63] Ign. *Phld.* 6.1. The exact meaning is debated (see p. 41, n. 6). Lieu thinks that Ignatius becomes "caught in his own rhetoric" here (*Image and Reality*, 278).

[64] Attempts, mostly by Seventh-Day Adventist scholars, to argue that early Christians did not meet on Sunday are dismissed by Schoedel as "strained" (*Ignatius of Antioch*, 123, n. 3).

presbyters and deacons are expected to obey and support the bishop (which they do) and that the church is to obey the three-part hierarchy of leadership (which they do not always do). All the other intriguing matters of the development of structures of authority and of the duties of the distinctive offices are left unaddressed.

Ignatius's letters contain a few clues about the kinds of members who made up the early churches and the behavior expected of them. Several hints appear in Ignatius's letter to Polycarp, which gives more specific instructions about such matters. One focus of these instructions is on the charitable role of the church. Widows are mentioned, but the instructions are unspecific: they are not to be "neglected" (Ign. *Pol.* 4.1)—ambiguous instructions, doubtlessly more helpful to the widows of Smyrna than to modern investigators. Virgins are included in the group of widows. Some degree of novelty appears to have been present, for Ignatius makes a special note of "virgins who are called widows,"[65] which seems unnecessary if the inclusion of virgins in the group of widows had been a long-standing practice (Ign. *Smyrn.* 13.1). The only other mention of widows is in a polemical passage against schismatics. There Ignatius indicts the separatists for their disregard of widows and their neglect of a host of other groups in need of assistance, such as orphans, the sick, the poor (referred to as the "hungry" and "thirsty"), and prisoners (Ign. *Smyrn.* 6.2). We cannot, however, take at face value Ignatius's somewhat blanket criticism of the negligent charitable activities of the schismatics, for such comments were stock polemic fodder.[66] Nonetheless, these comments would have been, for the most part, ineffective if Ignatius's own church circle were not engaged somehow in alleviating the distress of these groups, whatever the practice of other groups might have been.[67]

---

[65] The Greek reads, τὰς παρθένους τὰς λεγομένας χήρας.

[66] Judith Perkins, for example, assumes the accuracy of Ignatius's description of the schismatics' charitable neglect in her comment that "Most other contemporary social institutions likewise shared such a lack of concern. Ignatius named precisely those categories exempted from the prevailing social power relations" (*The Suffering Self: Pain and Narrative Representation in the Early Christian Era* [London: Routledge, 1995], 192). But this is an insufficiently nuanced view of the matter, although she is right to relate the church's service to needs that were generally not being met adequately or for which additional relief would have made a difference. Trevett, whose reading of Ignatius's comment likewise lacks nuance, thinks that Judaizers are ruled out as the target of Ignatius's criticism because those rooted in Hebrew Scriptures would not have neglected widows (*A Study of Ignatius*, 161). All that Ignatius's words convey here, however, is that the schismatics' treatment of widows is not adequate, which is a matter of perspective and, in a polemical context, perhaps only loosely accurate. Recall a similar charge of neglecting widows in the earliest complaint between Hellenist and Hebrew Christians in Jerusalem (Acts 6:1). There the context is definitely Jewish.

[67] Widows, orphans, and the poor are also recipients of charity in Polycarp's circle (Pol. *Phil.* 6.1).

Concerning orphans, early Christian literature expresses a general concern that the church protect these children.[68] We can conclude from this that the structures of the larger society were not meeting some needs. However, this does not mean that only Christians or Jews, with whom the Christians shared many of their social concerns, had kindly sensibilities. In the first century, some wealthy Roman citizens in some cities of Italy founded *alimenta,* trust funds of sorts, to support orphans and the children of the poor. Some emperors of the late first and second centuries made the care of these children an element of their social policy.[69] Orphans were a concern for Ignatius also, which indicates not only that there were orphans in the churches but that among them were orphans whose plight was grave. Some orphans would have had the good fortune to be adopted or raised by relatives. But there also seem to have been orphans in Christian churches who did not have support from extended families. This suggests that perhaps some families who joined the church had no relatives in the assembly or at least none who could take over the care of children in the event of the parents' death. If, as some scholars contend, the church grew mainly as a result of its social networks, we may have a clue here to the economic level of some of the early Christians. Given a situation where church members often would have had relatives within the assembly (assuming conversion through social networks) and orphans needed the care of the church, some families may have been too poor to take one more child, even a relative, under its care. On the other hand, the situation might suggest that the church was taking orphans under its care who had had no previous relationship to the church and was thereby bringing them for the first time into its orbit. The exact situation, however, is unknown.[70]

---

[68] The following is a list of the earliest or most influential references: James 1:27; *1 Clem.* 8.4; *Barn.* 20.2; Ign. *Phil* 6.1; Ign. *Smyrn.* 6.2; *Herm. Sim.* 1.8; 5.3.7; 9.26.2; *Herm. Mand.* 8.10; *Herm. Vision* 2.4.3; Aristides of Athens, *Apologia* 15; Justin, *1 Apol.* 67; *Apostolic Constitutions* 2.25; Tertullian, *Adversus Marcionem* 4.14. A full list of such references would be extensive.

[69] Pliny the Younger set up such a system out of private funds in his hometown, Comum, as did many wealthy individuals in various cities in the first century. The emperors Nerva, Trajan, and Antoninus were associated with such initiatives. The intention in these cases seems to have been to stabilize the declining population of Italy. See F. C. Bourne, "The Roman Alimentary Program and Italian Agriculture," *TAPA* 91 (1960): 47–75; G. Woolf, "Food, Poverty, and Patronage: The Significance of the Epigraphy of the Roman Alimentary Schemes in Early Imperial Italy," *Papers of the British School at Rome* 58 (1990): 197–228; Peter D. A. Garnsey, "Trajan's Alimenta: Some Problems," *Historia* 17 (1968): 367–81; Ramsay MacMullen, *Christianizing the Roman Empire (A. D. 100–400)* (New Haven and London: Yale University Press, 1984), 54.

[70] The first letter to Timothy offers fairly explicit instructions about widows. The expectation is that if a widow has grown children or grandchildren in the assembly, the family, rather than the church, is to provide support (1 Tim 5:4). This would free up the church's resources for the assistance of widows who do not have such family support

Ignatius's churches contained both slaves and free, as was probably the case in any early Christian assembly, given the prominence of the slave class in Roman society.[71] Of the slaves, there were both men and women. Ignatius's writings provide a clue that some of the slaves were seeking their freedom at the expense of the church. There is nothing surprising about slaves' seeking their freedom, for the purchase of freedom was a reasonable aspiration of many in a world where the various misfortunes of life could bring one into servitude.[72] The reason Ignatius

---

(5:16). Although a similar support of orphans is not mentioned, one might assume such an expectation. This sense of family responsibility was not sharply different from the view of the wider society, in which families often raised orphans of close relatives. The care of those who did not have such family support was offered by the church, and also by the occasional philanthropist in limited ways in the form of *alimenta* (see the immediately preceding note). To what extent 1 Timothy's instructions regarding widows reflects wider Christian practice is uncertain, but the influence of the Hebrew Scriptures would have served to remind Christians of their obligations to widows and orphans. Jews had a reputation of caring for their own (Martin Goodman, *The Ruling Class of Judea: The Origins of the Jewish Revolt against Rome, A. D. 66–70* [Cambridge: Cambridge University Press, 1987], 61–67). This sense of obligation carried over to the young Christian community, and it seems to have been one element of Jewish practice that Gentile converts to Christianity adopted, for the charitable emphasis of Christians became renowned and much later was seen by the pagan emperor Julian as an important factor in Christian success. Even Roland Smith, who cautions against attributing Julian's reforms to Christian influence, admits the influence of Christian ideas of charity (*Julian's Gods: Religion and Philosophy in the Thought and Action of Julian the Apostate* [New York: Routledge, 1995], 111).

[71] Ign. *Pol.* 4.3. Slaves are mentioned often as members of early Christian assemblies (1 Cor 7:21–22; 12:13; Gal 3:28; Eph 6:5, 8; Col 3:11, 22; 4:1; 1 Tim 6:1; Phlm 16; *1 Clem.* 55; *Did.* 4.13; *Barn.* 19.7). Newly enslaved people were constantly available for purchase. A primary source of slaves was Rome's continued expansion, in which a whole conquered people, or an element of it, could be taken into slavery. Another source was revolts within the empire; the Jews' various failed revolts contributed substantial numbers of new slaves. A third source was those who were in debt. For a collection of ancient sources on Greco-Roman slavery, see Thomas Wiedemann, *Greek and Roman Slavery* (London: Croom Helm, 1981).

[72] This would have been truer of domestic slaves than of agricultural slaves. The latter were usually worked into the ground, living short, brutal lives. Domestic slaves enjoyed better treatment; some possessed considerable skills before their enslavement and with these skills rose to prominent positions in the household. They would have naturally taken every opportunity to regain their freedom, and on some occasions the resources of the church were used, as may be implied by Ignatius's need to forbid the practice (Ign. *Pol.* 4.3). The matter would have been complicated further for the Christian church in Antioch if some of the slaves in Christian homes were Christian Jews who had been enslaved by Rome in the action against the Jews of Palestine during the failed Jewish War, which resulted in the enslavement of thousands of Jews. One can imagine the debate that such a situation would have produced. Antioch, which was near Palestine, would have been a likely center for the sale of slaves, since it was from Antioch that the Roman troops were sent against Judea and it was to Antioch that the booty of war was brought. Clearly, the

rejected the practice of using church funds to redeem slaves is unknown. There was no uniform Christian position; some Christians encouraged the redemption of slaves.[73]

Both marriage and celibacy were acceptable options in Ignatius's church (Ign. *Poly* 5.1–2). Vows of marriage or of celibacy were to be carried out with the knowledge of the bishop, although marriage would have had a more public recognition; knowledge of a vow of celibacy was between the celibate and the bishop. This raises the question whether the comment applies more to male celibates than to female, for, as already seen, there appears to have been a public recognition of celibate females (as virgins and widows).[74] If the situation was such that female celibates were publicly recognized and male celibates were not, this may be similar to what we find in Tertullian's North African churches a hundred years later, where celibate males seem to have been pressing for some public recognition within the Christian assembly.[75]

No doubt, life in Ignatius's churches was more complex and varied than this small window allows us to see.

The Centuries after Ignatius

The Christian community in Antioch likely lived in the shadow of the synagogue until late into the fourth century. According to John Chrysostom's estimate, only about one-third of Antioch was Christian by the late 300s. If we assume that the Christian population grew considerably as a result of the conversion of Constantine and the alliance of the Constantinian dynasty with the Christian church in the middle part of the 300s, then, the Christian population of Antioch, before this surge of growth, was probably smaller than the Jewish population, although it is not possible to determine how much smaller.

As already mentioned, much of recent scholarship has focused on the continuing attraction that Judaism and the synagogue held for elements of the Christian church in Antioch. There is a danger in this emphasis, however, for it represents only one side of the Christian movement's dynamic encounters with

---

freeing of slaves with church monies had been discussed at least in Polycarp's church, and it seems that Ignatius had already dealt with the matter in Antioch.

[73] Paul's comment in 1 Cor 7:21–22 sets a tone that is repeated in the post-Pauline literature (Col 3:22; Eph 6:5–6; 1 Tim 6:1), although *Herm. Mand.* 8.10 offers a counter position. Generally, however, Christianity accepted the reality of slavery, although it modified the treatment of slaves (Geoffrey S. Nathan, *The Family in Late Antiquity: The Rise of Christianity and the Endurance of Tradition* [New York: Routledge, 2000], 169–84).

[74] The expectation of chastity before marriage should be assumed. What Ignatius identifies is a vow of lifelong celibacy.

[75] Tertullian, *De virginibus velandis* 10.

the larger world. In addition to its engagements (both positive and negative) with Judaism, the Christian community in Antioch would have engaged in attacking paganism and successfully converting Gentiles. This dimension of Christian activity is important, for it reminds us that Judaism, though a constant and considerable element in early Christianity's social, cultural, and intellectual environment, was not the only element—nor was it likely the most important as Christianity made its way in the religious marketplace.[76]

Christianity in Antioch was also theologically a fertile field for the intra-Christian debates of the period. Early in the second century, the shadowy figure of Saturninus, an early Gnostic, was situated in Antioch, and Ignatius's anti-docetic arguments are almost certainly directed at an environment with which Saturninus might easily have identified.[77] According to Justin, Menander, a Samaritan and follower of Simon Magus, spent time in Antioch, promising immortality and attracting disciples. Justin claims that some of Menander's followers were still alive even in his time, which seems to suggest a considerably earlier origin for the movement in Antioch, close to Ignatius's time (1 Apol. 26). One must therefore be careful not to obscure the rich life of the Christian community by concentrating too much on the evidence of the attraction of the synagogue for some Christians. Judaism was but one facet of a considerably broader world in which Christians spread their message.

The attraction of Christians to the synagogue may also need to be seen in a new light, for scholarly discussion seems to have overlooked the most illuminating feature of the situation as it relates to the growth of Christianity. If aspects of the synagogue continued to attract Christians, we must ask who these Christians were. If they were Jews who had converted to Christianity but still retained some of their associations with the synagogue, this should be understood as a net gain for the Christian movement, not a loss as it is generally presented, for the primary identity of these individuals would have been Christian even though they were Jews.

If we assume, however, that few Jews were attracted to Christianity in the second and third centuries, then the Christians who were being attracted to the synagogue must have been Gentile converts to Christianity. With the

---

[76] Indeed, in his writings, Bishop Theophilus of Antioch (mid to late second century) is concerned with pagans, not Jews or the synagogue. Theophilus was a pagan convert to Christianity. In his *Apologia ad Autolycum*, he argues the Christian case against paganism. On the other hand, the world of Judaism considerably influenced Theophilus, according to Rich Rogers, who argues that Theophilus is closer to Hellenistic Judaism than any other author of an early Christian writing (*Theophilus of Antioch: The Life and Thought of a Second-Century Bishop* [Lanham, Md.: Lexington Books, 2000]).

[77] For a recent summary of discussions about Saturninus, see Alastair H. B. Logan, "Gnosticism," in *The Early Christian World* (ed. Philip F. Esler; 2 vols.; New York: Routledge, 2000), 2:916–20.

considerable Christian use of the Jewish Scriptures and with Judaism and the synagogue featured often in the distinctive Christian documents themselves, many Gentile converts to Christianity would have had their curiosity about Judaism awakened.[78] This likely led to a movement of *some* Gentile converts through Christianity into Judaism. In other words, Christianity attracted Gentiles but did not hold all of them. This is not surprising, as some Gentiles would have been exposed to the religious aspects of Judaism for the first time by their association with Christianity. Some Christian converts would have continued their religious pilgrimage into Judaism, and others may have experimented with aspects of Judaism even as they retained their primary identity with the Christian camp.

Such a situation should not be seen as negative for the Christian movement. It reflects the success, not the failure, of Christianity in the pagan world. The time came (probably earlier rather than later) when the Christian movement ceased to attract Jews in any significant numbers. At the same time, if some Christian converts moved through Christianity into Judaism, Christians would have come to experience a net loss in terms of transfer of members between themselves and Judaism. In other words, more Christians would have converted to Judaism than Jews to Christianity, although we have no way to determine whether such movement consisted of many or few. Overall, however, the Christian movement would have continued to grow as a result of new converts from paganism, most of whom found in Christianity a permanent calm for their religious restlessness. This would have created an environment where Christian sermons might well be directed against Judaism and its attractions—the very characteristic found in Christian literature of the first few centuries.[79] Such sermons and concerns should not be understood as pointing to a massive departure of membership from the Christian community into Judaism. It is just as likely, if not more so, that such sermons point to the success of Christians in attracting Gentiles, some of whom were further attracted to Judaism itself.

It is likely also that, to some indeterminable degree, the attraction of Christians to the synagogue that is reflected in some sermons (most of which are as

---

[78] The counter forces of Christian scriptures and preaching warned against association with the synagogue, but not everyone can be expected to dutifully follow the exhortations of the bishop or heed the warnings in the community's writings.

[79] In the view of Andres Klostergaard Petersen, anti-Jewish Christian literature indicates that the ways of Judaism and Christianity had not departed ("At the End of the Road—Reflections on a Popular Scholarly Metaphor," in *The Formation of the Early Church* [ed. Jostein Ådna; WUNT 183; Tübingen: Mohr Siebeck, 2005], 63). But one might as well argue that early Mormon attacks on traditional Christianity indicate that there had not been a separation of the ways between these two groups. The reality is that both groups would have recognized a separation, and neither would have wanted to be counted under the same umbrella as the other.

late as Chrysostom) arose from the considerable growth of the Christian movement after the conversion of Constantine and the favoritism shown to the church by the Constantinian dynasty.[80] If there were a significant attraction to Judaism, sermons against any such association are certainly not surprising. Although the degree of such an attraction is unknown, it is clear that, with the flood of untutored Gentiles into the church during the Constantinian dynasty, the numbers of Christians attracted to Judaism would have increased, for many would have had their first substantial exposure to elements of Judaism from within their new Christian environment, and some would have continued their religious journey into Judaism. This is mostly overlooked in discussions about the attraction of some Christians to Judaism.

The attention that Christian sermons give to the issue of Judaism indicates *where* members were being lost. Whether the loss was minimal or massive, Christian leaders would have addressed the matter, since they would have considered any loss an undesirable situation. The Christian criticism of Judaism makes sense in an environment in which some Christian converts ended up in Judaism, but such criticism does not require a major movement of Christians into Judaism or into Jewish practice.[81]

Did Ignatius Lose Control of the Church in Antioch?

Ignatian scholarship is accustomed to speak of Ignatius's loss of control in Antioch.[82] Trevett, for example, wonders why Ignatius does not name a single individual from Antioch in his letters although he mentions a number of others from elsewhere.[83] The suggestion seems to be that Ignatius must have lost all support in Antioch. But Trevett may be making a mystery where there is none.

---

[80] Robert L. Wilken comments about the attraction of Judaism for Christians, "Finally a word about judaizing Christians or Jewish Christianity in Antioch. Here too the most extensive evidence comes from the 4th century, specifically in the writings of John Chrysostom, and in other works from Syria" ("The Jews of Antioch," *SBL Seminar Papers, 1976* [Missoula, Mont.: Scholars Press, 1976], 73). But he then reverses the significance of the evidence by arguing that such attraction was much the same in the earlier period. Given the considerably changed character of the membership in the Christian church as a result of Constantine's conversion, we must rethink our questions about Christian attraction to, or curiosity about, Judaism.

[81] Lieu suggests that some of this polemic may have had a rhetorical character that resulted in a scholarly perception of "a more substantial threat than what the numbers justified" ("History and Theology in Christian Views of Judaism," in *The Jews among Pagans and Christians in the Roman Empire* [ed. Judith Lieu, John North, and Tessa Rajak; New York: Routledge, 1992], 89).

[82] Trevett, *A Study of Ignatius*, 48.

[83] Ibid., 52.

Ignatius seems to mention individuals by name in his letters mainly where there was a direct association of the individual named with the church addressed or with individuals who joined Ignatius en route, possibly as fellow martyrs.[84] There is no reason to mention individuals in Antioch. And it is unlikely that Ignatius could find no supporter to identify by name in Antioch when the evidence at least from Asia Minor shows that the prominent church officials from a wide area quickly rallied around Ignatius. Almost every scholar, including Trevett, thinks that the schism in Antioch was quickly healed after Ignatius's departure.[85] It seems unlikely that Ignatius had lost all support in Antioch, so that he could not name even one person as his ally, but a few days later had the membership return to his fold. Further, Ignatius's confidence in presbyters and deacons would be difficult to explain had he none of the clergy in Antioch on his side.

Ignatius makes several statements about being unworthy or being the least.[86] Many scholars have argued that Ignatius's sense of unworthiness was connected to a troubled situation within his church in Antioch and that Ignatius held himself responsible for the sorry state of affairs there.[87] This reconstruction has in fact become a near-consensus opinion.[88] But such a portrait of Ignatius seems profoundly flawed (see pp. 177–81 for a detailed critique of the popular view of Ignatius's dilemma). The aim here is not to rehabilitate Ignatius to the status he held in early Christianity but to show that the currently popular portrait of Ignatius is unsound. But first we need to look at the debate regarding the nature of the opposition that Ignatius confronted—one of the most heated debates in scholarship on Ignatius.

---

[84] Ignatius names eleven people who traveled to see him (p. 101, n. 49). All the other names he mentions are of individuals from Smyrna, where Ignatius was a guest for some days (Travia, Alce, Daphnus, Eutecnus [Ign. *Smyrn.* 13.2]; the wife of Epitropus, Attalus, Alce [Ign. *Pol.* 8.2–3]), except for Philo and Rheus Agathopus, deacons who joined Ignatius's company in Troas (Ign. *Smyrn.* 10.1).

[85] Trevett, *A Study of Ignatius,* 52.

[86] Ign. *Eph.* 21.2; Ign. *Magn.* 14.1; Ign. *Trall.* 13.1; Ign. *Rom.* 9.2; Ign. *Smyrn.* 11.1.

[87] Trevett, *A Study of Ignatius,* 59–66, argues that Ignatius willingly submitted himself to arrest, influenced by passages in *1 Clement* that encouraged individuals to depart from their churches if it meant that this could bring peace to the church. But Clement's situation was quite different from that of Ignatius. Clement wants the new leadership to withdraw so that the church can have peace *under the old leadership.* Ignatius is not leaving his church in Antioch in order to make way for new leadership, and if he were, this would not be in step with Clement's recommendation. Granted, Ignatius may have misread Clement's advice, but this is unlikely.

[88] For a recent detailed exposition of this position, see John-Paul Rogers, *Ignatius and Concord: The Background and Use of the Language of Concord in the Letters of Ignatius of Antioch* (Patristic Studies 8; New York: Peter Lang, 2007).

Ignatius's Opponents

The Problem

Ignatius had enemies. We know that some were outside the church, for Ignatius, who had an evolved view of Christian suffering and martyrdom, was under arrest and on his way to Rome to be executed "for the Name."[89] This suggests that not everything was hospitable for Christians in the larger environment of Antioch.

It is not the identity of the opposition from outside the church, however, that has sparked debate; rather, it is the identity of the opposition from within. The debate is old; the matter, unresolved.[90] Influenced by works on Ignatius by J. B. Lightfoot and Theodor Zahn, older scholarship generally maintained that Ignatius confronted only one group of Christian opponents.[91] In more recent years, challenges to this view have become common, and the two-group hypothesis has gained considerable support.[92] A few scholars, seeing the difficulty of resolving the matter so neatly, introduce a third group.[93]

---

[89] Although many scholars argue that Ignatius's plight arose from internal disputes within the church (a reconstruction challenged in ch. 5), Ignatius sees the matter primarily as the consequence of carrying "the Name" (Ign. *Eph.* 1.2; 3.1; Ign. *Magn.* 1.2; possibly Ign. *Smyrn.* 4.2). This phrase became the common expression by which Christians specified the basis of the external opposition to the Christian movement (Acts 15:26; 26:9; 1 Pet. 4:14; Pliny the Younger, *Ep.* 10.96.2; *Herm. Sim.* 8.6; 9.28; Athenagoras of Athens, *Legatio pro Christianis* [or *Apologia*] 2; Justin, *1 Apol.* 4; Justin, *2 Apol.* 2; Justin, *Dial.* 39; 96. Tertullian opens his *Apologeticus* with a lengthy discussion of what he considers the offensive and strange legal procedure of convicting Christians merely because of "the Name" (1–3).

[90] Matti Myllykoski provides a recent review of the debate ("Wild Beasts and Rabid Dogs: The Riddle of the Heretics in the Letters of Ignatius," in *The Formation of the Early Church* [ed. Jostein Ådna; WUNT 183; Tübingen: Mohr Siebeck, 2005], 341–77). For a summary of scholarly positions up to the early 1970s, see J. J. Gunther, *St. Paul's Opponents and Their Background* (Novum Testamentum Supplements 35; Leiden: E. J. Brill, 1973). Trevett gives a brief summary of some more recent scholars (*A Study of Ignatius*, 150–52), after which she devotes about one-third of her book to an attempt to identify the groups Ignatius confronted (146–215). C. K. Barrett ("Jews and Judaizers," 220–44) gives a shorter analysis of the various positions.

[91] Lightfoot, *S. Ignatius, S. Polycarp*; Theodor Zahn, *Ignatius von Antiochien*.

[92] Recent major monographs supporting the two-group or multigroup thesis include Schoedel, *Ignatius of Antioch*; Corwin, *St. Ignatius*; Charles Thomas Brown, *The Gospel and Ignatius of Antioch*; and Trevett, *A Study of Ignatius*. As seen earlier in this chapter, Zetterholm offers a different kind of interpretation.

[93] Christine Trevett, "Prophecy and Anti-episcopal Activity: A Third Error Combatted by Ignatius," *JEH* 34 (1983): 1–18. Often the third group includes a mingled mass of characteristics that seem not to fit pure Judaizers or Docetists.

What is primarily at issue is whether one group could have had both a docetic and a Judaizing character, for both perspectives seem to be explicitly confronted and condemned in Ignatius's letters. In certain passages Ignatius seems to object to unambiguous Judaizing tendencies;[94] in other passages he seems to object to tendencies that are just as unambiguously docetic.[95] On this point almost everyone agrees. Further, individual letters seem to be focused on one or the other of the problems, not on both. What is at dispute is a handful of passages that seem to suggest a mixture of these ideas: sometimes seemingly anti-docetic language is used against what appear to be Judaizing opponents,[96] and in several passages anti-Judaizing language is used against opponents who are more clearly docetic.[97] The question is, Where does the confusion lie—1) with Ignatius, who sometimes failed to keep two groups separate; 2) with the heretics, who, though only one group, appropriated a mixture of somewhat unrelated beliefs; or 3) with the nature of the evidence, in that Ignatius was not writing systematic rebuttals of his

---

[94] Esp. Ign. *Magn.* 8–11; Ign. *Phld.* 6; 8–9.

[95] Ign. *Trall.* 9–10; Ign. *Smyrn.* 1–5; 6.2. Although modern discussion usually speaks confidently of a docetic position, the issue is not so clear-cut. Docetism is a scholarly construct, built mainly from comments in the letters of Ignatius and supplemented with reference to less precise comments in the letters of John. Polycarp, almost certainly addressing the issue that concerned Ignatius, connects Johannine language to the Docetists (Pol. *Phil.* 7.2). Cerinthus perhaps is to be associated with such ideas also; Kurt Rudolph calls him "the first Docetist," but little information about him is available (*Gnosis: The Nature and History of Gnosticism* [ed. and trans. Robert McLachlan Wilson; Edinburgh: T&T Clark, 1984], 165). What is known of Cerinthus comes from a few comments by Irenaeus (*Haer.* 3.3.4; 3.11.1) and Eusebius (*Hist. eccl.* 4.14.6). There is also a modern assumption that the developed gnostic systems of the mid-second century were outgrowths, in some way, of an earlier docetic position. With such limited primary data, we cannot dismiss the possibility that gnostic/docetic theological reflection grew out of Judaism or contains, in addition to its distinctive docetic message, more traditional Jewish concepts as well. For a repudiation of the very category "Gnosticism," see Michael A. Williams, *Rethinking "Gnosticism."*

[96] In Ignatius's letters to the Magnesians and to the Philadelphians, both of which are widely thought to challenge a Judaizing tendency, Ignatius uses what appears to be anti-docetic language (Ign. *Magn.* 8.1; 9.1; 11; Ign. *Phld.* 8.2; 9.2).

[97] This is the least significant piece in the puzzle. The passages usually appealed to (Ign. *Magn.* 8–11 and Ign. *Phld.* 8–9) do not demand a docetic interpretation and are reasonably explained from a Judaizing or Jewish standpoint by Paul J. Donahue ("Jewish Christianity," 83–87). Donahue goes on to argue for a distinct Judaizing opposition, in addition to a docetic opposition that no one disputes. But he perhaps overstates his case when he claims that "a close examination of the passages alleged to show the gnostic character of Ignatius's Jewish Christian opponents actually supports the two heresy view rather than refutes it" (p. 87). For a defense of the one-heresy position, see Einar Molland, who argues that any of the supposedly Judaizing aspects of the opponents' position can be understood within the framework of Docetism ("The Heretics Combatted by Ignatius of Antioch," *JEH* 5 [1954]: 1–6).

opponents' beliefs but calling churches to unity under their bishops, a unity he believes would go far in neutralizing the danger from the opposition, whatever its complexion?

A representative sample of scholarly positions will give a sense of how nuanced and heavily qualified the proposed reconstructions of Ignatius's opposition are. Bauer attributes what he takes to be the confused description of the heretics in Ignatius's writings to Ignatius's "complex personality."[98] Schoedel charges that Ignatius "invented" the link between docetic and Judaizing tendencies, combining the two.[99] Lieu speaks of Ignatius's "harmonizing rhetoric."[100] Hammond Bammel proposes that the two systems were perhaps "not entirely separate," for if the Docetists tried to infiltrate churches in Ignatius's camp, they may well have tried also to infiltrate the churches of the Judaizers and, in so doing, could have also picked up some ideas from the Judaizers.[101] Sumney thinks that Ignatius is most accurate when he describes the opponents in the cities he visited (Philadelphia and Smyrna), and that Ignatius tends to reflect his situation in Antioch when he addresses Asia Minor churches that he has not visited. Sumney finds no discernable error in Magnesia. He argues that the problematic two-sided error that seems to be reflected in Magnesia (Ign. *Magn.* 8–11) does not reflect a real group but merely Ignatius's mixing of situations.[102] Trevett thinks that Ignatius's description of the Judaizers reflects a "collage," combining elements from Antioch and Asia Minor.[103] Molland argues for one group, Docetist in character, whose only Judaizing element is an appeal to the Jewish Scriptures in defense of its position.[104] Barrett argues that aspects of Jewish reflection influenced the development of Gnosticism and thus a heresy of mixed gnostic and Jewish elements would be natural enough; the Judaism of this heresy would, however, be unorthodox.[105] Such comments

---

[98] Bauer, *Orthodoxy and Heresy,* 88.

[99] William R. Schoedel, "Theological Norms and Social Perspectives in Ignatius of Antioch," in *The Shaping of Christianity in the Second and Third Centuries* (vol. 1 of *Jewish and Christian Self-Definition;* ed. E. P. Sanders; Philadelphia: Fortress, 1980), 31–32; idem, *Ignatius of Antioch,* 118, 124–25.

[100] Lieu, *Image and Reality,* 43.

[101] Hammond Bammel, "Ignatian Problems," 83. The assumption that there were churches of the Judaizers is problematic. The Judaizers seem to be situated in Ignatius's churches or only recently separated from them. If there already were churches of the Judaizers, one would expect Judaizing Christians to have joined these assemblies rather than churches within Ignatius's orbit. No doubt, the situation is complex, but it does not help resolve the difficulties to introduce Judaizing churches without more substantial evidence.

[102] Jerry L. Sumney, "Those Who 'Ignorantly Deny Him': The Opponents of Ignatius of Antioch," *JECS* 4 (1993): 345–65.

[103] Trevett, *A Study of Ignatius,* 183.

[104] Molland, "The Heretics Combatted by Ignatius of Antioch."

[105] C. K. Barrett, "Jews and Judaizers." Barrett thinks that Judaizers were always easier to define sociologically than theologically (p. 244).

illustrate nicely the complexity of suggestions that have been offered to clarify the situation of Ignatius's opponents, but they generally do not help much in resolving the problem. Almost every author who attempts to identify Ignatius's opponents offers some such interpretation of problematic material in the Ignatian letters.[106]

Those who argue for two groups of opponents posit a docetic group and a Judaizing group. Although there is almost general agreement on the character of the docetic group,[107] opinions differ considerably regarding the composition of the Judaizing group—from native-born conservative Jewish Christians[108] to Essene Christians,[109] to proselytes or God-fearers, to Gentiles with an interest in the Jewish

---

[106] Most attempts to identify the opposition in the Ignatian letters recognize that the matter is complicated by the nature of the evidence. See the cautious comments of Donahue, "Jewish Christianity," 81.

[107] Myllykoski takes a different approach. He challenges the common view that the heretics in Ephesus, Tralles, and Smyrna were Docetists. They are somewhat vaguely described by Myllykoski as a group relying on "earlier Jewish-Christian influences" ("Wild Beasts and Rabid Dogs," 374). He considers the heretics in Magnesia and Philadelphia to be Jewish Christians (pp. 372–74).

[108] Corwin argues that the Judaizers could not have been orthodox Jews because they do not practice circumcision (St. Ignatius, 58). The passage on which Corwin bases her conclusion, however, does not support such a definitive description of the Judaizers. Ignatius simply says that "it is better to hear Christianity from the circumcised than Judaism from the uncircumcised" (Ign. Phld. 6.1). The group in question can only be said not to require circumcision; Jews within this group may have continued to practice circumcision, much like Paul's own native-born Jewish followers.

[109] Corwin maintains that the Judaizing group consists of former members of the Qumran community (St. Ignatius, 61–65). But her description of the Ignatian Judaizers as Essenes is unconvincing. The Dead Sea Scrolls had been discovered eight years after Corwin's 1937 Yale dissertation, and the first photographic edition of the manuscripts was released in 1956, a few years before the revision of her dissertation was published in 1960. It is in the excitement of this discovery that her reconstruction should be viewed. Her selection of the Essenes as the Judaizers of the Ignatian letters is puzzling if, as she contends, a number of theologically distinctive and isolated Christian communities existed in Antioch (p. 49). Surely Ignatius's group, which had so little sympathy for Judaism of any kind, would have been the least likely home for these former Essenes. Corwin also fails to explain why the Essenes sought out any home group. If Christianity in Antioch was composed mainly of theologically distinct and isolated house-church groups, the Essene immigrants to Antioch could have maintained their identity as an Essene group with their own house-church unit. Ignatius's church, if one of many independent Christian communities, would have offered nothing in terms of group identity or group benefits that was not offered by other more congenial groups or that the Essenes themselves did not already have. If they were already Christians before their move to Antioch and if Antioch was filled with numerous and diverse Christian options, churches within Ignatius's orbit would have been among the least likely to attract such hypothetical Essene Christians to their membership. Further, Corwin also must qualify the nature of this Essene group, because they no longer practice circumcision, and one would have expected Essenes to have been circumcised (p. 63). C. K. Barrett ("Jews and Judaizers," 229), who argues

heritage of Christianity (the uncircumcised of Ign. *Phld.* 6.1). Most opt for the last position, viewing the Judaizers as Gentiles who converted to Christianity but were attracted to elements of Judaism beyond that sanctioned by Ignatius's church.

The proponents of the two-group hypothesis frequently dismiss the one-group hypothesis by contending that no other early Christian group existed with both Judaizing and docetic tendencies.[110] There is a growing consensus in favor of some version of a two-group hypothesis.[111] The burden of proof, however, must be laid on the shoulders of those who argue for more than one group, for two primary reasons.

First, the passages in the Ignatian letters where anti-docetic attacks seem to be directed at a Judaizing group or anti-Judaizing attacks seem to be directed at a docetic group are problematic only for the two-group hypothesis, whereas such passages offer strong support for the one-group hypothesis, where docetic and Judaizing elements are mixed. Second, the main argument against the one-group hypothesis—that a group with both docetic *and* Judaizing tendencies did not exist in the early period—has weight only if it can be shown that the Ignatian letters distinguish between two groups of opponents. Unless this is established, these letters themselves may witness to the existence of a group with such a mixture.

The discussion that follows examines a range of arguments made in support of the two-group hypothesis. It is my contention that most are overly ingenious or suspiciously nuanced. The examination groups relatively similar points and treats only arguments that appear to have substance or are frequently repeated.

In focusing my criticism on the two-group hypothesis, I do not mean to identify with the one-group proposal. Rather, I wish to separate myself from all camps that try to identify the particular heretical character of Ignatius's opposition. Counting one or two or three distinctive heretical groups demands a precision that neither Ignatius's letters nor the ecclesiastical circumstances of his day allow.[112]

---

for one group of opponents, warns that given gnostic tendencies in Qumran, Corwin's argument is "in danger of destroying itself," although the strength of Barrett's objection depends on how gnostic the Essenes were, a position that itself seems to lack convincing support. Corwin's Essene thesis has not gained a following.

[110] This argument is being challenged by new views of the opponents as a single group. Now, instead of seeing the group as Docetists, some scholars argue that the group was Jewish. Michael Goulder, for example, contends that the group reflects a form of Ebionism ("Ignatius's 'Docetists,'" *VC* 53 [1999]: 16–30). Along a similar line, John W. Marshall argues for one group that reflects angel Christology ("The Objects of Ignatius's Wrath and Jewish Angelic Mediators," *JEH* 56 [2005]: 1–23).

[111] Donahue, for example, maintains that "we know of no such mélange as Jewish Christian Gnosticism" ("Jewish Christianity," 87).

[112] Although Ignatius addresses some of the same cities as does the author of Revelation (Ephesus, Smyrna, and Philadelphia), it is impossible to establish the precise

Different Heresies in Different Cities

The claim is made that in most of Ignatius's letters, Ignatius addresses one group of heretics or the other but not both. Some communities appear to be threatened by one group; other communities by the other, and Ignatius addresses them accordingly. The letters to the Magnesians and to the Philadelphians are said to be directed at the Judaizing tendencies; the letters to the Trallians and to the Smyrnaeans, at the docetic views. The letter to the Ephesians does not point as clearly to identifiable opponents, but Ignatius does reject certain people and hints of an anti-docetic concern mark some of the language.[113] The letter to Polycarp does not specifically address either tendency, but it does not contradict what Ignatius says in his Smyrnaean letter, which is addressed to the same church situation as the letter to Polycarp. The letter to the Romans has a different focus altogether and shows no interest in combating specific heretical positions.

If we assume that there were two quite distinct heresies, it would seem that both heresies were familiar to Ignatius in Antioch. His response to each seems informed and nuanced, and thus it is unlikely that he developed his counter positions on the spot as he came upon unfamiliar heresies on his journey through Asia Minor to execution in Rome.[114] The question then becomes whether Ignatius's church in Antioch, for whatever reason, is the only church with both groups active. How is it that no church in the province of Asia seems to have had both? And even if this were the case, why would Ignatius not warn of the danger of the other when addressing each heresy? Two of the churches, those at Tralles and Magnesia, are only fifteen miles apart, yet according to the two-group hypothesis, Magnesia was challenged by a Judaizing group and Tralles by a docetic group. Is it likely that the churches and their problems were so starkly different, given their close

---

relationship between the churches addressed in Revelation and the churches addressed by Ignatius. While Ignatian scholars often contend that the opposition in Philadelphia is Judaizing and that in Smyrna is docetic, Revelation uses the same language to address opponents in both cities: "those who say they are Jews and are not, but are a synagogue of Satan" (Rev. 2:9; 3:9). How do we make sense of what appears to be a different assessment of the opposition by the author of Revelation and Ignatius? It may be that the author of Revelation used similar language to address two distinctive groups; it may be that a Jewish group of some kind lost influence in Smyrna shortly after Revelation was written, and a docetic group became a threat there by the time Ignatius passed through about a decade later. Or it may be that the author of Revelation and Ignatius are addressing different communities altogether, although what these communities were and how they differed would be guesses at best. Corwin thinks that Revelation's comments may apply to Essene Christians in Smyrna and Philadelphia (*St. Ignatius,* 61).

[113] Ign. *Eph.* 7.2; 18.2.

[114] Corwin thinks that Ignatius's attack on the schismatics reflects most clearly the situation in Antioch, where he may have had some years to develop his response to such opposition. Donahue maintains the same position ("Jewish Christianity," 82).

proximity and the certainty of regular contact between them? Surely a danger in one assembly could spread to the other, and prior warning of such danger would have been in order and expected.[115]

Further, many scholars have pointed out that Ignatius seems to draw the lines more sharply than the Asian churches were accustomed to.[116] If this is the case, then some churches may have been unaware that they even had a "problem" until Ignatius called attention to the matter. This cautions us further against assuming that the divisions were neat and clearly identifiable within particular cities.[117]

If there were two heretical options, it is likely that Ignatius would have viewed each church at some risk from both. A more nuanced reading of the Ignatian letters probably goes beyond the available evidence.

Anti-Docetic Comments to Judaizing Churches

If the opponents are distinguishable and they are not active in the same cities, as the two-group hypothesis generally assumes, then one must explain comments of Ignatius that appear in a letter directed at one group but seem more appropriate to the other group. Corwin, for example, a defender of the two-group hypothesis, contends that the most problematic passage in this respect is in the letter *to the Magnesians*, whose church supposedly was affected by a Judaizing heresy: why does Ignatius comment about the birth, passion, and resurrection

---

[115] One might ask whether it is likely that any church at this time would have escaped some attraction in the direction of Judaism, whatever the degree of Docetism's appeal.

[116] This raises the question how Ignatius supposedly knew the situation in each church so intimately that he was able to direct specific attacks against dangerous beliefs in their midst. If the local leaders had not been aware of such distinctions, how would they have been able to describe their situations so clearly to Ignatius that he was able to respond as precisely as he did?

[117] Donahue notes, "Early Christianity was an extremely varied movement, a spectrum spanning the range from an extreme Jewish Christianity that rejected Gentile Christianity altogether to a dualism that cut Christianity's tie to Judaism. The middle ground was occupied at every point" ("Jewish Christianity," 92). But Donahue's conclusion from this observation goes beyond the evidence: "As long as the private home remained the principal locus for Christian worship, Christians in a metropolis like Antioch could go their diverse ways with a minimum of conflict. Christians from different religious and social backgrounds tended to form different congregations." The evidence from Ignatius about Antioch and the cities in Asia Minor suggests just the opposite. Whatever the conflict in Antioch, it seems recent, and if it involves a schism, the schism is fresh. In the cities of Asia, schism is apparently the exception. Where there is schism, Ignatius confronts it as an abnormal situation. But according to Donahue's reading of the evidence, a conflict resulting in the formation of a new group would have fit quite naturally into the diverse and fragmented structure of Christianity that existed in the early period. However, if Ignatius's argument against schism and separate assemblies is taken seriously, such division must have been the exception, not the norm.

of Jesus—themes that normally have an anti-docetic ring? Corwin attempts to resolve the problem by arguing that the Judaizers accepted Jesus as a teacher but not the bringer of grace,[118] and thus Ignatius wants to focus their attention on the more central aspects of the Christian understanding of Jesus—his birth, death, and resurrection. But in the passage that Corwin highlights, Ignatius seems to be emphasizing that Christ *is* the teacher, which is a strange emphasis if this is not a point of contention between Ignatius and his opponents. Ignatius talks about being found "disciples of Jesus Christ, our only teacher," and he points out that "even the prophets who were his disciples in the spirit awaited him as their teacher" (Ign. *Magn,* 9.1–2). It would appear, then, that this is an issue of contention—not of agreement—between Ignatius and his opponents, and so Corwin's reading of the matter is problematic. Corwin contends that the opponents do not accept Jesus as the bringer of grace, yet quite the opposite is the thrust of Ignatius's comment that "if we have lived according to Judaism until now, we admit that we have not received grace" (Ign. *Magn.* 8.1).[119] It appears that the opponents do think of Jesus as the bringer of grace and would have seen themselves recipients of this grace, but Ignatius wants to disabuse them of this assumption. If they are still living according to Judaism, they have *not* received grace. Corwin admits that the passage is a difficult one for her two-group hypothesis.[120]

Ignatius's Theological Sensitivities

It is sometimes argued that Ignatius modifies his theological language in some letters so as not to offend Jewish sensibilities; in other letters, no such sensitivity is shown. Given that the letters in which such sensitivity is supposedly shown are letters that appear, on the basis of other evidence, to address a Judaizing element, the selective use of sensitive language seems to confirm that Ignatius is addressing two groups and is conscious of this.

Donahue, for example, who considers the letters to the Magnesians and the Philadelphians to be directed against the Jewish heresy, points out that only in these letters does Ignatius refrain from calling Jesus "God."[121] Surely it is expecting far too much of Ignatius to look for such nuance and sensitivity in his writing. If the Judaizing group can be offended, they will have been sufficiently offended

---

[118] Corwin points to Ign. *Magn.* 8–9 (*St. Ignatius,* 59–60).

[119] The translation follows Ehrman, except for substitution of the word "grace" for Ehrman's "God's gracious gift." The Greek reads simply χάριν, and most translators have rendered it as "grace."

[120] Corwin, *St. Ignatius,* 60. In a similar way, Brown, another defender of the two-group hypothesis, tries to mute the force of the "ostensibly anti-docetic statements" in Ign. *Magn.* 11.1 by making them into anti-Judaizing statements (*The Gospel and Ignatius,* 183).

[121] Donahue, "Jewish Christianity," 87.

by the other sharp comments Ignatius has made about Judaism.[122] Yet Ignatius is unequivocal and unrestrained enough in other attacks he makes on Judaizing practices in these letters. Further, Ignatius's comments in his letter to the *Romans,* which is addressed to a church where there was likely a large Jewish element, show no such restraint of language.[123] There Ignatius calls Jesus "God" three times (Ign. *Rom.* intro. [twice]; 3.3). He speaks also about the passion of his God (6.3). It is highly unlikely, then, that Ignatius checks his language in his letters to the churches in Magnesia and Philadelphia, as Donahue contends, and that the omission of some phrase referring to Jesus as God in those letters is either significant or intentional on Ignatius's part.

Donahue's argument is further complicated by the fact that he admits that both heresies were present in all the churches. He thinks that Ignatius judges the Gnostics as a far more serious threat in all the churches except Magnesia and Philadelphia, and thus refrains from denouncing the Judaizers who might be present in these churches.[124] But if Ignatius is sensitive to the Jewish element in some of the churches, why doesn't he avoid calling Jesus "God" in all of his letters?[125] Each church would have had a Jewish element that could be offended, and tensions would thereby have been provoked where little had existed previously. The overly nuanced analysis of Ignatius's language put forward by Donahue therefore is not convincing.[126]

In the same vein, some scholars contend that Ignatius was careful to distinguish between the two groups of opponents and that he treated the opponents differently—rejecting the Docetists completely but holding out hope for the Judaizers. For example, Trevett claims that for Ignatius, the Judaizers were errorists, not heretics.[127] But Trevett treats Ignatius's caustic comments about Judaism and Judaizers too lightly, and the distinction she draws between an errorist and a heretic probably does not make sense until long after Ignatius's time.

---

[122] Ign. *Magn.* 10.2–3; Ign. *Phld.* 6.1.

[123] The evidence for a significant Jewish element in the church at Rome includes Paul's letter to the Romans, which seems particularly focused on answering a range of issues about Judaism that arose from major theses of his message, and the letter from Clement of Rome to Corinth (*1 Clement*), which, with its rich appeal to the Jewish Scriptures, suggests a congregation familiar with the Jewish world.

[124] Donahue, "Jewish Christianity," 90, n. 17.

[125] It is doubtful that Ignatius would have viewed his comments about Jesus being "God" as inflammatory or offensive. More likely, he would have considered the censure of such language inflammatory and offensive. This language rolls comfortably off Ignatius's lips. There is nothing to suggest that such words would have offended the original readers of Ignatius's letters.

[126] Hammond Bammel agrees with Donahue that Ignatius intentionally avoids referring to Jesus as θεός in certain letters ("Ignatian Problems," 88).

[127] Trevett, *A Study of Ignatius,* 165–73, 178.

Different Attitudes to the Jewish Scriptures

It is sometimes argued that the heretical groups had different attitudes to the Jewish Scriptures and that Ignatius's differing treatment of these scriptures in his letters is best explained by his awareness of these differences. Corwin, for example, argues that the docetic position led to contempt for Jewish writings, and since she cannot see how this attitude could apply to those with Judaizing tendencies, she contends that there must be two groups.[128] But the passage on which she builds her argument is far less decisive. Ignatius simply says that his opponents are not persuaded by "the words of the prophets nor the Law of Moses, nor, until now, by the gospel" (Ign. *Smyrn.* 5.1). He could have easily thrown this kind of accusation at Judaizers, for he believes that Jews in general and Judaism as a system have failed to understand the Hebrew Scriptures. Those who did understand, such as the Hebrew prophets, waited for and hoped in Christ.[129]

Uncircumcised Judaizers

According to the two-group hypothesis, the opposition in Philadelphia is Judaizing, which would lead one to expect that the group had been promoting circumcision—the issue generally assumed to be a key component of Judaizing parties. Circumcision, however, does not seem to have been an emphasis of Ignatius's Judaizers. At least in Philadelphia, according to one of Ignatius's comments (Ign. *Phld.* 6.1), the opponents who are preaching Judaism seem to be uncircumcised. Donahue counters this evidence by arguing that Ignatius's comment about the uncircumcised is not to be taken at face value. For Donahue, Ignatius means nothing more than that a law-free gospel does not permit distinctions among Christians.[130] The Judaizers, then, according to Donahue, are circumcised, in spite of Ignatius's comment that seems to point in the opposite direction. Although it is no doubt true that Ignatius believed that a law-free gospel does not permit distinctions among Christians, Ignatius would have confused his case by less-than-straightforward language here. Although Ignatius's comment about hearing Judaism from the uncircumcised need not mean that all the Judaizers were uncircumcised, it would make little sense if none of them were uncircumcised. When Ignatius says that some of his opponents were uncircumcised, we can take it that some were uncircumcised. That Ignatius's comment means more than this is likely; that it means less or means something different is neither required by the evidence nor probable.

---

[128] Corwin, *St. Ignatius*, 56–57.

[129] Ign. *Phld.* 5.2. Lake treats this as a probable reference to Christian prophets, but most translators understand the comment as referring to Hebrew prophets. Schoedel (*Ignatius of Antioch*, 128) follows Lake.

[130] Donahue, "Jewish Christianity," 89.

Another problem of Donahue's argument is that he sometimes advocates the position that the Judaizers were God-fearers.[131] This position conflicts, however, with his argument that the opposition was circumcised. Surely God-fearing Judaizers would not have been circumcised, for this was what generally distinguished God-fearers from full proselytes. Further, as argued in chapter 2, God-fearers were probably not much of a factor at the time of Ignatius. Supposing, however, that they were, the puzzle would then be why God-fearers suddenly became a focus for Ignatius's uncompromising, vehement attack or how they came to be associated with Ignatius's church circle in the first place when such a variety of more compatible Christian options supposedly were available.

Donahue attempts to strengthen his argument by pointing to Ignatius's comment that "if someone walks in a strange doctrine then he would have no part in the Passion" (Ign. *Phld.* 3.3).[132] Donahue contends that this kind of comment could apply only to Jewish Christians, since Gnostics denied the passion.[133] But he is asking the language to bear too much here. Ignatius may well have wanted to say that Gnostics, who denied the passion, had no part in the passion. We must remember that Ignatius is writing to churches that are mainly on his side, and writing for their sake. It is, then, largely irrelevant, for example, whether a comment about the passion is more effective against Judaizers or Docetists, for the comment is not made for their benefit. It is made for Ignatius-like Christians regardless of their opponents, and such Christians would have found Ignatius's comment about the passion meaningful. Ignatius's statement is broadly dismissive: *anyone* who walks in a strange doctrine has no part in the passion. Most of his readers would have agreed.

So Many Christianities, So Few Opponents

Whether one understands that Ignatius's opponents consisted of one group or two, the opposition reflects a considerable breadth of theological speculation—from Judaizing to docetic tendencies. This opposition appears to have been part of Ignatius's church circle until shortly before Ignatius wrote his letters, and some of the opponents may have considered themselves still part of this church. But if the Christian movement at this time was as diverse as some scholars contend, with a host of competing and largely isolated visions of Christianity, each meeting separately, one has to wonder why such groups ever associated with Ignatius's circle in the first place.

---

[131] Ibid.

[132] Donahue uses Lake's translation. Ehrman's translation is different: "No one who follows someone creating a schism will inherit the kingdom of God; anyone who thinks otherwise does not agree with the Passion."

[133] Donahue, "Jewish Christianity," 92.

Corwin, for example, thinks that Antioch had several theologically distinct and isolated Christian groups, yet she does not see the Docetists and Judaizers as part of this diversity. Rather, these two groups were either still part of Ignatius's group or only recently separated from it and still viewing themselves as belonging to his group: "A somewhat open situation is suggested, rather than the struggle of obstinate groups frozen into irreconcilable opposition."[134] These schismatic groups rejoined Ignatius's church shortly after Ignatius left for martyrdom in Rome, and news of this brought about the peace Ignatius speaks of in his letters from Troas. But this view raises a question: what theologically distinct Christian groups could not have fit into Ignatius's church if the Judaizing and docetic extremes could exist there and were separated from Ignatius's church only briefly?

Ignatius's church, as represented by his letters, simply does not fit the current scholarly speculation on the situation of early Christian assemblies, where each nuance of belief had its own isolated and independent assembly. Surely the separate existence of the Judaizing and docetic groups in Ignatius's circle would have been well established, and their contact with Ignatius's church long severed, if there ever had been such contact between such diverse communities in the supposedly multiform world of early Christianity. In such a splintered Christian world, Ignatius's church was the least likely home for Judaizers or Docetists, who could have found more comfortable environs in almost any other Christian community or in an assembly of their own. That such varied groups are found in some kind of association with Ignatius's church suggests a much more inclusive and broad sense of the Christian community in the time of Ignatius than is possible in recent reconstructions that emphasize the diversity and segmentation of early Christianity.

Another Approach to Ignatius's Opponents

Perhaps the debate has been framed too sharply in terms of identifiable heretical groups, especially since so little of what Ignatius says is directed toward a specific heresy.[135] Further, as already noted, most reconstructions of the situation have to put serious qualifications on Ignatius's comments to make them fit.

Instead of assuming that Ignatius's comments demand either one group or two groups of opponents, we should ask whether there is any evidence that Ignatius would have understood a question framed in this way. Does Ignatius view

---

[134] Corwin, St. Ignatius, 52–54; quote, p. 54.

[135] Sumney is less driven to find specific and identifiable opponents in each of Ignatius's letters ("Those Who 'Ignorantly Deny Him'"). Instead of trying to identify the number of distinctive groups of opponents, Frederick W. Norris focuses on Ignatius's attempts to mark the "inside" and the "outside" ("Ignatius, Polycarp, and I Clement: Walter Bauer Reconsidered," VC 30 [1976]: 30–33).

the opposition as neat, identifiable groups, each easily labeled and refuted, or is his focus more clearly on what he holds as true, from which perspective he dismisses everything that does not measure up?[136] I suggest that Ignatius works with a simple dualism: one is either in the bishop's church or outside it, one is either on God's side or on the side of the prince of this world.[137]

Many of Ignatius's arguments against schism are broad rather than specific, catching in their scope schism of any stripe. His sweeping terms of dismissal of his opponents could fit Judaizers, Docetists, or almost any other group he chose. For Ignatius, there are two coinages (Ign. *Magn.* 5.2); one is either a believer or an unbeliever; there is one body of the church, in which are believers, whether among the Jews or among the Gentiles (Ign. *Smyrn.* 1.2); one either comes under the authority of God and the bishop or under the power of the prince of this world—the real enemy for Ignatius. Ignatius's opponents, of whatever stripe, are part of that evil order.[138]

A number of other passages employ identical or similar language to describe groups that are supposedly quite diverse.[139] Proponents of the one-heresy theory often point to such language as proof that Ignatius has only one group in mind. Against this view, Donahue objects that the use of common language indicates only that Ignatius considers the Docetists (or Gnostics, as Donahue labels them) and the Judaizers both as *heretical*, not that he considers them to be *identical*. This is correct, but one might respond to Donahue in kind: Ignatius's use of common language indicates that Ignatius considers the opposition *heretical* and, as heretical, without need of more precise definition or distinction. Indeed, the concern to identify distinctive groups may be of little interest to either Ignatius or his readers.

---

[136] Ign. *Eph.* 5.2–3; 14.2; 18.1; Ign. *Magn.* 5.1–2; 10.3; Ign. *Trall.* 3.1; 6.1; 7.2; 11:1–2; Ign. *Phld.* 2.1; 3.1–2; 4.1; 6.2; 7.2; 8.1; Ign. *Smyrn.* 8.2; 9.1.

[137] Adelbert Davids suggests that Ignatius had little interest in distinguishing between heretical groups, although different groups did exist ("Irrtum und Häresie: 1 Clem.-Ign. von Antiochien-Justinus," *Kairos* 15 [1973]: 165–87). I differ from Davids in that I do not think the opposition was yet formed into distinctive enough groups to be sharply distinguished from each other. They still saw themselves largely as part of the bishop's church in spite of some activities done without the bishop's approval. That two groups (and no others) clearly stood as identifiable entities in Ignatius's world is unlikely. Are we to suppose that the two groups each had only one house-church unit? If so, the opposition must be viewed as minimal. If each group had more than one house-church unit, what kind of alliance did they have with each other except through the bishop's church? Anything more than two house churches, one containing Judaizers and one containing Docetists, would likely have seemed to Ignatius as general opposition, not as two distinctive communities of opponents.

[138] Ign. *Eph.* 17.1; 19.1; Ign. *Magn.* 1.2; Ign. *Trall.* 4.2; Ign. *Rom.* 7.1; Ign. *Phld.* 6.2.

[139] See Donahue, "Jewish Christianity," 83. Ignatius uses the same term, *heterodoxia*, for beliefs in Smyrna (Ign. *Smyrn.* 6.1) and in Magnesia (Ign. *Magn.* 8.1), whose churches supposedly are confronted by different opponents.

Ignatius draws boundaries that mark off the inside—whatever is not *in* is *out*.[140] The evidence does not demand that Ignatius saw things more precisely divided or that his readers or even the schismatics themselves did. The groups identified so distinctly by scholars may not have viewed themselves as all that distinct.[141] Two criteria stand out by which Ignatius measures those whom he rejects. One is their attitude to Jesus, the other their attitude to the bishop. On either point, Ignatius is prepared to dismiss individuals without much discussion beyond these two criteria and sometimes with general descriptions that make it difficult to identify particular groups.[142] Even supposing that Ignatius saw the true church challenged by two distinctive and dangerous opposition groups, it is unlikely that he would have sought to keep the groups separate, arguing against one group in some letters and against the other group in other letters. It is more likely that he would have warned all churches of the two dangers, and indeed he does, on occasion, warn of dangers not yet present in some of the churches.[143] Further, he certainly is aware that a church might be threatened by both, for his responses to each aberration suggest a familiarity with both that he probably gained in Antioch. If such was the danger in his own church, he likely would have considered these beliefs a potential threat to all churches.

The evidence from Ignatius's letters suggests that he does not think in terms of a number of neatly distinguishable groups of opponents. There is one church and there is one opposition. The opposition is not defined as much by precise aspects of their distinctive beliefs as by their independence of, or separation from, the bishop.[144]

---

[140] Brown captures a sense of Ignatius's method when he points out that Ignatius's answer to disunity, whether stemming from docetic or from Judaizing tendencies, is the gospel (*The Gospel and Ignatius*, 183). See also Henning Paulsen, *Die Briefe des Ignatius von Antiochia und der Brief des Polykarp von Smyrna* (Handbuch zum Neuen Testament 18; Die Apostolischen Väter 2; Tübingen: J. C. B. Mohr [Paul Siebeck], 1985), 64–65.

[141] A group in Smyrna holds separate assemblies but admires Ignatius (Ign. *Smyrn.* 5.1; 7.1; 8.1–2); a group in Magnesia honors the bishop but holds separate meetings or conducts aspects of religious life beyond the authority of the bishop, at least in Ignatius's view (Ign. *Magn.* 4.1; 6.1–7.1).

[142] See Davids, "Irrtum und Häresie," 172–79. Some scholars maintain that Ignatius had little interest in providing a clear picture of the opponents (see Trevett, *A Study of Ignatius*, 150).

[143] Ign. *Trall.* 8.1; Ign. *Smyrn.* 4.1

[144] C. K. Barrett warns that although it is possible that Ignatius combined the features of his opponents into a "sweeping assault, . . . a grossly inaccurate account of them would have done him and his readers little service" ("Jews and Judaizers," 222). Barrett does think, however, that Ignatius confused elements of his own situation in Antioch with the situation in Asia Minor. Donahue cautions against expecting that the number of opponents confronted in Ignatius's letters can be determined with certainty ("Jewish Christianity," 81).

CHAPTER 4

Religious and Ethnic Tensions in Antioch

Ignatius and the Climate of Suspicion

Various attempts have been made to explain how Ignatius became a victim of governmental action. The most common view during the last several decades is that an internal church dispute brought Ignatius to the attention of the authorities. According to this view, the Jewish authorities were not involved in any way, and the Roman authorities acted only after the matter threatened public order.

This theory, however, has serious weaknesses. First, the arguments put forward to support the theory of an internal church conflict are unconvincing. They are based on flawed linguistic conclusions and manipulated statistical work. Further, they leave a number of major questions unanswered. These weaknesses will be discussed further in chapter 5. Second, the Jewish and Christian movements in Antioch around the time of Ignatius operated in a world of heightened religious and ethnic suspicion, where questions of boundaries and identity were profoundly important. In some cases, suspicion led to concrete action, and having the wrong identity could have fatal consequences. Ignatius and his community were caught between two worlds, the Jewish and the Greco-Roman, at a time when relationships between these two groups in Antioch were at their most fractured. And the Christian group may have had reason to be fearful of both.

This chapter summarizes the evidence for religious and ethnic tensions in Antioch, building on some recent detailed studies, so as to offer a general sense of the religious and ethnic rivalry affecting Jews and Christians in Antioch. As will be shown, Ignatius's developed view of martyrdom fits well a situation in which Christians could be and were jeopardized as Christians. This is more probably the situation of Ignatius than the view that ties all of Ignatius's problems to a fight in his local church, with non-Christians looking on as disinterested bystanders.

Jewish-Gentile Tensions in Antioch

Jewish-Gentile relationships in the ancient world seem rarely to have been uniform over space or over time.[1] Each period, area, or incident deserves its own examination, without any assumptions about what the *normal* situation might be. The one exception perhaps is that after the rise of the Roman Empire, the conditions for Jews may have come to differ less substantially from area to area, since Rome seems to have adopted and enforced a fairly favorable policy toward the Jews in the empire.[2] It is unlikely, for example, that the conditions for Jews in the two largest centers of Judaism in the Diaspora, Alexandria and Antioch, differed as substantially as some of Josephus's comments might suggest. He states that the hostility of the residents of Alexandria against the Jews there was "perpetual" (*J. W.* 2.487). In his comments about Antioch, the contrast could not be starker: Jews had "undisturbed tranquility" there (*J. W.* 7.43). The reality, however, seems to have been more nuanced. Alexandria provided a pleasant enough home for perhaps hundreds of thousands of Jews over many centuries, though with occasional tensions and, in the first century, perhaps increasing hostility. The situation for Antioch was much the same. There is adequate evidence for an uneasiness in the relationship between the Jewish community and the larger Gentile population. Some authors have paid particular attention to Jewish-Gentile crises in Antioch. Stephen Cummins, for example, notes that "periodically" the Jewish community in Antioch "came under attack in ways that would have evoked notable precedents."[3] Magnus Zetterholm summarizes several situations from Antiochus IV to Titus, but he probably exaggerates the situation when he contends that "many Jews in Antioch lived under the constant threat of one day being burnt at the stake by a former neighbor."[4]

On the whole, the situation for Jews in Antioch could not have been routinely hostile, for Antioch remained for centuries a city of choice for Jewish immigration. Antioch was inviting to Jews, with the Jewish population growing under normally amicable conditions there. However, on occasion, the winds seemed

---

[1] For an extensive review of the evidence, see Louis H. Feldman, *Jew and Gentile in the Ancient World.*

[2] Jews would have been affected by the booms and busts that their Gentile neighbors experienced, and some cities may have been more receptive to their Jewish component than others. But under Rome, Jews had certain basic rights guaranteed. See Tessa Rajak, "Jewish Rights in the Greek Cities under Roman Rule," in *Studies in Judaism and Its Greco-Roman Context* (vol. 5 of *Approaches to Ancient Judaism*; ed. William Scott Green; BJS 32; Atlanta: Scholars Press, 1985).

[3] Stephen Anthony Cummins, *Paul and the Crucified Christ in Antioch: Maccabean Martyrdom and Galatians 1 and 2* (SNTSMS 114; Cambridge and New York: Cambridge University Press, 2001), 139.

[4] Magnus Zetterholm, *The Formation of Christianity in Antioch,* 121.

to shift and an influential part of the population turned on the Jews. How can we balance these two realities? Probably we need look no further than the mixture of tensions that are part of the social and political dynamics common in any city. One group appears to gain at the expense of another; personal jealousy is fanned into group animus; distant hostilities place local immigrant communities under suspicion and at risk.[5] But community life seems to have flourished for Jews in Antioch, and thus these troubles must have been the occasional, not the constant, reality.

With moments of jeopardy in an atmosphere of tolerable and perhaps amicable relationships, a community may well remember and memorialize their periods of crises. Even in good times, then, we could expect that a community's self-understanding and identity would be shaped by defining moments of crises, perhaps some of which were in the distant past. Such seems to have been the case with the Jews in Antioch.[6]

The interest here is not to examine every crisis for Jews in Antioch but to study the period of Ignatius. Our focus is not on the particulars of each crisis, but on the general atmosphere fostered by such tensions. By the time of Ignatius, Jews had lived in Antioch for about four hundred years. Early tensions, even if we could discover these in the scarce evidence available, need not have had much relevance in Ignatius's time, although attitudes, once shaped, may have set the tone for the relationships for years afterwards. Yet little suggests a hostile relationship during

---

[5] Both modern and ancient examples of such behaviour abound. Local residents slaughtered Romans living in areas of Asia Minor when Mithradates drove out the Roman armies from Asia in 88 B.C.E. (Tacitus, *Ann.* 4.14). The Esther story, written in an environment in which many Jews lived in foreign lands as resident aliens, is propelled by a threat of hostilities from the local people. In the modern period, Japanese residents of Canada and the United States, many of whom had been born in North America or had lived for years in these lands as responsible citizens, were deprived of basic rights because of the conflict with Japan in World War II. The literature on this topic is extensive; for a selection of readings, see Alice Yang Murray, ed., *What Did the Internment of Japanese Americans Mean?* (Boston: Bedford/St. Martin's, 2000).

[6] There is evidence that the Jews in Antioch had an interest in, or memory of, the crisis in Jerusalem under Antiochus IV, which provoked the Maccabean revolt. Robert L. Wilken points out that rabbinic literature speaks of three distinct exiles, placing one in Daphne, just outside Antioch, and that John Chrysostom, too, spoke of such a captivity ("The Jews of Antioch," 67–68). According to Malalas, Antioch had a synagogue called the "synagogue of the Hasmonaeans," in which supposedly were buried the bones of martyrs of the Maccabean revolt (Elias Bickermann, "Les Maccabées de Malalas," *Byzantion* 21 [1951]: 63–82; Cummins, *Paul and the Crucified Christ in Antioch*, 83–86). It is difficult to judge the historical worth of these reports, but each suggests that the Maccabean crisis had importance that somehow shaped the Jewish community in Antioch. Perhaps Antiochus had brought Jewish captives from Palestine to Antioch who carried the memory of that crisis with them, with the stories retold from generation to generation.

most of the period.[7] Where there is evidence of tension, it is usually later, closer to the time of Ignatius, and thus is perhaps more relevant.

A survey of incidents of tensions in the 250 years before Ignatius gives a sense that some elements of the population in Antioch bore a distinct dislike for the Jewish community there. Such hostility was displayed most sharply at the time of the Jewish revolt in 66–70 C.E., although earlier events may have planted seeds of enmity.[8] It is not possible to determine how widespread or prolonged these tensions were.

Maccabean Influences

Some scholars believe that in the second century B.C.E., antagonism likely developed between Jews and Gentiles in Antioch over the crisis in Jerusalem caused by Antiochus IV and the resulting Maccabean revolt, although exactly what form it took is not known.[9] Two decades later, Jews in Antioch were compromised when Jewish troops under the Maccabean Jonathan came from Judea to help Demetrius, one of the claimants to the Seleucid throne, gain control of Antioch against the wishes of the population of the city. These Jewish troops appear to have joined in the plundering and burning of parts of the city. An increasingly negative attitude toward Jews in Antioch would have developed from this incident, but we do not know how intense or widespread this feeling was or how long it lasted.[10]

---

[7] If a Jewish element was part of the original settlement of the city, as is likely on the basis of Jewish assistance as mercenaries in the army of the victorious Seleucus I, then the initial situation of Jews in Antioch would have been advantageous, whether this included full citizenship rights and obligations or not. We know little about Jewish life in Antioch during the first hundred years, but there were crises in Antioch in the early period. The Ptolemaic army advanced northward along the coast and captured Seleucia and Antioch in 248 B.C.E. How this action affected the Jewish population that lived in Antioch at this time is unknown, but they may have experienced no greater uncertainties than other residents of Antioch.

[8] Both Cummins (*Paul and the Crucified Christ in Antioch*, 66–72) and Zetterholm (*The Formation of Christianity in Antioch*, 112–21) examine first-century crises that could have strained the relationships between Jews and non-Jews in Antioch. Although one must be cautious about drawing upon incidents from the more distant past in discussing specifics of Ignatius's situation in Antioch, it is nonetheless important to take note of events over the centuries prior to Ignatius that reflect some element of tension between Jews and the rest of the populace in Antioch. Such incidents could have left resentments and suspicions that may have survived through times of less troubled relationships, perhaps providing an even more ready environment for hostile action when tensions again began to develop.

[9] Downey, *A History of Antioch*, 109; Zetterholm, *The Formation of Christianity in Antioch*, 21; Cummins, *Paul and the Crucified Christ in Antioch*, 139.

[10] First Maccabees 11:20–52 and Josephus, *Ant.* 13.137–142, report the incident. Whatever the exaggeration in the details of the story, Zetterholm thinks that the action

The Roman Civil War

In the first century B.C.E., Rome was plunged into a civil war stemming from the assassination of Julius Caesar. One of the Roman claimants, Cassius, exacted heavy tribute from Antioch and other cities in Syria (Josephus, *Ant.* 14.272). Zetterholm suspects that Jews were more heavily taxed and thinks that this reflects a negative attitude toward Jews: "It may have been easier for the people of Antioch to endure a heavy tax burden if they knew that the despised Jews had to contribute even more."[11] This conclusion goes beyond the evidence, however, and assumes what Zetterholm hopes to establish: that the general attitude toward the Jews in Antioch was clearly negative. The reality was that all of Syria was heavily taxed; further, evidence suggests that the Jews *in Judea* were more heavily taxed.[12] That the citizens in Antioch would have felt themselves benefited by the heavier tax on Judea is unlikely.

If there is substance to Josephus's account, one incident in this series of events could have sparked or increased hostility toward the Jews. According to Josephus, Antony, having defeated Cassius, ordered various cities, including Antioch, to restore what the Jews lost to Cassius.[13] Although Josephus does not say how the matter resolved itself, one can imagine a situation in which disputes arose over exactly what was lost and what was to be restored—claims and counterclaims, perhaps many or most irresolvable. Nor is it clear to what degree a city such as Antioch would have been responsible for restoring what may never have been in the city's possession, for much of the Jewish loss was in tribute paid to Cassius, not in monies unfairly exacted by the civic authorities in Antioch. Further, given that no comparable effort seems to have been made by Antony to restore to Antioch and other cities the tribute that Cassius had exacted from them, a sense of injustice may have been fostered and some degree of animosity toward the Jews provoked.

Perhaps Josephus simply got his information wrong about Antioch. The reference to Antioch is an aside in Josephus's story. The primary issue is the

---

would have influenced the shaping of a "generally negative attitude towards Jews" (*The Formation of Christianity in Antioch*, 21–23). But one must remember that the incident occurred 250 years before Ignatius—a span of numerous generations and various shifts in the population of Antioch. One should note, too, that both accounts are in Jewish writings. Whether the man on the street in Antioch knew this story in Ignatius's time is difficult to say, although strains from old hostilities often can have a life of their own long after the original dispute.

[11] Zetterholm, *The Formation of Christianity in Antioch*, 23.

[12] Josephus comments that Cassius taxed mainly Judea (*Ant.* 14.272). Josephus is speaking about a situation 150 years after the event, and it is not possible to be certain about the accuracy of this report.

[13] Josephus, *Ant.* 14.319–323.

seizure of Jewish territory by Tyre, and it is to Tyre that both decrees recorded by Josephus are addressed (*Ant.* 14.314–322). Certainly the matter would have been less clear-cut for the situation in Antioch, if Antioch was addressed at all in the decrees.

The Incident of Caesar's Statue

In 39–40 C.E., Emperor Caligula ordered that a massive statue depicting him deified as Jupiter be placed in the temple in Jerusalem.[14] This was a potentially explosive situation, which the Roman governor Petronius, who was assigned to carry out the order, recognized. According to Josephus, the Jews of Antioch and other locales attempted to intervene.[15] The matter ended either with Caligula's assassination or with the emperor's decision to cancel his decree, a point on which the ancient evidence differs.[16]

Many scholars have given weight to the report by John Malalas that a serious riot broke out in Antioch in the third year of Caligula's reign, that is, in 39–40 C.E. According to Malalas, many Jews were killed and synagogues burned in the initial onslaught. He states that this repression propelled the Jewish high priest in Jerusalem to attack Antioch with thirty thousand troops, killing many of the residents there. Although Malalas's story has elements of exaggeration and error, the thread of the story may have roots in real difficulties of that period. Malalas's details of the Jewish counterattack are considered more fanciful.[17]

Although we cannot be certain of many of the particulars of the crisis and the response, no one disputes that Caligula ordered that his statue be set up in the Jerusalem temple. It is equally certain that Jews would have resisted, although whether with decorum or in near riot cannot be determined from the evidence. Even though the matter was resolved in favor of the Jews, it is probable that the incident introduced some further element of animosity into Jewish-Gentile

---

[14] Cummins (*Paul and the Crucified Christ in Antioch,* 66–72) discusses the matter in detail. See also Anthony A. Barrett, *Caligula: The Corruption of Power* (London: B. T. Batsford, 1989), 188–91.

[15] Josephus, *J. W.* 2.184–203; *Ant.* 18.256–309; A. A. Barrett, *Caligula,* 189.

[16] For a brief summary of the evidence, see F. J. Foakes-Jackson, *Josephus and the Jews: The Religion and History of the Jews as Explained by Flavius Josephus* (New York: Richard R. Smith, 1930), 158–59. Nicholas H. Taylor argues that the plan to install the statue was made by the governor while he was in Antioch and that it was here that the first Jewish protests arose ("Caligula, the Church of Antioch, and the Gentile Mission," *Religion and Theology* 7 [2000]: 4–5).

[17] On the basis of comments by Malalas, Cummins thinks that Jews were killed and Jewish synagogues burned in Antioch in the pagan reaction to the Jewish protest of Caligula's edict (*Paul and the Crucified Christ in Antioch,* 140). Taylor holds the same view ("Caligula" 5).

relationships both in Palestine and in cities with influential Jewish populations such as Antioch.

Some scholars, most recently Nicholas Taylor, following Gerd Theissen, think that the Caligula incident resulted in a deterioration of Jewish-Christian relations partly because of differing responses to the effort of Caligula reflected by the Jewish and Christian communities.[18] It is clear that the possibility of a statue being placed in the temple provoked a crisis of considerable magnitude—probably the most significant crisis for that generation of Jews. The intended sacrilege would have recalled to every Jewish mind the story from two centuries earlier of the pollution of the temple by Antiochus IV and the apocalyptic predictions of the despoiled temple in the book of Daniel, written about the time of the crisis under Antiochus. Given the critical stance toward the Jerusalem temple reflected in the gospel traditions, in the Stephen speech, and in other early Christian literature, it appears that the attitude to the temple was a matter of dispute in Jewish-Christian relationships.[19] If Christians had developed a negative or ambivalent attitude to the temple from early on, they could have read a threat to the temple as part of God's plan—as they did later, the destruction of the temple. This may have visibly tempered their response to the crisis under Caligula, which would make them suspect in the eyes of Jews who felt propelled to action by the events.

Riots in Alexandria and Edicts in Antioch

Other reports suggest a heightened tension between Jews and Gentiles about this time. One surrounds a serious riot that broke out in Alexandria. Jews

---

[18] Nicholas H. Taylor, "Palestinian Christianity," 13–41; idem, "Caligula"; Gerd Theissen, *The Gospels in Context: Social and Political History in the Synoptic Tradition* (Minneapolis, Fortress, 1991). For a review of the scholars who see consequences for Christians from the incident, see Cummins, *Paul and the Crucified Christ in Antioch,* 66–72.

[19] The Synoptics and John address the destruction of the temple (Mark 13:1–2; 14:58; 15:29; Matt 24:1–2; 26:61; 27:40; Luke 21:5–6; John 2:19–21). In addition to forecasts of destruction, the Matthean tradition speaks of Jesus as greater than the temple (Matt 12:6). Acts reflects a similar tension regarding the temple. Paul is accused of speaking against the temple (Acts 21:28; 24:6). Although he denies the charges (24:12–18; 25:8), it is clear that attitudes to the temple had become an issue of controversy and grounds for defamation, as Stephen's speech suggests (7:48–54). Much of the New Testament literature spiritualizes the temple idea, a move that had the potential to reduce the importance of the physical temple. Christians were not alone, however, in holding such views or in forecasting the destruction of the temple (see Oskar Skarsaune, *In the Shadow of the Temple,* 155–60). This does show that one could be Jewish and at the same time somewhat "anti-temple"; still, such views were on the fringe rather than in the mainstream. For an argument that Stephen's speech is not anti-temple, see Jeffrey S. Siker, *Disinheriting the Jews: Abraham in Early Christian Controversy* (Louisville: Westminster John Knox, 1991), 123–25.

asserted their rights in an audience with Claudius, but the emperor ordered the Jews not to demand rights beyond what were traditionally theirs. Claudius's edict was sent to various cities of the empire, including Antioch, [20] suggesting that the clashes in Alexandria had some effects on the Jews of Antioch. However, we do not know to what degree ordinary life and rights were affected there or whether Jews in Antioch staged some public protest against the repression of the Jews of Alexandria. The fact that Claudius expressly prohibited Alexandrian Jews from increasing their numbers through immigration provides some evidence of the threat from the Jews felt by the Gentile population.[21] Even if we cannot establish with certainty every detail of the story, we can at least conclude that the edict published in Antioch would have sharpened the tension between Jews and Gentiles there, whether or not Jews from Antioch had any concrete involvement in the unrest in Alexandria. Indeed, if Malalas is correct about the riots in Antioch at the end of Caligula's reign, the riots in Alexandria about the same time must have caused Rome considerable concern. The eastern part of the empire would have appeared unstable in its two most important cities. Whatever actions Rome took to address the tensions between Jews and their neighbors, nothing could have been done to erase completely the sharpened bitterness between Jews and Greeks that the riots reflect.

Accusations of a Plot to Burn Antioch

Josephus also reports a situation in Antioch where a prominent Jew named Antiochus betrayed his community by accusing Jews of plotting revolt and arson against the city (*J. W.* 7.47–53). Later, when a fire did break out in the marketplace, Antiochus again pointed to Jews as the culprits.[22] Even though the investigation of the governor halted the initial violence against the Jews and they were cleared of the charges, their reputation would have been damaged at least to some degree in some quarters, and suspicions would have been heightened on both sides. Perhaps worse for the Jewish community, suspicions may have become more pronounced

---

[20] Josephus, *Ant.* 19.287–291.

[21] See p. 36, n. 131.

[22] Two actions against Jews occurred in Antioch about the time of the Jewish revolt. The first incident took place in 66/67, when Antiochus made his allegations; the second was three to four years later, when Jews were targeted with similar charges related to a fire had broken out in the center of Antioch. Josephus paints Antiochus as the villain in the story, but others may have seen the matter differently. Josephus admits that Antiochus had been highly respected among the Jewish people, but Josephus attempts to dismiss such respect by saying that it was only because of the position of his father, the *archōn* of the Jews in Antioch. One has to wonder why Josephus reports information about Antiochus's reputation, only to turn around and dismiss it. One senses that Josephus may know more than he is willing to admit (Josephus, *J. W.* 7.47–57).

in the relationships between individual Jews. Who could be trusted? Had not one of their own provoked the situation in the first place and kept the matter alive?

Some scholars think that Christians may have been a focus of the attack, even though Josephus does not mention Christians in the account.[23] He does say that both resident Jews and "foreign" Jews were blamed.[24] Given that the Jewish War had broken out just months earlier in Palestine, we might expect some influx of Jewish refugees into Antioch. Nothing would demand that the refugees be Christian, but nothing would exclude the possibility that many of those who sought refuge in Antioch were Christian.[25]

The situation mentioned by Josephus is as explosive as any we can find in Jewish-Gentile relations in Antioch. Josephus notes that the Jewish War had just broken out and everyone had come to hate all Jews. While the report is obviously exaggerated, it reflects an atmosphere of extreme tension. Reports of Jewish slaughter of the non-Jewish populations in towns of Palestine and Syria would have fanned Gentile suspicion of their Jewish neighbors in Antioch. And this suspicion would have been heightened by any influx of Jewish refugees. Word of a Jewish plot to attack Antioch in some way (by arson, according to Josephus) would have fit the mood of the moment well. In such an explosive atmosphere, residents of Antioch must have been ready to believe almost any rumor. The Jewish community, accused of a most serious charge, may have looked for a scapegoat. In the midst of mob violence, Christians may have been an easy scapegoat for the threatened Jewish community in Antioch or the suspicious Roman authorities there.

E. Mary Smallwood contends that the arson accusation targeted Christians not as a peripheral element in the conflict but as the primary focus.[26] She is

---

[23] C. K. Barrett, "Jews and Judaizers," 231; Smallwood, *The Jews under Roman Rule*, 361–64. Virginia Corwin thinks it unlikely that Christians in Antioch "wholly escaped this excitability" (*St. Ignatius,* 47).

[24] Some scholars think that Josephus has some details of the story wrong. Although Josephus is not always a reliable source, we cannot simply dismiss his comments without good reason. Josephus is specific in his comments here: Antiochus was the accuser; his father, the *archōn* of the Jews in Antioch, was burned to death as a result, as were other Jewish residents of Antioch. Further, the Sabbath was outlawed and Jews were forced to "sacrifice in the manner of the Greeks" (*J. W.* 7. 47–53). Josephus's mention of the involvement of "foreign Jews" (ξένους Ἰουδαίους (*J. W.* 7.47)] leads some to suspect that the plot was blamed on these foreign Jews or on another identifiable group of Jews distinguishable from the general body of Jewish residents of Antioch. Who these foreign Jews were is difficult to say. They could have been Jews who were not residents of the city or Jews whose residency had not been formalized in some way. Most likely, they were newly arrived Jews. Why such Jews were said to be connected to the false charges is not clear; perhaps the addition of a "foreign" element made the plot seem more sinister.

[25] See p. 236, n. 110.

[26] Josephus's comment does not mean that these Jews could not have been Christians. We do not know how Josephus viewed Christians or whether he would have made a point of distinguishing them.

impressed particularly by the fact that an identical charge was laid against Christians in Rome only three years earlier.[27] According to Josephus's account, the leader of the Jews, who was betrayed by his own son, was burned to death. Smallwood suggests that this leader had become a Christian and that he was betrayed for this reason.

Smallwood further contends that the action was directed only at one element within the Jewish community.[28] She bases this on the fact that a test was given to identify the plotters among the Jews. Why would a test have been necessary at all if the whole Jewish community was viewed as the culprit? Their Jewishness alone would have made them guilty. The test forced the suspects to sacrifice "in the manner of the Greeks." This would have caught any pious Jew or Christian, whether a suspect in the plot or not. The plotters must first have been identified in some other way. After identification of the suspect group in some other way, the test could then be applied. What better suspects in an arson plot than Christians, a group already tainted by this charge in the fire at Rome three years earlier?

Although the reconstruction proposed above is highly provisional and speculative, it illustrates well how Christian Jews would have been caught in any general crackdown on the Jewish community.[29] Further, the charge of arson may have made Christians a more easy scapegoat and a more likely target, particularly if they had already become a problem for the Jewish community in Antioch. What easier way to take the heat off a community than to finger one small element associated with it, whose members already have come under suspicion elsewhere for an identical crime and who are already an irritant to the larger Jewish community?

If Christians were involved in any way—either as the cause or the scapegoat—in any of the incidents of tensions affecting the Jewish community in Antioch, the matter would have had some importance in setting the tone of future relationships between the Jewish and Christian communities there. Although there is no explicit report of a Jewish-Christian clash in Antioch, it is unlikely that relations were friendly and unfractured, given 1) the tension between Jews and Christians that is reflected in almost every early Christian document associated with the area, 2) the coining, in Antioch, of a distinctive label for the Christian movement so as to provide Christians with an identity separate from Judaism, 3) incidents involving Jews that may be better explained by specifying a Christian element as

---

[27] Smallwood, *The Jews under Roman Rule*, 362.

[28] Ibid.

[29] The Gentile backlash could have struck more generally at the most distinctive feature of Judaism, Sabbath observance. In the heat of the rumors and accusations, the larger Gentile population would not, and perhaps could not, distinguish among the assortment of groups within the Jewish community. We need only look at the reaction to Islamic terrorists in the last few years to see how easily an entire community might be tarred with the same brush as some of its most extreme members.

a primary target, and 4) Ignatius's harsh language that pronounces the sharpest of breaks between Christianity and Judaism.

The Request to Expel the Jews

Josephus reports an incident in which inhabitants of Antioch petitioned Titus to expel the Jewish residents of Antioch.[30] The request came at the most opportune moment for anti-Jewish sentiment in Antioch, for Titus had just defeated the Jews.[31] Jews had surely discredited themselves in the eyes of the Romans by their revolt and dogged resistance to Rome in Palestine and their slaughter of Gentile residents in many areas of Palestine and Syria.[32] The petitioners had some hope that Titus would be sympathetic to anti-Jewish voices and would allow Antioch to expel its Jewish population.[33]

Titus rejected the petition, however, according to Josephus.[34] Some scholars have pointed out that the situation may not have been quite as favorable to Jews

---

[30] Josephus, *J. W.* 7.100–103; 109.

[31] Titus had acquired command after his father, Vespasian, the newly acclaimed emperor, turned his attention to crushing the opposition to his imperial claim.

[32] Antioch was one of very few areas in Syria where the Jews did not suffer retaliation during the Jewish War (Josephus, *J. W.* 2.479). It could be that since Jews in Antioch had not attempted any action against their Gentile neighbors, as had occurred in bloody clashes elsewhere, they did not experience a backlash. Yet non-Jews in Antioch must have had some level of uncertainty about their Jewish neighbors, particularly since credible reports were circulating about brutal attacks and retaliations among Jews and Gentiles in scores of nearby places. For whatever reason, the Jews in Antioch did not take up arms then or half a century later, when Jews throughout much of the eastern Roman Empire revolted. Josephus attempts to explain the quiet in Antioch by pointing to the imbalance in the size of the populations and the pity that the non-Jews had for those who had not taken part in the revolts. Josephus is clearly baffled by the restraint shown by the non-Jewish residents, and he seems to be fumbling for an adequate explanation. His explanation, however, seems to overlook the fact that not much pity was shown in any other action of the residents of Antioch toward their Jewish neighbors in this period. Zetterholm thinks that the restraint of the population may have had something to do with the presence of Roman troops in the city (*The Formation of Christianity in Antioch*, 117). This appears to be a better explanation than that offered by Josephus.

[33] As Josephus reports, Titus had already thrown many Jewish captives to the beasts or forced them into deadly gladiatorial combats (*J. W.* 7.37–40).

[34] Titus had a Jewish love interest, Berenice, the daughter of Herod Agrippa. It is not possible to determine to what degree this relationship tempered Titus's response to the Jewish situation in Antioch, but it may be that the Jews gained some benefit from this association. Berenice's brother, King Agrippa II (44–94?), a friend of a series of Roman emperors, intervened on behalf of the Jews from time to time. Further, Josephus's patrons were Vespasian and his successors; for a discussion of how this might have influenced his work, see Tessa Rajak, *Josephus: The Historian and His Society* (London: Gerald Duckworth, 1983; Philadelphia: Fortress, 1984), 185–222.

as Josephus paints it. Titus had set up cherubim from the Jerusalem temple at
the southern entrance to Antioch. This was near the Jewish quarter in the city
and on the road to Daphne, where many Jews lived and which was the same road
Jews used when coming to Antioch from Palestine.[35] Such a display would have
been a constant reminder of the recent Jewish defeat and an affront to the Jews
of Antioch and to any Jewish visitor to the city. But even if Josephus colors the
story a little, he does reflect the temper of the situation correctly: Jews in Antioch
were not subject to expulsion or loss of liberties in spite of events in Palestine that
could have put them very much at risk.

One does get a sense, however, that events could have gone in the opposite
direction just as easily. Titus's response to the situation seems to have surprised
both Jew and non-Jew. From Josephus's account, the request for action against
the Jews did not come from a small circle of insignificant opportunists but from
the general population and leadership together.[36] Further, it is clear that the Jews
themselves feared greatly what might happen.[37] Given the vicious and unstrained
ethnic slaughter in the previous four years that marked the engagement between
Jews and their Gentile neighbors throughout Palestine and areas of Syria, almost
to the doorstep of Antioch, suspicion and resentment must have been close to
the surface in Antioch. Although Antioch's initial reaction to its local Jewish residents during the Jewish War was restrained, this is hardly proof that there was
nothing sour in the relationship between Jew and Gentile in Antioch up to that
point. The throng of Antiochene residents attempting to force Titus into action
against the Jews, coupled with the Jews' own fear that Titus might agree to this
request, provide evidence of a deep antagonism in the relationship between Jews
and other residents of Antioch.

An Atmosphere of Distrust

We have examined several reports of incidents over the two centuries prior
to Ignatius. Such stories, notwithstanding points of exaggeration and cases of
outright fabrication, suggest that all was not harmonious between the Jews in
Antioch and their Gentile fellow residents. Each group would have been quite
keenly aware of the other, and certain kinds of suspicion and fear probably sim-
mered just below the surface for many. Josephus's report of incidents during the
Jewish War probably does not capture a significant change in attitude toward the
Jews in Antioch—from the friendly to the hostile—although there would have
been some shift in public opinion against the Jews because of the Jewish revolt
and its bloody excesses. Josephus's stories may simply indicate that a potentially

---

[35] John Malalas, *Chronographia* 10.45.

[36] Josephus, *J. W.* 7.107.

[37] Josephus, *J. W.* 7.104.

more receptive political environment had arisen in which a long-standing anti-Jewish attitude might have greater currency. It is not possible to determine from these incidents whether all non-Jews, or even the majority in Antioch, counted themselves adversaries of the Jews, but from the accounts, it does not appear that there was a silent and sympathetic majority.[38]

Given such an atmosphere of latent hostility and occasional violence, Jews may have been particularly diligent not to cause offense where it could be avoided. The Jewish leadership would have been keenly aware of Jewish groups whose activities had the potential to create unnecessary jeopardy for the larger Jewish community. In so far as the Jewish leadership had the ability, they may have attempted to check, contain, or expel the sources of potential problems for the Jewish community in Antioch. Indeed, Jews in Antioch may have been generally less willing than Jews elsewhere to involve themselves in risk and conflict. They did not participate in the Jewish War, as Jews in many of the cities of Syria did, nor did they participate in the widespread revolts against Trajan fifty years later, although we cannot determine why.[39] It is possible, then, that the majority of the Jewish community in Antioch was not particularly tolerant of fringe groups in Judaism that might threaten the security of the whole community of Jews. As we shall see later, this may have had implications for the Christian community in Antioch.

Internal Jewish Tensions in Antioch

Whatever tensions were created for Jews in Antioch from external adversaries, one should not discount the tensions arising from elements within the Jewish community itself. Indeed, there are at least as many accounts of internal conflicts as of external conflicts, although this may be somewhat slanted by the nature of the evidence.[40]

---

[38] Zetterholm speaks of "a profound fear and hatred of the 'Jews'" among the population of Antioch; he also thinks that "the masses of Antioch needed few excuses to start massacres" of the Jews (*The Formation of Christianity in Antioch,* 119) and that "many Jews in Antioch lived under the constant threat of one day being burnt at the stake by a former neighbor" (p. 121). These may be too sweeping generalizations. Zetterholm himself says that "it would be an oversimplification to describe the relations between Jews and Gentiles in the Syrian cites as wholly antagonistic" (ibid.). Yet Zetterholm is certainly right to call attention to the less-than-hospitable atmosphere Jews would have experienced from time to time in Antioch.

[39] This is not to say that the Jewish community in Antioch was passive. Jewish actions in the Caligula incident suggest that they could be provoked into resistance over religious matters, even those unrelated to their situation in Antioch.

[40] The literature is mainly from Josephus and Christian writers. All of the Christian writers reflect tensions stemming from the dispute between Christians and Jews over membership and the proper appropriation of the Jewish heritage. One account in

It is not surprising that internal tensions arose. The Jewish community in Antioch was not monolithic. Jews who had settled there would have differed in cultural background (Mesopotamian, Palestinian, Seleucid, Syrian), in religious practice (paralleling the diversity of Judaism in Palestine), and in attitudes toward Gentiles (from accommodating to isolationist). Further, by the first century, the significant Jewish community in Antioch already had a long history. It is hardly likely that this community had been or remained monolithic; surely, various religious options were explored, and rejected or embraced by segments of the Jewish population. That all Jews there were observant is unlikely; that they reflected some degree of the rich diversity found among Jews in first-century Palestine is probable.[41] Undoubtedly, some found city life in Antioch almost intoxicating and liberating and their Judaism embarrassingly outdated and quaint. Others must have retreated defensively, becoming conspicuously observant to make a statement or to protect boundaries and retain Jewish identity—not unlike the range of responses to the dominant culture found in immigrant communities today.[42] Two forces would have pulled at them: the cosmopolitan complexion of thriving Antioch and the intimate comfort of familiar Judaism and the Jewish social world.[43] Coupled with these influences would have been the impact of the

---

Josephus suggests a certain discord within the Jewish community itself (*J. W.* 7.47–57). Although, as we have seen, Josephus sets up the conflict as between Jews and Gentiles (with one apostate Jew making accusations against his fellow Jews), some scholars read the account as revealing a controversy within the Jewish community itself.

[41] Trevett thinks we should speak of "Judaisms" in Antioch rather than "Judaism" (*A Study of Ignatius*, 39). She also points out that "Tannaitic and later Jewish teachers were not convinced that Antiochene Jewish orthopraxis was all it should be" (p. 38), although she offers no sources in support of this statement.

[42] One must be cautious about drawing parallels in anything more than a general way, although some scholars have endeavored to use the modern situation of immigrants to illuminate the ancient world in a more substantial way. Much of Zetterholm's work reviews the discussion of the impact of immigration on communities, relating some modern cases to the situation of Jews in Antioch ("The Cultural and Religious Differentiation," in *The Formation of Christianity in Antioch*, 53–111). But modern examples may not help much, for the ancient world generally fostered loyalty to one's ancestral traditions in a way that the modern, secularized Western world does not.

[43] Some of the current reflection on the question of observant Judaism suggests that Diaspora Judaism was only minimally observant (Tessa Rajak, "The Jewish Community and Its Boundaries," 18–19). But to call such Jews "minimally" observant uses the perspective of their opponents, who promoted a more detailed observance of Torah. Most Diaspora Jews, regardless of their degree of observance, would have considered themselves observant, for their own standards, not the standards of others, would have specified what the appropriate level of observance was. Further, patterns of observance could have changed over time or differed from place to place, as perhaps regarding the wearing of phylacteries (Judith Lieu, "History and Theology," 86). Of course, there were Jews who were not observant by anyone's standards—the apostates from Judaism or,

devastating Jewish War in Palestine, with the resulting loss of the temple and the Jewish homeland. However individuals related to the distant Jerusalem and the temple, its destruction would have become a continuing focus of Jewish reflection and concern.

Through all such tensions and pressures, the Jewish community at Antioch was able to remain identifiable as Jewish over a period of hundreds of years prior to Ignatius's time, although some Jews must have lost this identity completely and others must have related to it in a range of ways.[44] It is also likely that some of the tensions between Jews and Samaritans surfaced in Antioch, for Antioch would have been a natural second center for Samaritans as well as Jews, and perhaps more so after the Maccabean revolt and the Jewish conquest of Samaria. The debate over the Christian message would have been but one of many areas of dispute within the Jewish community.[45]

Whether Ignatius caught the nuances of the diversity within Judaism in Antioch is not clear. It is possible, and perhaps likely, that Ignatius knew of some of the diversity within Judaism but chose to treat Judaism as monolithic. It is Judaism as a whole that he speaks about—a religious system that, regardless of its nuances and diversity, stands in contrast to Christianity and ranks inferior, according to him.

Jewish-Christian Relations in Antioch

Evidence of Tension and Separation

Current scholarship makes much of the similarity between Judaism and early Christianity. In some cases, it so emphasizes the similarity that the distinctive identities of these movements are called into question. Emphasis on the common ground is not particularly helpful, however, in determining a group's sense of its distinctive self-understanding. Such a fixation on the similarities can cause one to overlook the sense of newness and difference that Christians such as Ignatius held to be crucial and definitive.

---

from another perspective, converts to Greco-Roman religious sensibilities. We should not assume that no Jews were attracted to the dominant religion of the day or that, if they were, there must have been political or social rather than religious reasons for the change.

[44] To the outsider, religious groups often appear more monolithic than they really are. We learn of the rich diversity of Judaism in the first century from Jewish and Christian writings, reflecting the perceptions of those most intimately acquainted with Judaism. Greco-Roman writers investigating Judaism or Christianity rarely captured such nuance, although some, such as Celsus, managed to be quite informed and perceptive.

[45] The references to Jewish-Christian tension in the early period are read here as reflecting a degree of realism and not as mere rhetorical constructs. Granted, the evidence is from Christian sources, but it is widespread and substantial. See p. 160, n. 112.

To illustrate this, suppose one were to lump Judaism and Greco-Roman religions together based on their shared concepts of temple, priesthood, sacrifice, and divinity.[46] Such a linking of religious sensibilities in the ancient world would not necessarily produce a more accurate picture of the individual movements—indeed, it might well obscure important distinctions. We might at times wish to consider ancient religion in its broadest dimensions, but we would never claim that a more specific examination of Judaism (or any other religion) would misrepresent either ancient religion or Judaism. In the same way, the consideration of only the common elements of Judaism and Christianity can obscure defining differences and prevent a serious examination of the distinctive identity of the Christian (or Jewish) movement.

Consequently, the examination here of earliest Christianity is intentional in not focusing on what is retained from Judaism. The matters that are primary for early Christian identity do not necessarily lie in this common ground. Rather, Christian identity is most profoundly marked by the elements of Judaism that early Christians forsook or modified by their boundary markers or that were brought together into a new cluster and focus by the Christian movement. Christian self-awareness was most sharply defined at points where the Christian community was reshaping the boundaries or revising the core of its Jewish heritage. Conscious, intentional, and reflective decisions would have been demanded at these points. Thus the most accurate understanding of the early Christian community's self-identity can be gained by an examination of the essential core (the Christ confession) and of the perimeter or boundary markers, which were defined largely in reference to Judaism. The common ground shared by Judaism and Christianity is common because it is largely uncontroversial—and thus mostly irrelevant in defining distinctive Christian identity over against Judaism.

For the early Christian movement, developing as it did out of a Jewish environment, its natural and necessary markers would have been shaped in response to Judaism. That Christianity initially defined itself mainly in contrast to Judaism is not surprising,[47] nor is it surprising that such a definition reflects varying

---

[46] Lieu speaks of "a shared identity" of pagans, Jews, and Christians (*Christian Identity in the Jewish and Graeco-Roman World* [Oxford: Oxford University Press, 2004]: 143). Lieu is asking a different question from that explored here, and so it is likely she will obtain a different answer—one that she recognizes will be different from the answer that the ancient texts sought to supply.

[47] Our primary interest here is in the relationship between Jews and Christians in Antioch. All of the explicit evidence about this subject is Christian. The pagan and the Jewish literature of this period rarely mention Christians at all, and neither mentions Christians in Antioch or their relations with the Jewish community there, although some scholars believe that a few comments in non-Christian literature may have some information about the Antiochene Christian movement living within the shadow of the Jewish community. For recent examinations of Jewish-Christian relationships in Antioch

degrees of tension and hostility.[48] These are natural conditions in the process of separation and the establishment of a new and distinct identity.

As will be seen, some recent scholarship on the Christian movement in Antioch downplays the tension with the Jewish community.[49] According to this view, Christian leaders objected to Christian Judaizers who misused the Jewish traditions, but they had no issue with Judaism itself. However, this is an unlikely interpretation of the evidence. Christians cannot understand themselves as a distinctive entity without some sense of the "other," which, for Christianity in its earliest days, was Judaism. This sensibility is reinforced in a wealth of early Christian literature. Although this literature does not capture the distinctive identity of Christians in a uniform way, the Christian movement forcefully asserts its *claim* to a distinctive identity against Judaism, perceived broadly or narrowly.

Judaism's Awareness of Christianity

A more debatable issue regarding Jewish-Christian relationships in Antioch is whether Christianity was important enough even to gain notice from Jews. Although Judaism was the "other" against which Christianity defined itself, there is no necessary counter relationship that establishes Christianity as Judaism's "other." Judaism's main identity is marked off by the larger world of Greco-Roman paganism; this is its primary "other."[50] To understand Ignatius and Jewish-Christian relations however, we must ask whether Christianity featured *in any way* in Judaism's reflection in the early second century.

---

reflected in the early literature, see Zetterholm, *The Formation of Christianity in Antioch*; Cummins, *Paul and the Crucified Christ in Antioch*, 138–60; Michelle Slee, *The Church in Antioch*; Michele Murray, *Playing a Jewish Game: Gentile Christian Judaizing in the First and Second Centuries CE* (Waterloo, Ont.: Wilfrid Laurier University Press, 2004), 43–72; Brown and Meier, *Antioch and Rome*.

[48] Paul's letters come to mind, particularly Romans and Galatians and the Thessalonian correspondence. The Gospels also reflect this tension through stories highlighting the tensions between Jesus and Jewish leaders. The preservation and prominent place of such stories in the gospel traditions suggest that the tension was felt by the Christian church decades after Jesus' own conflict with Judaism, whatever that might have involved. The *Epistle of Barnabas* and the *Didache* likewise reflect sharp tension. Indeed, almost all of the earliest Christian literature offers at least a hint of conflict with Judaism. Ignatius's letters, then, are not anomalies when they reflect such tension.

[49] See pp. 148–53, 223–25.

[50] This does not mean, however, that the Jewish identity and sense of boundary cannot be marked in terms of other groups also. In Palestine, the Samaritans probably played as significant a role as paganism in terms of being Judaism's "other." Christianity perhaps does not rise to the level of the primary "other" for Judaism until after the christianization of the Roman Empire.

Inasmuch as the key issue that routinely appears in Christian reports about Antioch concerns questions of Jewish and Christian identity,[51] it is difficult to imagine that struggles within the Christian community about some of these more explosive matters entirely escaped the notice of the Jewish leadership in Antioch. According to the witness of Acts and Paul, the rise of the Christian movement had not escaped the notice of the authorities in Jerusalem.[52] Given a network of communication that even the fledgling Christian groups in Jerusalem and Antioch had developed with each other, it is almost certain that the Jewish officials in Jerusalem had at least as effective and as established a network with Jewish officials in Antioch.[53] It is therefore likely that the Jewish authorities in Antioch were alerted to the Christian problem, since the suppression of the Christians of Palestine seems to have forced some of them to flee to Antioch and other areas.[54] It is equally likely that the intra-Christian dispute over the admission of uncircumcised Gentiles did not escape the notice of the Jewish authorities in Antioch, for this seems to have been a major Christian dispute and any investigation of the Christian movement by Jewish authorities would have revealed it.

Indeed, the internal Christian debate over the status of Gentiles may have had something to do with the attempt of Christians to accommodate themselves to the dominant Jewish presence under which Christians lived and worshiped in the earliest period. Given the animosity towards Jews around this time from the larger population of Antioch, the Jewish authorities may well have been

---

[51] Paul puts the matter bluntly: "If you, though a Jew, live like a Gentile, and not like a Jew, how can you compel the Gentiles to live like Jews?" (Gal 2:14). In the same letter, Paul speaks of his earlier life and successes in "Judaism" (1:13–14). He makes circumcision an issue (2:3) and places Jews and Gentiles together in a new relationship in Christ (2:15–21; 3:28–29; 5:6, 11; 6:15). Regardless of what interpretation is put on these words, it is difficult to free the situation in Antioch completely from questions of status, boundaries, identity, and religious conduct and scruples.

[52] Gal 1:13–14. Acts frequently includes Jewish officials in the opposition to Christians (e.g., Acts 4:1–30; 5:17–18, 27–40). Even if the presentation in Acts contains rhetoric, it seems highly unlikely that the Jewish leadership did not take some interest in silencing the followers of Jesus, given that Jesus had been recently executed by the Romans. If Acts had included no story of the opposition of Jewish authorities to the Christian movement, we likely would have assumed some such opposition simply on the basis of the story of Jesus' execution and our knowledge of Roman concerns about revolt in frontier provinces.

[53] S. Safrai, "Relations between the Diaspora and the Land of Israel," in *The Jewish People in the First Century: Historical Geography, Political History, Social, Cultural, and Religious Life and Institutions* (ed. S. Safrai and M. Stern; 2 vols.; CRINT 1; Assen, Neth.: Van Gorcum; Philadelphia: Fortress, 1974–1976), 1:181–215.

[54] The evidence comes from Acts, and although caution needs to be used with such material, the report of persecution matches Paul's own testimony of his activities as a persecutor (see p. 3, n. 10), and the reported flight of persecuted Christians from Palestine to other centers makes sense.

particularly sensitive to disruptions that would bring the Jewish community to the attention of the authorities in any unfavorable way. It is unlikely that the first impression Christianity made with the Jewish authorities in Antioch was positive. Any disturbances caused by Christians would have been a matter of concern to the Jewish community. This fact seems to be indicated by Christian literature from the period, which often reflects the hostility that the young Christian community encountered from the Jewish authorities—and sometimes, it seemed to some early Christian writers, from the whole of the Jewish people.[55]

Where, then, is the evidence of Jewish hostility toward the Christian movement? Almost everywhere. Document after document from Christianity's first hundred years reflects conflict with elements of the Jewish leadership, people, institutions, practices, or theology. Supposing the worst-case scenario—where all the surviving Christian stories provide completely false or highly exaggerated reports of conflicts—we would nonetheless still have evidence of tension between Christians and Jews in the mere fact that the Christian community's literature is colored so profoundly by such stories, for it would be impossible to imagine a community producing this kind of literature without some truth in the tale.[56] The sweeping dismissal of these stories leaves too much residue behind that demands explanation.

Paul is the first and perhaps the most convincing witness to the Jewish hostility that the early Christian community faced, for, as he confesses, he was himself a zealous persecutor of the followers of Jesus[57] and, after he converted, he found himself at the receiving end of the abuse he had earlier zealously meted out. Several items stand out about Paul's involvement. The attack on Christians was deliberate, directed at Christians specifically, and approved and administered by some level of formal authority.[58] The attack was either against all Jewish Christians or perhaps more specifically against the Hellenists. Paul does not make a distinction here, and he offers no clue that he persecuted only the Hellenist component, whatever that distinction might have meant at the time of Paul's attack against the church. Even supposing it was only the most extreme liberalizing position that was attacked it would have been mild compared with the extreme positions soon to be put forward in the Christian movement. If the early Hellenist position caused the

---

[55] Matt 27:25; Acts 13:46; 28:25–28; 1 Thess 2:14–16.

[56] Denying that stories of the Jewish persecution of Christians have captured at least some of the historical reality reflects a radical and unproductive skepticism, what Lightfoot calls, in another context, "the kind of skepticism that bordered on insanity" (Lightfoot, S. Ignatius, S. Polycarp, 2.1.54).

[57] Gal 1:13–14, 22; 1 Cor 15:9; Acts 22:19. See Martin Hengel, "Der vorchristliche Paulus," Theologische Beiträge 21 (1990) 174–95.

[58] Although Paul does not say explicitly that he had formal authority, as does Acts (9:1–2; 22:5; 26:10), his description of his repression of Christians suggests some degree of formal sanction (Gal 1:14).

Jewish leadership concern, matters can hardly have improved when one of their agents switched sides and encouraged an even more radical stance—acceptance of uncircumcised Gentiles as full members!

Paul's own record is explicit on the matter. As much as scholars have found differences between the portrait of Paul presented in Acts and what can be constructed from Paul's own letters, there is agreement on Paul's persecution of the church, although the accounts in Acts offer considerably more detail.[59] Whatever we wish to make of each detail, the point still stands that Paul, as a loyal adherent to Judaism, was a persecutor of the early Christian movement. The notion that he was the only Jewish persecutor or that the persecution of the Christian movement stopped with his conversion cannot be reasonably sustained. Indeed, Paul serves as a useful and credible witness that the Jewish pursuit of Christians continued well beyond his own participation in the repression, for he records his own encounters with Jewish opposition after his conversion, as does the book of Acts.[60]

The evidence for tensions between Jews and Christians in Antioch is more indirect. Matthew's Gospel, for example, presents an atmosphere of tension between Christians and Jews, but the specifics are obscured because the tension is reflected in the mirror of stories about Jesus and the situation decades earlier in Palestine rather than described in an account of the contemporary situation of Antioch.[61] And Ignatius distinguishes sharply between Christianity and Judaism but recounts no particular clash between the two groups.

There are only a few stories and comments that offer hints of a conflict between the Christian and the Jewish communities in Antioch. Yet these situations, if interpreted in a particular way, can account for the atmosphere of tension between Jews and Christians that we find in much of the literature. In some cases, other reconstructions of the stories are possible and perhaps even as probable. Nonetheless, given the tone of much of the early Christian literature, some effort to make sense of the chilly environment between Jews and Christians is required, no matter how provisional the reconstructions must be.

Early Christian literature supports the notion that when the Jewish community was offended by certain Christian innovations, it could and did take repressive action against the Christians. Themes of tension with, and rejection by, the

---

[59] Acts 7:58; 8:1–3; 9:1–31; 22:1–20; 26:1–15.

[60] 2 Cor 11:24; 1 Thess 2:14–16. Acts offers extensive support for Paul's reports in his letters that he or others had been persecuted by the Jews (Acts 9:22–25; 11:19; 12:1–5; 13:45, 50; 14:1–6, 19; 17:5–9, 13). Whether the details in Acts have any substance is a matter of debate, but the mere composing of such accounts reflects a degree of animus in Jewish-Christian relations—even if all of these reports were unreliable in their detail.

[61] This assumes that Matthew was composed in Antioch and reflects, to some extent, the situation there.

synagogue are numerous.[62] Even if we were to suppose that much of the Christian presentation is idealistic and in some cases even fictional, we cannot escape the overall weight of the evidence through a range of diverse documents. If early Christian literature reflects the hostility and intervention of the Jewish community in matters related to Christian groups or individuals,[63] it is highly unlikely that Christians invented all such charges of repression and that Jewish authorities were, in fact, benign, and allowed Christians to go unchecked and unchallenged. It is equally unlikely that the Jewish community in Antioch tolerated the most highly offensive innovation of Christians—the inclusion of Gentiles. Such a measure was troubling enough to Jewish Christians themselves. Indeed, it would be a far more curious and unlikely story if the Jewish community in Antioch took no action against Christian innovators there, particularly if early Christians operated initially within the orbit of Jewish authority.

Scholars who read between the lines to find evidence of Jewish-Christian tensions in stories that seem to focus only on a Christian incident or on a Jewish incident are on a more sober path than those who reject the accounts of explicit persecution as mere rhetoric. Tension between the two communities is highly probable. Stories that do not explicitly mention both communities may be relevant and revealing of the Jewish-Christian controversy, and to these stories we now turn.

The Jerusalem Council and Innovations in Antioch

Some early Jewish Christians in Antioch took a daring step in opening membership and table fellowship to Gentiles. This caused a schism in the Christian group, and details of the friction and attempts to resolve the crisis are reflected in Acts 15:1–35 and Gal 2:1–10, which appear to speak of the same incident.[64] The

---

[62] The word "synagogue" is used here in a general way for the recognized Jewish leadership and community of an area. Although this word was a favorite of Christians for the Jewish component of an area, Jews used a variety of terms. The debate about what the words meant remains unsettled (see p. 73, n. 101).

[63] Matt 10:23; 23:34; Luke 21:12; John 9:22; 12:42; 15:20; 1 Thess 2:14; and Paul's own pre-Christian activity (see p. 145, n. 57).

[64] For a discussion of this oft-treated matter, see C. K. Barrett, "Paul: Councils and Controversies," in *Conflicts and Challenges in Early Christianity*, by Martin Hengel and C. K. Barrett (ed. Donald A. Hagner; Harrisburg, Pa.: Trinity Press International, 1999), 42–74; Slee, *The Church in Antioch*, 36–52; Philip F. Esler, *The First Christians in Their Social Worlds: Social-Scientific Approaches to New Testament Interpretation* (New York: Routledge, 1994), 50–67; Stephen G. Wilson, *Luke and the Law* (SNTSMS 50; Cambridge: Cambridge University Press. 1983), 71–102; Peter J. Tomson, *Paul and the Jewish Law: Halakha in the Letters of the Apostle to the Gentiles* (CRINT 3.1; Assen, Neth.: Van Gorcum; Philadelphia: Fortress, 1990), 222–30.

story as we have it reflects only the debate within the Christian community. The degree to which the local Jewish community in Antioch would have taken offense at these innovations among the liberalizing Christian group is not addressed. It is difficult to believe, however, that these innovations within the Jewish-Christian group in Antioch escaped the notice of Jews in Antioch, who probably had already been forced to deal with the claims of the Christian group there before Christians began to experiment with greater openness to Gentiles.[65] The Christian movement was, at this time, not yet distinct from Judaism, nor was it likely free of the authority of the leadership of the Jewish community in Antioch.[66] It is unlikely that Jews in Antioch as a whole would have been less offended by this innovative approach to Gentiles in their community than were some Christian Jews in Antioch and Christian Jews in the mother church at Jerusalem. It is also unlikely that the Jewish authorities knew nothing of the dispute.

Muting the Tension between Jews and Christians

This portrait of tension has been challenged. Modern scholarship mutes in some way almost every report of Jewish-Christian tension reflected in the early Christian literature. The first significant modern attack on the early Christian presentation of a hostile relationship between Jews and Christians focused on the Gospels. The claim was that this material was deliberately presented in a certain way so as to indict the Jewish officials and populace in the death of Jesus when in fact it was the Roman authorities who were responsible.[67] The view of Jewish-Christian disputes in Acts was similarly challenged,[68] and Paul's mainly

---

[65] According to Acts 11:19, some early followers of Christ fled to Antioch because of the persecution that broke out in the area of Judea at the time of the martyrdom of Stephen. There is nothing improbable in the story. If Christians fled to Antioch from persecution in Jerusalem, the Jewish authorities in Antioch may have become aware of the new Christian movement soon after its beginnings.

[66] See p. 72, n. 95, for Christian submission to synagogue discipline.

[67] The most influential study along this line was Paul Winter, *The Trial of Jesus* (Berlin: de Gruyter, 1961). For wider examinations, see Douglas R. A. Hare, *The Theme of Jewish Persecution of Christians in the Gospel according to St Matthew* (SNTSMS 6; Cambridge: Cambridge University Press, 1967); Judith Lieu, "Accusations of Jewish Persecution in Early Christian Sources, with Particular Reference to Justin Martyr and the Martyrdom of Polycarp," in *Tolerance and Intolerance in Early Judaism and Christianity* (ed. Graham N. Stanton and Guy G. Stroumsa; Cambridge: Cambridge University Press, 1998), 279–95; idem, *Image and Reality*; Paula Fredriksen, "What 'Parting of the Ways'?" 56–61.

[68] On the historicity of stories in Acts, see esp. Ernst Haenchen, *The Acts of the Apostles* (Philadelphia: Westminster, 1971); Martin Hengel, *Acts and the History of Earliest Christianity* (Philadelphia: Fortress, 1980). Haenchen tends to be skeptical; Hengel tends to accept the accounts unless problematic in some way. For our purpose here, it matters not which scholar offers the better treatment of these stories. For a general review of ap-

uncomplimentary interpretation of Judaism and his radical vision of Christianity were removed from the near-normative position they had held in reconstructions of the early church and were relegated to a much less influential position or radically reinterpreted so that Paul remained within the orbit of Judaism.[69] Stories of conflict between the church and the synagogue were also reinterpreted, often by moving them from the realm of reality to the realm of rhetoric.[70]

Although such theories are useful for asking new questions about a number of issues related to early Christianity, the newer approaches are less successful in providing convincing answers to these questions. Further, the various revisionist approaches have not been able to mute fully the radicalism of early Christian literature.[71] There is something about Judaism that disturbs early Christian authors, and Christians express an attitude toward Gentiles that disturbs traditional Judaism. Most radical of the Christian innovations is that Gentiles and Jews are included in an affiliation that they did not share before. It is not a matter critical to the debate whether the "Christian" proponents of this new understanding at first saw themselves as Christians or Jews or something else altogether. In so far as they created a new community that could not operate within the boundaries of Judaism as perceived by Christians, by Jews, or by the larger society, the Christian movement generated a profoundly revolutionary religious experiment. To borrow the language (but not the thinking) of the revisionists, who speak of a *paradigm shift* in the contemporary understanding of Paul and of Jewish-Christian

---

proaches to Acts, see Joseph B. Tyson, "From History to Rhetoric and Back: Assessing New Trends in Acts Studies," in *Contextualizing Acts: Lukan Narrative and Greco-Roman Discourse* (ed. Todd Penner and Caroline Vander Stichele; Society of Biblical Literature Symposium Series 20; Atlanta: Society of Biblical Literature, 2003), 23–42; and Daniel Marguerat, *The First Christian Historian.*

[69] For a review of the history of this revisioning of Paul and for a new contribution to the effort, see Terence L. Donaldson, *Paul and the Gentiles: Remapping the Apostle's Convictional World* (Minneapolis: Fortress, 1997). Donaldson admits that Paul's language sets up various relationships between Israel and the Gentiles (pp. 29–33). He thinks that the tangle of Paul's language can be resolved by making a distinction "between the surface elements of the text and an underlying set of basic commitments or convictions" (33). This may be the case, but for understanding the development of early Christianity, this resolution fails. Whatever Paul's underlying clarity on the relationship of Israel and the church, it is Paul's *expression* of his ideas (even if rhetorical and situational) that is transmitted to later generations. Although it is important to probe for what Paul (and any other ancient) "really meant," we must be careful not to lessen the impact of how Paul was heard. It is Paul's rhetoric—blunt, unnuanced, and polemical—that defined Paul for the early church, probably even within Paul's lifetime.

[70] James W. Parkes, *The Conflict of the Church and the Synagogue* (London: Soncino, 1934). For a review of the influence of Parkes, see Becker, *The Ways That Never Parted,* 8–11, 16–17.

[71] Attempts to dismiss Paul's language as mere rhetoric do not adequately address such radicalism.

relations, my contention here is that Ignatius is part of a paradigm shift that takes a Jewish-colored movement out of its place in Judaism and sets it distinctly apart from Judaism as a new religion.[72] However much the Christian movement was shaped within the matrix of Judaism and however much its concerns and goals were set in a Jewish framework, the radical novelty and consequences of its vision resulted in a fundamentally new sensibility. It is largely irrelevant whether Paul and other early Christians who stood in some tension with Judaism envisioned such a dramatic development. The reality is that such a development occurred, not as a peripheral offshoot but as the mainstream of the movement.

There is no need here either to counter or commend any of these revisionist readings in detail, as Ignatius is the focus of interest in this study. All that is required is to show that a certain explicit level of hostility existed between the early Christian movement and Judaism[73] and that such tension would not have been absent in Antioch, where the Christian movement, as a religious option distinct from Judaism, took its most distinct shape.

Various reconstructions mute or completely deny a tension between Ignatius and Judaism. This is despite the fact that the early Christian literature often reflects what appears to be tension between Jews and Christians and that Antioch seems to figure prominently in disputes about Jewish and Christian identity. Such reconstructions tend to consider all negative allusions to Judaism as referring to an aberrant form of Judaizing Gentile Christianity, the followers of which are charged with misappropriating the heritage of Judaism found within the Christian church.

Lloyd Gaston, for example, contends that Ignatius had no feud *per se* with Judaism.[74] It is not clear whether Gaston thinks that Ignatius simply had no interest in Judaism other than when it appeared in questionable form within Christianity or that Ignatius had no objection to Judaism as such. Gaston does quote with approval this comment of Harald Riesenfeld: "There is no controversy against Judaism in its orthodox form in the letters of Ignatius."[75] Other scholars present a similar view of Ignatius's comments about Judaism and Judaizing.[76]

---

[72] Donaldson recognizes that by the time of Justin, the Christian perception was no longer Paul's both-and, but rather an either-or: Jew *or* Christian (*Paul and the Gentiles*, 306). In Ignatius's writings, situated between Paul and Justin, the either-or dichotomy is clearly the defining vision. As Donaldson himself admits, even Paul was coming to recognize that his vision of the both-and unity as the people of God was unlikely to come about (305–6).

[73] Robert H. Gundry, *Matthew: A Commentary on His Handbook for a Mixed Church under Persecution* (2d ed.; Grand Rapids: Eerdmans, 1994); Bruce J. Malina, "Establishment Violence in the New Testament World," *Scriptura* 51 (1994): 51–78.

[74] Lloyd Gaston, "Judaism of the Uncircumcised in Ignatius and Related Writers," in *Separation and Polemic* (vol. 2 of *Anti-Judaism in Early Christianity*; ed. Stephen G. Wilson; SCJ 2; Waterloo, Ont.: Wilfrid Laurier University Press, 1986), 33–44.

[75] Ibid., 36, n 20.

[76] See pp. 223–25.

It is no surprise to discover that Ignatius's negative comments about Judaism are directed toward Judaizing elements within the Christian church—he is writing to Christian churches and dealing with problems there. Although one can agree with Gaston and others that Ignatius's remarks are specifically directed against Judaizing elements within the church, it is quite another matter entirely to conclude that Ignatius has no issue with Judaism. Ignatius's attack is more basic and more profound than Gaston's characterization. The stark and uncompromising language that Ignatius employs against Christian Judaizers of whatever stripe must carry over more broadly to Judaism as a whole if the language is to have the impact it is intended to have. When Ignatius says, "If anyone should interpret Judaism to you, do not hear him" (Ign. *Phld.* 6.1), he is not speaking simply of some aspect of the Judaizing position, although this may be included and indeed may even be primary in the context of the letter. Ignatius is speaking, rather, of any interpretation of Judaism that is at odds with the Christian message, and in his mind, every interpretation of Judaism fits that bill, whether traditional or novel, whether orthodox or esoteric. It is not merely "bad" or "inadequate" interpretations of Judaism that concern Ignatius; it is Judaism itself. Only because Ignatius's language has this broad scope can it have an effective, narrow, and precise application to the situation at hand—the Judaizers in Christian assemblies. The same is true when Ignatius charges, "It is outlandish to proclaim Jesus Christ and practice Judaism" (Ign. *Magn.* 10.3), or when he comments, "If we have lived according to Judaism until now, we admit that we have not received God's gracious gift" (Ign. *Magn.* 8.1). Such comments strike at Judaizing tendencies in the church, but they strike effectively because Ignatius uses an unqualified approach to the issue. It is Judaism itself—not some twisted and uninformed Gentile misappropriation of an element of Judaism—that is the problem. Ignatius brings an indictment against Judaism as a whole.

This becomes even clearer in other passages of Ignatius's letters. Judaism is, in Ignatius's mind, at best *passé* or, more likely, something quite worse.[77] His very use of the term "Christianity" as an appropriate term to stand in contrast to Judaism forcefully suggests this. "Lead Christian lives," he says, "for whoever is called by a name other than this does not belong to God" (Ign. *Magn.* 10.1). He does not intend to make an exception for Judaism; indeed, by using the name "Christian," it is likely that he has Judaism in mind as the most obvious contrast. Ignatius's list of negative comments about Judaism continues: "Christianity did

---

[77] C. K. Barrett says that, for Ignatius, Judaism and Docetism were "equally destructive of Christianity" and that Christianity had "replaced" Judaism ("Jews and Judaizers," 221). Michele Murray takes somewhat of a middle position: Jews are not causing problems for Ignatius; it is Christian Judaizers who are. Murray admits, however, that "While it is true that Ignatius does not denounce Jews generally, in his own way, he denies the Jewish scriptures and history any intrinsic validity" (*Playing a Jewish Game*, 90).

not believe in Judaism, but Judaism in Christianity—in which every tongue that believes in God has been gathered together" (Ign. *Magn.* 10.3). "Both of them [the circumcised and the uncircumcised], unless they speak of Jesus Christ, are to me tombstones and sepulchers of the dead," Ignatius proclaims (Ign. *Phld.* 6.1). These are blunt rejections of Judaism, not merely of some twisted appropriation of Judaism by elements within Christianity.

Further, whatever validity the Judaism of old had, its continuing validity can no longer be maintained given the appearance of Christ, according to Ignatius's view. Speaking of the Hebrew prophets, Ignatius says that "those who lived according to the old ways came to a new hope, no longer keeping the Sabbath but living according to the Lord's Day" (Ign. *Magn.* 9.1–2). His conclusion is that there is no option other than Christianity. Clearly, for Ignatius, Judaism is not the second best choice—it is no choice at all. Ignatius also contends that Christ "is the door of the Father, through which Abraham and Isaac and Jacob and the prophets and the apostles and the church enter" (Ign. *Phld.* 9.1). He can hardly mean that the ancient Hebrew prophets hoped in Christ but Jews of his own time do not need to or that Jews may enter a door other than that through which the patriarchs and the prophets have entered.

Ignatius's language of anti-Judaism would have no weight against specific Judaizing groups unless it had weight against Judaism in general. Ignatius already has made a decision about Judaism: it is irrelevant or worse. In his letters he evaluates certain groups within the Christian church. Once he has judged these groups to be unacceptable by labeling them "Jewish" or counting them as part of "Judaism," he can easily discredit and dismiss them. Such a strategy works only if Judaism itself has been discredited and dismissed. The close analysis, by Gaston and others, of the Judaizing characteristics of Ignatius's opponents does not succeed in muting or redirecting Ignatius's harsh criticism of Judaism as a whole.

Some have attempted to mute Ignatius's negative analysis of Judaism by appealing to the fact that there are no references to Jews or Christian Jews in the Ignatian letters but only to Judaizers.[78] Gaston contrasts Ignatius's opponents to the opponents in the Pauline writings, who were more clearly Jews. But such a contrast reveals little. Ignatius stood at the end of the process.[79] The legitimacy of Judaism was no longer a question of debate; this matter had been long settled in the tradition in which Ignatius was at home. The separation was perhaps decades old by then. Terms of distinction had been formulated or appropriated, and Ignatius employed such labels without further argument to reinforce the distinctive self-understanding of the Christian community. To imply that Ignatius had no

---

[78] Gaston, "Judaism of the Uncircumcised," 40.

[79] "The exemption from circumcision and accordingly from the Jewish law is a matter of course for [Ignatius], and clearly for his adversaries as well" (Einar Molland, "The Heretics Combatted by Ignatius of Antioch," *JEH* 5 [1954]: 2–3).

issue with Judaism but only with Gentile Judaizers is to overlook the stage re-flected by Ignatius in the process of disengagement and to disregard the definitive kind of language employed by him.

In a further effort to mute the force of Ignatius's anti-Jewish comments, some have argued that Ignatius has a less dismissive stance toward Judaizers than to-ward Docetists.[80] But as argued elsewhere in this work, such an overly nuanced reading of Ignatius's letters overlooks how Ignatius intended his words and how his readers understood them.[81]

Ignatius's position is clear. The question is whether Ignatius is an anomaly. All of the Christian literature associated with Antioch reflects a deep hostility or distance between Judaism and Christianity. It may be unlikely that such literature represents the full scope of Christian relationships with Judaism, but it is even less likely that it represents a minority position. Ignatius's sharp distinction between Judaism and Christianity is probably as characteristic a reflection of the attitudes of Christians in Antioch as we are likely to find.

Christian Reflection on Persecution and Martyrdom

Ignatius's Reflection on Martyrdom

Ignatius's letters are marked by frequent, developed references to martyrdom and discipleship. Such mature reflection does not seem to fit a situation where these ideas developed overnight in response to a completely unexpected arrest. Nor does this reflection seem to be the idiosyncratic musings of a leader out of touch with the everyday realities of the life of his congregation. Martyrdom seems to have become such an issue of contention for churches in Ignatius's orbit that Ignatius uses his own march to martyrdom to refute the position of his op-ponents on the subject.[82] His docetic opponents already have reflected on this matter and have developed their own view of Jesus, which negates the reality of Jesus' suffering and death. The clash of views seems to have been serious enough to lead finally to schism of some kind.[83] Ignatius argues pointedly against the schismatics' position.

---

[80] Trevett, *A Study of Ignatius,* 170–73. J. Rius-Camps thinks that Ignatius's language toward the Judaizers was "slightly gentler" (*The Four Authentic Letters of Ignatius,* 50–51), but Hammond Bammel ("Ignatian Problems,"83) lists a range of comments made by Ignatius about the Judaizers that seem to mute the force of Rius-Camps's contention.

[81] See pp. 120–21.

[82] Ignatius's opponents who hold this view are commonly referred to as docetic in cur-rent scholarship. Ignatius does not have a label for them (Ign. *Trall.* 10.1; Ign. *Smyrn.* 4.2).

[83] The nature of the schism in Antioch is unknown, since Ignatius does not explicitly address the issue of schismatics in his city. In his letters, the comments that are explicit

There is nothing particularly original about making Docetism a central element in the situation at Antioch.[84] It has merit because it presents martyrdom as a solid issue regarding which there could have been a serious dispute. Further, this dispute is clearly supported by documentary evidence, as it is reflected in comments in Ignatius's letters and in other references to docetic tendencies in Antioch and elsewhere. Such a dispute would also account for Ignatius's emphasis on the reality of Jesus' death and the necessity of Ignatius's own approaching martyrdom. Most important, this reconstruction can make sense of Ignatius's continued desire to embrace martyrdom even after learning that peace had been restored in Antioch, for if the substance of his opposition to the Docetists was that Christians should not try to escape martyrdom, his own escape from martyrdom could seriously blunt his argument.

Ignatius considers the docetic position linked closely to attitudes regarding martyrdom and the passion of Christ.[85] But why are they related? The threat of persecution and execution would have prompted Christians to reflect on the death of Jesus and past heroes as examples of faithfulness, calling others to follow such examples and embrace martyrdom should it come. There are certainly frequent enough references in early Christian literature to indicate that Christians reflected on the theme of martyrdom and on the death of Jesus; Ignatius's own letters provide some of the clearest examples. The docetic side would have tried to negate these powerful examples.

The primary consideration is whether this kind of reflection and debate is likely to have developed outside a context of persecution, in an atmosphere of congenial relations for the Christian community in Antioch.[86]

The Jewish Roots of Martyrdom

Christian ideas and behavior often developed within the environment of Judaism. Some elements were borrowed unaltered, some were revised, and some

---

about schism or separate eucharists are directed to churches in Asia Minor. Ignatius's deep concern about schism, however, suggests troubles in Antioch also.

[84] See, for example, Norbert Brox, *Zeuge und Märtyrer: Untersuchungen zur frühchristlichen Zeugnis-Terminologie* (Munich: Kösel, 1961), 211–15. We need not fall back to the earlier position that a specific persecution was instigated against Christians. All that is required is that Christians were occasionally the subject of repression. Much of the evidence from the ancient world is dismissed as rhetoric, even if it points to some degree of trouble for Christians in their larger world.

[85] Ign. *Magn.* 9; Ign. *Trall.* 10–11; Ign. *Smyrn.* 1–7.

[86] A short time after Ignatius, as Gnosticism came into its own, the themes of martyrdom and persecution provided one of the dividing lines between some gnostic groups and the church led by the bishops. See "The Passion of Christ and the Persecution of Christians," ch. 4 in Elaine Pagels, *The Gnostic Gospels* (New York: Random House, 1979), 70–101.

were discarded. No overarching explanation can account for every aspect of Jewish influence on Christian development, nor can it be assumed that Jewish influence produced uniform development in every area of Jewish-Christian contact. We would not be far amiss, however, to look for some Jewish influence in most of the developments in Christianity in the first century. The theme of martyrdom is of particular interest here. This theme dominates much of Ignatius's writings, and it would be unwise to attempt to understand Ignatius's attention to this theme without an examination of this concern in Antioch's political and religious environment, particularly as it relates to Judaism. As already seen, an atmosphere of suspicion marked Jewish-Gentile relations in Antioch in the years prior to Ignatius. Christians, so closely connected to Judaism, would have been at risk along with Jews in a world where boundaries and identity were still matters of dispute. The Jewish reflection on martyrdom in periods of such crises probably would have some audience in Christian circles also.

It has been customary to attribute most of the features in the Christian view of martyrdom to mainly Jewish influence.[87] Some scholars, however, dismiss or qualify Jewish influence on early Christian ideas of martyrdom.[88] G. W. Bowersock rejects the Jewish connection outright, identifying a Gentile environment

---

[87] Michael J. Wilkins, "The Interplay of Ministry, Martyrdom, and Discipleship in Ignatius of Antioch," in *Worship, Theory, and Ministry in the Early Church* (ed. Michael J. Wilkins and Terence Paige; Sheffield: JSOT Press, 1992), 306–8. Wilkins points to the influence of Karl H. Rengstorf, "μαθητής," in *Theological Dictionary of the New Testament* (ed. G. Kittel and G. Friedrich; trans. G. W. Bromiley; 10 vols.; Grand Rapids: Eerdmans, 1964–1976), 4:415–61. Robert M. Grant argues that it is likely that Ignatius's ideas of martyrdom reflect traditional views ("Scripture and Tradition," 51–52). W. H. C. Frend, who wrote a major work on martyrdom, finds compelling Jewish connections for the Christian view of martyrdom (*Martyrdom and Persecution in the Early Church* [Oxford: Blackwell, 1965]). For a brief summary of Frend's position, see his "Martyrdom and Political Oppression," in *The Early Christian World* (ed. Philip F. Esler; 2 vols.; New York: Routledge, 2000), 2:815–39.

[88] See the collection of articles in Jan Willem van Henten, ed., *Die Entstehung der jüdischen Martyrologie* (Leiden: E. J. Brill, 1989). See also Arthur J. Droge and James D. Tabor, *A Noble Death: Suicide and Martyrdom among Christians and Jews in Antiquity* (San Francisco: Harper, 1992); and esp. G. W. Bowersock, *Martyrdom and Rome* (Cambridge: Cambridge University Press, 1995). But such approaches have not escaped criticism. Robin Darling Young (*In Procession before the World: Martyrdom as Public Liturgy in Early Christianity* [Père Marquette Lecture in Theology, 2001; Milwaukee: Marquette University Press, 2001], 5) dismisses Bowersock's rejection of the Jewish influences on Christian martyrdom and points to other recent works of importance on the theme. Bowersock is challenged, too, by Daniel Boyarin, "Martyrdom and the Making of Christianity and Judaism," *JECS* 6 (1998): 577–627; repr. in modified form as ch. 4 in *Dying for God: Martyrdom and the Making of Christianity and Judaism* (Stanford, Calif.: Stanford University Press, 1999). See also Frend, "Martyrdom and Political Oppression," 817–19. For a collection and discussion of primary texts, see Jan Willem van Henten and Friedrich

in which the idea of martyrdom—or noble death—developed: "Without the glorification of suicide in the Roman tradition, the development of martyrdom in the second and third centuries would have been unthinkable."[89] Bowersock is thinking, in particular, of the heroic suicides of Stoic philosophers and of the popular legends of Lucretia and Scaevola.[90] He even maintains that "*without Rome, a* μάρτυς *would have remained what he or she had always been, a 'witness' and no more.*"[91] In other words, the concept of a witness *standing firm till death* would not have arisen without the idea of a positive dimension of suicide in the Greco-Roman philosophical tradition.

Without dismissing useful insights in Bowersock's work, there are two fundamental problems with his approach that leave open the possibility of early Jewish concepts of martyrdom. First, Bowersock seems to assume that Jews could not have had a concept of martyrdom without also having a fixed technical term to identify the concept. At least, his argument is primarily about when the word μάρτυς and its associated cognates came to be used in the ancient Mediterranean world in a restrictive way to denote "heroic death"—or what we know as "martyrdom."[92]

Bowersock makes a number of observations that he considers important to the discussion. He points out that "Ignatius betrays no knowledge of the language *or concept* of martyrdom," and that Ignatius "never once availed himself of the term 'martyr.'"[93] Yet Bowersock is prepared to admit that Christians had "an intense and seemingly irrational desire to die at the hands of persecutors" before the creation of the terminology and that Ignatius "certainly longed for death."[94] Bowersock then makes a most questionable distinction: "As the case of Ignatius reminds us, one must consider *the desire for death* in conjunction with the concept of *martyrdom*. But they are not the same."[95] There is a fundamental problem with Bowersock's distinction. Were we to change Bowersock's phrase "desire for death" in the quotation to "desire for death *for a cause*," which is certainly in Ignatius, are we not then speaking of martyrdom, and if not, how delicately can we split this hair?

Bowersock's point seems to be that until the middle of the second century, Christians did not use the word μάρτυς to speak of voluntary death. Yet this fact in itself does not mean that such an association is completely absent from the

---

Avemarie, *Martyrdom and Noble Death: Selected Texts from Graeco-Roman, Jewish, and Christian Antiquity* (New York: Routledge, 2002).

[89] Bowersock, *Martyrdom and Rome*, 72.

[90] Ibid., 73.

[91] Ibid.

[92] Bowersock argues that the term μάρτυς was not employed in a technical sense until the middle of the second century C.E. (ibid., 5, 13). The earlier use of the term meant "witness," and it was used in a wide variety of contexts.

[93] Ibid., 15 (emphasis added).

[94] Ibid., 6.

[95] Ibid., 7 (emphasis added).

term. The fact is that the word μάρτυς did later become the technical term for the concept of martyrdom, and it is doubtful that the association came to mind out of the blue, without reference to any past sensibilities. Bowersock himself admits that Ignatius "sounds so much like a martyr"[96] and that Ignatius "would undoubtedly qualify as a voluntary martyr in terms of his actions."[97] We can at least conclude on the basis of this evidence that the *idea* of witness was probably a dominant or favorite association that early Christians made with martyrdom and, indeed, that such an association is necessary to explain how the term for the concept of witness became the technical term for martyrdom.[98]

The *concept* of martyrdom is certainly recognizable through much of early Christian literature even though it was not tagged with a technical term of its own.[99] If the concept of martyrdom could be a topic of reflection in earliest Christianity without a distinctive technical term to identify it, surely such could have been the case in Judaism also, and this weakens Bowersock's claims. His position is further weakened in that he too readily dismisses material that could be taken to indicate that Jews had developed a concept of martyrdom before attaching a technical term for it. For example, he says that the story of the fiery furnace "hardly constitutes anything like martyrdom" because it "had a happy ending."[100] One might argue against Bowersock, however, that stories with a happy ending are the more powerful stories of the witnessing aspect of martyrdom, for it is only the concept of witness—the term later used for martyrdom—that is featured; death does not occur. In addition, the stories of the fiery furnace and Daniel in the lions' den, both of which have "happy endings," become important themes in Christian art and literature about persecution and martyrdom.[101] Further evidence still against this claim is the perception of informed Romans on the matter: Tacitus, for example, says that Jews think that those who die in battle or torture are immortal and that for this reason they have a contempt of death (*Hist.* 5.5). Such a comment suggests that an ideal of martyrdom likely was present in Jewish thinking by the time of Ignatius. This view is not different from how Josephus saw the matter, where Jews would die rather than violate their religious sensibilities (*Ag. Ap.* 2.33).

---

[96] Ibid., 8.

[97] Ibid., 6.

[98] As van Henten and Avemarie note, "The phenomenon of martyrdom is older than the Christian or Jewish terminology that indicates it" (*Martyrdom and Noble Death,* 3).

[99] The idea of being faithful in face of death is a theme throughout much of early Christian literature before this time. Such material frequently highlights suffering, persecution, and executions—granted, without technical terms but not without a clear *concept* of martyrdom.

[100] Bowersock, *Martyrdom and Rome,* 7.

[101] More information about the use of these themes appears in Christian material. Both Daniel and the Hebrews of the fiery furnace story are counted as victims of persecution in *1 Clem.* 45.4–8 and in Tertullian, *De jejunio adversus psychicos* 9. The apocryphal *Acts of Paul* 7 describes Paul's encounter with a lion as an event of similar kind to Daniel's encounter.

Another problem for Bowersock's thesis is that it fails to explain why early advocates of Christian martyrdom routinely appealed to Jewish examples in support of their case and how they were able to do so without explaining to their audiences that the Jewish victims were themselves proper martyrs in the same sense as were the executed Christians.[102] The identification of pious victims of civil violence in the Hebrew Bible as "martyrs" seems to be assumed by author and audience alike. This being so, it is much more likely that the traditional view of Jewish influence on Christian themes of martyrdom remains a reasonable hypothesis. Bowersock, in his appeal to philosophical suicides in the Roman world, shows, at most, possible influences on the *development* of Christian concepts of martyrdom and the story tradition in which martyrdom is preserved, but this is not the same as locating the *origins* or the *dynamism* of the concept. Christian reflection on martyrdom was sufficiently early and widespread to require that if the idea was not borrowed from Judaism, it was a creation of the Christian genius itself but, even then, probably not without some reflection on the Jewish past.[103]

Bowersock spends too much time tracing the development of a *term* for martyrdom instead of the development of the *concept* of martyrdom. His line of argument cannot bear the weight he places on it.[104]

The Religious Test

Greco-Roman religion was not designed to produce martyrs. It was generally tolerant of a diversity of beliefs, mainly because the divine world was viewed as diverse and each power deserved its particular recognition and respect.[105] Gods

---

[102] Matt 5:12; 23:29–37; Acts 7:52; Rom 11:3; 1 Thess 2:15; Jas 5:10. Ignatius follows this tradition (Ign. *Magn.* 8.2), as does *Barnabas* (5.11), and *1 Clement* (54). The book of Revelation mentions the killing of prophets several times; some scholars think that these instances may be references to Christian prophets.

[103] The examination of the Jewish contribution to ideas of martyrdom often focuses on the Maccabean martyrdom traditions (Cummins, *Paul and the Crucified Christ in Antioch*, 54–90; Jan Willem van Henten, *The Maccabean Martyrs as Saviours of the Jewish People: A Study of 2 and 4 Maccabees* (Supplements to the Journal for the Study of Judaism 57; Leiden: E. J. Brill, 1997). More specifically, the debate centers on whether Ignatius was familiar with 4 Maccabees, a debate that revolves mainly around the date of the book. Trevett argues for at least the plausibility that Ignatius's thinking was shaped by an "environment where ideas and language like those of *IV Maccabees* were present" (*A Study of Ignatius,* 25). There is general agreement that if Ignatius did not use 4 Maccabees, both Ignatius and the author of 4 Maccabees shared the same milieu, which even Bowersock recognizes (*Martyrdom and Rome,* 79). See also Allen Brent, *Ignatius of Antioch,* 116–18.

[104] It is another matter, and one much debated, how the word "witness" (μάρτυς) became the technical term "martyr." Bowersock points to Brox, *Zeuge und Märtyrer,* still the standard work on the subject.

[105] The view of the widely tolerant religious attitudes in the Greco-Roman world may overstate the situation. See Rebecca Lyman, "Hellenism and Heresy," *JECS* 11 (2003): 209–22.

would be honored at the appropriate occasions, and in times of personal crises or national action, the gods would be consulted. Generally, there seems not to have been armies of zealous crusaders, fighting and dying for the gods.[106] The gods had their own fights—family squabbles that one had best avoid.

Even the Jews, whose much more exclusivist religious perspective stood in sharp contrast to the more tolerant Greco-Roman attitudes, generally were left unmolested by the larger society, even though Jewish particularism appeared odd and provoked curiosity and comment from time to time.[107] On only a few occasions did Jewish religion become the focus of attention and action by the larger society, putting the pious Jew in jeopardy and in a few cases forcing Jews to choose between life and religious faithfulness. Even then, religion rarely seems to have been the primary cause of the crisis. Other matters provoked the crisis, and religion became a useful way to identify or compromise opponents.

Josephus reports an incident that delineates a test that was used to identify suspects. Jews under suspicion of plotting to burn the city of Antioch were required to sacrifice "in the manner of the Greeks."[108] Those who refused to do so were condemned as plotters against Rome and were executed. The irony in this is that what to the Romans was a test of political loyalty was to the Jews a test of religious loyalty, and the test could really only accurately reveal the latter, as Tertullian caustically pointed out when the test was applied to Christians.[109] We do not know whether the situation Josephus described reflects the first use of the test under the Romans; tests of similar kind had been employed in Palestine under the Hellenizing efforts of Antiochus IV almost three hundred years earlier.[110] The consequence of refusing to sacrifice was clear: Jews would be executed. Thus

---

[106] Van Henten and Avemarie, *Martyrdom and Noble Death*, 5.

[107] Tacitus, *Hist.* 5.1–13.

[108] Josephus, *J. W.* 7.50–51. Pliny the Younger used a similar test to identify unrepentant Christians. He had Christians repeat a formula of invocation to the gods and make an offering of wine and incense to Trajan's statue. Josephus does not indicate that Jews had to sacrifice to the emperor, although, given the circumstances, it is at least probable. With Pliny's test for Christians, a special component was added: they were forced to revile the name of Christ. Pliny's method was simply to ask the accused three times whether they were Christians. A repeated affirmative reply on the third posing of the question would lead to execution. See W. H. C. Frend, "The Persecutions: Some Links between Judaism and the Early Church," *JEH* 9 (1958): 141–58; note esp. pp. 144–46 for comments on the effort to force Jews to profane God's name and to offer sacrifice.

[109] Tertullian, *Apologeticus* 35–37.

[110] 1 Macc 1:41–64. Although a number of offenses are listed for which execution could result, it appears that the routine and easiest test was to require Jews to sacrifice (1:51; 2:15, 23; see also 2 Macc 6:7–9). Sometimes the emphasis is on eating pork or meat that had been offered to idols. The stories in Daniel fit the situation of the times, with pious Hebrews refusing to eat the proscribed foods or bow in worship to an image of the emperor (Dan 1:5–16; 3:5–28).

there seems to have been a clear connection established in Judaism between religious loyalty and martyrdom before any Christian reflection on the matter, although Jews rarely found themselves facing such stark choices.[111]

The Christian Evidence

Early Christian literature on martyrdom stands in line with Jewish reflection, routinely addressing the suffering[112] and death[113] that the faithful might face. Ignatius's own reflection on the theme, however nuanced to fit his particular situation and mental state, is not out of step with early Christian attitudes. In other Christian literature associated with Antioch, the same theme surfaces. Even aside from the most obvious, numerous, and powerful references to suffering and death— those of Jesus himself—Matthew's Gospel is surprisingly full of warnings of the persecution and killing of the faithful.[114] Matthew 5:11–12 assumes that Christians will be persecuted on account of Christ, and he compares the persecution of Christians to the persecution of the Hebrew prophets as experiences of the same

---

[111] Granted, the crisis was not empire-wide, but the incident reported by Josephus was in Antioch, and it was there that Ignatius's ideas of martyrdom most likely took shape. The probable composition of 4 Maccabees in the late first or early second century in Antioch suggests a situation in which incidents of religious tension could place the Jewish community in jeopardy or focus their reflection on the theme of persecution and martyrdom. That Christians would have escaped such pressures is unlikely.

[112] This section omits all references to suffering (of which there are many) that are not explicitly located in a context of hostile action from outsiders or might not easily be read this way by early Christians (Matt 5:10–12, 44; 10:23; 23:34; John 15:20; Acts 9:16; Rom 12:14; 1 Cor 4:12; 2 Cor 1:3–11; Gal 4:29; 5:11; 6:12; Phil 1:29; 3:10; Col 1:24; 1 Thess 2:2, 14; 3:4; 2 Thess 1:4–5; 2 Tim 1:8, 12; 2:3, 9; 3:11–12; 1 Pet 2:20–21; 3:17; 4:1, 13–19; 5:9–10). There is also Paul's own confession that he persecuted the church (1 Cor 15:9; Gal 1:13, 23; Phil 3:6), together with traditions supporting Paul's claim (Acts 7:57–8:3; 9:1; 22:4; 26:11; 1 Tim 1:12–16); see Martin Hengel, "The Pre-Christian Paul," 29–52. The theme is found in other early Christian literature (1 Clem. 5; Did. 1.7; Martyrdom of Polycarp 12.3; Justin, Dial. 110.4; 131.2; 133.6; 1 Apol. 1.31). In early Christian literature, Christians often name Jews as their persecutors, although such accusations are thought to have been exaggerated. See Lieu, "Accusations of Jewish Persecution in Early Christian Sources." See also Abraham J. Malherbe, The Letters to the Thessalonians: A New Translation with Introduction and Commentary (AB 32B; New York: Doubleday, 2000), 172–79.

[113] Matt 10:28; 23:34, 37; John 16:2; 24:9; Acts 5:33; 23:12–14; 1 Thess 2:15; Rev 2:10, 13; 6:11; 11:7; 13:15. In addition, the early Christian writings routinely refer to the killing of Jesus. Many of the early apostles seem to have suffered martyrdom, and however legendary some of the traditions are, the martyrdom or persecution of some notables seems certain: Peter and Paul (1 Clem. 5), James the brother of John (Acts 12:2), James the brother of Jesus (Josephus, Ant. 20.200–201), and John the author of Revelation (Rev 1:9).

[114] The correlation between the comments about persecution in Matthew's Gospel and the real situation is the subject of debate. See Gundry, Matthew, 649; and Hare, The Theme of Jewish Persecution of Christians.

sort, much as Ignatius does (see Ign. *Magn.* 8.2). Such warnings surface again a few chapters later in Matthew's Gospel: believers are like sheep among wolves; they will be brought before councils, governors and kings; they will be flogged in synagogues, betrayed by family, and persecuted from town to town—all because of the Name. The one who endures to the end will be saved (Matt 10:16–23). Then follows a series of short admonitions that would become routine words of encouragement to future Christian martyrs: "do not fear those who kill the body but cannot kill the soul"; "everyone therefore who acknowledges me before others, I also will acknowledge before my Father"; "whoever does not take up the cross and follow me is not worthy of me"; "those who lose their life for my sake will find it" (10:28, 32, 38, 39). The theme of taking up the cross is repeated a few chapters later, as is the paradoxical promise that those who lose their life for Christ's sake will find it (16:24–25). Later Jesus indicts his opponents as the "descendants of those who murdered the prophets," and he charges that they themselves will do the same to the prophets sent to them—killing, crucifying, flogging in synagogues, and pursuing from town to town—so that, says Jesus, "upon you may come all the righteous blood shed on earth, from the blood of the righteous Abel to the blood of Zachariah" (23:29–35). The apocalyptic warnings in Matthew set out similar conditions: believers will be tortured and put to death for the Name, but the one who endures to the end will be saved (24:9–13).[115]

If Matthew's Gospel was written in Antioch or Syria (as most think likely), it bears witness to an environment in which Christians could expect persecution and even execution. This gospel is replete with the expectation of persecution. Its tone certainly makes the situation faced by Ignatius and his response to it seem in tune with the character of the times. Yet much of the recent scholarship on Ignatius asserts the opposite, ruling out Jewish or Roman initiation of the action in Ignatius's case and contending that some internal problem in the Christian community must have provoked governmental intervention. Even a hasty reading of Matthew's writing, coming from the same area as Ignatius, makes it difficult to understand why many Ignatian scholars seem unwilling to consider the possibility of placing the responsibility for Ignatius's situation on the doorstep of the synagogue or the civil government.[116]

---

[115] It matters not that this alert is in a passage of eschatological warning. The passage would have caught the attention of early readers of Matthew's Gospel as something particularly relevant to their situation.

[116] The *Didache*, which is particularly influenced by Matthew or by a world shared with Matthew, is likewise associated with Antioch or Syria by many scholars. Although the Didache does not portray a community under threat from Jews, as does Matthew, the document does begin and end with admonitions suggesting that such a threat lies near the surface of the community's reflection. The document begins by encouraging readers to bless those who curse them, pray for their enemies, fast for those who persecute them, and love those who hate them (*Did.* 1.3). The tone at the end is similar: people will hate

Judaism and Ignatius's Dilemma

In much of contemporary scholarship, Ignatius is removed far from any contact with Judaism or Jews, friendly or hostile. His plight arises from some internal church dispute. Even those who are prepared to admit that Ignatius's difficulties stemmed from external matters usually seek the root in a civil persecution of the Christian community without specifying the matter that provoked the intervention of the authorities.

Ignatius mentions that he is in bonds for the Name,[117] and he routinely connects his status as prisoner with the cause of Christ, as do those who meet him.[118] In only one place does Ignatius offer what might be a hint about the source or cause of persecution. Pointing to the Hebrew prophets, he says that they were persecuted because they lived according to Christ rather than according to Judaism (Ign. *Magn.* 8.1–2). He then connects the new hope in which Christians live with some kind of endurance (Ign. *Magn.* 9.1–2), a word that he sometimes associates with martyrdom.[119]

It is difficult to know exactly what this comment means, for Ignatius rarely speaks explicitly about why he faces martyrdom. There is no suggestion of anything else having prompted his conviction. Ignatius seems to present his situation as one that developed from external hostilities from either Jews or the larger Greco-Roman society.[120] Even if we cannot be certain that such was the case, this is a far more likely hypothesis than one that puts the blame on an internal crisis in the church at Antioch against a backdrop of a benign world of Jews and pagans (see the next chapter).

---

one another and persecute and betray, but "they who endure in their faith shall be saved" (16.4–5). The document is less clear about whether this threat arises from those outside the community, those inside, or both.

[117] Ign. *Eph.* 1.2; 3.1; Ign. *Magn.* 1.2.

[118] Ign. *Eph.* 11.2; Ign. *Trall.* 1.1; 5.2; 10.1; 12.2; Ign. *Rom.* 1.1; 4.3; Ign. *Phld.* 5.1; Ign. *Smyrn.* 10.2; 11.1; Ign. *Pol.* 2.3.

[119] Ign. *Eph.* 3.1; Ign. *Magn.* 1.2; Ign. *Smyrn.* 4.2, 5.1.

[120] Chadwick links the two: Ignatius tried to "widen the gulf between the Christian house churches and the synagogues; the resulting disturbances bring in the Roman authorities" (*The Church in Ancient Society*, 68).

CHAPTER 5

The "Peace" in Antioch

The Traditional View

The Roman authorities convicted Ignatius of a capital offense and sentenced him to death in the Roman arena. Scholars have differed about what led to Ignatius's plight. According to the older view, Ignatius was the victim of an anti-Christian persecution.[1] This makes some sense of the evidence. Ignatius was on his way to martyrdom, and the situation entailed Roman action of some sort. If the charge stemmed from organized governmental action against Christians, Ignatius's church would have been equally at risk. Indeed, the church would have been perhaps even more at risk now that their leader was convicted and absent and the authorities were scrutinizing the Christian movement more closely. Ignatius, every bit the proper bishop, was more concerned about the plight of his threatened church than about his own plight, an attitude clearly reflected in his letters, written on his journey to martyrdom in Rome.

This understanding of Ignatius's situation in Antioch, put forward in detail by J. B. Lightfoot, has been challenged and largely dismissed by scholars who have contended that there is no historical evidence of a persecution in Antioch at this time.[2] They maintain that the civil authorities generally left Christians unmolested until the Christians themselves created a situation that demanded intervention. In the case of Antioch, they contend, a bitter internal conflict in the church finally became so out of hand that it poured into the streets, so to speak, making governmental intervention necessary for the common good. Only then did the Roman authorities take action. The clearest target was Ignatius, the leader of the church, who either willingly offered himself to absorb the wrath of the government or was fingered by opponents within the church as the man responsible. Thus the Roman government was involved only as a secondary player.

---

[1] P. N. Harrison provides a good review of the positions (*Polycarp's Two Epistles*, 79–106), although he has little sympathy for the traditional view. He points out that as early as the seventeenth century, an alternative view was available (p. 81).

[2] Lightfoot, *S. Ignatius, S. Polycarp*, 1:1–22.

If it can be established that the problem in Antioch was mainly an *internal* church dispute, it becomes easy to point to Ignatius, the bishop, as the individual who had failed in some way. According to the now popular view of the situation, Ignatius's frequently expressed concern about unworthiness in his letters would then make sense. External persecution, unprovoked by Christian internal conflict, would not have made Ignatius accountable for the situation in Antioch, and his sense of unworthiness would be puzzling, so it is argued.

This newer reconstruction, put forward in detail in 1936 by P. N. Harrison, is the dominant view. It has been adopted and developed by Hammond Bammel, Schoedel, Rius-Camps, Swartley, Trevett, and most other leading Ignatian scholars,[3] with few dissenting voices.[4] Schoedel, in his influential commentary on Ignatius, contends that the church at Antioch was fractured by dissent and that it was likely that "the secular authorities of Antioch chose to try to frighten Christians into conformity or to maintain a lower profile by removing their leader."[5] Hammond Bammel, quoting Rius-Camps with approval, maintains, "There had been a public disturbance due to internal discord in the church at Antioch. . . . This had attracted the attention of the authorities and . . . Ignatius [gave] himself up as responsible."[6] Trevett examines the various options others have offered and concludes that internal conflict is the most likely explanation of the situation in Antioch.[7]

To some extent, scholars find the newer reconstruction convincing because of Harrison's detailed analysis of Ignatius's vocabulary and the even more detailed statistical analysis of vocabulary offered by Willard Swartley almost four decades after Harrison's study. Schoedel, for example, describes Harrison's argu-

---

[3] Hammond Bammel, "Ignatian Problems," 62–97; Schoedel, *Ignatius of Antioch;* idem, "Theological Norms and Social Perspectives in Ignatius of Antioch," in *The Shaping of Christianity in the Second and Third Centuries* (vol. 1 of *Jewish and Christian Self-Definition;* ed. E. P. Sanders; Philadelphia: Fortress, 1980), 30–56; J. Rius-Camps, *The Four Authentic Letters of Ignatius;* Willard M. Swartley, "The Imitatio Christi in the Ignatian Letters," *VC* 27 (1973): 81–103; Christine Trevett, "Ignatius 'To the Romans' and I Clement LIV–LVI," *VC* 43 (1989): 35–52; Frederic W. Schlatter, "The Restoration of Peace in Ignatius's Antioch," *JTS* 35 (1984): 465–69; Corwin, *St. Ignatius;* Robert Joly, *Le dossier d'Ignace d'Antioche* (Éditions de l'Université de Brussels, 1979); Judith Lieu, *Image and Reality,* 25.

[4] An exception is Mikael Isacson, "Follow Your Bishop! Rhetorical Strategies in the Letters of Ignatius of Antioch," in *The Formation of the Early Church* (ed. Jostein Ådna; WUNT 183; Tübingen: Mohr Siebeck, 2005), 322–23.

[5] Schoedel, *Ignatius of Antioch,* 11. Although Schoedel links government action to a conflict within the church at Antioch, the reality is that the authorities could have taken the action they did for any number of reasons.

[6] Hammond Bammel, "Ignatian Problems," 78.

[7] Trevett, "Ignatius 'To the Romans.'"

ments as "persuasive"[8] and quotes Swartley's work with approval;[9] others echo this opinion.[10] But these studies, though widely praised, are seriously flawed, and any reconstruction built on Harrison's or Swartley's work needs to be reconsidered. This chapter offers a detailed examination of the arguments put forward by Harrison and Swartley, since so much of our understanding of Ignatius depends on their reconstruction of the situation in Antioch at the time of Ignatius's arrest.

Harrison's Study of Ignatius's Vocabulary

Everyone grants that Ignatius was deeply troubled when he passed through Asia Minor. This might be expected, as his journey to hungry beasts and execution in Rome grew nearer each day. But what makes Ignatius's worried state so strange is that he is not distressed that he is going to die. Quite the opposite: he is distressed that he might escape death either by his own weakness or by the intervention of friends.[11] He also has a second concern, related to an unspecified situation affecting his church in Antioch, which he left a few weeks earlier.[12] The two concerns may be related, but they need not be.[13]

The main problem facing any reconstruction of the situation in Antioch is that we have only the comments of Ignatius himself about the matter, and these are ambiguous.[14] In each letter to churches in Asia Minor and Rome, Ignatius

---

[8] Schoedel summarizes eight points he finds convincing in Harrison's argument ("Theological Norms," 37). But as we will show, there is little that is compelling in Harrison's argument, and there is less in the argument of Swartley, which Schoedel also accepts.

[9] Schoedel, *Ignatius of Antioch*, 11.

[10] Trevett may be the exception. Although she closely follows Harrison's arguments regarding vocabulary, she makes no reference to Swartley's work. Whether this reflects her opinion of Swartley's arguments is not clear ("Ignatius 'To the Romans,'" 34–40).

[11] See especially Ignatius's letter *To the Romans*, which is profoundly shaped by the concern that Ignatius's martyrdom might be prevented or might fail. Other letters offer hints of this concern as well (Ign. *Eph.* 1.2; 3.1; Ign. *Smyrn.* 7.1).

[12] Ignatius is not specific in his request for prayer for the church in Antioch (Ign. *Eph.* 21.2; Ign. *Magn.* 14; Ign. *Trall.* 13.1; Ign. *Rom.* 9.1). Only after he receives good news that the matter in Antioch is resolved does he mention that the church there has gained "peace" (Ign. *Phld.* 10.1; Ign. *Smyrn.* 11.2; Ign. *Pol.* 7.1–2).

[13] Trevett connects the two issues (*A Study of Ignatius*, 60). Others seem to assume such a connection.

[14] There is also a comment by Polycarp in his letter to the Philippians that seems to refer to other martyrs at the time of Ignatius (Pol. *Phil.* 9.1–2). This could point to a more significant persecution than proposed by Harrison and others, but the matter is debated. Trevett thinks that other Christian prisoners may have been in the transport to Rome ("Ignatius 'To the Romans,'" 37). Hammond Bammel comments on the matter briefly. Although she thinks that Ignatius's plight is better explained by internal church conflict, she notes the evidence for the possibility of persecution, pointing to Ignatius's comments

writes of the situation in his home church, first urging prayer for the church of Antioch and then, upon hearing the good news that the church has gained peace (εἰρηνεύειν), encouraging church leaders to travel to Antioch to congratulate the church on its new and happy state. Unfortunately, the words that Ignatius uses to describe the circumstances in Antioch are general enough to apply to almost any situation where security or concord is gained in the face of a perceived threat or open conflict. Ignatius's descriptions of the situation in Antioch do not tell us much more than that a bad situation has been changed into a good one.

Harrison was convinced that he could wrestle more from Ignatius's language.[15] But in spite of the wide acceptance of Harrison's analysis, the evidence he offers only weakly supports his conclusions. His case rests on five words used by Ignatius when speaking of the situation in Antioch. All five are ambiguous but clearly positive. Scholars who support a persecution thesis have found the words amenable to a description of the termination of civil repression. Scholars who argue for a thesis of schism in Ignatius's church find the language equally amenable to a description of the restoration of unity. Harrison recognized that if his reconstruction were to be convincing, he would need to demonstrate that the words under examination could not fit a context of persecution.

Two of the words Harrison examines are drawn from the world of shipping and travel (εὐδία [calm weather] and λιμήν [haven]). The first is employed once by Ignatius (Ign. Smyrn. 11.3), the second twice (Ign. Smyrn. 11.3, Ign. Pol. 2.3). These words, however, are too general to be of any help in determining the precise situation at Antioch. Harrison's effort to preclude the use of "haven" and "calm weather" from describing the cessation of persecution[16] and the efforts of others to link such words to secession of internal strife[17] fail to give adequate weight to the primary sense of these words. The words indicate security—but security specifically from what must be determined by other clues Ignatius might offer.

(Ign. Rom. 5.2; 10.1) and Polycarp's mention of Zosimus and Rufus as possible prisoners (Pol. Phil. 9.2) ("Ignatian Problems," 78, n. 2). One might also point to Polycarp's comments in Pol. Phil. 12.3: "Pray also for kings and magistrates and rulers, as well as for those who persecute and hate you and for the enemies of the cross." The most natural reading of this passage suggests civil persecution. Harrison, though admitting the possibility of other martyrs, points out that nothing demands that these individuals be from Antioch (Polycarp's Two Epistles to the Philippians, 90–91). Although this is true, the best guess is that they were. And does it really matter to the issue here if they were not?

[15] Harrison's hypothesis builds on the slightly earlier work of Streeter, who had argued that Ignatius's distress was rooted not in civil persecution of Christians but in conflict over the establishment of the episcopate as a monarchical office. According to Streeter, Ignatius remained distressed until he learned, while at Troas, that his candidate had been appointed in Antioch and that the monarchical office was secure (The Primitive Church, 170).

[16] Harrison, Polycarp's Two Epistles to the Philippians, 87–90.

[17] Trevett, "Ignatius 'To the Romans,'" 30.

The third word, σωματεῖον (corporate body), which is extremely rare in Greek literature, appears only once in Ignatius (Ign. *Smyrn.* 11.2). As with the first two words, σωματεῖον is general, indicating a positive state but supplying no details about this condition. Although Harrison and others have tried to demonstrate that this word could not have been used to describe the end of persecution, the case is not convincing.[18] Advocates of this position sometimes merely assume that the restoration of σωματεῖον must have involved a return to unity. For example, Schoedel argues that the word is positive rather than negative.[19] One could well agree with Schoedel on this point. But he goes on to conclude that therefore Ignatius must be speaking of unity. This conclusion does not necessarily follow.

To summarize our critique of Harrison's case to this point: three of the words upon which his hypothesis of internal conflict depends provide nothing more than a house of linguistic cards. The words specify a positive condition but generally nothing more specific. We would be little worse off in our attempt to specify the exact problem in Antioch had Ignatius used only words such as "good" and "bad."

The fourth word, μέγεθος (greatness), is also an ambiguous word, although, like the other words examined above, the meaning is clearly positive. This word appears three times in Ignatius (Ign. *Rom.* 3.3; Ign. *Smyrn.* 11.2; and Ign. *Eph.* intro.). Harrison points out that in two instances, Ignatius employs the word to identify a characteristic of a healthy church (Ign. *Rom.* 3.3; Ign. *Eph.* intro.). He then concludes that Ignatius must mean the same thing in the remaining passage (Ign. *Smyrn.* 11.2), which identifies the condition that the church in Antioch has recovered—internal peace, not peace from external persecution.[20] But Harrison has misread the evidence. Suppose we agree with Harrison that the use of the word μέγεθος for describing the situation in Antioch is ambiguous and in need of clarification from Ignatius's two other uses of this word.[21] One of the other

---

[18] Harrison, *Polycarp's Two Epistles to the Philippians,* 86–87.

[19] Schoedel, *Ignatius of Antioch,* 250–51. A negative interpretation arises because of another word of similar spelling (σωμάτιον), with which it is sometimes confused by scribes (Harrison, *Polycarp's Two Epistles to the Philippians,* 86).

[20] Harrison, *Polycarp's Two Epistles to the Philippians,* 84–86. Corwin agrees with Harrison (*St. Ignatius,* 28–29). She adds that the intensity with which Ignatius describes his opponents betrays a bitterness that makes best sense if a schism had damaged the church in Antioch but had not yet fractured the churches of Asia Minor. She further points out that Ignatius's anti-docetic polemic is "the warp and woof of his thinking" and something that he had been preaching in Antioch "perhaps for years" (p. 29), which she feels strengthens the seriousness of the case for schism in Antioch. But one can admit schism in Antioch without making it the cause of Ignatius's plight. Indeed, the longer the period of Ignatius's confrontation with the Docetists, the less likely a recent schism explains Ignatius's dilemma.

[21] The sentence reads, "For they have found peace and have recovered their own *greatness,* and their own corporate body has been restored to them" (Ign. *Smyrn.* 11.2; italics added).

instances of the word is equally ambiguous.[22] As with the other words already mentioned, this word has value in identifying a positive state, but it lacks any content for specifying what this positive state might be or how it arose. Indeed, on the basis of two of the three uses of the word μέγεθος, nothing more can be said about the state of the church in Antioch than that a positive condition has been recovered. Only in the third passage is there support for Harrison's position: "Christianity is a matter of greatness [μέγεθος], when it is hated by the world" (Ign. *Rom.* 3.3). Harrison's conclusion is that, given Ignatius's association of the word with being hated by the world, the church in Antioch would not have lost its μέγεθος from persecution but rather would have gained it. But Harrison's conclusion requires that he restrict the meaning of the word μέγεθος to this one kind of context.

We can evaluate the merits of Harrison's argument by examining the use of the English word "greatness," one of the meanings of μέγεθος. That anyone would confine an author's use of the English word "greatness" as much as Harrison confines the Greek word μέγεθος for Ignatius is doubtful. An author might well say that Christianity is a matter of greatness when it is hated by the world and in another letter say that a church that has just come through a period of persecution has recovered its greatness. Although Harrison does make a valid point about one way in which Ignatius is known to have used this word, the word is too general to bear the weight Harrison places on it.

Harrison's argument is also not helped by the fact that three of the five words he presents as crucial for understanding the situation in Antioch occur in one paragraph (Ign. *Smyrn.* 11). One can hardly conclude that Ignatius's letters are ripe with the kind of language essential to Harrison's reconstruction—whether ambiguous or otherwise.

The fifth word of Harrison's study is "peace," in both a noun form (εἰρήνη) and a verb form (εἰρηνεύειν).[23] In the three letters written from Troas, Ignatius uses these words to describe the state of his church at Antioch.[24] These words could be employed to indicate either the end of civil repression or the end of internal conflict. Harrison senses that he needs to dismiss the use of these words for specifying the end of persecution in Ignatius's case. He argues that the noun εἰρήνη was not used to describe the absence of persecution until after the period of the New Testament and

---

[22] "To the church that is blessed with *greatness* by the fullness of God the Father" (Ign. *Eph.* intro.; italics added).

[23] The order of Harrison's presentation is reversed here. He deals with the cognate "peace" first, then looks at other words that might be supportive of his case. Here, however, these supplementary words are examined first and their usefulness to the question is challenged; then Harrison's first point is examined. Although I agree with Harrison that the cognate "peace" is his strongest point, I disagree that his is the only possible interpretation.

[24] Ign. *Phld.* 10.1; Ign. *Smyrn.* 11.2; Ign. *Pol.* 7.1; 12.2.

the Apostolic Fathers, and he contends that the verb εἰρηνεύειν was never employed in this way.[25] Harrison then concludes that Ignatius must have intended the other possible meaning of the word—an absence of internal conflict—which would place Ignatius in the company of other Christian writers of the period.

Harrison too quickly disallows, however, the connection between the idea of peace and an end of persecution. Such a connection is found explicitly in 4 Maccabees,[26] a document with which many scholars think Ignatius was particularly familiar.[27] Furthermore, ancient writers frequently employed the word "peace" to indicate the cessation of war or a state opposite to war,[28] and Ignatius himself connects the two concepts in one case.[29] This indicates that the two terms ("war" and "peace") were commonly linked and that Ignatius was familiar with— and had used—this connection. Further, given that early Christians often spoke of their persecution by the state as "war" (as Harrison himself recognizes),[30] one would expect that Christians might easily have used words with the meaning "peace" to characterize the end of persecution. Thus, contrary to what Harrison contends, we might well anticipate Ignatius's use of the word "peace" to indicate the end of persecution. Further, Harrison's claim that Ignatius (or early Christian writers generally) *never* employed the word "peace" to describe the end of persecution is too sweeping, for Harrison fails to indicate what word these writers would have used *had they addressed the topic* of the end of persecution.[31] Finally, as Harrison himself admits, passages in the New Testament make a connection between peace and the end of persecution or repression of some kind,[32] and later

---

[25] Harrison, *Polycarp's Two Epistles to the Philippians*, 83–84.

[26] 4 Macc 18:3–4.

[27] Ignatius rarely quotes clearly, and the reader often must guess whether Ignatius is likely to have had a particular passage in mind or is simply using a common tradition. Nonetheless, a sense of the importance of the linguistic world of 4 Maccabees to Ignatius's thought is gained when one observes, for example, that of forty-two passages from the Old Testament and intertestamental writings that Schoedel considers in his commentary on Ignatius, about one-quarter are from 4 Maccabees (*Ignatius of Antioch,* 289).

[28] Homer's *Iliad* uses εἰρήνη and εἰρηνεύειν to indicate a state in which hostilities have ceased or in which hostilities are absent (2.797; 5.792; 6.37; 11.47; 21.571; 22.131).

[29] Ign. *Eph.* 13.2. This passage most clearly connects the word "peace" to the end of internal strife, and Harrison is justified in maintaining that Ignatius could use the word "peace" in this way. But even here, Ignatius connects the word "peace" with "war." Ignatius's use of these terms shows a range of meaning that Harrison fails to appreciate.

[30] Harrison, *Polycarp's Two Epistles to the Philippians*, 83. The book of Revelation, for example, is filled with this kind of language (Rev 9:7, 9; 11:7; 12:7, 17; 13:4, 7; 16:14; 17:14; 19:11, 19; 20:8).

[31] Harrison, *Polycarp's Two Epistles to the Philippians*, 83.

[32] John 16:33; Acts 7:31; Matt 10:34; Luke 14:32; 19:42–44; Acts 12:20; Rev 6:4. The word εἰρήνη has a considerable range of meanings in Christian literature, much as the English word "peace" has today. It may also be contrasted to division (Luke 12:51; Acts 7:26; 1 Cor 14:33). It is the latter meaning that Harrison emphasizes.

writers also used the word "peace" to describe the end of persecution.[33] Harrison fails to demonstrate convincingly that Ignatius could not have done the same or why, in light of the known link in Ignatius's mind between the terms "war" and "peace," Ignatius would not have turned to the word "peace" quite naturally to describe the end of persecution.

Harrison and others following him have shown that the word "peace" was used in a variety of ancient writings for the end of schism or group strife.[34] The significance of this observation is diminished, however, when we note that Ignatius frequently speaks of internal peace in churches *without* using the word εἰρήνη, a word that has become so central in the recent reconstructions of the situation at Antioch. In fact, Ignatius's favorite words for internal peace in a church are not based on the cognate εἰρήνη at all but on a complex of words such as "harmony" and "concord."[35] Thus, when Ignatius uses the word εἰρήνη to speak of the situation in Antioch, he does not draw from the stock of terms that he routinely employs to describe peace in the churches of western Asia Minor. Since the words that Ignatius uses to describe peace, harmony, or unity in the churches of Asia Minor are more than adequate to describe the resolution of internal conflict, one at least must wonder why Ignatius focuses on the word εἰρήνη for his description of the resolution of the problem at Antioch. Ignatius had a range of ways in which he could have expressed the resolution of internal disorder at Antioch, and the word εἰρήνη is *not* one of his favorites.

Perhaps the most telling point is that Ignatius never uses εἰρήνη to describe harmony or concord in the churches of Asia Minor.[36] Surely, if Ignatius's church in Antioch had recovered what the churches in Asia Minor had retained, Ignatius

---

[33] *Polycarp's Two Epistles to the Philippians,* 83.

[34] Harrison, *Polycarp's Two Epistles to the Philippians,* 83–84; Schoedel, *Ignatius of Antioch,* 212–13.

[35] See, for example, ἐν μιᾷ ὑποταγῇ (Ign. *Eph.* 2.2); συντρέχειν τῇ τοῦ ἐπισκόπου γνώμῃ (Ign. *Eph.* 4.1); τοὺς ἐγκεκραμένους (Ign. *Eph.* 5.1); ἐνώθητε τῷ ἐπισκόπῳ (Ign. *Magn.* 6.2); εἴ τις σχίζοντι ἀκολουθεῖ (Ign. *Phld.* 3.3); μερισμός (Ign. *Phld.* 8.1). Ignatius uses cognates of the word ἕνωσις twenty-five times and the word ὁμόνοια eight times. He uses a cognate of the word εἰρήνη or its cognate only six times (Ign. *Eph.* 13.2; Ign. *Trall.* intro.; Ign. *Phld.* 10.1; Ign. *Smyrn.* 11.2; 12.2; Ign. *Pol.* 7.1), and in only one instance of the word εἰρήνη is the context related to freedom from internal conflict (Ign. *Eph.* 13.1–2; see n. 36 below).

[36] The one possible instance of Ignatius's use of "peace" to indicate internal harmony is Ign. *Eph.* 13.2. Even here the connection is indirect. Ignatius mentions concord in the context of coming together more frequently and comments, "Nothing is better than peace, by which every battle is abolished, whether waged by those in heaven or by those on earth." But we cannot be sure, even from this case, that there were separate assemblies in Ephesus. Ignatius does say much earlier that one who does not come to the assembly has separated himself (5.3); this need not imply, however, separate assemblies, as it may mean merely infrequent attendance in the assembly, for whatever reason.

would have employed such positive vocabulary to describe the restored state of the church in Antioch. But he does not do this; rather, he employs a different term. Thus Ignatius's use of the word "peace" to describe the situation in Antioch, instead of clarifying the situation, introduces a new question.

All Harrison can reasonably conclude is that the five words he examines *could* have been used to indicate the cessation of internal conflict in the church at Antioch. He cannot demonstrate that these words could not have described just as adequately the cessation of persecution. These terms all have an element of ambiguity, as they are general enough to describe a wide range of situations where an issue that produced distress or conflict has been resolved. Unless the context is unambiguous, one must be careful not to force a more specific meaning than this on the vocabulary.[37]

Swartley's Study of Ignatius's Vocabulary

Building on Harrison's thesis, Willard Swartley argues that Ignatius's sense of unworthiness is affected by the situation in Antioch. By a detailed statistical analysis of vocabulary, Swartley tries to demonstrate that Ignatius's concern about his worthiness drops sharply when he hears that the church at Antioch has gained "peace."[38] Swartley concludes that "peace" must have meant the restoration of internal harmony rather than the end of a persecution and that Ignatius held himself personally responsible for the schism.

On the surface, Swartley's analysis of the change in Ignatius's sense of worthiness seems to provide a convincing statistical demonstration that Ignatius's self-doubts are related specifically to the lack of unity in his church at Antioch and that Ignatius's attitude is changed when he hears that his church has gained peace.[39] But a close examination of Swartley's statistical work shows that his data do not support his conclusions and cannot serve as a basis for confirming anything about the situation in the church at Antioch.[40]

Swartley's primary contention is that the vocabulary of the letters written before Ignatius learns the good news about Antioch differs from that in the letters written after this news. Swartley does not count the frequency of single words but

---

[37] Minute analysis of vocabulary often falls into the trap of confining the definition of a word to its meaning in a particular passage. Like the error of the old adage "Once is never, twice is always," we make too sweeping a statement on the basis of too little evidence.

[38] Swartley, "Imitatio Christi," 98.

[39] Ibid., 93.

[40] The criticism here of Swartley's article is limited to his attempts to determine what situation is described by Ignatius's comments that the church in Antioch had gained "peace." Although this is not the only matter treated in Swartley's article, it is a crucial matter and the one that has had the most influence on Ignatian scholarship.

of word clusters that he has determined to have similar meaning or interest. This can be a tenable procedure, for it permits one to pursue a *concept* rather than a mere word. But care must be taken to ensure that the cluster is meaningful and relatively complete, and here Swartley's analysis falls short. He puts an array of terms into what he calls his "ethical" cluster: thirteen words in addition to several compound words based on one of the words in the cluster.[41] Words suggesting worthiness, discipleship, and imitation might indeed fit together, but to allow words such as εὑρίσκω (find), πρέπω (be fitting), τυγχάνω (attain, happen), or ἐπιτυγχάνω (obtain) into the cluster compromises the integrity of the cluster as a meaningful, consistent group.[42] The last four words are general terms, yet these words account for 44 percent (62 of 142 instances) of the word occurrences that Swartley considers. We might overlook an occasional word or two that does not seem to fit the cluster were it not for the high stakes here. On the basis of the word clusters he compiled, Swartley finds "a very significant inverse correlation between the terms in the ethical cluster and the terms in the cluster on unity" reflected in the two groups of letters:[43]

> How does one explain this sudden lack of terms expressing Ignatius's concern that he be *worthy* of his immediate martyrdom? The increase of terms denoting unity is perhaps itself the answer. Further, since it is in this epistle (10.1) that Ignatius first knows that the church in Syria is now at peace, it is readily apparent that . . . *the unity of the church in Syria is the key that unlocks the door to understanding Ignatius's use of these ethical terms.*[44]

An examination of the evidence, however, does not support this conclusion. Even were we to generously grant some degree of integrity to Swartley's word clusters, his evidence can be challenged and his arguments refuted at almost every point.

First, Swartley's statistics do not demonstrate any clear differences between the vocabulary of the letters written before Ignatius received good news about Antioch and the letters written after, despite Swartley's contention. He can make his point only by appealing to the most extreme examples. According to his own figures, the significant change in vocabulary appears only in the letters to the *Romans* and the *Philadelphians* (Ign. *Rom.* 35; Ign. *Phld.* 9). None of the other letters

---

[41] Swartley complicates his investigation by choosing ambiguous labels for his clusters: "ethical," "Christological," "unity," and "obedience." He says that the last cluster "penetrates" the other three clusters ("Imitatio Christi," 90).

[42] Swartley does attempt to remove occurrences of these words that do not fit the clusters, identifying such passages as either "interpretation too problematic to evaluate" or "use is non-significant" (ibid., 96). Nonetheless, his effort is not convincing.

[43] Ibid., 91.

[44] Ibid., 93 (italics original).

shows any such changes.[45] Taking Swartley's own figures from his table A (line 2 of table A below), in the number of words from the ethical cluster, the letters to the *Smyrnaeans* and to *Polycarp,* written after the news, show no significant difference from the letters to the *Magnesians* and the *Trallians,* which were written before (fourteen and fifteen compared with twenty and seventeen). Swartley's conclusion can be made only by taking the two most extreme figures as representative cases. No letter has a greater wealth of ethical language than the letter to the Romans; none less than the letter to the Philadelphians. No letter has a greater wealth of language expressing unity than the letter to the Philadelphians; none less than the letter to the Romans. The thesis that Ignatius's vocabulary changes after he learns of the peace of the church in Antioch is not supported by the language of the majority of letters in the Ignatian corpus. Swartley's statistical analysis is flawed, for it rests on atypical cases, and the other letters in the corpus refute it.

Table A
"Ethical" Vocabulary in the Ignatian Letters

	written from Smyrna before "peace"				written from Troas after "peace"			
	Eph	Mag	Tral	Rom	Phld	Smyr	Pol	Total
1. lines	186	112	102	111	107	120	85	823
2. ethical words	32	20	17	35	9	14	15	142
3. ratio	5.8	5.6	6	3.2	11.9	8.6	5.7	5.8[46]

Second, Swartley does not usually consider the varying lengths of the letters in spite of the importance that document length has on questions of word frequency. Line 3 in table A indicates the frequency of ethical vocabulary on the basis of the length of the letters, in terms of the ratio of ethical cluster words to the number of lines. Clearly, when length is given due consideration, only the letters to the *Philadelphians* and the *Romans* may be counted as substantial anomalies. Thus Swartley's contention that the letters written before the news contain the greater number of ethical terms fails. Three of the letters (two written before the news and one after) are almost identical in the proportion of ethical words (5.8, 5.6, 5.7).

---

[45] The letter to the Ephesians (with thirty-two such words) appears to fall into line with that to the *Romans* (with thirty-five), but when the length of the letters is factored in, this similarity disappears, as will be shown in more detail below.

[46] The data in tables A and B are from Swartley's work or from my calculations based on Swartley's: line 1 (Swartley, pp. 96–97); line 2 (Swartley, p. 92); line 3 (calculated from lines 1 and 2).

Third, as mentioned previously, the word clusters are neither self-evident nor compelling. Other groupings could as reasonably have been made. We will look at a specific instance of the problem here. For example, why does Swartley add εὑρίσκω (find) to his list of ethical terms? By his own reckoning in his table B, one-third of the occurrences of this word are not relevant, and of the remaining sixteen, almost all appear within a passage with a noun from the same ethical cluster, which Swartley has already counted.[47] Indeed, in many cases εὑρίσκω acts as the verb to one of these nouns and clearly should not be counted as a separate occurrence for the ethical cluster, since to do so would artificially inflate the count. The data in line 3 of table B below show the ratio of ethical words to lines, with all occurrences of εὑρίσκω removed. Again, the results do not support Swartley's hypothesis. The letters to the *Romans* and the *Philadelphians* are the anomalies. The other letters, whether written before or after the news from Antioch, are grouped together in the middle, with three of these five letters (two from before the news of Antioch and one from after) being almost identical (7.4; 7.8; 7.1).

Table B
"Ethical" Vocabulary in the Ignatian Letters
with occurrences of εὑρίσκω omitted

	written from Smyrna before "peace"				written from Troas after "peace"			
	Eph	Mag	Tral	Rom	Phld	Smyr	Pol	Total
1. lines	186	112	102	111	107	120	85	823
2. ethical words	25	19	13	29	7	13	12	118
3. ratio	7.4	5.9	7.8	3.8	15.3	9.2	7.1	7.0

Fourth, other words that Swartley overlooked should have been included in the ethical cluster.[48] And the data should have included passages reflecting the sense of a word in Swartley's ethical cluster though not containing the precise word. Consider this passage: "But whatever he approves is acceptable to God, so that everything you do should be secure and valid" (Ign. *Smyrn.* 8.2). Or "Nothing will be lost to you. . . . Neither will the perfect hope, Jesus Christ, be ashamed of you" (Ign. *Smyrn.* 10.1–2). Should these passages not be included in the ethical

---

[47] Swartley, "Imitatio Christi," 94–95.

[48] Consider, for example, words from the cognate πιστ (faith). Ignatius says that "faith cannot do what is faithless nor can faithlessness do what is faithful" (Ign. *Eph.* 8.2). In Ign. *Eph.* 14.1, one is encouraged to "completely adhere to the faith and love that are in Jesus Christ." About fifty cognates of πιστ appear in the Ignatian letters. Surely some of these words deserve to be included in Swartley's various clusters.

cluster, containing words such as "worthy," "attaining," and "proper"? Yet neither passage is included in Swartley's lists. This observation could be repeated throughout the letters, and each omission from Swartley's list weakens further the credibility of his analysis.

Fifth, Swartley attempts to introduce the "context" into the statistical counts. In doing so, eleven different symbols or combinations of symbols are used to analyze the ethical terms associated with Ignatius's concern about his future and the terms associated with concerns about church unity.[49] Use of these symbols, however, introduces a cumbersome complexity into data that are already suspect. Yet the symbols are important to Swartley's contention that there is a connection between the ethical terms and Ignatius's concern about his future and his conclusion that it is the news from Antioch that explains certain differences—what Swartley calls a "more decisive" demonstration.[50] He contrasts the ethical terms associated with Ignatius's concern for his future with the ethical terms associated with his concern for church unity. On the basis of a detailed list of passages marked by codes to indicate the theme, Swartley tries to establish three main points:

(a) the number of ethical terms that show Ignatius's anxiety for his future will be proportionately higher in *Ephesians* to *Romans* than in *Philadelphians* to *Polycarp;*

(b) the number of ethical terms which show Ignatius's anxiety will constitute a higher percentage of the total number of ethical terms in the letters of *Ephesians* to *Romans* than in the letters of *Philadelphians* to *Polycarp;* and

(c) there will be significant indication throughout all the letters that the ethical terms are related to Ignatius's concern for church unity.[51]

For the sake of argument, let us accept Swartley's identification of the passages that show a concern for the future, or a concern for unity, or a mixture of these concerns (he offers four levels of mixture), even though, as just seen, there is little to encourage confidence in the identification. Let us grant, too, Swartley's first two points—(a) and (b)—for they follow from the undisputed fact that Ignatius reflects more anxiety about his future in the letters written from Smyrna than in the letters written from Troas. If Ignatius reflects less anxiety about his future in the letters written from Troas—*for whatever reason*—then certainly there will be fewer passages reflecting anxiety to which Swartley's ethical cluster might be attached. Nothing more revealing than this surfaces from Swartley's first two observations.

---

[49] Swartley, "Imitatio Christi," 96.

[50] Swartley, "Imitatio Christi," 97. Line 4 of table C below provides Swartley's percentages of ethical terms that reflect some concern by Ignatius for his future.

[51] Ibid., 93, 96.

Here again Swartley's methodology is suspect. He argues that three times as many ethical terms are related to concerns about church unity as to concerns about Ignatius's own future (totals of line 2 contrasted with totals of line 3, table C below—*with Romans omitted*), which would suggest, so Swartley contends, that Ignatius's self-doubts are related to the situation in Antioch. Since the calculations tell us only that Ignatius spoke about church unity more than about his future, Swartley's attempt to make this into something significant in support of his larger thesis fails.

It is Swartley's point (c) that, if supported, is substantial. The numbers Swartley offers (table C, line 3) seem at first to support his claim that after Ignatius hears about the unity of his church in Antioch, his ethical vocabulary drops.[52] But the striking differences evaporate when one examines the various passages closely, for many of the passages in which Swartley finds a link between ethical terms and concerns for church unity are dubious. For example, of the eleven passages identified within the letter to the Ephesians, at least six seem to reflect almost nothing about the theme of church unity (2.1; 2.2; 9.2; and 21.2, which Swartley lists three times). Indeed, the only way the theme of unity can be gleaned from Ign. *Eph.* 21.2 (which contains half of Swartley's count) is to assume that schism was the problem at Antioch. But this is the very thing that Swartley's statistical work is supposed to demonstrate.

Table C
"Ethical" Vocabulary in the Ignatian Letters
(expressing "future" and "unity" concerns)

	written from Smyrna before "peace"				written from Troas after "peace"			
	Eph	Mag	Tral	Rom	Phld	Smyr	Pol	Total
1. lines	186	112	102	111	107	120	85	823
2. future	8	3	8	22	1	1	0	43
3. unity	12	16	15	7	6	8	7	71
4. unity*	10	5	8	3	5	8	7	46
5. ratio (#1 to #4)	18.6	22.4	12.6	37.0	21.4	15.0	12.1	17.9[53]

omitting passages requiring the larger context

---

[52] Ibid., 97.

[53] The data in this table are from Swartley's work or from my calculations based on Swartley's data: lines 1 and 2 (Swartley, pp. 96–97); line 3 (Swartley, p. 97); line 4 (line 3 minus passages where Swartley had to appeal to the "larger context"); line 5 (line 1 divided by line 4). There are two discrepancies in Swartley's data. In his text, he reports 11 unity passages for Ephesus, but he offers 12 on his chart. He counts 7 unity passages for Philadelphia, but he offers 6 on his chart. The figures here are consistent with those on his chart C.

Sixth, many of the passages that Swartley identifies depend on what he calls "the larger context" rather than the immediate concern.[54] The problem for Swartley's analysis here is that the theme of unity is so dominant in Ignatius's letters that when we look to the wider context of almost any passage, we very likely will come into contact with some aspect of the theme of church unity. Should such passages be included in Swartley's tables? Line 4 of table C above provides the number of passages in which the theme of church unity is linked to ethical vocabulary, with those passages *excluded* that Swartley could identify only by appealing to the larger context. Swartley puts forward the data given in table C, line 3, showing the difference between the letters written from Smyrna (forty-two) and those written from Troas (twenty-two). A more reliable contrast is drawn from line 4, which excludes passages that Swartley could include only by appealing to the wider context. There the difference evaporates: the letters from Smyrna have twenty-two such words; the letters from Troas have twenty-one. We could look at things from another angle, with similar results, if we examine the ratio of ethical words by taking into account the length of each letter. The letter to the Magnesians, written from Smyrna, and the letter to the Philadelphians, written from Troas, are almost identical (22.4 to 21.4), as are the letters to Tralles (from Smyrna) and to Polycarp (from Troas) (12.6 to 12.1). Thus the supposed sharp contrast in vocabulary between the letters from Smyrna and the letters from Troas does not exist.

Seventh, among the three letters written after Ignatius learns that the church at Antioch has gained peace, only in one case does Swartley include a term under the category of "unity" based on the wider context. Yet for the letters written before the news, Swartley includes twenty-six passages by appealing to the wider context (with the letter to the Romans omitted, twenty-two). The appeal to the wider context thus distorts the numbers substantially in favor of the conclusions Swartley wishes to draw.

For all the reasons presented here, Swartley's thesis must be set aside.

The Cause of Unworthiness

In the context of comments about the situation in Antioch, Ignatius frequently mentions his unworthiness. In four of his letters, he says that he is the last of the faithful in Antioch;[55] in three letters, he speaks of his unworthiness.[56] As already seen, many modern reconstructions of Ignatius's situation relate his sense of unworthiness to a crisis that affected his church in Antioch. Indeed, the

---

[54] Ibid., 96. These are placed in parentheses in Swartley's charts.
[55] Ign. *Eph.* 21.2; Ign. *Trall.* 13.1; Ign. *Rom.* 9.2; Ign. *Smyrn.* 11.1.
[56] Ign. *Magn.* 14.1; Ign. *Trall.* 13.1; Ign. *Smyrn.* 11.1.

most popular form of this reconstruction, just examined, claims to find a dramatic easing of Ignatius's sense of unworthiness after he hears that the crisis in the church at Antioch is over.

In addition to the detailed arguments above, several other observations call into question the adequacy of such a reconstruction of Ignatius's sense of unworthiness. First, there is no neat association between Ignatius's being the last of the church in Antioch and his feeling unworthy. Consider Ignatius's closing comments in the letter to the Ephesians, written *before* learning of the peace in Antioch:

> Pray on behalf of the church in Syria; I am being taken from there to Rome in chains—even though I am the least of those who believe there—since I have been deemed worthy to be found honorable to God. (Ign. *Eph.* 21.2)

The massive sense of unworthiness that Ignatius allegedly reflects before learning about the resolution of the situation in Antioch is not found here. Quite the reverse. He speaks of his *worthiness*, not his *unworthiness*, in spite of the unresolved situation in Antioch and even while admitting that he is the least of the believers in Antioch. Too much has been made of Ignatius's comments about being the "least" in this passage; not enough has been made of his clear sense of worthiness here. On the other hand, in the letter to the Smyrnaeans, written *after* learning of the peace, Ignatius continues to speak of his unworthiness in much the same way as he had in some comments before learning of the peace:[57]

> Your prayer has gone out to the church in Antioch in Syria. I greet everyone, having come from there bound in chains that are most acceptable to God; but I am not worthy to be from there, since I am the least of them. Still, I have been deemed worthy according to God's will. (Ign. *Smyrn.* 11.1)

The same can be said about the letter to the Philadelphians: Ignatius continues to have concern, saying, "Even though I bear my chains in him, I am even more afraid, since I am still not perfected" (Ign. *Phld.* 5.1). Such should not be the case, if Ignatius's sense of unworthiness derives from the situation in Antioch, for which he held himself accountable and the resolution of which, much to his relief, he learns before writing the letters from Troas. Some scholars who promote this hypothesis have noticed such inconsistencies, but they have not convincingly explained them.[58]

---

[57] Note the similar tone in Ign. *Eph.* 21.2, quoted above.

[58] Swartley appeals to the "wider context" to understand the passage, turning the obvious meaning of the statement "that I may attain to God by the lot that I have been mercifully assigned" away from the idea of martyrdom to Ignatius's position as bishop ("Imitatio Christi," 97–98). This proposal, however, is strained and unconvincing.

More problematic for this reconstruction is that Ignatius provides a second concern around which the language of unworthiness much more easily clusters—the idea of discipleship and martyrdom.[59] Ignatius repeatedly emphasizes that he has yet to attain martyrdom, although he is constantly treated as though he had. This places him in such celebrated company that he is embarrassed, for he has yet to endure the test and prove himself worthy of the name and the fame. Immediately after mentioning that he may not deserve the attention given him by the church at Ephesus (Ign. *Eph.* 2.2), Ignatius adds,

> I am not giving you orders as if I were someone. For even though I have been bound in the name, I have not yet been perfected in Jesus Christ. For now I have merely begun to be a disciple and am speaking to you as my fellow learners. For I have needed you to prepare me for the struggle in faith, admonishment, endurance, and patience. (3.1)

A similar connection of concerns appears later in the letter when Ignatius associates himself with the worthy Ephesians and with Paul, provided he goes on to martyrdom (11.2–12.2). The situation in Antioch does not seem to play a role in Ignatius's sense of worthiness here; it is martyrdom yet to be grasped that is relevant.

In the letter *to the Magnesians* also, thoughts of unworthiness arise (Ign. *Magn.* 11.1–12.1). Here again it seems that Ignatius's approaching martyrdom plays a role. He even proudly calls attention to his chains and then draws back, saying that, even with the chains, he does not compare to the Magnesians. The theme is developed even more clearly in the letter to the *Trallians,* where, in connection with his chains and approaching martyrdom, Ignatius is prepared to make boastful statements (Ign. *Trall.* 3.3–5.2). Yet he realizes that he is not yet a disciple and there are ordeals that lie ahead (5.2; 12.2). In particular, he asks that the church pray for him that he might obtain what his heart is set on (martyrdom) and that he might not be found reprobate (12.3). Again the sense of worthiness is associated with martyrdom, which Ignatius recognizes he has yet to attain (13.3).

Swartley makes much of the sharp drop in Ignatius's anxiety about his future between the letters written from Smyrna and those written from Troas, and Swartley associates this change with the news that the church at Antioch has gained "peace":[60] "When Ignatius knew that the church over which he was bishop attained unity, then his own concern about being worthy, being a true disciple, attaining God, etc. appears to be relieved and virtually non-existent!"[61] But as already seen, the data do not support Swartley's contention that Ignatius's concerns

---

[59] Corwin (*St. Ignatius,* 26–28) lists a few subjects that cause Ignatius some sense of unworthiness, but she highlights the situation in the church at Antioch, like Harrison.

[60] See table C, line 2.

[61] Swartley, "Imitatio Christi," 93.

about being worthy disappear after learning of the resolution of the situation in Antioch. Another fundamental problem with Swartley's procedure is that he links the news of peace in Antioch with Ignatius's lack of anxiety about his future in a causal way. There need be no such causal relationship, however, and certainly no causal relationship that makes Ignatius responsible for a fractured church in Antioch.

Swartley does not address another factor that comes into play between the letters from Smyrna and those from Troas that could account for Ignatius's new confidence. This is the *writing* of the letter to the Romans itself.[62] Ignatius's recurring worry is that he might fail, in the final scene, to be a true disciple. He states this repeatedly in his letters, and his letter to the Romans is taken up almost entirely with this theme.[63] Our best explanation for Ignatius's anxiety is the one that Ignatius himself offers often and frankly. He fears that his martyrdom might be diverted in some way, and for one so zealously seeking death, the possibility of being denied this much-longed-for and important goal could be the direct and primary, if not the full, cause of the level of anxiety detected in his letters.

If Ignatius's anxiety stems from his fear that his martyrdom might be prevented in some way, what could put his mind at peace? Most likely, the key to any assurance would be the disabling of the potential agency through which his death sentence might be overturned. Ignatius tells us plainly what this is: the intervention of the Roman church.[64] Why else would Ignatius send a letter such as the one to the church at Rome unless he was convinced that their good intentions could deny him the martyrdom he so willingly embraced and longingly sought? Ignatius goes out of his way to set up the situation in advance so that when he arrives, the path to martyrdom will be unhindered. It is the goodwill of the Roman church that is causing Ignatius anxiety, so much so that his letter to them is filled with one theme: *Please let me be a martyr!*

---

[62] Although the order of the writing of the letters from Smyrna cannot be determined, Ignatius does say in his letter to the Romans that he is writing to all the churches (Ign. *Rom.* 4.1). This suggests that some letters may have already been written. If so, the letter to the Romans could well have been the last letter from Smyrna. The other letters written from Smyrna may have been written at one sitting, as they share similar concerns and style.

[63] Ign. *Eph.* 2.1; 3.2; Ign. *Magn.* 9.1; 14.1; Ign. *Trall.* 5.2; 12.2–3; 13.3; Ign. *Rom.* 1.2; 2.1; 4.1–2; 5.3; 9.2; Ign. *Phld.* 5.1; Ign. *Smyrn.* 11.1; Ign. *Pol.* 7.1.

[64] It is a matter of some debate how the Roman church might have been able to intervene on Ignatius's behalf. The seriousness with which Ignatius confronts its potential intervention should warn us against dismissing the matter too hastily. Corwin speculates that Christian influence in the imperial court is a possibility (*St. Ignatius,* 23–24). Her thesis assumes that the charges of atheism and of the adoption of Jewish customs, as recorded by Dio Cassius about a situation about twenty years earlier, be taken as a reference to Christianity (*Hist. rom.* 67.14). Cf. Eusebius, *Hist. eccl.* 3.18.4.

Once Ignatius gives clear instructions to the Roman church not to prevent his martyrdom, would his mind not be somewhat set at ease? Would he not have fewer doubts about being a *true* disciple if the only possible source of intervention has been dealt with? And surely, now that he has dealt with the situation that might have prevented his path to martyrdom, a new peace and assurance might be reflected in his future correspondence. Given the existence and focus of the letter to the Romans, this is the most obvious analysis of the situation.

Someone may wish to argue that Ignatius could not have been so concerned about the possible intervention of the Roman church that he was driven to anxiety of the kind expressed in his letters. Why would he not have realized earlier that he could simply write the Roman church and thus assure his stage for martyrdom? And if he knew this, why would he be genuinely anxious about an intervention that he could so easily control? But any such view does not do justice to the intensity of Ignatius's concern expressed in his letter to the Romans. For him, the matter is not superficial, nor is his concern feigned. Furthermore, such dismissal of the legitimacy of Ignatius's concern does not adequately diagnose what can cause anxiety and how solutions to problems may suddenly come into focus. Nor does it recognize the impact on a person that a perceived solution to a discerned crisis can have. Ignatius's sense of the resolution to the matter that might have prevented his martyrdom is the most telling element to account directly, naturally, and fully for Ignatius's new confidence. There is no need to appeal to the situation in Antioch, the details of which are a theoretical construct, when a substantial explanation for the source of Ignatius's anxiety is available in the letter to the Romans.

After writing his stirring "last will and testament" to the Roman church, Ignatius moves much more confidently toward his martyrdom, and herein most likely lies the key to the difference in tone reflected in the letters written from Troas in contrast to the letters written from Smyrna. This is not to say that the resolution of the situation in Antioch brought no sense of relief. It is, however, a secondary relief in comparison with Ignatius's relief about the completion of his discipleship in martyrdom now that he has dealt with the potential intervention of the Roman church.

Unanswered Questions

As mentioned, much of recent scholarship has spoken confidently about Ignatius's sense that he was somehow to blame for the situation in Antioch, maintaining that his anxiety was related mainly to that situation. But the lynchpin of this reconstruction is a handful of seriously flawed linguistic and statistical arguments. With these arguments largely gone, the case for connecting Ignatius's plight to internal conflict in the church at Antioch becomes much more difficult to make. Making matters more serious, Harrison, Swartley, and others who promote this portrait of Ignatius and the church in Antioch fail to explain many facets of the situation in Antioch and Asia Minor that their reconstructions presuppose. These are now addressed.

The Appointment of a New Bishop

Some scholars have suggested that matters at issue in Antioch must have been fairly concrete to convince Ignatius that the issue in the church there had been resolved and that the decision had gone in favor of his position. One proposed event is the appointment of a successor bishop from among Ignatius's supporters. But this is a guess at best, and it raises more questions than it answers.

The idea that one of Ignatius's supporters had been appointed in Ignatius's place is not likely to have been the condition that eased Ignatius's concern about the church in Antioch.[65] For one thing, it is not obvious that a new leader would have been chosen so quickly, within days of Ignatius's departure. Ignatius was still bishop of the church, even though he was on his way to martyrdom. It is not clear, then, that a new bishop would have been considered *before* Ignatius was executed. Further, since there appears to have been a possibility that Ignatius might be freed—knowledge that the church in Antioch must have had[66]—it seems even more improbable that the first act taken after Ignatius's departure would have been the election of a new bishop. Finally, even if a new bishop had been elected, it is not clear that such an event would have been judged a solution to the problem at Antioch. The church could still have been fractured—perhaps now even more so—and separate assemblies and eucharists may have continued. Merely having a bishop in place was not enough. The churches of Asia had bishops, yet these churches were in danger, according to Ignatius's assessment of the situation, and

---

[65] Everything Ignatius says about presbyters and deacons indicates that he has full confidence in the leadership of the churches. Nothing in his letters offers a hint that the presbytery is fractured, with each side promoting its candidate for the bishop's office. Nor is there a suggestion that candidates with sharply different agendas or with questioned orthodoxy are competing for the bishop's office. Ignatius praises the presbytery and demands obedience of all to the bishop and presbyters.

[66] Ignatius worries that his martyrdom might be prevented. This has puzzled commentators and has led to speculation about the nature of the charge against Ignatius or the legality of his conviction. One would expect that Ignatius's church would have been as aware of any of these nuances as Ignatius was himself. If there were irregularities in the case against Ignatius, perhaps the door would be opened for friends in Rome to intervene. Unfortunately, no information is available about how Ignatius came to be convicted, and even if there were a full record, it might not enlighten us as to what strategies for his release Ignatius feared from his well-intentioned friends in Rome. See the recent suggestions by Brent, *Ignatius of Antioch,* 16–19.

he uses his last moments to address the matter. The appointment of a supportive bishop, then, was not likely the solution that eased Ignatius's concern about the church in Antioch. Nor, on the other hand, would such an appointment have caused Ignatius's increased concern, as seems to be suggested by Trevett.[67]

Schism and the Bishop's Accountability

As discussed, many scholars have argued that Ignatius's sense of unworthiness arose from his conviction that he, as the bishop, was personally accountable for a schism that broke out under his watch. According to this view, when Ignatius hears that the schism in Antioch has been healed, he is relieved and supposedly his sense of worthiness is restored.[68] Consider, for example, Schoedel's assessment:

> Ignatius's self-effacement is connected with the unsettled state of affairs in Antioch, that what the other churches and their bishops have that he lacks is a clear claim to having preserved what he regards as the supreme blessing inherited from the apostolic age—namely, concord and unity.... Thus a challenge to Ignatius's authority in Antioch would be the clearest evidence of disunity and would call into question the value of his ministry there.[69]

Several points in this reconstruction fail, however. For one thing, the supposed contrast between Ignatius's fractured church in Antioch (for which Ignatius is blameworthy) and the supposedly harmonious and unified churches in Asia (for which the Asian bishops can be praised) is exaggerated. Separate assemblies and divisions of some sort existed in at least some of the churches of Asia,[70] which Schoedel admits. This calls into question Schoedel's contrast of situations between Antioch and Asia. Further, the supposed connection between Ignatius's

---

[67] Trevett thinks that Ignatius's ecclesiology was at the heart of the dispute in Antioch and that he recognized the "adverse effect of his own considerable personality on the peace of Christian Antioch" (*A Study of Ignatius*, 66). Such a hypothesis fails, however, in light of the considerable attention that Ignatius gives to the office of *bishop* as the defense against schism and error throughout the letters that he wrote to the churches of Asia. It is unlikely that Ignatius would have promoted in Asia what he judged to be a deterrent to peace in Antioch. See the section "Schism and the Bishop's Accountability," pp. 183–84.

[68] Harrison, *Polycarp's Two Epistles to the Philippians*, 101–4. Schoedel makes this central to his reconstruction (*Ignatius of Antioch*, 13).

[69] Schoedel, *Ignatius of Antioch*, 13.

[70] Ibid., 160. He points to Ign. *Eph.* 11.2–12.2; Ign. *Rom.* 4.3; 7.1. But there is nothing in these passages that speaks of Antioch or schism at all. It is only by first concluding that there was a schism in Antioch that one can use these passages to hint at such a situation. Schoedel (pp. 29, 201) assumes Swartley's conclusions, but Swartley's work is inadequate.

sense of unworthiness and a schismatic situation in Antioch is sharply at odds with Ignatius's view of schism and responsibility elsewhere. For churches in Asia, Ignatius does not blame the bishop for schism; he defends the bishop. The schismatics are the ones at fault, and they are to be avoided. Where there is schism, the schismatics are challenged directly and ordered to desist and submit to the bishop.[71] Ignatius's advice to Bishop Polycarp is to make no accommodation with the schismatics (Ign. *Pol.* 3.1; 4.1). Further, Ignatius does not recommend that bishops sacrifice themselves to heal schism (as he himself is supposedly doing according to reconstructions such as Schoedel's).[72] Schoedel and others, therefore, are forced to maintain that Ignatius held himself, as bishop, accountable for matters in Antioch that he excuses the bishops for in Asia Minor, and that he fails to recommend as a solution to schisms in Asia Minor the action he has himself taken to restore unity in Antioch. Although such a double standard is possible, it is not a convincing reading of the evidence. The reasonable conclusion is that Ignatius would have done in Antioch much as he explicitly advises bishops to do in Asia Minor: fight the schismatics and hold them accountable for any schism.

Ignatius's sense of unworthiness, if connected to the situation in Antioch, seems, then, to relate to something other than his failure to prevent schisms.

The Schismatics' Response to Ignatius in Antioch

Whatever the problem facing the church in Antioch, the matter appears to have been resolved within days of Ignatius's leaving the city under armed guard. The messenger bearing the good news caught up with Ignatius in Troas, before Ignatius wrote his final three letters.[73] We do not know how long Ignatius was delayed along the way. If it was a couple of weeks at most, then the resolution of the problem in Antioch must have happened within days of Ignatius's departure. Even if a longer delay is granted, it cannot be reasonably maintained that the resolution in Antioch occurred more than a very few short weeks after Ignatius left.

---

[71] Ign. *Eph.* 5.2–3; 20.2; Ign. *Magn.* 3.3–4.1; 6.1; 7.1; 13.2; Ign. *Trall.* 2.1–2; Ign. *Phld.* 3.1–4.1; 8.1; Ign. *Smyrn.* 8.1–2.

[72] Nowhere does Ignatius suggest that he sees his sacrifice as a key to the resolution of the situation in Antioch. He does repeatedly say that by his death he will become a true disciple (Ign. *Eph.* 1.2; 3.1; Ign. *Rom.* 4.2; 5.1–3; Ign. *Magn.* 5.2; 9.1; Ign. *Trall.* 4–5; Ign. *Pol.* 7.1), and he is explicit that this is his intense desire (a theme throughout his letters and the central theme in his letter to the Romans).

[73] This determination is made by observing that the letters written from Smyrna speak of the situation in Antioch as unresolved and those written from Troas as resolved. Further, since Ignatius informs both the church and the bishop in Smyrna that the situation in Antioch has been resolved, it is improbable that the messenger caught up with Ignatius in Smyrna after the letters from Smyrna had been written, for, had this been the case, Polycarp and his church in Smyrna presumably would have heard the news and would not have needed such information in letters written to them by Ignatius from Troas.

Many scholars contend that such an immediate resolution of the problem suggests that the crisis was caused and controlled by the Christians themselves, as would be the case with an internal schism. The theory contends that when internal conflict in the church became public enough for the authorities to intervene, Ignatius quickly offered himself up to divert further attention from the church. Ignatius's "voluntary martyrdom" then pricked the conscience of the schismatics, who repented when they saw the consequences of their defiance.[74] This repentance supposedly was the good news that Ignatius learned about in Troas, much to his relief.[75] Corwin, for example, argues that the peace indicates the return of the schismatics. Such quick return indicates that the "divisions were not irreparably deep"; the situation did not include "a struggle of obstinate groups frozen into irreconcilable opposition."[76]

The popular view that Ignatius's plight provoked the repentance and return of the schismatics must assume that not only the arrest, trial, and conviction of Ignatius were done speedily but the transport as well. Although this is possible, the likelihood must at least be considered that there was delay at some stage in this process. Then the question is, If Ignatius's opponents were prepared to repent within days of Ignatius's removal from Antioch, why would they not have responded in a similar way earlier, when Ignatius first offered himself as a scapegoat, or at the trial, when they might have been able to influence the deliberations, or as Ignatius awaited transport? Surely Ignatius could have detected some initial sign of sorrow in his opponents, some small evidence of repentance that would have relieved him of his fears *before* his departure for Rome, if his opponents supposedly repented so quickly on his leaving, as Harrison, Swartley, Corwin, and others suppose.

Trevett's judgment on the matter is more cautious. She dismisses the hypotheses contending that the repentance of the schismatics resolved the situation in Antioch. She thinks that such divisions were not so easily remedied. She points to Ignatius's own view of the near impossibility of the repentance of schismatics,

---

[74] The phrase "voluntary martyrdom" appears in Hammond Bammel, "Ignatian Problems," 78–79.

[75] Ign. *Phld.* 10.1; Ign. *Smyrn.* 11.1; Ign. *Pol.* 7.1.

[76] Corwin, *St. Ignatius*, 54. This is a popular explanation, but it is too easy a solution, and Brent's recent appeal to the psychology of "scapegoating" is still unconvincing (*Ignatius of Antioch*, 44–47). If Ignatius's opponents so quickly repented, one wonders how deep the opposition was and why Ignatius made the matter one of such grave importance. Schoedel has a better read on the situation (supposing the basic assumption of internal church conflict is correct). He thinks the situation was "delicate and required careful negotiations" (*Ignatius of Antioch*, 213). Schoedel's explanation is itself weak, however, for if the matter required delicate and careful negotiations, why does Ignatius request only prayer until *after* the matter has been resolved? Ignatius does not ask for any kind of negotiations or intervention to resolve the matter—sensitive or brash.

which, as she notes, he holds even in letters written from Troas, after he has heard that the church at Antioch has gained peace.[77]

Further, given the sharply conflicting interpretations of Jesus held by Ignatius and the Docetists, it seems inconceivable that schism would have been healed within days of Ignatius's departure. From what we know about Ignatius, there was no possible compromise with the Docetists. The Docetists likewise do not seem to have been prepared to compromise their position. They were even less likely to repudiate their position entirely and affirm in its place the theological position of Ignatius.

We cannot assume, then, that Ignatius's sentence or death would have healed the rift in Antioch. We do not know the nature or severity of the supposed rift. With Ignatius's death, the sides could have become even more firmly set against each other, with Ignatius's side blaming the other for the loss of their leader. Ignatius certainly does not promote his approaching martyrdom as a cure for the situation in Antioch. He does use his status as prisoner and future martyr as an argument against the docetic position, but when schismatics praise him as a martyr, he rebuffs them. This does not suggest an atmosphere of easily healed hurts.

The argument that Ignatius's condemnation healed a significant schism—crucial to many of the current reconstructions of the situation in Antioch—is not compelling.

The Schismatics' Response to Ignatius in Asia Minor

The popular reconstruction of Ignatius's situation portrays Ignatius as facing a harsh and hostile opposition in Antioch. Ignatius did face opposition. His ready-made arguments against schismatics and his call for submission to the bishop suggest that he had encountered schism and opposition in his own church. But reconstructions of the situation in Antioch often go wrong in their descriptions of the nature of the opposition. A violently hostile opposition in Antioch is not supported by a strand of explicit evidence. Indeed, we know almost nothing about the opposition to Ignatius in Antioch, although the popular understanding of Ignatius's plight depends solely on a supposedly internal (and largely undefined) conflict proposed by some scholars. We do not know who the opponents were. We do not know whether there was one group or many or whether they were united in their opposition to Ignatius or fractured. We do not know how significant a minority or majority the opposition was. Nor do we know what happened to the opposition after the church in Antioch had gained its peace.

---

[77] Trevett, "Ignatius 'To the Romans,'" 43. Trevett maintains that the situation in Antioch concerned an internal dispute. By dismissing the repentance of the schismatics as the solution, however, she narrows considerably the range of events that could constitute a restoration of peace in Antioch.

Clearer information, however, is available about the schismatic tendencies of other churches within Ignatius's orbit. This evidence comes from Ignatius's comments about the schismatics in the churches of Asia. It is far safer to use the kind of opposition for which there is explicit information (in the churches of the province of Asia) to sketch out the probable nature of the opposition in Antioch than to appeal to merely imaginative constructs for the opposition in Antioch, uninformed by local evidence or by situations elsewhere. It is likely, though not certain, that there were substantial links between the schismatic tendencies in Asia and those in Antioch. Certainly, Ignatius and the bishops of Asia Minor enjoyed substantial links, as did the churches of Asia and the church at Antioch, with a network of visits, financial and personnel support, and exchanges of letters.[78] Although it is possible that the schismatic tendencies lacked such translocal links, a far more likely scenario is that they had links similar to those connecting Ignatius's churches, particularly when there is evidence that some of the schismatics came from other areas as visitors, which suggests a measure of translocal contact.[79] Yet if the popular construction of the opposition in Antioch is correct, the schismatics seem to differ in their treatment of Ignatius. In Asia the schismatics were sympathetic and friendly to Ignatius and rendered at least token support to their bishops;[80] in Antioch the schismatics supposedly were hostile and perhaps culpable in Ignatius's conviction. They appear to have loved Ignatius in Asia but hated him in Antioch.[81]

The point is that where we have explicit evidence for the schismatics' attitude to Ignatius, it stands at odds with the attitude assumed by currently popular portraits of the opposition in Antioch, for which there is no explicit information. This does not mean that Ignatius faced no opposition in Antioch. But any portrait of the opposition in Antioch must pay careful attention to the portrait of the opposition in Asia and be informed by it. No other standard for comparison is available.

Ignatius's Response to Schismatics in Asia Minor

Ignatius's response to the schismatics in Asia is equally intriguing. They like him, but he does not like them, nor is he swayed even slightly by their respectful

---

[78] For such evidence, see p. 187, n. 119.

[79] Ign. *Eph.* 1.9; Ign. *Smyrn.* 4.1.

[80] Ign. *Magn.* 4.1; Ign. *Phld.* 7.1–2. The latter passage hints at some activity within the bishop's church. Those who are involved in some kind of "division" apparently are still meeting in the bishop's church for some of their activities, and it appears that it is within that setting that they meet Ignatius.

[81] It is possible that the situations were different in Antioch and Asia Minor, although no one argues for starkly different kinds of opposition in the two areas—Judaizing and docetic tendencies in one area, something altogether different (whatever that could have been) in the other area.

treatment of him. Ignatius dismisses their recognition of the bishops as hollow, and he deals with them sharply both in public and in his writings.[82]

The theory that is now widely accepted, however, reads the Antioch schismatics' attention in an entirely different way. According to this view, Ignatius welcomes news of the return of the schismatics to his church, and his anxiety and sense of unworthiness evaporate. He supposedly accepts the return of the schismatics at face value and does not question their sincerity or suspect their motives. But this is not the Ignatius we know in Asia Minor. He distrusts the schismatics' positive approaches to him and to the bishops in Asia. Recognition of the bishops by the schismatics and their praise of him mean nothing to Ignatius.

As already mentioned, some scholars have argued that Ignatius makes a distinction between the schismatics: he holds out no hope for the Docetists, but he thinks the Judaizers can be reconciled.[83] As argued earlier, however, Ignatius has no interest in so discriminating between schismatic positions.[84] Even if it were the case that Ignatius clearly distinguished between two different schisms and was more conciliatory to the Judaizing schismatics, his language toward the Judaizers reveals a strong skepticism about the likelihood of the repentance of either group.[85]

Further, there is no evidence that Ignatius is more hopeful in the letters from Troas that schisms could be healed. Surely he would be more positive about reconciliation if the news from Antioch were that the schism there had been healed. He does not mention such a healing, nor does he indicate in any way that the matter is relevant to the schismatic tendencies in Asia Minor.

The Roman Involvement

Ignatius was a condemned prisoner. Those who are convinced that Ignatius was not the victim of an orchestrated persecution by the civil authorities have offered various explanations for Ignatius's status as a condemned prisoner. Harrison merely hints that Ignatius was probably falsely condemned by elements within the church[86] and he contends that he was at pains not to be explicit about the

---

[82] Ignatius does not even wish to remember their names. They are blasphemers; they have attempted to deceive him. He has no place for their praise (Ign. *Phld.* 7.1–2; Ign. *Smyrn.* 5.2). He shows the same dismissive attitude toward those who try to deceive their bishop (Ign. *Magn.* 3.2–4.1).

[83] The more positive statements about repentance are in the letter *to the Philadelphians* (3.2; 8.1; 9.1). The passage in Ign. *Eph.* 10.1 seems to refer to nonbelievers, not to schismatics.

[84] See the section, "Another Approach to Ignatius's Opponents," pp. 124–26.

[85] Ign. *Eph.* 7.1; 16.1–2; Ign. *Smyrn.* 4.1.

[86] Harrison, *Polycarp's Two Epistles to the Philippians*, 97–104.

situation in Antioch.[87] Harrison's contention here has little merit, for it assumes what Harrison is attempting to prove: that there was in Antioch a failed situation for which Ignatius was responsible and about which Ignatius was embarrassed and did not desire to speak. Harrison attempts to probe the silences and the psyche of Ignatius in order to establish his theory. Ignatius did not give specifics about the situation in Antioch. But it does not follow that there is something suspect in this silence.[88] Indeed, it is quite likely that the churches addressed by Ignatius knew what had happened in Antioch and that Ignatius therefore did not need to deal with the matter in his letters or defend his role in the events. Had Ignatius been seen in some way as the one at fault for the plight of the church in Antioch, one might have expected some defense of his innocence. There is, however, no hint of a need or an effort to do that.

Harrison's explanation of the situation in Antioch is further weakened in that it leaves unexplained what kind of charge was brought against Ignatius, why the civil government accepted the accusation and then proceeded to convict Ignatius,[89] why it sent Ignatius to Rome under heavy guard, and why others, in like matter, were charged in the same way.[90] Supposing that Harrison is correct in his assertion that members of Ignatius's own congregation had falsely accused him, a number of questions remain unanswered. What kind of accusation could have been made against Ignatius that would have been serious enough to be counted a capital offense? If it were that he was a Christian, would anyone within

---

[87] Ibid., 95–100.

[88] Trevett's charge that Ignatius was "reticent about what *did* happen in Antioch" is incorrect (*A Study of Ignatius*, 61). Since Ignatius is silent about what happened, Trevett must read certain judgments into the situation to conclude that Ignatius was reticent. There is nothing in Ignatius's letters to suggest that the churches in Asia Minor do not know what happened in Antioch, yet they do not hold Ignatius in contempt for the situation there; rather, they praise and adore him. Ignatius is reticent about only one matter— the honor that he is receiving before he has finished his discipleship as a martyr. He would have had this kind of hesitation regardless of the situation in Antioch. To tie Ignatius's self-effacement to a specific failure in Antioch is to cheapen Ignatius's profound view of discipleship, which is never perfect or perfected (in spite of whatever accomplishments he has had already) until the beasts have ground God's wheat—as Ignatius colorfully phrases his martyrdom (Ign. *Rom.* 4.1).

[89] We should not think that only a cursory examination was done. Although some cases may have been tried quickly, Pliny the Younger's careful actions provide evidence that Roman authorities could investigate matters quite thoroughly. We know nothing of Ignatius's trial except that it ended in conviction. For an attempt to read between the lines regarding Ignatius's legal matters, see Stevan L. Davies, "The Predicament of Ignatius of Antioch," *VC* 30 (1976): 175–80.

[90] Harrison recognizes that he needs to keep martyrs to a minimum for the good of his theory, and he suggests that Ignatius might have been the only martyr (*Polycarp's Two Epistles to the Philippians*, 90–91). But the evidence points to other martyrs at the time, as will be seen in the next section.

the church have wanted to call the government's attention to this?[91] All credibility within the church would have been lost for the betrayer, whether an individual or a group,[92] and such charges might place Ignatius's accusers in as much jeopardy as Ignatius himself. If, on the other hand, the charge was a false one, what kind of investigation was done of this serious offense? How was it that the civil government believed the accusation? And why did Ignatius not fight the charge? Would Ignatius have wanted to leave behind a leaderless church now brought under serious suspicion from the civil authorities by false charges brought against him?

Streeter is more specific about the issue of conflict in the church. He thinks that it had something to do with Ignatius's election as bishop and his attempt to establish the episcopate as a monarchical office.[93] Bauer made much of this idea in his classic work, and both Hammond Bammel and Rius-Camps favor this view.[94] As noted above, Hammond Bammel goes so far as to speak of Ignatius's "voluntary martyrdom," which is supposed to have healed the rift that this innovation had caused in the community.[95] This reconstruction places Ignatius in control of the situation in a crucial way: he causes the conflict by insisting on the authority of the monarchical office; he minimizes governmental intervention into the affairs of the church by offering himself as a scapegoat; he restores the church to harmony by his self-sacrifice.

However, Hammond Bammel's reconstruction fails, like Harrison's, to account for the possible martyrdom of others at the time,[96] to explain in what way a voluntary martyrdom would have healed the rift,[97] or to account for the judgment of the civil authorities that the matter was serious enough to be considered a capital offense.[98]

---

[91] Some scholars have suggested that the Judaizing schism in Ignatius's church rejected the name "Christian." Although it is possible that the Judaizing group favored another name, there is nothing to suggest that they would have been viewed as different from their fellow members should the authorities have to intervene.

[92] This would not occur if an anonymous accusation were made against Ignatius. A letter of Pliny the Younger, written around the time of Ignatius (*Ep.* 10.96), mentions such accusations against Christians in Bithynia. We should not assume, however, that anonymous accusations were accepted legal procedure. In the case of Pliny, the anonymous accusations did not occur until after Pliny had already started his trials and sentences. He had reservations about such accusations, and when he inquired regarding imperial policy, persons named in anonymous accusations were not to be pursued (*Ep.* 10.97).

[93] Streeter, *The Primitive Church*, 169.

[94] Walter Bauer thinks that Ignatius was in a minority position and hoped to gain control of the church through promotion of the monepiscopal office—an office to which Ignatius thought his group would be able to elect one of their own, given how splintered the opposition supposedly was (*Orthodoxy and Heresy*, 61–65). Harrison is more cautious (*Polycarp's Two Epistles to the Philippians*, 82, n. 3).

[95] Hammond Bammel, "Ignatian Problems," 78–79.

[96] See the next section, "Was Ignatius the Sole Martyr?" pp. 191–94.

[97] See "The Schismatics' Response to Ignatius in Antioch," pp. 184–86.

[98] It is difficult to know how much risk a Christian suffered when a complaint was made or how deeply the investigation would proceed beyond determining whether the

Was Ignatius the Sole Martyr?

The possibility of other victims of persecution at the time of Ignatius's crisis must be examined in more detail because it has considerable relevance to the question of the nature of Ignatius's dilemma and the extent of action against Christians. So crucial is the matter that Harrison thinks it necessary to argue that Ignatius was the only martyr at that time, and other scholars follow him.[99] Unfortunately, most simply assume that Harrison is correct, even though the evidence in favor of multiple martyrs is strong. This section examines in detail the neglected passages.

Ignatius describes the church in Ephesus as a passage for "those being taken up to God," a phrase that translators have taken to mean "martyrs."[100] Although he mentions only Paul by name, he uses the plural. It is doubtful that Ignatius is describing the Ephesian church as a highway for victims "of all kinds" and not just Christian victims, as Trevett suggests.[101] Even though victims of all kinds must have passed through the busy port of Ephesus, Ignatius has in mind only those "taken up to God"—Christian martyrs, as he himself will soon be. Further, in other letters, Ignatius mentions people by name who may have been facing the same fate; he writes in the letter *to the Philadelphians* that Rheus Agathopus has "bid farewell to life" (Ign. *Phld.* 11.1), and perhaps Philo as well.[102] Although some scholars

---

person was a Christian, which seems to have been deemed sufficient to bring a capital conviction, at least according to Pliny the Younger's evidence. Pliny's action, however, stemmed specifically from complaints brought against Christians apparently by those with some stake in the economy of the temples (Pliny the Younger, *Ep.* 10.96.10). Most Christians who came to the attention of the authorities may have been targeted by their accusers for other reasons, but the charge of being a Christian was probably attractive because it was easier to prove and the consequence of conviction was more dire. For a detailed examination of informants in the empire (but without reference to the issue of Christians), see Steven H. Rutledge, *Imperial Inquisitions: Prosecutors and Informants from Tiberius to Domitian* (New York: Routledge, 2001).

[99] Harrison, *Polycarp's Two Epistles to the Philippians*, 95–100. Schoedel says simply that the phrase "said farewell to life" indicates "any serious commitment that counts the cost" (*Ignatius of Antioch*, 214, n. 14). But it is doubtful that this is the meaning Ignatius intends here. Ignatius has repeatedly emphasized his need to be a martyr in order to complete his discipleship. Death and life are the stuff of his language, and he is saying his farewell to life. Granted, the phrase could mean something less than martyrdom; the question is whether it could mean less than this in the context of Ignatius's immediate situation. Trevett's position (*A Study of Ignatius*, 8) is similar to Schoedel's.

[100] Ign. *Eph.* 12.2. Ehrman translates, "those slain for God"; Holmes translates, "those who are being killed for God's sake."

[101] Trevett, *A Study of Ignatius*, 8–9.

[102] The verb is singular and applies more directly to Rheus Agathopus, but conceivably Philo is to be associated with Rheus in the same situation.

suggest that such a phrase is "insufficiently explicit"[103] to conclude that Rheus Agathopus was facing martyrdom, it seems curious that in letters dominated by the theme of martyrdom, Ignatius would have used a phrase that was easily and naturally applied to martyrdom if he meant something else by this phrase. Another letter describes Philo and Rheus Agathopus as those who have "followed" Ignatius "in the word of God" (Ign. *Smyrn.* 10.1). Such an expression is ambiguous, but the context is suggestive. Ignatius goes on to thank the church for its kind treatment of his friends, and his mind seems to turn to the church's treatment of him a few days earlier as he mentions his chains, concerning which the church in Smyrna showed no embarrassment. Although it does not follow that Ignatius's friends were likewise in chains, it is a possibility.[104] This potential scenario is strengthened by Polycarp's reference to Ignatius, Zosimus, and Rufus in Pol. *Phil.* 9.1, which is followed by a series of comments that, in the most natural reading, suggest martyrdom: "None of them acted in vain"; "They are in the place they deserved, with the Lord, with whom they also suffered"; "They did not love the present age" (9.2). At the end of the letter, Polycarp asks whether the Philippians have heard anything more definite about Ignatius and those with him (13.2). His inquiry may suggest that those with Ignatius were in the same predicament as he was. If they were merely traveling to Rome, the request for more definite information about them appears a little odd, whereas this request makes full sense for Ignatius and anyone else with him facing execution. The importance of the issue is this: if there were other martyrs from Antioch or areas nearby, this would suggest a wider governmental action than proposed by some of the modern reconstructions that portray Ignatius as a lone martyr and his situation as confined to an internal conflict within his church.

Further, one need not demand specific corroborating evidence of a persecution in Antioch during Ignatius's final days there.[105] Roughly at the same time as

---

[103] Trevett, *A Study of Ignatius*, 8.

[104] The question is why those mentioned by Ignatius (Ign. *Smyrn.* 10.1) are different from those mentioned by Polycarp (*Phil.* 9.1–2). Schoedel denies that Philo and Rheus Agathopus, who are mentioned by Ignatius, were prisoners but grants that Zosimus and Rufus, who are mentioned by Polycarp, were. Thus, although there were other Christian martyrs, they were not from Antioch but were added later, according to Schoedel (*Ignatius of Antioch*, 11). But, in fact, it is unclear where these individuals are from; Antioch cannot be ruled out. For the sake of argument, however, let us rule out Antioch as their hometown. This would indicate that Roman action against Christians was more widespread than we would guess from Ignatius's letters. In order to deny governmental persecution of Christians, should we conclude that these individuals had been bishops of their own fractured churches and that they offered themselves up to take the pressure off their congregations when interchurch conflict disturbed the public order? A more likely scenario is that Christians were coming to the attention of the Roman authorities (see Pliny's letter) and that Ignatius and others were caught in governmental action—what early Christians called persecution.

[105] Some scholars have tried to find a specific politically sensitive incident that could make sense of the various facets of Ignatius's situation (see Trevett, *A Study of Ignatius*,

the crisis in Antioch, Pliny the Younger wrote about his action against Christians. Pliny's letter is useful here for two reasons: it offers a detailed record of how a governor might treat Christians, and it provides evidence for an early persecution no other record of which has survived.

Pliny received accusations that certain individuals were Christian, and on the basis of these accusations, he arrested and examined the accused.[106] If the accused admitted to being a Christian and refused to sacrifice, they would then be sentenced to death. This does not mean that each governor would have followed Pliny's exact procedure, for Pliny himself was uncertain about aspects of the process. It can be argued, however, that other governors would have followed procedures similar to those of Pliny, for Pliny acted as he thought proper, and when he seeks advice from the emperor, Pliny shows that he has read the imperial policy well. This is not to say that a fixed imperial policy was in place at the time of Ignatius, but Pliny's account does contain a detailed description of the actions of a responsible governor. Lacking evidence to the contrary, it seems safe to assume that governors in other provinces generally would have followed a somewhat similar policy.[107]

Pliny's evidence works effectively against reading too much into the lack of corroborative evidence of a specific persecution in Antioch at the time of Ignatius. Requiring such corroboration would impose an unreasonable standard of evidence. This period of the early church is not richly documented. As mentioned, the persecution of Christians in Bithynia under Pliny, for example, is not documented at all in the contemporary Christian sources.[108] We know of a persecution

---

3–8, for a review of some suggestions). Instead of looking for a single year in Trajan's reign that could explain Ignatius's predicament, we might be more discerning simply to note that almost any year in Trajan's reign would do, from 98 to 117. The entire reign of Trajan is one of tremendous ferment. Rome invaded Dacia in 101 at considerable cost and again in 105, with victory finally celebrated with grand games in Rome in 107–108. Looking more to the east and the area around Antioch, Rome furthered its expansion by annexing Arabia in 106 on the heels of its success in Dacia. Early in 114, tensions with Parthia over Armenia came to a head, leading to attacks on Parthia. In the campaigns of 115, Trajan reached the Persian Gulf and established the new province of Mesopotamia in the conquered lands. Various groups in the newly conquered territories revolted, with a massive uprising of the Jewish population in some centers of the eastern empire.

[106] Trevett notes that Pliny's letter shows the important role of local grassroots hostility toward Christians in provoking governmental response (ibid., 7).

[107] For a discussion of scholarship on Pliny and the Christians, see A. N. White, *The Letters of Pliny* (Oxford: Clarendon, 1966), 691–712, 772–87.

[108] Indeed, Pliny's letter hints that other unrecorded persecutions may have occurred in the area before Pliny's action. He reports that some of those who were accused of being Christians confessed that they once had been Christians, in some cases two years before and in some cases as many as twenty (*Ep.* 10.96.6). Although there are a host of reasons a Christian might leave the movement, the possibility exists, given the theme of

in that area only because of an overly cautious governor who wrote routinely to the emperor about various matters, the problems of Christians being but one. Even Pliny's supposed ignorance of how to handle Christians speaks for, rather than against, unrecorded early persecutions of Christians.[109] He mentions that he has never attended trials of Christians, implying that there were trials of Christians of which Pliny was aware but that he had not observed. Nothing in the record corroborates these persecutions, yet it would be an unhealthy skepticism to deny the incidents. Lightfoot, whose work on Ignatius remains the richest and most insightful study despite being written more than a century ago, makes the following observation:

> It is generally supposed that the historian of the early Church, in order to arrive at the truth with regard to the extent of the persecutions, has only to make deductions for the exaggerations of Christian writers. In other words, it is assumed that *the Christians forgot nothing, but magnified everything.* This assumption however is shown to be altogether false by the history of the manner in which the record of this Bithynian persecution has been preserved.[110]

Although the circumstances in Bithynia cannot be tied to the contemporary situation involving Ignatius in Antioch, we must be careful not to dismiss the possibility of persecution in Antioch during Ignatius's last days there. Given the paucity of evidence for the period, Ignatius's plight can itself be evidence of persecution, unless there is evidence that the predicament has another cause. Indeed, the Ignatian letters themselves and the body of early Christian literature as a whole document an environment of persecution. These sources remain significant even after efforts to qualify the reports and despite the failure to find corroborative evidence of persecution in non-Christian sources.

Ignatius's Stance in Asia Minor

If the situation in Antioch was primarily an internal church matter that became so disruptive that the civil authorities had to intervene (at which time Ignatius offered himself as a scapegoat so that the remainder of his community would not suffer), how does one explain Ignatius's actions in western Asia Minor? There he encouraged the churches to draw lines more sharply

---

persecution that haunts most of early Christian literature, that persecution of some kind played a role in some of the apostasies identified in Pliny's letter.

[109] Even if Pliny's knowledge of Christians is "slight and largely second-hand," as Robert L. Wilken maintains (*The Christians as the Romans Saw Them* [New Haven: Yale, 1984], 16), Pliny is not ignorant of the existence of the Christian movement or of the fact that Christians have been brought to trial.

[110] Lightfoot, *S. Ignatius, S. Polycarp*, 2.1.17.

than boundaries seem to have been drawn previously,[111] and this would have led, in all probability, to the kind of bitter church conflict that turned the civil authorities against the church in Antioch. Yet this was the very situation in Antioch that Ignatius had hoped to reverse by offering himself to the authorities for execution, according to one hypothesis. Is it likely that Ignatius would have encouraged the kind of action in Asia Minor that, according to Harrison and others, had brought the church in Antioch to the attention of the civil authorities—a predicament that Ignatius hoped to reverse in Antioch by the sacrifice of himself?

Further, if an explosive internal conflict provoked civil intervention in the church at Antioch, why does Ignatius not use the outcome of the crisis in Antioch to warn about similar dire consequences of schism in the churches of western Asia Minor? He employs every other imaginable argument against schism.[112] Why not use the most painful, immediate, and obvious argument—the likelihood of civil intervention, prosecution, and execution?

Given Ignatius's lack of a conciliatory approach to the schismatics in western Asia Minor,[113] he seems to have created a situation there in which conflict was likely to become sharper and civil intervention more likely, according to Harrison's understanding of governmental action in matters of this sort. Ignatius's stance in western Asia Minor stands in sharp contrast, then, with the more conciliatory approach he is thought to have taken in his last days in Antioch. This would be puzzling behavior for a man who had learned, only days before, a hard lesson about schism.

The Response to Good News from Antioch

Whatever problem is proposed as the key to the state of affairs in Antioch, this problem must have sufficient power to explain the various responses that resulted from a resolution of the problem. Consider how Ignatius responds. He is relieved—little more. One would expect a considerably different response from

---

[111] Consider, for example, the tone in Ign. *Smyrn.* 7–11; Ign. *Phld.* 2–4; 6; Ign. *Smyrn.* 4–8. Many scholars note that Ignatius seems to draw the lines more sharply than had been done before. Schoedel, for example, thinks that Ignatius went "beyond local expectations" in drawing boundaries and that it was he who "polarized" the situation (*Ignatius of Antioch*, 13).

[112] In schism Christians lack the bread of God (Ign. *Eph.* 5.2); they violate the example set by Jesus himself (Ign. *Magn.* 7.1); they are not pure (Ign. *Trall.* 7.2); they are at risk from "wolves" (Ign. *Phld.* 2.2); they do not inherit the kingdom of God (Ign. *Phld.* 3.3); they serve the devil (Ign. *Smyrn.* 9.1). Ignatius's nowhere asserts that schism could lead to civil intervention in the church's affairs, a most obvious point if this was the reason for Ignatius's arrest.

[113] See, for example, Ign. *Smyrn.* 5; Ign. *Phld.* 7.

Ignatius on the basis of Harrison's accounting of the situation. Why does Ignatius continue to desire martyrdom? If the restoration of internal harmony was
achieved simply by Ignatius's offering himself to the civil authorities, has Ignatius
not accomplished what he had hoped to do? Would a willingness on Ignatius's
part to be delivered from the sentence of death have reversed the repentance of
a church that had been cut to the heart upon seeing Ignatius condemned and
carried off to his execution? In Harrison's reconstruction, one would have expected Ignatius to take full advantage of any possibility of release and to return
in triumph to his repenting church. But he did not do this; in fact, he made the
greatest effort to prevent it.

Harrison's explanation of Ignatius's continued desire for martyrdom is
particularly unconvincing. He notes that Ignatius's desire for martyrdom after
learning that the church at Antioch had obtained peace might be taken by some
to indicate that Ignatius was not particularly sane—that he had lost his grip on
reality. Harrison asks, "What of it? . . . It is not only the unhappy victim of some
old complex, who is liable to be thrown (in a sense) off his balance by the tragic
failure and maddening ironies of life."[114] Thus Harrison admits that Ignatius's reaction to the peace in Antioch is problematic to his reconstruction, but he evades
the problem by adding a new factor to the equation—Ignatius's mental health.
Harrison's reconstruction is cheapened by this kind of explanation, and it is in
fact only a less direct way of admitting that his reconstruction cannot adequately
explain Ignatius's reaction to the gaining of peace in Antioch.[115]

A further problem with reconstructions such as Harrison's is that Ignatius
does not use news of peace in Antioch to argue his case against schism. What
stronger argument against the schismatics in Asia Minor would there be than
the repentance of the schismatics in Antioch? The schismatics in Antioch supposedly have just handed in their weapons, so to speak, and have rejoined the
church. Yet Ignatius does not mention such information, although the news is
fresh and he is enlivened by it. Surely when he is writing to the Philadelphians
and the Smyrnaeans, whose assemblies have experienced, or are threatened
by, schism, such news would have some significance.[116] Ignatius's failure to
mention such information is baffling, especially since he has demonstrated
that he is willing to use almost any argument he can against schismatics. This
further weakens the case that the news from Antioch related to a healing of
the schism there.

---

[114] Harrison, *Polycarp's Two Epistles to the Philippians*, 102.

[115] Trevett defends Ignatius against such charges in "The Much-Maligned Ignatius,"
Expository Times 93 (1982): 299. Holmes, *The Apostolic Fathers*, 81, speaks of the "vivid,
almost macabre eagerness with which Ignatius apparently anticipates his death," but he
defends Ignatius against what he sees as "unwarranted criticism."

[116] Ign. *Phld.* 7.1–2; Ign. *Smyrn.* 7.1–8.2.

Ignatius's Requests to the Churches of Asia Minor

Ignatius first asks that churches in western Asia Minor pray for the church at Antioch; then, upon learning that the church in Antioch has gained "peace," he asks the churches to send a representative (deacon or bishop), and where this is not possible, he wants letters sent.[117]

Harrison recognizes the tremendous demands Ignatius makes of the churches in asking them to send representatives to Antioch.[118] He tries to explain why Ignatius would request this level of help *after* the problem in Antioch has been resolved. Harrison thinks that Ignatius acquired the idea from learning that churches near Antioch had sent representatives. Harrison recognizes that Ignatius's request to the churches is onerous and taxing, and this is why he thinks that the reconciliation in Antioch must have still needed major players to make their influence felt.[119] The problem with such an explanation is that if the healing of the schism in Antioch still requires this kind of weighty attention, how is it that Ignatius is supposedly relieved of anxiety on hearing a report about the matter? The situation in Antioch would be still uncertain; Ignatius would still have grave concerns for his church.

Equally problematic for Harrison's reconstruction is why Ignatius did not ask for high-powered help from the churches of western Asia Minor *before* the resolution of the crisis there, with the church at Antioch left leaderless by his arrest and Ignatius's faction backed into a corner by the schismatics? Certainly Ignatius could not have expected things to go in his favor after he left. He was clearly deeply concerned about the situation in Antioch. He surely would have wanted prominent and respected leaders to make their presence felt as soon as possible in a church that no longer had access to his leadership. At least this is what we would expect Ignatius to have done if Harrison is correct about the internal fight at the center of the problem in Antioch. Further, once harmony was restored, there would seem to be little need to go to the expense of sending

---

[117] Ign. *Eph.* 21.2; Ign. *Magn.* 14.1; Ign. Trall. 13.1; Ign. *Rom.* 9.1; Ign. *Phld.* 10.1; Ign. *Smyrn.* 11; Ign. *Pol.* 7.1–8.1.

[118] Harrison, *Polycarp's Two Epistles to the Philippians,* 92.

[119] Ibid., 92–95. Ignatius, in Ign. *Phld.* 10.2, reports that neighboring churches have sent bishops, presbyters, and deacons to Antioch. Harrison's proposal that Ignatius acquired the idea to ask for delegates to travel to Antioch from a report that nearby churches had done so is unconvincing. The situations are quite different. What nearby churches could routinely do is not what can be expected—even once—of distant churches, particularly when those churches had already made considerable effort to travel to visit Ignatius and support him on his journey. Further, the practice of the early Christian church and of Ignatius himself was to visit other churches and intervene where necessary. That the idea to send delegates to Antioch does not come to Ignatius's mind until *after* the church in Antioch gained peace suggests that the situation there is somewhat unusual.

a number of people to the church at Antioch. Letters would have been in order and sufficient.[120]

Trevett tries to support Harrison's analysis. She points to the practice of the Roman church reflected in *1 Clement,* which she contends provided a template for Ignatius's requests to the churches of Asia regarding the church in Antioch. *First Clement* 1 explicitly identifies the problem in Corinth as an internal church conflict. According to Trevett, the Roman church sent delegates "to secure peace in Corinth."[121] But Trevett's parallel between *1 Clement* and the Ignatian letters is weak, for Ignatius does not request that delegates be sent to Antioch, as the Roman church did to help resolve the Corinthian situation. Ignatius asks only for prayer during the crisis. Not until *after* the church in Antioch has peace does he ask for delegates. And this is the puzzle. Why not ask for respected members of the Asia Minor community to go to Antioch and intervene when it seems to have been a common practice of early Christian communities? The church at Rome concerns itself with the business of the church at Corinth (*1 Clement*); Polycarp concerns himself with the affairs of the church at Philippi in his letter to the *Philippians;* the author of Revelation concerns himself with the affairs of the "seven churches of Asia." Indeed, such intervention is the very practice Ignatius engaged in by writing letters to the churches in Asia. One would think that if there was schism in Antioch, the strategy would have been to bring in the "big guns" from other churches immediately, while the situation still needed solution, with things still unsettled and Ignatius the bishop removed.[122] Regarding Antioch, why does Ignatius ask for an approach different from his practice in other places and from the practice of Christian churches elsewhere?

It cannot be argued that visits from bishops of other cities would have been ineffective during schism because the local church would resist such intervention as meddlesome or irregular; there are too many examples of the intervention of one church in the affairs of another within early Christianity. Indeed, Ignatius's actions reflect such engagement. He spoke frankly and forcefully when he had opportunity to meet schismatics in person and wrote sharply to churches he could not visit. In other words, Ignatius meddles, and he thinks it can be effective. Thus nothing about Ignatius's own actions in Asia Minor suggests that he would have been reluctant to encourage outside high-level help during a schism in Antioch, especially with his side weakened by his removal.

---

[120] Robin Darling Young thinks that Ignatius wants delegates from the churches in Asia to go to Antioch in order to elect a bishop in Ignatius's place (*In Procession before the World: Martyrdom as Public Liturgy in Early Christianity* [Père Marquette Lecture in Theology, 2001; Milwaukee: Marquette University Press, 2001], 20). Yet Young may be assuming a practice of election not yet in place in the early second century.

[121] Trevett, "Ignatius 'To the Romans,' " 49.

[122] Harrison, *Polycarp's Two Epistles to the Philippians,* 91–94.

His simple request for prayer for the church during its crisis does not point favorably to Harrison's hypothesis.

If we allow for a persecution, however, better sense can be made of the requests. What more but prayer could the churches of western Asia Minor offer if the church in Antioch was being persecuted and Christian leaders were being sentenced to death? But once the persecution subsided, the situation was different. Church leaders from abroad could safely visit the church at Antioch, and their presence likely would have been welcomed as the church tried to recover from its recent terror.

Ignatius's Main Concerns

Emphasis on Ignatius's sense of unworthiness or his concern about the church in Antioch has often drawn attention away from several more primary concerns reflected in the Ignatian letters. Ignatius wants to (1) complete his discipleship by embracing martyrdom,[123] (2) discredit false teaching,[124] and (3) bring the church to unity behind the bishops.[125] As already argued, Harrison cannot explain Ignatius's continued desire for martyrdom after hearing that the church at Antioch has gained its peace. Harrison does not address the other two points, but surely, as primary concerns on Ignatius's mind as he is led from Antioch to martyrdom, they provide some insight into the problem in Antioch, and such themes must be central to any credible reconstruction.

Nothing in the evidence suggests that Ignatius connects the success of his martyrdom to the resolution of the problems in his church at Antioch, and certainly nothing suggests that Ignatius links the success of his martyrdom to the resolution of problems in all the churches, even those in Asia Minor, as Schoedel claims.[126] Rather than a successful martyrdom being dependent on the churches attaining peace, for Ignatius it is his own completed martyrdom that assures him of a successful *discipleship*. This is the major theme propelling his thinking. Calling on the church at Rome not to prevent his martyrdom, Ignatius pleads that he not only be called a Christian, but that he be found one.[127]

The theme of martyrdom fits most neatly into the realities of life in Antioch,[128] where group identity and labels mean something. In the last three decades of the

---

[123] True discipleship is presented in terms of martyrdom (Ign. *Eph.* 1.2; 3.1; Ign. *Rom.* 4.2; 5.1–3; Ign. *Magn.* 5.2; 9.1; Ign. *Trall.* 4–5).

[124] Docetic tendencies are addressed most directly in Ign. *Trall.* 9–10 and in Ign. *Smyrn.* 1–5.

[125] Ign. *Eph.* 20.2; Ign. *Magn.* 6.2; 7.1–2; Ign. *Trall.* 2.1–2; 7.1–2; Ign. *Phld.* 3.2–3; 4.1; 7.2; 8.1; Ign. *Smyrn.* 7–8.

[126] Schoedel, *Ignatius of Antioch*, 12.

[127] Ign. *Rom.* 3.2.

[128] For a detailed discussion of the tensions in Antioch, see ch. 4.

first century, Jews experienced an intensified level of suspicion from the larger society in Antioch. This charged situation of suspicion led to external repression and executions in the Jewish community, and Christians in Antioch would not have escaped unnoticed. Indeed, Christians may have come under suspicion from both sides, particularly as they challenged traditional group loyalties and changed long-standing boundaries of group identity for both Jews and Gentiles. By drawing both Jews and Gentiles into a new movement where each had equal status, the Christian group seems to have become more easily distinguishable from Judaism. In such an environment of suspicion and intolerance, martyrdom might well have become a prominent theme in the church's reflection, as indeed it is in Ignatius's letters, and Ignatius might well sense that he has become a prisoner for the Name.[129]

A Problem for the Persecution Thesis?

Fredric W. Schlatter raises an important objection to the persecution thesis. Ignatius received news from Antioch that the crisis facing his church there had been resolved. Yet how would the Christian community have known that their crisis was over and that peace had been restored? It is unlikely that a clear official pronouncement would have been made proclaiming the end of persecution; at best the Christians would have come to learn that persecution was over because days and weeks and perhaps months had gone by without governmental action on this front. Thus it is unlikely that the situation could have developed quickly enough for such news to be communicated to Ignatius in Troas. Since Ignatius is heartened by some news relating to the "peace" of the church in Antioch, the cessation of persecution cannot have been the news.[130]

Three matters make Schlatter's point less weighty. First, little is known about the treatment of Christians or their legal status in this period. Pliny's correspondence with Trajan regarding the Christian problem shows how rudimentary Roman policy was in dealing with Christians around the time of Ignatius and how inexperienced a senior official might be in this issue.[131] In fact, even at a later date, when Roman policy had more time to develop, the status of Christians was somewhat unclear, and scholars disagree over the legal status of the church.[132]

---

[129] Ign. *Eph.* 1.2; Ign. *Phld.* 5.1

[130] Schlatter, "The Restoration of Peace in Ignatius's Antioch," 466–67. Trevett (*A Study of Ignatius*, 57) follows Schlatter.

[131] Pliny the Younger, *Ep.* 10.96–97.

[132] The debate centers on the grounds for official Roman action against Christianity. Three suggestions have been proposed. Christians were prosecuted for (1) simply being Christians, against whom specific legal enactments were in place; (2) offenses already forbidden by law, for which a non-Christian might just as readily be guilty and as quickly

We simply do not know what provoked governmental action against Ignatius and other possible martyrs, and we are equally in the dark about what terminated the action against Christians.

Second, the alternative thesis of an internal church conflict faces a similar difficulty. Theories of either external persecution or internal conflict likewise require a clear and quick event that would relieve Ignatius of his anxiety. As already shown in this chapter, although several explanations have been offered in support of the theory that internal church conflict was the source of Ignatius's distress, none of these reconstructions would have offered Ignatius quick assurance that the crisis in Antioch was over.

Third, Schlatter argues that Christians would not have known for some time after the end of persecution that the action against them was really over. But there was a near-parallel situation in Antioch only a few decades earlier in which a persecution ended abruptly. Instead of Christians, as in Ignatius's case, the victims were Jews; otherwise the comparison holds. Josephus reports the incident.[133] Action was swift and brutal when Jews were accused of starting a fire; when investigation showed that others had started the fire, the persecution was halted. Although what provoked action against Ignatius is not known, one cannot argue, as Schlatter does, that the Christian community would not have learned quickly that the matter that placed them in jeopardy had been resolved.

Directions for Future Investigation

The puzzle of the crisis in Antioch remains unsolved. The currently popular thesis of internal church conflict as the key to the crisis is seriously flawed. The evidence simply does not support the thesis of an internal church conflict that rolled out into the streets. This idea gains much of its attractiveness only after a decision is made to dismiss the possibility of a civil repression. If there is no external persecution, Christians are entirely responsible for their situation, and Ignatius might be blamed—and might blame himself—for not controlling the situation.

If one admits the possibility of a local persecution of Christians, however, the puzzle pieces of the evidence fit together better. The atmosphere of suspicion and

---

prosecuted as a Christian (murder, illegal assembly, etc); and (3) disturbing the public order. The debate is discussed in detail in A. N. Sherwin-White, "The Early Persecutions and Roman Law Again," *JTS* 3 (1952): 199–213; Geoffery E. M. de Ste. Croix, "Why Were the Early Christians Persecuted?" *Past and Present* 26 (1963): 6–38; the brief debate between Sherwin-White, "Why Were the Early Christians Persecuted?—an Amendment," *Past and Present* 27 (1964): 23–27, and de Ste. Croix, "Why Were the Early Christians Persecuted?—a Rejoinder," *Past and Present* 27 (1964): 28–33. See also T. D. Barnes, "Legislation against the Christians," *Journal of Roman Studies* 58 (1968): 32–50.

[133] Josephus, *J. W.* 7. 47–53.

group animus that marked much of Jewish and pagan relationships in Antioch in the late first and early second centuries is the primary background for the Ignatian story. Questions of identity and group loyalty are important. The developing Christian church finds itself in a complicated situation, where its primary boundaries now fall outside the traditional lines for determining identity in the society. By bringing Jews and Gentiles together in a new vision, Christian loyalties are not fixed to any of the groups with which the new Christian members had previously affiliated. This new situation could have compromised the established but fragile relationship between Judaism and the larger society in ways that may have placed Christians in some jeopardy. As a result, the Christian movement may have come to the notice of the authorities as something distinctive from Judaism.

Even if the persecution thesis is rejected, we cannot easily go back to the thesis that an internal church conflict was affecting the church in Antioch and was the cause of Ignatius's sense of unworthiness. We would have to admit that the specifics of the conflict in Antioch and the restored "peace" remain unclear. We could, however, confidently assert that some elements in the popular reconstruction of the situation in Antioch need to be discarded. First, the evidence does not support the idea that Ignatius blamed himself for the situation, nor does he tie his worthiness to a successful resolution of the conflict in the church there. The popular reconstruction fails to make sense of the situation at several other points, and the linguistic argument, which seemed to offer compelling statistical support, was found to be based on a flawed methodology. Second, Judaism figures too strongly in Ignatius's reflection to be irrelevant to the situation in Antioch. Current reconstructions of Ignatius's situation that look only at an internal crisis fail to set the Christian movement in Antioch in its larger social reality.

The failure to find a widely convincing answer as to the cause of Ignatius's anxiety or the substance of the peace in Antioch is not a desirable outcome, particularly after a lengthy examination of the evidence. It is, however, better than a wrong answer. Current reconstructions of Ignatius's situation in Antioch fail, relying as they do on substantially flawed linguistic and statistical arguments. They also leave several questions unanswered about the behavior of the various individuals and parties involved. We would be better off to admit that Ignatius's situation remains unexplained than to settle for a hypothesis that starts from a weak central premise about the cause of Ignatius's anxiety and ends with so many issues unresolved.

CHAPTER 6

Boundaries, Identity, and Labels

The Ignatian Boundary Terms

The subject of this study is Ignatius, but any study of Ignatius is, of necessity, also a study of Christianity and Judaism.[1] And herein lies a problem. Recent scholarship has balked at the terms "Judaism" and "Christianity," particularly regarding their usefulness or accuracy in the period during which the Christian church emerged.[2] This is precisely the period of Ignatius. And these

---

[1] The term Ἰουδαϊσμός (Judaism) appears to have been coined in the Maccabean period, probably during the first century B.C.E. (2 Macc 2:21) (Judith Lieu, "'Impregnable Ramparts and Walls of Iron': Boundary and Identity in Early 'Judaism' and 'Christianity,'" *NTS* 48 [2002]: 305). Ignatius may have coined the term Χριστιανισμός (Christianity, or more accurately, "Christianism," as Lieu points out [p. 312]). At any rate, Ignatius is the first known user of the term. If he did coin the term, he did so in quite conspicuous opposition to the term "Judaism," for this is the way he uses the term in his letters (Ign. *Phld.* 6.1; Ign. *Magn.* 10.1–3). See also Judith Lieu, *Neither Jew nor Greek? Constructing Early Christianity* (New York: T&T Clark, 2002), 6; idem, "The Christian Race," ch. 8 in *Christian Identity in the Jewish and Graeco-Roman World* (Oxford: Oxford University Press, 2004), 239–68. Daniel Boyarin contends that the term "Judaism" did not identify a religion until the term "Christianity" was created as its counterpart. For Boyarin, Christianity creates the concept of "religion" ("Semantic Differences; or, 'Judaism'/'Christianity,'" in *The Ways That Never Parted: Jews and Christians in Late Antiquity and the Early Middle Ages* (eds. Adam H. Becker and Annette Yoshiko Reed; Texte und Studien zum antiken Judentum 95; Tübingen: Mohr Siebeck, 2003), 67–74; idem, "Justin Martyr Invents Judaism," *Church History* 70 [2001]: 427–61). Boyarin offers what is probably an overly nuanced treatment of the issue, but if he is correct that Christianity is mainly responsible for the concept of "religion," then far more emphasis should be placed on the creative genius of early Christianity and leaders such as Ignatius than has been done by Boyarin and others. Regarding the general discussion of boundaries, identity, and labels, Lieu's contribution is the most substantial. Her work represents a widely informed and cautiously balanced reflection in a field that often tends to be marked by exaggeration and extremism.

[2] For a brief inquiry into ancient boundary drawing, see Lieu, "'Impregnable Ramparts and Walls of Iron,'" 297–313. The concepts of boundaries and identity are also addressed in many of the chapters in Lieu, *Christian Identity*.

terms, which are now suspect, were the crucial labels by which Ignatius defined his world.[3]

Although no proposed solution to the problem of terminology for the early Christian period has gained wide acceptance, there is a general sense (though not one I share) that the traditional terms of "Jew" and "Christian" or "Judaism" and "Christianity" or "Judaizer" are no longer adequate. But the proposed substitutions, instead of offering clarity and precision, have driven scholars into an almost hopeless terminological quagmire.[4] They cautiously put their terms in quotation marks or daringly coin hyphenated or compound words to try to capture the particular nuance of special meaning they intend. Those who were once described as Jewish Christians are now labeled with a cornucopia of choices: "Jewish movement of Jesus,"[5] "Jesus-believing Jews,"[6] and the five-word phrase "anti-Gentile-Christian Jewish Christianity,"[7] to list but a few. A similar list could be compiled for Gentile Christians. But no term stands out as having the potential for wide acceptance. Even Lieu's comparatively mild suggestion that we replace "Christianity" with "Christianism" is unlikely to be widely adopted.[8] Probably the most popular term to replace "early Christianity" is the label "the Jesus movement." But this term is itself problematic: it is as loaded as any other label, it is historically

---

[3] These words appear seventeen times, spread over six of the seven letters of Ignatius. "Christian": Ign. *Eph.* 11.2; Ign. *Magn.* 4.1; Ign. *Trall.* 6.1; Ign. *Rom.* 3.2; Ign. *Pol.* 7.3; "Christianity" (or "Christianism"): Ign. *Magn.* 10.1, 10.3 (twice); Ign. *Rom.* 3.3; Ign. *Phld.* 6.1; "Judaism": Ign. *Magn.* 8.1; 10.3 (twice); Ign. *Phld.* 6.1 (twice); "Judaize": Ign. *Magn.* 10.3; "Jews": Ign. *Smyrn.* 1.2.

[4] See the collection of articles in *Studies in Religion* 33 (2004): 147–234. This issue deals with "Names and Naming in the Ancient World," the subtitle of this particular volume. It offers a review of various aspects of the debate, with proposals (some more convincing than others) for how to resolve the concerns about terminology.

[5] Anne Fitzpatrick-McKinley, "Synagogue Communities in the Graeco-Roman Cities," in *Jews in the Hellenistic and Roman Cities* (ed. John R. Bartlett; New York: Routledge, 2002), 65, n. 75. But after using this term, Fitzpatrick-McKinley then uses the term "Christian": "Later Roman officials and opponents of the Jewish movement of Jesus identified Christian groups with such clubs and associations." She follows up with a reference to Pliny, who himself uses the term "Christian." Use of the term "Christian" would have worked adequately throughout Fitzpatrick-McKinley's discussion.

[6] Magnus Zetterholm uses this term and "Jesus-believing Gentiles" throughout *The Formation of Christianity in Antioch.*

[7] This is the title of section 10.2 in Jürgen Becker, *Paul: Apostle to the Gentiles* (trans. O. C. Dean Jr.; Louisville: Westminster John Knox, 1993), 263.

[8] Lieu's term is a simple transliteration of the Greek without the Greek ending, and so it more accurately reflects the spelling of the ancient term than does "Christianity" ("'Impregnable Ramparts and Walls of Iron,'" 312). Lieu's term, however, is not necessarily an advance. It does highlight the parallel between the ancient terms for the two religions, Christian*ism* and Juda*ism*, but this parallel is clearly conveyed to any modern reader by the terms "Christianity" and "Judaism."

without support, and it is less accurate—hardly an improvement on the more traditional term "Christianity" regardless of the difficulties that burden the latter term.[9] Bengt Holmberg thinks, with good reason, that terminology has become "unwieldy":

> If "Christian" is a term used about a specific group of people and their specific faith and ethos by others and themselves already in the first century, it is hard to understand why modern anxieties about how the term might be misunderstood should prevent its use in historical investigation of this very phenomenon.[10]

Tim Hegedus is of a similar opinion, and he makes a reasoned case for using the term "Christian" for even the first-century followers of Jesus.[11]

In the midst of the intense debate about boundaries and identity, the question arises as to how important it is to get the terms "just right." The general assumption in recent scholarship seems to be that it is crucial, making the effort at nuanced definition and terminological exactitude the focus of much of the scholarship in the field. Lieu, for example, expresses the concerns of many regarding the modern application of the terms "Jewish" and "Christian" (and related cognates) as labels for groups and literature in the ancient period that did not explicitly use these terms: "How far are we imposing a false sense of unity and of difference?"[12] The question is a fair one. We must be cautious not to misrepresent the ancient situation by imposing inadequate or inaccurate labels. But Lieu's question does not touch the heart of the matter. The crucial issue is whether there was a distinctive Christian self-understanding, not whether the group in question had

---

[9] As far as is known, no one in ancient times called early Christianity "the Jesus movement." From the beginning (or as near to the beginning as can be determined), Christianity's distinctive confession had something to do with Jesus as the Christ, and he was judged worthy to be followed precisely for this reason. The term "Jesus movement" is not more theologically neutral. It tends to reflect theological sensitivities of the modern scholar—not neutral sensitivities.

[10] Bengt Holmberg, "The Life in the Diaspora Synagogues: An Evaluation," in *The Ancient Synagogue from Its Origins until 200 C.E.: Papers Presented at an International Conference at Lund University, October 14–17, 2001* (ed. Birger Olsson and Magnus Zetterholm; Coniectanea biblica: New Testament Series 39; Stockholm: Almqvist & Wiksell, 2003), 219–32. Zetterholm tries to counter Holmberg's position by arguing that the term "Christian" was probably used only *later* in the first century and that it is not clear what group was tagged with the label (*The Formation of Christianity in Antioch*, 16–17, n. 21). Even if Zetterholm is correct, this need not prohibit the use of this general term for a discussion of the first century. It is not clear that the dismissal of general terms has given a "higher degree of analytical precision" (which presumably implies greater clarity as well) in the description of early Christianity, as Zetterholm maintains.

[11] Tim Hegedus, "Naming Christians in Antiquity," *SR* 33 (2004): 175. His article provides good summaries of aspects of the debate as well as balanced comments on many of the issues.

[12] Lieu, *Neither Jew nor Greek?* 6.

a particular label, for a community need not have a distinctive *term* for itself in order to have a clear *sense* of its separate and distinctive identity. We must be cautious not to overlook or underestimate a group's sense of identity and distinction merely on the grounds that it has yet to develop some formal labeling or that it uses labels it will later discard for others.

As to the matter at hand—whether we can use the broad categories "Jew" and "Christian" for Ignatius's period—monolithic labels distinguishing broad categories of Jews, Christians, and pagans were appropriate by the time of Ignatius and perhaps even earlier. Indeed, it might be argued that to understand Ignatius, these monolithic terms must be retained. As seen, these are his terms, and they are terms that make the larger world in which he lived intelligible. This is not to say that these terms are without problems, or that they reflect permanently fixed and universally clear categories. Indeed, these terms often were used in older scholarship as more fixed than the terms in fact were in the ancient world. But the modern debate often demonstrates the excesses at the opposite end of the discussion, where terms such as "Judaism" and "Christianity" are dismissed as of little use. The remainder of this chapter argues against this contemporary extremism.

Whatever the level of sophistication in the debate over terminology —and it is quite varied—the debate is really simply a debate about words. Although this may seem a trite comment, it is an important point. Too often the terms with which we work—boundary terms associated with group identity—are treated as words of a special kind, and we are warned that such terms are flexible, or evolving, or subject to negotiation and change. We also are warned that the texts in which such terms are used present idealized or desired worlds, not the world as it really was—image versus reality. But such comments apply to language and literature generally, and we must not make the terms of our interest or the literature of our focus (matters related to Christian and Jewish identity) special in a way they are not, or consider our debate more exotic than it is. The words of our concern— boundary labels and terms of group identity and distinction—are like all words of our language: they define things.[13] And they define things always within a community of coiners and users. They are the tools by which communities shape and organize their vast and multiform world into a world that can be comprehended and communicated. Granted, there can be misuse of categories, forcing things to appear more alike than they really are. But this is not a defect of categories; it is a defect of scholars who are expecting too much of categories.

---

[13] An observation frequently made in studies of religion—mainly due to the influence of Jonathan Z. Smith—is that the term "religion" is an artificial construct, or an invented category, or a fabrication (surprisingly, it seems) of humans (William E. Arnal, "Definition," in *Guide to the Study of Religion* [ed. Willi Braun and Russell T. McCutcheon; New York: Cassell, 2000], 22). We might well ask what term does not have these characteristics.

The categories "Judaism" and "Christianity" are highly significant and pro-foundly loaded words for Ignatius.[14] This study has used the terms "Christianity" and "Judaism" without apology. Where it was useful, these terms have been quali-fied to avoid confusion. But they have not been qualified where it seems that the confusion arises from an artificially created, overly nuanced web of hyphenated, bracketed, or otherwise decorated language, so imprinted with the code of each modern author's interests that terms come to convey a privileged meaning that only the coiner really knows.[15]

Identifying Judaism and Christianity

The trend today is to minimize the differences between Judaism and Chris-tianity, at least in the first two or three centuries of their common existence. This newer approach can provide a welcome corrective to some of the more theologi-cally motivated views that emphasized the differences and, more pointedly, the supposed inferiority of Judaism to Christianity.[16]

But the modern trend has a serious problem. It tends to mute the significance of the differences that clearly existed between early Christianity and Judaism. Explicit pronouncements by ancient groups regarding their self-understanding

---

[14]Klutz offers judicious comments about Ignatius's language ("Paul and the Develop-ment of Gentile Christianity," 1:168–70).

[15]Brian E. Daley critiques the argument of one publication in the field: it is "half-buried in the coquettish, self-conscious language of all-too-clever literary theory" (review of Daniel Boyarin, *Dying for God: Martyrdom and the Making of Christianity and Judaism*, *First Things* 115 [2001]: 68).

[16]It was often said that Judaism emphasized the law whereas Christianity emphasized faith and grace or that Judaism reflected a restrictive particularism whereas Christianity proclaimed a sweeping universalism. The assumption was that, in each case, the Christian option was better. Modern scholarship has dismissed both portraits as caricatures of Judaism. For a review of the issue and a discussion of the literature, see Terence L. Don-aldson, "Jewish/Christian Relations," in *The Early Church: An Annotated Bibliography of Literature in English* (ed. Thomas A. Robinson *et al.*; Metuchen, N.J., and London: Scare-crow, 1993), 229–46. Also see idem, *Paul and the Gentiles*, 3–27; C. J. Roetzel, "*Oikoumene* and the Limits of Pluralism in Alexandrian Judaism and Paul," in *Diaspora Jews and Ju-daism: Essays in Honor of, and in Dialogue with, A. Thomas Kraabel* (ed. J. A. Overman and R. S. MacLennan; South Florida Studies in the History of Judaism 41; Atlanta: Scholars Press, 1992), 163–82. Another useful review of the history of the debate is offered in the first half of Andrew S. Jacobs, "The Lion and the Lamb: Reconsidering Jewish-Christian Relations in Antiquity," in *The Ways That Never Parted: Jews and Christians in Late Antiq-uity and the Early Middle Ages* (eds. Adam H. Becker and Annette Yoshiko Reed; Texte und Studien zum antiken Judentum 95; Tübingen: Mohr Siebeck, 2003), 95–108. Ja-cobs's adoption, in the second half of his article, of postcolonial criticism to analyze the problem of Jewish-Christian relationships is less helpful (pp. 109–18).

and their sense of boundaries are now often treated as flawed, imperceptive, or unimportant—a mere image rather than the concrete reality. It has become fashionable in some scholarly works to treat such internal or insider perspectives almost as data of inconvenience, although this is seldom explicitly admitted. The "correct" view now is whatever happens to be the current scholarly pronouncement on where a group's boundaries *really* stood and who was *really* a member of what, in spite of how the ancients may have identified themselves and drawn their boundaries.

Regarding Judaism and Christianity in the ancient period, modern scholarship has muted the differences or minimized the significance of the "parting of the ways" regarding Judaism and Christianity. Six approaches are explored below.[17] Each point has its value, each its danger.

Perspective 1: Siblings

Some scholars speak of Christianity and Judaism (at least in its rabbinic form) as siblings.[18] This portrait of the relationship is thought to be more accurate than the mother-daughter paradigm that used to be more commonplace.[19] The sibling metaphor recognizes that both Christianity and rabbinic Judaism have a claim to roots in a common religious world and that they emerged around the same time—"twins," as Alan Segal portrays the relationship,[20] or an even closer sibling relationship, "twins, *joined at the hip*," as Daniel Boyarin puts it.[21] But the danger

---

[17] There are other possible approaches. Andres Klostergaard Petersen, for example, argues that the metaphor of the "parting of the ways" reflects the idea of a broken marriage ("At the End of the Road—Reflections on a Popular Scholarly Metaphor," in *The Formation of the Early Church* [ed. Jostein Ådna; WUNT 183; Tübingen: Mohr Siebeck, 2005], 51).

[18] The most influential work in this regard is Alan F. Segal, *Rebecca's Children: Judaism and Christianity in the Roman World* (Cambridge: Harvard University Press, 1986), although more than a decade earlier Roy A. Eckardt discussed the same imagery (*Elder and Younger Brothers: The Encounter of Jews and Christians* [New York: Schocken Books, 1973]). Daniel Boyarin briefly examines the Jacob-Esau paradigm in relation to Christianity and Judaism (*Dying for God*, 1–21). See also Philip S. Alexander, " 'The Parting of the Ways' from the Perspective of Rabbinic Judaism," in *Jews and Christians—the Parting of the Ways, A. D. 70 to 135:* The Second Durham-Tübingen Research Symposium on Earliest Christianity and Judaism, Durham, September, 1989 (ed. James D. G. Dunn; WUNT 66; Tübingen: J. C. B. Mohr [Paul Siebeck], 1991), 1–25.

[19] Even though Martin Hengel sees the value in the sibling metaphor, he sometimes uses the mother-daughter language ("Early Christianity as a Jewish-Messianic, Universalistic Movement," 8, 34; 6, 9, 31, 36).

[20] Segal, *Rebecca's Children*, 1.

[21] Daniel Boyarin, *Border Lines: The Partition of Judaeo-Christianity* (Philadelphia: University of Pennsylvania Press, 2004), 5.

in this perspective is that it may miss how contentious the relationship was, even from its beginning,[22] or it may attempt to force a historical situation into a metaphor that is untidy and misleading beyond its most general and obvious insight.[23]

This criticism of the kinship metaphor is not meant to suggest that the Christian movement and rabbinic Judaism shared nothing or that they failed to recognize their shared worlds.[24] The danger of the kinship metaphor is that the focus is drawn to the similarities. It is, however, the differences that define and distinguish, regardless of the number of similarities between the groups. A group's sense of the need to have boundaries and its efforts to draw these lines have a significance that cannot be muted by the group's similarity to the other groups that come to be distinguished from it by such marking. The boundaries mark the "them" and the "us" in the consciousness of the group in profound ways, whether the group marked off is almost a twin or a polar opposite. It would therefore be a mistake to minimize the significance of boundaries merely because the groups on either side of the new borders are similar. In fact, this condition of similarity generally should be expected.[25]

Such is the case with early Christianity and Judaism. Although it is important to recognize how substantially the Christian world overlapped with Judaism, such

---

[22] Segal recognizes that these siblings generally have not been on speaking terms, even from the beginning (*Rebecca's Children*, 142–62). Early Christian literature is marked by its negative references to Judaism (see n. 26 below).

[23] Boyarin notes the untidiness of the Jacob-Esau sibling metaphor. He describes the relationship between Jews and Christians as "not a single, unambiguous, clear, linear story, but one of doublings and doublings back, of contradictions and obscurities," and he proposes that kinship metaphors be abandoned (*Dying for God*, 6–8). But Boyarin overstates the case. Although he may capture the character of the periphery, the core understanding of Jewish and Christian identity and relationship was much clearer, as I have argued throughout the present study.

[24] We know far more about how Christians understood these shared ideals simply because much more of the surviving literature that addresses the matter is Christian. According to the author of Acts, Paul appealed to ideals he shared with the Pharisees (Acts 23: 6–10). Moreover, according to Acts, some Pharisees were part of the early Christian movement (15:5). These passages suggest a shared world between some Jews and some Christians. At the same time, however, the storyline of Acts does not present the Pharisees as friends of the church—quite the opposite. Acts is not an apologetic for Pharisees but for the Christian movement.

[25] Lieu calls attention "to the selectivity, to 'the particular, chosen traits'" in the drawing of boundaries, pointing out that "difference is never absolute, even if it is represented as such; rather, the invention of 'the other' involves the selection of some—the boundary markers—while ignoring similarities" (*Christian Identity*, 270). This is correct, but I would want to point out that this is normal, not negative. Further, insiders can see differences where outsiders see similarities; again, this is normal and expected. See also Albert I. Baumgarten, "The Rule of the Martian as Applied to Qumran," *Israel Oriental Studies* 14 (1994): 121–42.

closeness should not deny Christianity a distinctive identity apart from Judaism. More important than the shared areas of interest are the areas that Judaism and Christianity did not share. There the boundaries are frequently sharp, the "family" connections forcefully and explicitly denied. Often neither side recognized a sibling in the other; each was, in its judgment, an only child. Recognition of such a self-perception is crucial for understanding these movements. The scholarly conclusion that the two groups shared a large common world, though true, should not be taken as more insightful or informative than the denial by these groups that they shared such a world, for it is through the latter perception that the ancient world came to be redefined and realigned. The perception of difference is critical in a primary way for all who would later analyze the early Christian movement.

Ignatius does not recognize a family relationship to Judaism. He does recognize sharing, but it is not mutual sharing. Judaism is indebted to Christianity; Christianity is not indebted to Judaism.[26] Ignatius stands in line with many early Christian thinkers who assert that Christianity and Judaism are not twins, or brothers, or half-brothers, or even friendly acquaintances. The early and recurrent position in much of Christian literature is that Christianity has replaced Judaism and that Judaism is now obsolete, with no ancient core worthy of restoration other than the parts that Christians themselves have appropriated.[27] Judaism

---

[26] Ignatius's closest admission of a relationship between Judaism and Christianity is his comment "Christianity did not believe in Judaism, but Judaism in Christianity" (Ign. *Magn.* 10.3). Ignatius presents the Hebrew prophets more as Christians-in-waiting than as Jews (Ign. *Magn.* 8.2–9.2).

[27] It is not just a group's sense of being different from others that is important here. A group can recognize itself as distinctive without dismissing other groups. A group might even view other groups somewhat negatively but see them in one positive light at least: as misguided siblings whom they hope to influence to return to the "purity" of a tradition that they all share. Some passages in early Christian documents reflect this tone. It is Paul who perhaps struggles most trying to find a continuing role for Israel (see esp. Rom 11). But even he sees the *Christian* message directed to the Jews as well as to the non-Jews. Although he sets his focus on non-Jews, it is not because Jews do not need the Christian message but because they already have responsible carriers of this message to them in Peter and the other apostles (Gal 2:7–9), and even then Paul hopes to win some Jews himself (1 Cor 9:20). E. P. Sanders, in one of his many writings on the topic, puts the matter starkly: Paul "*explicitly denies that the Jewish covenant can be effective for salvation, thus consciously denying the basis of Judaism*" (*Paul and Palestinian Judaism: A Comparison of Patterns of Religion* [Minneapolis: Fortress, 1977], 551; italics original). Sanders, James D. G. Dunn, and others of like mind offer a consistently more natural reading of the relevant texts than the recent revisionist efforts to mute the force of Paul's negative comments about Judaism and Torah. The comments about a role for Israel or a message directed to Israel that are scattered throughout early Christian documents must be seen as always set against a particular backdrop: both author and reader believe that for the most part, Israel has rejected the Christian message and has opposed its messengers. Even Paul leaves the issue of Israel unaddressed in most of his writings or addressed in a way that minimizes

has lost its place in the divine scheme, whatever its role was before the rise of Christianity. Judaism is simply an actor whose part in the play is over or an actor who has been released from the cast for not following the script. Christianity is presented either as the original intent of God or something radically new from God. Judaism is not the erring sibling who can be reformed. Judaism has, at best, a temporary role; with the coming of Christ, it is replaced.[28]

Many scholars have noticed the starkness of Ignatius's language in distinguishing Christianity from Judaism. Lieu summarizes Ignatius's position: "The only relationship between the two is a one-way passage which virtually renders Judaism obsolete."[29] Stephen Wilson speaks of the "entirely negative view of 'Judaism'" in Ignatius.[30] Virginia Corwin uses the phrase "incomplete and inadequate" to summarize Ignatius's view of Judaism, contrasting this with Ignatius's view of Christianity as "full and final."[31] Magnus Zetterholm observes that "Ignatius understood Judaism to be *something profoundly different from Christianity*."[32] It is such a sensibility that propels Christianity into its place as a religion in its

---

the role of Israel. When his situation forces him to address the issue, as in his letter to the Romans, there is "a startling lack of logical consistency," "anguished arguments," "curious logic," "tortuous line of argumentation," and "irreducible tension" that even those who see a continuing role of Israel in Paul's vision must recognize (Donaldson, *Paul and the Gentiles*, 220, 221, 226, 305). John G. Gager maintains that Paul is often misunderstood when he speaks of Judaism and Israel (*Reinventing Paul* [Oxford: Oxford University Press, 2002]). But even Gager has to admit that Paul failed in his efforts to correct the mistaken "anti-Israel" readings of his comments (p. 105). See also Oskar Skarsaune, who argues that Paul's vision never went much beyond the synagogue (*In the Shadow of the Temple*, 174). The problem with all of these new readings of Paul's view of Torah, Judaism, and Israel is that whatever Paul meant, it was the forceful rejection of Torah and Judaism that became the early and standard reading of Paul's writings, and it was this reading that became the "Paul" of early Christians—even the Jewish Christians who hated Paul. It was not what Paul supposedly *thought* but what Paul *was thought to have said* by his earliest readers that is Paul's real contribution to early Christianity.

[28] For a survey of early Christian views of Judaism, see Judith Lieu, "History and Theology," 79–96; Wayne A. Meeks, "Breaking Away: Three New Testament Pictures of Christianity's Separation from the Jewish Communities," in *"To See Ourselves as Others See Us": Christians, Jews, "Others" in Late Antiquity* (ed. Jacob Neusner and Ernest S. Frerichs; Chico, Calif.: Scholars Press, 1985), 93–116; Jeffrey S. Siker, *Disinheriting the Jews*; and Stephen G. Wilson. *Related Strangers: Jews and Christians, 70–170 C.E.* (Minneapolis: Fortress, 1995). Martin Goodman captures nicely the sense of the early distinctive identity that developed among Christians (*Mission and Conversion*, 100–101).

[29] Lieu, "History and Theology," 93.

[30] Stephen G. Wilson, "'Jew' and Related Terms in the Ancient World," *SR* 33 (2004): 162.

[31] Corwin, *St. Ignatius*, 189.

[32] Zetterholm, *The Formation of Christianity in Antioch*, 2. Note his other comments on the issue (pp. 1–3).

own right, distinct from Judaism and the world of paganism. And this sensibility obtains very early.

This does not mean that there were no other views about Judaism expressed in the Christian movement. But a dominant sensibility in early Christian literature generally dismisses or heavily qualifies Judaism, and this sensibility best explains the coming of Christianity early to distinctive and recognized identity. One might attempt to argue that much of the pro-Jewish Christian literature has been lost, but the reality is that a tension with, or opposition to, Judaism marks most of the Christian literature that is preserved, dating from the earliest years of the Christian movement.

If Judaism and Christianity were siblings, they lived in a house early and profoundly divided.

Perspective 2: Subspecies

Some scholars contend that it is a fiction to speak of Christianity as anything but a subspecies of Judaism, at least in the early period. The emergence of Christianity as a religion in its own right is pushed from the first or early second century, which was the traditional understanding,[33] into the fourth century, when Emperor Constantine allied the forces of the empire with the cause of the church.[34] Some make the same claim for Judaism or, more particularly, for rabbinic Judaism.[35] Rosemary Radford Ruether puts it bluntly: "The fourth century is the first century for Christianity and Judaism."[36] Andres Petersen concedes that "it make sense to acknowledge a general separation of Judaism and Christianity when one focuses on the fifth and the sixth century," but he qualifies even this

---

[33] Probably the majority of scholars still posit an early break between Jewish and Christian identity. Stephen G. Wilson, for example, who has worked extensively on such questions, comments, "By the 2d century (if not before) the two communities effectively operate as separate entities despite their intimate past and a few surviving anomalies such as the Jewish Christians" ("'Jew' and Related Terms," 168).

[34] James W. Parkes appears to have been the first to make Judaism and Christianity "fourth-century religions" (*The Conflict of the Church and the Synagogue,* 153). A brief review of the issue can be found in Boyarin, *Dying for God,* 6–7. Boyarin describes as "cutting-edge scholars" those who refer to the *fourth* century as the *first* century of Christianity and Judaism ("Semantic Differences," 66). It remains to be seen, however, how future scholarship will judge them.

[35] Jacob Neusner, *Judaism and Christianity in the Age of Constantine: History, Messiah, Israel, and the Initial Confrontation* (Chicago Studies in the History of Judaism; Chicago: University of Chicago Press, 1987), ix.

[36] Rosemary Radford Ruether, "Judaism and Christianity: Two Fourth-Century Religions," *SR* 2 (1972): 1–10. Boyarin agrees: "It was then that Judaism and Christianity finally emerged from the womb as genuinely independent children of Rebecca" (*Dying for God,* 6).

concession: "But that, of course, does not necessarily imply that the separation took place at all levels of society."[37] Paula Fredriksen reaches even to the end of the seventh century, and "possibly beyond":

> To conceptualize relations between ancient Jews and Christians in terms of a "Parting of the Ways" is to misconstrue the social and intellectual history of Judaism, of Christianity, and of majority Mediterranean culture at least up through the seventh century, and possibly beyond.[38]

Fredriksen compromises her proposal, however, by introducing a third element—Mediterranean culture. The effort to bind Judaism and Christianity together for long centuries fails to recognize the fact that Christianity soon found another partner, the Gentiles. The pronounced Gentile equation in Christianity makes suspect any view of Christianity that denies it a distinct identity from Judaism until centuries after its beginnings.

The attempt to deny an early parting of the ways for Judaism and Christianity is in fact a version of the traditional view that Christianity was born from Judaism—the mother-daughter metaphor. The modern view is different, however, in contending that Christianity should be viewed as a subspecies of Judaism for hundreds of years longer than was traditionally understood. Rather than a gestation of decades, as most scholars used to allow, Christianity had a gestation of centuries.

Those who argue for the fourth-century date (or later) for the emergence of Christianity and Judaism as independent religions in their own right have not discovered some new truth that challenges the traditional view of an early separation of Christianity from Judaism. These scholars have merely focused on the end of the process by which the movement came to be recognized as distinctive by the larger society, and even then they appear to have stretched out the process over a much longer period than is required. But supposing that the process of separation did extend in some substantial way into the fourth century, there is nothing that makes this the point at which to grant one movement the status of a separate entity from the other group. Equally valid, if not more so, is the point at which one movement recognizes or declares itself to be a separate entity and in so doing validates its own distinctive existence. This is particularly the case if disinterested or neutral outsiders come to make this distinction also.

For Ignatius, Christianity and Judaism are separate entities and have always been separate.[39] Modern scholarship's refocusing to the fourth century misses

---

[37] Petersen, "At the End of the Road," 62.

[38] Paula Fredriksen, "What 'Parting of the Ways'?" 38.

[39] Ign. *Magn.* 8.1; 10.3; Ign. *Phld.* 6.1. Ignatius does admit that the Hebrew prophets had been part of Judaism, but as mentioned earlier, he sees them as waiting in hope for the coming of Christ (Ign. *Magn.* 8.2–9.2). Lieu thinks that not only Ignatius but early Christian writers generally held this view ("History and Theology," 88), or as Lieu says

the sense of newness and the sharp differentiation from Judaism that is found widely in early Christian literature. The modern perspective can hardly be called more accurate than that of Ignatius. Indeed, the modern view requires such a considerable qualification of the terms used by the ancients that they lose their value for helping us understand the world of the ancients. In that world Jews and Christians were clearly distinguished and terms such as "Jew" and "Christian" could be employed to effectively indicate the distinction.

Perspective 3: Christianities and Judaisms

In recent years it has become fashionable to speak of Judaisms and Christianities[40] and to discount any meaningful use of the singular forms of these terms.[41] To complicate the debate even further, some scholars have challenged

---

in another place, it is not law and grace that Ignatius sets in opposition but Judaism and grace (Image and Reality, 28).

[40]Robert A. Kraft ("The Weighing of the Parts: Pivots and Pitfalls in the Study of Early Judaisms and Their Early Christian Offspring," in The Ways That Never Parted: Jews and Christians in Late Antiquity and the Early Middle Ages (eds. Adam H. Becker and Annette Yoshiko Reed; Texte und Studien zum antiken Judentum 95; Tübingen: Mohr Siebeck, 2003), 88, n. 3) attributes the popularity of the term "Judaisms" to Jacob Neusner, William Scott Green, and Ernest S. Frerichs, eds., Judaisms and Their Messiahs at the Turn of the Christian Era (Cambridge: Cambridge University Press, 1987). See also Jacob Neusner, Studying Classical Judaism: A Primer (Louisville: Westminster, 1991), 17–36. The parallel term "Christianities" followed shortly thereafter, although the idea has been around since Bauer, Orthodoxy and Heresy. Note, for example, the following works: Jonathan Z. Smith, Drudgery Divine: On the Comparison of Early Christianities and the Religions of Late Antiquity (Chicago: University of Chicago Press, 1990); Ehrman, Lost Christianities; Willi Braun, ed., Rhetoric and Reality in Early Christianities (SCJ 16; Waterloo, Ont.: Wilfrid Laurier University Press, 2005); and, complete with diagrams of the Christianities, Sheila E. McGinn, "Internal Renewal and Dissent in the Early Christian World," in The Early Christian World (ed. Philip F. Esler; 2 vols.; New York: Routledge, 2000), 2:893–906. Kraft thinks that fewer people now speak of "Christianities" ("The Weighing of the Parts," 88). Against the trend to use the plural form of these terms, some scholars have found that the singular term "Judaism" does have usefulness in identifying a cluster of shared ideas and attitudes that constituted, in a nonarbitrary way, something often referred to simply as "common Judaism." For descriptions of the boundaries of a definable Judaism, see, for example, E. P. Sanders, Paul, the Law, and the Jewish People (Philadelphia: Fortress, 1983); idem, Judaism: Practice and Belief, 63 BCE–66 CE (London: SCM; Philadelphia: Trinity Press International, 1992); and James D. G. Dunn, The Partings of the Ways between Christianity and Judaism and Their Significance for the Character of Christianity (London: SCM, 1991).

[41]Daniel Boyarin, speaking of terms such as "Judaism," "Christianity," and "Judaeo-Christianity," goes too far when he asserts, "These categories have to be, if not abandoned, thoroughly reconfigured by the new research, which we are introducing here" ("Judaeo-Christianity Redivivus," JECS 9 [2001]: 418).

the adequacy of other "monolithic" terms, such as "early Christianity," "Jewish," "Gentile," "pagan," and "Greco-Oriental."[42]

Added to this is an overly careful policing of terms to prevent any anachronistic employment.[43] What is inadequately appreciated is the fact that monolithic terms, by their nature, include ambiguities on the edges, whether of subject or of time. Such terms may well have a proper "anachronistic" use, in that the terms, by their nature as monolithic terms, can identify movements from their early stages, before the time a formal label was coined and applied.

Granted, the rejection of such traditional terms as "Christianity" and "Judaism" does have some shock value in reminding us that ancient movements were not monolithic constructs: each had a range of diverse approaches and expressions. But such nuancing of the debate often fails to appreciate that the larger world in which Jews and Christians lived commonly employed such general and sweeping terms to identify Jews and Christians.[44] The ancients almost entirely

---

[42] David Frankfurter examines the debate ("Jews or Not? Reconstructing the 'Other' in Rev. 2:9 and 3:9," *HTR* 94 [2001]: 403–25). See also William Scott Green, "Ancient Judaism: Contours and Complexity," in *Language, Theology, and the Bible: Essays in Honour of James Barr* (ed. S. E. Balentine and J. Barton; Oxford: Oxford University Press, 1994), 293–310; Gabriele Boccaccini, "Middle Judaism and Its Contemporary Interpreters (1986–1992): Methodological Foundations for the Study of Judaisms, 300 BCE to 200 CE," *Henoch* 15 (1993): 207–33.

[43] Frankfurter, "Jews or Not?" 407. Lieu states, "To suggest that Christianity and Christians could exist prior to and independently of their fashioning of parameters" is "an impossible position" (*Christian Identity*, 145). But she overlooks the fact that Christians sensed some kind of distinctive identity from the start, and however much this identity may have been viewed from within a familiar world of Judaism (a hardly surprising scenario), it blossomed into something quite different. A seed is not a flower, but there is something substantial that links one to the other.

[44] Christians and pagans employed the terms "Christianity" and "Judaism" quite early. Although "Christian" is not widely used in our earliest literature, where the term is employed, the readers are apparently familiar with it. The word appears three times in the New Testament (Acts 11:26; 26:28; 1 Pet 4:16). Although it seems at first to have been a label applied to Christians by others, Christians do not seem to have resisted the name. Ignatius readily uses the term (Ign. *Eph.* 11.2; Ign. *Magn.* 4.1; Ign. *Trall.* 6.1; Ign. *Rom.* 3.2; Ign. *Pol.* 7.3), and this suggests that it was intelligible in Christian circles from Antioch to Rome. The following Greco-Roman authors, who are contemporaries of Ignatius, likewise employ the term: Tacitus, *Ann.* 15.44; Pliny the Younger, *Ep.* 10.96 (and Trajan's reply); and Suetonius, *Nero* 16. In the middle of the second century, the term is used frequently by Lucian (*De morte Peregrini* 11, 12, 13, 16; *Alexander* [*Pseudomantis*] 25, 38, 39). For both the Christians themselves and the Roman courts, "Christian" was the key term of identity at trials conducted by Pliny and at the trial of Justin Martyr and his friends (*Acts of Justin Martyr*). We do not know what term, if any, Jews used of Christians at the time of Ignatius. It may be that Jews adopted the language of the larger society to identify Christians, but it does not matter much to the discussion when or if Jews came to use the term "Christian." If the Christian group itself and the larger Greco-Roman world

missed the diversity that many modern reconstructions see as the most distinctive aspect of these movements. Louis D. Feldman's observation is particularly important: "Pagans, throughout the entire period of antiquity, viewed the Jews as a group, making almost no differentiation among subgroups of Jews."[45] Yet the Romans were able to distinguish between Jews and Samaritans, as Feldman points out.[46] The point of interest here is the Roman ability to discriminate between Jews and Samaritans while showing no interest in discriminating among the various species of Judaism. In much the same way, the Romans came to distinguish between Jews and Christians. The general terms "Jews," "Christians," and "Samaritans" (or other monolithic terms by which ancient groups were distinguished) do not appear to be loosely used and poorly applied categories of the ancients; rather, they appear to be perceptive and discriminating terms. There seems to have been something about the groups in question that allowed such general labeling, and the modern perspective is deficient when it lacks the ability or interest to understand the broad use of these terms for the early period. Scholars should attempt to understand such general and broad terms as substantial and insightful ways of perceiving and categorizing the world in which Ignatius lived, however much the terms may be problematic for modern concerns.

The increasing fondness in scholarship for a word such as "Christianities" fits well into a climate where the multiform character of Christianity is assumed. Scholars are generally convinced of the diversity of early Christian communities, basing this view mainly on peculiarities and distinctive elements found in early Christian documents and from these constructing distinct religious communities that supposedly created and preserved the documents.[47] Sometimes an even more nuanced reading of a document is attempted in a further effort to discover redactional layers within the document and from these layers either to trace the historical development of a community or to identify splintering trajectories within the

---

were using the terms, then the distinctive identity of the Christian group was largely established. Lieu addresses aspects of this question, including the use of the terms "Jew" and "Judaism," in *Image and Reality*, 57–102; " 'The Parting of the Ways,' " 19–20.

[45] Louis H. Feldman, *Jew and Gentile in the Ancient World*, 45. He offers a range of evidence (pp. 45–51).

[46] Ibid., 45. There are other ways of grouping that reflect the interests of those defining the boundaries. Justin, for example, could group Jews and Samaritans together as Israel when he wanted to contrast the multitude of Gentile believers to the few Jewish and Samaritan believers (*1 Apol.* 53).

[47] Robert L. Wilken offers a balanced assessment of the development of the interest in diversity that marks the contemporary study of early Christianity, pointing to its benefits and its dangers ("Diversity and Unity in Early Christianity," *SecCent* 1 [1981]: 101–10). He thinks that there has been a loss of the sense of a center—a conclusion he reached more than twenty-five years ago (pp. 105–7). In part, the inability of scholars today to recognize the usefulness of monolithic terms such as "Judaism" and "Christianity" is a consequence of this loss.

community. Whatever merit there might be to such procedures, scholars often overlook the fact that a document may reflect the thinking of an individual, the author, or, perhaps more accurately, merely one stage in the thinking of the author rather than the thinking of an entire unique and isolated community.[48]

Early Christian communities tended to encompass a range of diversity and to use a variety of documents that could be minutely analyzed into a number of distinctive and even competing theological perspectives.[49] Ignatius's church is one in which a variety of documents and traditions were appropriated.[50] If one were to try to reconstruct Ignatius's church from any one document or tradition that Ignatius employs, this reconstruction would misrepresent the diverse character of Ignatius's church. Yet this method is routinely employed on a host of early Christian documents, and communities are defined on the basis of individual documents. Where we do have a clearer picture, as in Ignatius's community, the method falls short.[51]

The Ignatian letters challenge the standard reconstructions of diverse Christian assemblies in another way. Ignatius confronts some groups because they are separate from the bishop's church either in practice or in attitude.[52] What complicates the matter for the "Christianities" thesis is that Ignatius's opponents range over the entire theological spectrum of early Christianity, from Judaizing to docetic.[53] Under a scenario where there is a multitude of early Christianities,

---

[48] Frederik Wisse is skeptical about the practice of hypothesizing gnostic groups on the basis of the existence of gnostic-colored documents ("The Nag Hammadi Library and the Heresiologists," *VC* 25 [1971]: 205– 23; idem, "Stalking Those Elusive Sethians," in *The Rediscovery of Gnosticism* [ed. Bentley Layton; 2 vols.; Leiden: E. J. Brill, 1980–1981], 2:563–78). His caution might well be applied to other ancient documents.

[49] Lieu is one of a few voices warning about the danger of reconstructing differentiated communities on the basis of differentiated interpretations (*Christian Identity*, 164).

[50] See pp. 79–81, 86, and p. 80, n. 130.

[51] Does my objection to creating distinctive communities on the basis of distinctive documents lay a trap for me when I wish to describe the church in Antioch or Asia Minor by appealing to Ignatius's letters? I think not. Ignatius's letters explicitly address distinct churches, naming their leaders, commenting on beliefs and practices, drawing boundaries, and specifying membership. More important, such letters frequently reveal a range of theological idioms and literary influences shaping the sensibilities of the community. On the other hand, a document such as the Gospel of Matthew less easily offers up this kind of information, although this is not to say that some sense of an original audience or situation cannot be suggested from the content. But even when it is possible, we must be careful not simply to assume an independent and distinctive community in which this document had its life. Ignatius's community is able to use traditions from the conceptual world of the Gospel of Matthew *as well as* from a variety of other sources. To maintain that "Matthew's community" had only the influences of the conceptual world of the Gospel of Matthew is to assume what remains to be shown.

[52] See p. 80, n. 129.

[53] Chapter 3 discusses in detail the identity of Ignatius's opponents.

each largely independent and self-contained, one would have expected the Judaizing and docetic positions to have, from the start, their own assemblies, each accommodating some nuance of Judaizing behavior or docetic speculation. But this is not found on close examination of the situation in Antioch or Asia Minor. There Judaizing and docetic groups are within churches in Ignatius's orbit or are only recently separated from the churches. If we look at a concrete expression of Christianity in these churches, we find a significant range of theological positions and literature within one Christian community. Ignatius's Christian world is starkly different from what many of the recent reconstructions of early Christianity would lead us to expect; it is far more inclusive of the literature or traditions it appropriates and far more diverse in the beliefs and practices of its members. However much Ignatius may have wished to make belief and practice more uniform and however successful this effort toward uniformity became within the Christian church, the reality is that at the time of Ignatius, where we can examine individual living Christian assemblies, diversity is contained *within* individual assemblies.[54] The church we see is not composed of small, scattered, independent, theologically distinctive and isolated groups.

Further, Ignatius's debate with Judaism was expressed and can be understood only in terms of the broadest categories. For Ignatius, there is one Judaism and one Christianity. He is not interested in analyzing Judaism at more than the monolithic level. As for Christianity, there is one church, one bishop, and one Eucharist—in other words, one Christianity. There can be no "Christianities." Granted, this vision is idealistic, but it is far more consistent with other ancient descriptions of the church than many of the modern reconstructions that have no place to fit Ignatius's concrete church, which uses a range of theological traditions and has members from across the Christian theological spectrum.

One final qualification must be raised about use of the word "Christianities." The word is routinely paired with "Judaisms," but better parallels would be with the Essene community or with the group around John the Baptist. Do we find the same degree of diversity within the Essene or the Baptist movement? Whatever the diversity within these movements, no one posits a diversity there anything like the diversity assumed to be the essence of the early Christian movement. It is not obvious that Christianity must have expressed itself in a multitude

---

[54] It is difficult to determine how uniform Ignatius thinks the church should be. He is opposed to those who hold different opinions or separate meetings, but such comments are probably directed at the extremes of differences within his church, not all differences that existed there. Ignatius's church uses a range of theological traditions and idioms. When Ignatius challenges differences, they seem closely related to specific ideas central to Ignatius: views of Jesus, attitudes to suffering and discipleship, Judaism and Judaizing, and opposition to the bishop. Other differences are not addressed, and one cannot conclude that every difference rose to a level of serious concern for Ignatius.

of independent communities unless such diversity was the normal character of other submovements within Judaism. But nowhere in the debate has this matter been considered. Instead, the diversity within Judaism is taken as sufficient grounds to expect similar diversity within Christianity.

Perspective 4: Fluid Boundaries and Flexible Membership

Another way scholars have tried to show ambiguous borders between Christianity and Judaism is to place all Jewish and Christian groups on a shared continuum. Boyarin places the Marcionites on one end and the "Jews for whom Jesus meant nothing" on the other end. "In the middle," he argues, "were many gradations that provided social and cultural mobility from one end of this spectrum to the other." He contends that the boundaries were so fluid between Christians and Jews that individuals hardly knew in which group they were members, and that it was "impossible to declare phenomenologically who is a Jew and who is a Christian."[55] Christians and Jews are better viewed as "complexly related subsystems of one religious polysystem."[56]

Boyarin tries to support his reconstruction by turning to a story regarding a charge of Christianity that was laid against Rabbi Eliezer.[57] The Roman authorities had charged Eliezer with being a Christian, but the charge was dropped when he came to trial. According to the story, the accused rabbi was bewildered by the charge, and even after racking his mind, he could not come up with any reason someone might have thought him to be a Christian. Finally, a disciple of the rabbi suggested that Eliezer might have heard something from a Christian that "caused him pleasure." On hearing this, Eliezer remembered one incident where he had heard a saying of Jesus and had apparently found it agreeable.[58] Boyarin claims that "what we learn then from this story is that the rabbis themselves understood that, in notably significant ways, there was no difference between Christians and Jews, and the difference had to be maintained via virtual discursive force, via the tour de force."[59]

The story, however, actually confirms the opposite. It shows that boundaries between Jews and Christians were important and clear. Had the boundaries been vague, the rabbi might have wondered which of a number of things may have provoked his situation. Even if it were granted that Eliezer had Christian sympathies,

---

[55] Boyarin, "Martyrdom and the Making of Christianity and Judaism," *JECS* 6 (1998): 577–627, here 584; repr. in modified form as ch. 4 in *Dying for God*.

[56] Boyarin, *Dying for God*, 92.

[57] The brief story is found in the Babylonian Talmud, *'Abodah Zarah* 16b–17a. An even shorter version of the story is found in the Tosefta, *Ḥullin* 2.24.

[58] Boyarin, "Martyrdom and the Making of Christianity and Judaism," 579.

[59] Ibid., 591.

this rabbi does not represent the normal engagement between Christianity and Judaism. Eliezer's association with Christianity would have been secret rather than public, and it is condemned rather than tolerated. The incident reflects a situation where boundaries are sharp and distinctive identities clearly in place for Jews, Christians, and Romans. The question is not whether there were a distinctive Judaism and a distinctive Christianity. The question is, rather, with which group Eliezer's loyalties really were tied. Any attempt to hold a middle ground is rejected by the Jewish circle of which Eliezer was a part and, indeed, by Eliezer himself.

Boyarin also says that the Quartodeciman practice "actually implies that these Christians were in some sense followers of the Jewish religious leadership, as well."[60] Yet while the Quartodecimans dated their Christian celebration of Easter to the Jewish celebration of Passover, they identified with the Christian community, not the Jewish community. The debate was over the date of the *Christian* celebration of Easter, not over which should be celebrated—the *Jewish* Passover or the *Christian* Easter. When Bishop Polycarp of Smyrna, a Quartodeciman, traveled to Rome, he visited the Christian church, not the Jewish synagogue. There is no confusion of boundaries or stumbling over unclear identities here.[61]

Boyarin's effort to dismiss the substantial distinctive identities of the Christian and Jewish movements leads him to some extreme statements. For example:

> These religio-cultural histories were inextricably intertwined to the point where the very distinction between syncretism and "authentic" Judaism, Christianity, and "paganism" finally seem irrelevant.[62]

In another place, Boyarin expresses a similar view:

> Social contact and the gradations of religious life were such that, barring the official pronouncements of the leaders of what were to become the "orthodox" versions of both religions, one could travel, metaphorically, from rabbinic Jew to Christian along a continuum where one hardly would know where one stopped and the other began.[63]

Boyarin's comments place too much significance on the vagueness of the boundary. It is similar to arguing that color labels are inadequate because the boundary between two colors is indefinite. This creates an unworkable situation in which

---

[60] Boyarin, *Dying for God,* 13.

[61] Irenaeus, *Haer.* 3.3.4; Eusebius, *Hist. eccl.* 5.24. Boyarin looks at other events where he considers that the boundaries between Christianity and Judaism were not clear. As in the case of the Quartodeciman debate, all that is illustrated by these incidents is that some Christian practices were borrowed from, or informed by, Judaism, not that Christians were profoundly confused about the boundaries with Judaism or about their distinctive identity.

[62] Boyarin, *Dying for God,* 12.

[63] Ibid., 9. One could quite easily grant that in some cases, individuals moved from one group to another. It is quite another matter to suggest that most did or that any but the most unusual case involved individuals moving from one end of the spectrum to the other.

people no longer can speak of "blue" or "purple" because there is an indefinite area on the border where one person might call something "blue" while another calls it "purple."

Boyarin thinks that he has found a way to handle what he describes as "a situation in which there are recognizably separate entities within a given field but no way to articulate the borders between them," which he thinks describes the relationship between Judaism and Christianity.[64] In perhaps his most radical statement, Boyarin comments,

> There is, perhaps, one feature that constitutes all as members of the Judaeo-Christian semantic family: appeal to the Hebrew Scriptures as revelation. In all other respects, the category of Jews/Christians constitutes a family in which any one sub-group might share features with any other (on *either* side of that supposed divide) but not all features with any, and there is no one set of features that uniquely determines a Christian group (except, of course, for some appeal to Jesus, which is simply an analytic statement and therefore tautologous) over and against a non-Christian Jewish group.[65]

Tautology, however, is the nature of a definition. Boyarin's proposal for grouping all those who appeal to the Hebrew Scriptures as revelation is also tautologous.

Consider a modern parallel: the Mormons. If we accept the definition that Christians are those "who appeal to the New Testament as revelation," yet at the same time reject as tautologous the definition that Mormons are those "who make some appeal to Joseph Smith," we overlook an essential criterion of identification. In our case, if we cannot allow the "appeal to Jesus" behavior (or something like that) to serve as the mark by which a group is identified as Christian, we are living in a reality that does not correspond to the ancient world. These terms and the distinctions they implied were understood and became the basis of specific actions and attitudes.

Following a line similar to Boyarin, Gabrielle Boccaccini contends that the term "Judaism" should include rabbinism, Karaism, Samaritanism, and Christianity.[66] Boccaccini's broad definitional brush makes the term "Judaism" practically useless in identifying a particular group.

---

[64] Boyarin, "Semantic Differences," 78. Boyarin is using the work of Chana Kronfeld, *On the Margins of Modernism: Decentering Literary Dynamics* (Contraversions 2; Berkeley: University of California Press, 1996).

[65] Boyarin, "Semantic Differences," 79. Petersen follows the same line of thinking in grouping Christianity within Judaism ("At the End of the Road," 56–58). But this is little more than semantics.

[66] Gabriele Boccaccini, *Middle Judaism: Jewish Thought, 300 B.C.E. to 200 C.E.* (Minneapolis: Fortress, 1991), 20. Boccaccini comments that his view "may be shocking" (p. 15); Zetterholm responds, "I would, however, go further—it is simply incorrect" (*The Formation of Christianity in Antioch*, 2).

Boyarin's emphasis on the vagueness of the boundaries fails to give the core identity of these movements their due. Boyarin justifies his focus on the peripheries by appealing to theories of culture that emphasize hybridity—for example, those of Homi Bhabha.[67] We may certainly debate whether we have an enlightening parallel between the rise of Christianity and minority traditions in the modern world, but the dismissal of broad terms such as "Judaism" and "Christianity" is surely overkill. Granted, these are large, sweeping terms, and as such, they do not catch the nuances of the diversity that lies beneath all broad, general terms.[68] But this is the nature of general terms. There is nothing inherently

---

[67] Homi K. Bhabha claims that it is "the in-between space . . . that carries the burden of the meaning of culture" and that "cultures are never bounded and singular entities" (*The Location of Culture* [London: Routledge, 1994], 38).

[68] We are accustomed to seeing the long list of options representing the rich diversity of first-century Judaism displayed in every discussion of first-century Palestine: Sadducees, Pharisees, Herodians, Essenes, Zealots, *sicarii*, scribes, miracle workers, and baptizers of various stripes, including Christians. And these groups become further subdivided: family conflict among the Sadducees; Pharisees split between the followers of the "conservative" Shammai and those of the "liberal" Hillel (whatever these terms might mean in that ancient context); Essenes differentiated from the Qumranites; Christians split by modern scholars into a dozen trajectories; Zealots fractured into rival groups with loyalties to various strongmen; and Jews who did not want to be Jews at all. Judaism seems to have encompassed everyone, from the rich, elite bedfellows of the occupying Roman authorities to guerrilla terrorists and everything in between. In modern terms, we would say that they had hawks and doves of various kinds: pro-peace parties, politically disengaged religious visionaries, rock-throwing youths, suicide bombers, and inflamed apocalyptical agitators. No doubt, in the midst of all this toiled a mass of the ordinary— tired of everyone's line and hoping for an adequate supper and a good night's rest. Eric M. Meyers suggests that even after the destruction of Jerusalem, a range of diversity in Judaism is likely to have been found, for not all would have followed the developing rabbinic tradition ("Jewish Culture in Greco-Roman Palestine," in *Cultures of the Jews* [ed. David Biale; Westminster, Md.: Schocken Books, 1999], 169). Samaritans stood somewhere close. No doubt, they were not significantly less diverse than their Jewish neighbors, although this point is rarely recognized. The microscopic focus on the diversity of first-century Judaism in Palestine has yet to be applied to the diversity of perspective among the Samaritan people. Were not some pro-Herodian? Some resentful of both the Jewish and the Roman presence? Some innovative and some traditional in their treatment of Torah? Some observant? And some, with reputations lost, merely drawing water at the well? We know of Simon Magus (Acts 8:9–24) and followers such as Menander (Justin, *1 Apol.* 26); those who awaited the coming prophet (John 1:25; 6:14; 7:40); Samaritans who joined the Christian movement, implied by stories in the Gospels about the good Samaritan and the Samaritan woman at the well and explicitly confirmed by statements about the Christian mission (Luke 10:25–37; John 4:7–30, 40; Acts 1:8; all of ch. 8; 9:31; 15:3), although, according to Justin, Samaritans do not seem to have constituted a significant part of the Christian movement by his time (*1 Apol.* 53). These examples show mixed religious perceptions and hopes among the Samaritans. We could expect even more evidence for Samaritan diversity had a rich corpus of Samaritan literature

wrong with them. In particular contexts, they can be misleading and can obscure the experience of minority traditions; in other contexts, however, they can be not only profoundly insightful but also perhaps essential in capturing the heart of a community's consciousness.

To return to the example of the Mormons, the movement arose within and had its identity shaped in terms of the larger Christian movement. Although subgroups developed within the Mormon movement and each subgroup rejected the other Mormon subgroups, it is possible to use the broad term "Mormonism" as a meaningful, monolithic term. We are not more perceptive when we reject the term "Mormonism" for the term "Mormonisms" or for some new term altogether, such as the "Joseph Smith movement." The monolithic term to which we are accustomed carries within it, as a monolithic term, a sense of that variety and nuance for the informed reader of Mormonism.

By the time of Ignatius, a minority group, as Christianity was within the larger world of Judaism and Greco-Roman society, found its power and distinctive identity by employing and perhaps creating general, monolithic terms. In doing so, it propelled itself quickly to a status on a par with the group in which it had existed initially as a subspecies. In other words, it became a religion recognizable in its own right. Groups in the Christian movement that chose to remain quite consciously subspecies within Judaism (e.g., the Ebionites) had no such success within either Judaism or Christianity, and by the middle of the second century, they were mostly without status in either group. The Ebionites perhaps best represent culture's in-between—the undefined land described by Boyarin. The creative action is elsewhere, however, and much of it is in Ignatius's circle.

Perspective 5: Narrowing the Labels

Another way scholars attempt to diminish the traditional force of the terms "Judaism" and "Christianity" as boundary markers in the ancient period is to narrow the scope of the labels. This has been particularly useful in muting Ignatius's language, which seems unmistakably bold and uncompromising in drawing boundaries between Judaism and Christianity. The tactic is to admit the harshness of the language (which is too explicit to deny) but then to deflect the reference away from Judaism to some troubling, esoteric, and unrepresentative form of Jewish or Judaizing Christianity.[69]

---

survived, since communities are generally far more aware of the diversity within their communities than are outside observers.

[69] Lieu notes that recent scholarship often points out that "many of the attacks against the 'Jews' are in reality directed against 'Judaizing Christians'—Christians adopting Jewish beliefs or practices" ("History and Theology," 88). Petersen follows the same line ("At the End of the Road," 85).

Lloyd Gaston, for example, implies that Ignatius had no feud with Judaism; it is Christian misappropriation of Judaism that was Ignatius's concern.[70] In much the same way, Shaye Cohen modifies and narrows Ignatius's language. He recognizes that the language of Ignatius is clear: for Ignatius, the terms "Judaism" and "Christianity" are "antithetical categories," and Judaism and Christianity are "mutually exclusive."[71] Yet Cohen then changes the meaning of the terms to give them a narrower range. Cohen is forthright about what he is doing. He contends that we cannot be certain about what Ignatius meant by the terms "Judaism" and "Christianity" because the terms are not transparent and Ignatius does not define them.[72] Thus we cannot assume that Ignatius's use of these terms coincides with what we mean now, and to make this distinction within his article, Cohen puts the terms in quotation marks when he is using them for Ignatius's "hypostatized" Judaism and Christianity.[73] Similarly to Gaston, Cohen concludes, "The trouble with Judaism according to Ignatius is that when mingled with 'Christianity' it leads to error and 'heresy.'"[74]

> In both *Philadelphians* and *Magnesians* the "Judaism" that arouses Ignatius's attention and anger is within the church. This "Judaism" is the "Judaism" of Christians within the Christian community, not the "Judaism" of Jews "out there" beyond it.[75]

Cohen so limits the scope of the labels "Jewish" and "Judaism" in Ignatius's vocabulary that he is forced to argue that Ignatius had almost no familiarity, contact, or interest in broader Judaism, and Cohen extends this rather sweeping and unlikely conclusion to members of Christian churches who were accused by Ig-

---

[70] Lloyd Gaston, "Judaism of the Uncircumcised," 33–44. Gaston quotes with approval H. Riesenfeld's comment that "there is no controversy against Judaism in its orthodox form in the letters of Ignatius" (p. 36, n. 20).

[71] Shaye J. D. Cohen, "Judaism without Circumcision and 'Judaism' without 'Circumcision' in Ignatius," *HTR* 95 (2002): 398.

[72] Ibid., 397. To contend that Ignatius does not define his terms ("Judaism" and "Christianity") does not mean that the terms were not clear. In fact, that he sees no need to define them suggests that Ignatius senses that he is addressing communities where such terms would work in the way that he intended them. Further, if Ignatius is coining the word "Christianity" to parallel the term "Judaism" (as many think), it would have been important that the term "Judaism" have absolute clarity to the readers. This makes it highly unlikely that Ignatius's use of the term "Judaism" has some special, esoteric nuance, for this would render equally blurry the term "Christianity," the label of primary importance to Ignatius and the one by which he defined his world.

[73] Ibid., 398. Cohen says that Ignatius's terms are "not (necessarily) our own." My sense is that Ignatius's use of the terms is considerably closer to the way the terms have been used from Ignatius's time to our own than the way many modern researchers in the field now are qualifying them and how Cohen himself uses them.

[74] Ibid., 399.

[75] Ibid., 396. See also p. 401.

natius of Judaizing.[76] Much the same approach is taken by Michele Murray, who finds early Christian criticism of Judaism generally directed not at Jews as such but at Gentile Judaizers.[77]

Approaches such as those of Gaston, Cohen, and Murray overlook a key point: Ignatius's attacks on Judaizing forms of Christianity are effective only if both Ignatius and his audience recognize that there is something profoundly problematic with Judaism itself. The slur that something is "Jewish" or "Judaizing" is disqualifying only if Judaism in its broadest and most general representation has been disqualified.[78] Stephen Wilson, who recognizes that Ignatius's specific target of attack is Judaizing influences within the church, nonetheless clearly characterizes Ignatius's assessment of Judaism: "While Jews may not have been the immediate target, a negative view of Judaism is required for the rhetorical contrast to work: Judaism as an entity is inferior (even posterior!) to Christianity."[79]

Lieu briefly notes the matter from another angle, commenting on "the absence of a sustained conflict with Jewish Christians, so often seen as the real targets for Christian polemics against 'the Jews.'" She notes Justin's remarkably irenic attitude to Jewish Christians and points out that Jewish Christians were "not inspiring anti-Jewish diatribe."[80] It seems that the second century is marked by Christian anti-Jewish rhetoric that is directed with fuller force at Judaism itself. If Christian writers of the second century were primarily opposed to Judaizers rather than Judaism itself, as some contend, why is the more heated attack on the less worrisome matter? Lieu thinks that there was more than rhetoric here; there was encounter between Jews and Christians—and some of it was hostile.[81]

---

[76] Ibid., 403. Cohen's view runs counter to much of contemporary scholarship, which sees close contact between Christians and Jews at all levels even as late as the fourth century. See Donaldson, "Jewish/Christian Relations," 229–46. Feldman, for example, notes that "Ignatius here shows awareness of and mentions several specific practices of the Sabbath that were observed by Jewish Christians, namely, eating things that had been prepared on the previous day, drinking lukewarm drinks, walking only within a prescribed distance from their dwelling place, and dancing" (*Jew and Gentile in the Ancient World*, 584, n. 56). Feldman is referring to a comment that Ignatius makes about the Sabbath (Ign. *Magn.* 9.1). Although the quote is from the long recension of the Ignatian letters (probably fourth century), Ignatius may have had this kind of detailed knowledge of Judaism in the second century, for such details perhaps were common knowledge for any relatively informed individual living in a city with a sizeable Jewish population.

[77] Michele Murray, *Playing a Jewish Game*.

[78] Murray sometimes shows some awareness that the matter is more nuanced (ibid., 90). The section "Muting the Tensions between Jews and Christians," pp. 148–53, deals with Ignatius's attitude toward Judaism.

[79] Wilson, "'Jew' and Related Terms," 163.

[80] Lieu, *Image and Reality*, 284.

[81] Ibid., 286.

Perspective 6: Elite Labels

A final way in which scholars have minimized the significance of the labels "Judaism" and "Christianity" and other general terms of group identification is to contend that such labels, though used by the ancients, were tools of the elite and not reflective of the real situation.[82] This contention has been promoted for some time as scholars have attempted to recover voices of the past that were not represented in the literature of the elite.[83]

The current interest in the perspective of the non-elite has sometimes caused the perspective of the elite to be neglected or treated as profoundly flawed or as unrepresentative of the broader community. There seems to be an assumption that the perspective of the elite always stands in contrast to the perspective of the masses and stifles the aspirations of the non-elite. This could be the case in some situations, but there is no necessity that such routinely be the case. Particularly in a new religious movement, one may find that the perspective and aspirations of the elite and the masses correspond closely. Converts often join a new movement because they are attracted to a message formulated by the elite within that movement, or if they join for other reasons, they are quickly brought into the mental world proclaimed by the elite—if it is meaningful even to speak of the elite and the masses as significantly distinctive groups in the early stages of a religious movement.[84] The supposed struggle between the elite and the masses,

---

[82] Lieu, for example, says, "The texts reflect the experience or aspirations of a male literary elite, while the equally valid experience of others, particularly of women, is rarely directly available to us. The relationship between social experiences and the world constructed by the texts remains problematic" ("Impregnable Ramparts and Walls of Iron," 298). See also Jacob Neusner, *Judaism in the Matrix of Christianity* (repr., with new preface and introduction; South Florida Studies in the History of Judaism; Atlanta: Scholars Press, 1991), xvi; see also Zetterholm, who states, "Ideology as expressed in literary texts reflects mainly the view of the cultural elite and not that of ordinary people" (*The Formation of Christianity in Antioch*, 53). Petersen comments, "Sources . . . to a great extent stem from male elitist circles, but these sources can only with great difficulty be used to reconstruct what was taking place on 'the ground' " ("At the End of the Road," 62).

[83] Reconstructing the sensibilities of the non-elite is a task fraught with almost insurmountable problems. Material on the non-elite perspective is scarce. The efforts to hear these voices have been varied and generally less successful than is claimed. Such efforts resemble something like the works of the great Renaissance artists, who often captured more of their own world than the world of antiquity they claimed to paint when they featured scenes of the biblical world: colorful, compelling, intelligible—and wrong. The architecture is too modern, the dress too much from the fashions of the artist's world.

[84] Regarding early Christian conversion, the recent tendency has been to downplay the role of "belief" or "doctrine" in conversion; see Ramsay MacMullen, *Christianizing the Roman Empire*; Chad Kile, "Feeling Persuaded: Christianization as Social Formation," in *Rhetoric and Reality in Early Christianities* (ed. Willi Braun; SCJ 16; Waterloo, Ont.: Wilfrid Laurier University Press, 2005), 219–48.

then, is probably less significant in movements that are in their early stages and where members are often recent converts, finding the aspirations of their religious quest in the proclamation and focus of this movement rather than another. And for those born into the movement and perhaps isolated from other religious influences, their intelligible world is the world proclaimed by the elite. The elite and masses of such movements are likely to share considerable common ground that holds them together.[85] Later, as options narrow and structures become more institutionalized and opportunities become more limited, a feeling of "us" (the masses) and "them" (the elite) may well develop.

For early Christianity, to paint a portrait of the elite and the non-elite as forming two competing religious tendencies seems inappropriate.[86] It is far more likely that the two groups saw themselves sharing a common world, energized by a common spirit, bound together as a family, in one body, to use Christian language, and set against the hostile larger world on the outside.[87]

Perceptions: The Essence of Boundaries

It has become popular in modern scholarship, when speaking of how ancient Jews and Christians understood their distinctive identities, to distinguish between image and reality—between the ways things were perceived and the way things really were. There seems to be an underlying assumption that image distorts reality. Lieu, for example, sometimes seems to be speaking more pointedly not of "image *and* reality" (the title of one of her books) but of image *or* reality.[88]

---

[85] Lieu's comment "We should not . . . construct too complete of a divorce between the world of literature and that of most people's daily lives" is relevant here, although she stresses some distance between the two (*Image and Reality,* 278).

[86] The debate about the social and economic level of early Christian churches is unsettled. See Justin J. Meggitt, *Paul, Poverty, and Survival* (Edinburgh: T&T Clark, 1998); also *JSNT* 24.2 (2001), with review articles by Gerd Theissen and Dale Martin, along with Meggitt's response.

[87] Perhaps an examination of some modern North American religions in their early stages could be informative here. The adherents of groups such as the Mormons, Adventists, Jehovah's Witnesses, Christian Scientists, and Pentecostals often (though not always) would have expounded and defended their distinctive beliefs with as much zeal as any of their leaders.

[88] Lieu, for example, correctly points out that authors "may be seeking to represent a position that would not have been visible or persuasive to all those concerned" (*Neither Jew nor Greek?* 2). We could sharpen and broaden her point: no position would have been visible or persuasive to everyone. This observation does not point to a defect in the disputed perception but merely to the nature of group boundaries and identity. Lieu does recognize a profoundly important feature of "image": " 'Image' does not belong to the literary world alone, and 'reality' to the external" (*Image and Reality,* 279).

Indeed, another equally valid reflection on the interplay between image and reality deserves consideration—image *as* reality. When we are dealing with boundary-marking terms—a crucial issue in understanding Ignatius—the perception (image) is the reality. To propose this kind of relationship between image and reality is not to suggest a return to a less critical reading of ancient texts or a routine acceptance of the portrait provided by a text as an accurate description of the ancient reality.[89] It is rather to recognize that boundary-marking terms define and that they thereby *create* reality. The reality is the perception, and the distinction between image and reality that is often proposed in modern scholarship is potentially misleading.[90] Boundary terms show, by their very coining and their use, the world *as perceived* by their users, and at this level, such terms are accurate. Boundary terms structure and alter the way the world is categorized. There is no greater reality to which boundary-marking terms must conform in order to be appropriate or accurate.

Instead of dismissing boundary-marking terms as mere rhetoric and as misrepresentations of reality, we should try to see rhetoric as providing an essential tool for mapping and describing new territory. Indeed, the rhetoric of group boundaries corresponds to the reality much as a political map corresponds to the physical world. Modern scholars often seem to be expecting a satellite image (the reality), dismissing rhetoric and literature when such materials do not provide an identical image. More revealing of the "real" world of group identity is the conceptual map. Much as a political map shows highly significant conceptual boundaries that a photo image or topographical map cannot capture, so the boundary mapping of group identity must be viewed at such a conceptual level. Photographs (the "reality" of much of the present debate) fail to pick up conceptual boundaries, yet conceptual boundaries are the important ones in establishing identity. When scholars imply that the modern understanding of the ancient world ("reality") is somehow more accurate than the perceptions of the players from that ancient era ("image"), the modern debate misses the point, for the ancient perceptions mapped the ancient world. The *perceived* world of the ancients was their *real* world. It is this perceived world that gave boundary terms their substance. To look for more substantial or accurate boundaries of group identity than these

---

[89] Without becoming an apologist for the errors of the past, I think that some of the modern dismissal of older scholarship lacks insight. Harnack, for example, is criticized for his misunderstanding of the early relationship between Judaism and Christianity (see Jacobs, "The Lion and the Lamb," 98–101). It is always easier to see the baggage that past ages have carried than to see our own. When current scholarship on early Christianity is analyzed a hundred years from now, our age will probably not escape criticism for its baggage of post-Holocaust and postcolonial supersensibilities.

[90] The Christian vision of Judaism cannot be dismissed as mere rhetoric. It is in part rhetoric, but it is more, for it reflects what is happening in the real world. Rhetoric is a fundamental tool in establishing identity and in marking boundaries.

is as fruitless as trying to determine the political boundaries of the world on a globe that presents only the physical features of the earth. The necessary data are conceptual; they work with perceptions of the world that exist more in the mind than in the soil.[91]

Modern scholars sometimes qualify or distance the perceptions of the ancients from the supposedly *real* world of the ancients by using the category of theology. Lieu writes: "The (theological) perception of the early Christian writers (at least outside the New Testament) is of two separate entities, Judaism and Christianity, which have been separated virtually from birth."[92] Lieu is correct in observing that such was the early Christian theological perception, but she need not have qualified this with the word "theological." Simply put, this was their perception. Of course, it was a theological perception—they had no other perspective on the issue. I have said above that the *perceived* world of the early Christians was their *real* world; we could say as well that their *theologically perceived* world was their *real* world. The point is not whether the perceived world is theological but whether it is real. It is. The matter is not image *or* reality but image *as* reality, for, regarding boundaries and group identity, perception and reality are profoundly linked in much the same way as political units correspond to boundaries on a map.

The lived reality and the literary image are not polar opposites, even if it cannot be argued that they are mirror images. Indeed, much of the literary image and the lived reality are probably almost mirror images, bound together substantially in a mutually creative relationship. In fact, of all the lived realities in the ancient world, none corresponds so closely to the literary image of a text as that of the community engaged with that text. The oppositional relationship now often regarded as incisive in describing the tension between the lived reality and the literary image often misses this important point. Members of Ignatius's church were members of this church because the "prescriptive image," of which the literary image was a part, corresponded in a positive and compelling way with how the members would have understood their real world. In other words, what is preached is practiced—not perfectly and not by all, but in a way that makes the preached and the practiced look more like wheel marks from the same wagon tracks than from different wagons branching off in different directions.

It may be argued that the makers and users of the boundary themselves disputed the boundaries. Although this is true, we are in no position to judge which boundaries of the ancients were right and which were wrong. When we position

---

[91] Although a map is not the same as the territory it depicts, a map is the only depiction that can register political (or group identity) boundaries. For a different look at this theme, see Jonathan Z. Smith, *Map Is Not Territory: Studies in the History of Religions* (Leiden: E. J. Brill, 1978).

[92] Lieu, "History and Theology," 88.

ourselves as judges of this sort, we have simply sided with a particular perception of the boundaries; we have not determined the better boundary. Boundaries, as expressions of perception and definition, have an inherent rightness about them. There is no ancient or modern template to which such perceptions and terminology must conform, although often the subject is approached as though there were such an ideal against which the ancients' claims might be measured. Lieu says that "for Ignatius Judaism and Christianity are two separate systems with typical 'phenomenological' characteristics" and that "the only relationship between the two is a one-way passage which virtually renders Judaism obsolete." Her assessment of Ignatius's perception is accurate. She then points out, however, that "this does not represent the real situation which he is addressing."[93]

But one must ask whether setting up a contrast between the perceived and the real, which is almost always done at the expense of the perceived, unfairly disadvantages Ignatius. What exactly is this "real" situation that modern scholars have grasped but Ignatius did not? Is it that Judaism and Christianity were *not* separate systems? Could any argument have convinced Ignatius of this? Would he not simply have insisted that they were separate, and that Judaism was obsolete, and that there was a one-way passage from Judaism to Christianity? Could Ignatius ever have identified in any way with this "real" without being forced to deny his perceived and profoundly more real world? But, one might ask, what about the evidence that Christians did sometimes move to Judaism, contrary to the one-way movement into Christianity that Ignatius touts? Does this not count against Ignatius's reality? Ignatius was hardly unaware of this situation, and he factored such evidence into his real world: these individuals were not the planting of the Father; these were not within the church.[94]

Historians are always checking ancient claims against ancient evidence. That is their work. But they must be particularly cautious not to be too hastily dismissive of the perceptions of the ancients regarding boundaries and identity, for such items are fundamentally matters of perception. It is one thing to question, for example, whether there was an empire-wide census that forced Mary and Joseph to make a trip to Bethlehem, a claim made by the ancient Christian writer of the Gospel of Luke. It is another matter entirely to question, for example, Ignatius's claim that "if we have lived according to Judaism until now, we admit that we have not received grace" (Ign. *Magn.* 8.1) or that "Christianity did not believe in Judaism, but Judaism in Christianity" (Ign. *Magn.* 10.3). To say that Ignatius's perception about the matter was simply *wrong* is not helpful in attempting to understand the ancient world that Jews and Christians shared. One must be

---

[93] Ibid., 93. Lieu thinks it was "a situation of weak or poorly defined boundaries." The boundaries may be disputed, but it is not necessarily the case that they were poorly defined.

[94] An individual who is a Judaizer has become "rotten," says Ignatius (Ign. *Magn.* 10.3). To live according to Judaism is to be lacking God's gracious gift (Ign. *Magn.* 8.1).

very careful not to assert what the "real" situation was when speaking of creative self-definition and boundary marking. To contend, for example, that Judaism and Christianity were not separate is not to grasp the real situation; it is merely to accept a different set of boundary markings from those set up by Ignatius. Historians are on firmer ground when they recognize a certain kind of "rightness" about perceptions of boundaries and matters of self-definition. At the very least, they should not contrast Ignatius's perception ("image") with some supposedly more meritorious "reality."

I would be prepared, with some hesitation, to allow Ignatius's "image" to be contrasted to a more substantial "reality" if it could be shown that Ignatius is clearly the lone voice set against a range of others explicitly expressing the opposite view. What we find, rather, is that a broad spectrum of Christian litera-ture takes a stance not generally inconsistent with the picture that Ignatius offers, whatever particular nuance each author may put on the problematic relationship between Judaism and Christianity. This is a point that Lieu herself recognizes:

> Even though we must avoid reading back into the first and second centuries later conceptions of orthodoxy, nonetheless Ignatius's perception represents the domi-nant and formative perception of the developing self-consciousness of the Church, as it was expressed in literature, liturgy, creed and structures.[95]

There appears to have been a growing sense within the early Christian com-munity that Jews and Judaism were "the other."[96] Early Christian literature is ripe

---

[95] Lieu, "History and Theology," 94.

[96] For a discussion of "the other" in marking boundaries, see Lieu, *Christian Identity*, 269–97. Sometimes Lieu raises problems where there is none. She says, for example, "To speak of 'the other' is to claim the power to define the other, denying them their own voice and self-description" (p. 271). The matter is not that serious. A group defines the other only as it helps to define itself; this is a natural part of the process of boundary marking—the other side of the fence, so to speak. One might ask whether any group could define itself without in some way defining the group from which it wishes to mark its separate identity—its "other." As for denying "the other" its own voice and self-description, all groups do this to their "other." To allow "the other" a voice within one's group is to some extent to deny or mute one's own voice. Of course Ignatius denies Judaizers and Judaism a voice in his community. If these voices were given part of the stage in his group, it would be an entirely different community. Part of the definition of a community is the determina-tion of who gets the stage. The silencing of "the other" is not so grievous or offensive when this context is considered. It is only within the group's own circle that its "other" is denied their voice and self-description. Such an identification of "the other" has no validity and often no influence beyond the walls of the defining community. Indeed, "the other" may not even be aware of a small break-off group's definition of them—and if aware, it may not care. "The other" has its own stage and its own audience. To say, for example, that the Republicans deny their "other" a voice on their stage is true (and unsurprising); to read from this some dreadful silencing of the Democrats is a misconception. Each has its voice and its audience; each denies the other its stage. This is the nature of group dynamics.

with this idea. The sense is perhaps most starkly displayed in John's Gospel, where the author uses the term "Jew" or "Jews" more than ten times as often as the Synoptic writers, setting Jews up as "the other."[97] Paul has a sense that the Judaism that once was his life is no more (Gal 1:13–14). He sees Christians being called *from* Judaism and *from* the pagan world into something new (Rom 9:24; 1 Cor 1:24; 12:13; Gal 3:28),[98] and his sentiment is retained in the Pauline tradition (Col 3:11). The author of Hebrews sees Judaism as never more than a shadow of reality, and in almost any passage in Hebrews, the point is driven home that Judaism is sharply inferior and ineffective, and therefore obsolete in light of the new and perfect way that came with Jesus. Judaism and Christianity are not siblings: one is the religion of a servant (Moses), the other the religion of the Son (Jesus) (Heb 3:1–6). When the new is established, the old is abolished (Heb 10:10). The author of *Diognetus* sees Christianity as a religion distinct from the religions of the Jews and the pagans (1.1; 3.1–2; 4.6). In his view, both Jews and pagans persecute Christianity as something apparently distinguishable from both (5.17). The author *of Barnabas* is equally certain that Judaism and Christianity are different entities, and most of his letter addresses details of these differences, always dismissing the Jewish position.[99] The author of the *Didache* makes few explicit references to Judaism, but when he does, he refers to it with the dismissive label "the religion of the hypocrites" (8.1–2).

The world of the early church is one of conflict with Judaism, no matter how much this image needs to be modified in light of recent work on early Jewish and Christian relations. Stories of the church's conflict with the synagogue cannot be dismissed as fabrications, although one must be careful to note their polemical nature. Lieu comments about the tension reflected in the literature, "It is not always easy to distinguish here between the real consequences of actual persecution and the creation of a mental world where persecution and conflict is the norm."[100] Although this is true, it is likely that there is some

---

[97] There is considerable debate about what the author intends by the term "Jew." See Urban C. von Wahlde, "'The Jews' in the Gospel of John: Fifteen Years of Research (1983–1998)," *Ephemerides theologicae lovanienses* 76 (2000): 30–55; Raymond E. Brown, *An Introduction to the Gospel of John* (ed. Francis J. Moloney; Anchor Bible Reference Library; New York: Doubleday, 2003), 157–75; John Ashton, "The Identity and Function of the *Ioudaioi* in the Fourth Gospel," *NovT* 27 (1985): 40–75.

[98] The debate over Paul's view of the Gentiles is part of the reimaging of Paul's thought now at the forefront of scholarship on Paul. Paul is seen to fit much more within Judaism, and the salvation of the Gentiles is placed within the framework of traditional (though slightly modified) Jewish eschatological thinking (see pp. 210–11, n. 27).

[99] Reider Hvalvik, *The Struggle for Scripture and Covenant: The Purpose of the Epistle of Barnabas and Jewish-Christian Competition in the Second Century* (WUNT 2. Reihe, no. 82; Tübingen: J. C. B. Mohr [Paul Siebeck], 1996).

[100] Lieu, *Image and Reality,* 282.

correspondence between the actual situation and the perceived situation. Literature of this kind is probably both exaggerated (in that it is part of a creative process of realignment, boundary marking, and identity creation) and accurate (in that it captures in the clearest way possible the sharpening perspective of the group). If early Christian literature generally depicts an environment of hostility between the Christian movement and Jews, however exaggerated these depictions are, it is unlikely that the reality was that Jews and Christians were the closest of friends.[101] Adam Becker asks, "Are we to understand that someone can think of Jews as satanic and yet not catch a whiff of sulphur when walking by a synagogue?"[102]

As we have seen, there is a trend in recent scholarship to treat boundaries as blurred and terms as ambiguous, allowing for an extended period—of centuries in some cases—where one could not with any certainty determine who was a "Jew" and who was a "Christian." Michelle Slee describes this "growing scholarly consensus" well:

> As regards the relationship between the early Church and the Judaism(s) of the period, the growing scholarly consensus is that the Church was long bound up with Judaism, that clearly defined and discernable separation, if it did take place, occurred at different rates in different geographical settings, and often on those occasions the Church was only concerned to define itself over against *one particular Jewish group* as opposed to the whole of first century Jewry.[103]

Slee limits her work to the first century, where such a description has some merit, although it fails to recognize the radical nature of the developing Christian identity even then. Such a description, however, does not fit the second century. Ignatius presents a portrait of Judaism and Christianity that is a strong and damaging challenge to this scholarly consensus. For Ignatius, Christianity and

---

[101] Miriam S. Taylor reviews some of the debate about the conflict between Judaism and Christianity in *Anti-Judaism and Early Christian Identity: A Critique of the Scholarly Consensus* (Studia post-biblica 46; Leiden: E. J. Brill, 1995). Her own approach, in which she emphasizes the symbolic and theological character of Christian anti-Judaism, has itself been challenged for its lack of attention to the social realities. For shades of the debate, see Laurence Broadhurst, "Melito of Sardis, the Second Sophistic, and 'Israel,' " in *Rhetoric and Reality in Early Christianities* (ed. Willi Braun; SCJ 16; Waterloo, Ont.: Wilfrid Laurier University Press, 2005), 49–74; William Horbury, "Jewish-Christian Relations in Barnabas and Justin Martyr," in *Jews and Christians—the Parting of the Ways, A. D. 70 to 135:* The Second Durham-Tübingen Research Symposium on Earliest Christianity and Judaism, Durham, September, 1989 (ed. James D. G. Dunn; WUNT 66; Tübingen: J. C. B. Mohr [Paul Siebeck], 1991), 315–45; and R. S. MacLennan, *Early Christian Texts on Jews and Judaism* (BJS 194; Atlanta: Scholars Press, 1990), 116.

[102] Adam H. Becker, "Anti-Judaism and Care for the Poor in Aphrahat's *Demonstration* 20," *JECS* 10 (2002): 309.

[103] Michelle Slee, *The Church in Antioch*, 7.

Judaism are distinctive entities; one is not the other.[104] And as I have argued, Ignatius is not an anomaly.

The process by which Christianity came to be distinguished from Judaism is simpler than most scholars now admit. The stages in the perception of the Christian group—as a movement distinguishable from Judaism—are few, closely clustered in time, and early.[105] First, the Christian group had to recognize its own distinctiveness and make an issue of it. Second, the larger world had to recognize the Christian identity as separate from Judaism. Both of these sensibilities developed early.[106] It makes little difference how the Jews (the group with which the Christian group was most likely to be confused or identified) felt about the matter, for the recognition of a distinctive Christian identity was not dependent in any way on Jewish acceptance or recognition of the Christian group as distinctive.

---

[104] Ignatius speaks bluntly about the matter: "It is outlandish to proclaim Jesus Christ and practice Judaism. For Christianity did not believe in Judaism, but Judaism in Christianity—in which every tongue that believes in God has been gathered together" (Ign. *Magn.* 10.3). Ignatius has no place for a Judaism that does not believe "in God"—by which he clearly means a Judaism that does not believe in Jesus.

[105] I use the term "Christian group" intentionally here, although some other nuanced description more acceptable to the modern debate could have been used. The deliberate choice of a monolithic term here fits with my contention that the use of monolithic terms to identify "Judaism" and "Christianity" is a valid way of speaking of the religious situation in the second century and a necessary way of speaking about the world of Ignatius. Kraft cautions against such simplicity: "Complexities get masked by the urge to make and keep things clear and simple." He points out that "while it is clear that the definitional simplicity of mutually exclusive self-understandings ('Jewish' means, among other things, not 'Christian,' and vice versa), where it exists, shows parted ways, it is not clear that historically, every user of these terms 'Jewish' or 'Christian' (or their functional equivalents) would accept the exclusivist element" ("The Weighing of the Parts," 92). I agree with Kraft that not everyone would have seen things in this way. Still, most people who used these terms did so in an exclusivist manner. The example that Kraft offers actually supports my point. It is true that Ebionites or Nazarenes would not have used the labels "Judaism" and "Christianity" to the maximum exclusivist potential of such terms, yet nearly everyone around the Ebionites who had related concerns about identity seems to have opted for the exclusivist sense, and this caused "Jewish Christians" who wanted to claim both identities to be rejected by each of the larger bodies with which they tried to mark their identity. As Jerome concludes, "But while they wish to be both Jews and Christians, they are neither Jews nor Christians!" (*Epistulae* 112.13). The passage is quoted by Kraft (ibid., 92–93, n. 12). He could have quoted a much earlier author who expresses the same sentiment (Justin, *Dial.* 47). To bind the larger whole to the definitional interests of a minor player, rejected by both sides of the clearly "parted ways," is counterproductive.

[106] Even the story of Rabbi Eliezer (see p. 219) suggests a clear distinction between Jew and Christian in the late first or early second century. For Ignatius, the distinction is crucial. Evidence around the same time from Roman action against Christians (e.g., the trials under Pliny the Younger) suggests the same, as does the mid-second-century trial of Justin.

This is not to say that Jewish views on the matter can offer no fruitful areas of exploration. It is undeniable that Jews and Christians shared a large common world and that their communities were not formed into mutually exclusive enclaves as once assumed. But recognizing areas of contact and of common perspective does not preclude a recognition that the Christian and Jewish communities had come to have separate identities. Granted, sometimes the evidence is read in different ways. For example, the *Didache* commands Christians to fast on Wednesday and Friday, not on Monday and Thursday, as the Jews do (8.1–2). We could say that the Jews and Christians were similar because both fasted on two days of the week, or we could say that Jews and Christians were different because Christians intentionally fasted on different days. What we cannot say from texts of this kind is that the boundaries were blurred. Granted, some Christians would have been attracted to certain practices of the synagogue; indeed, there is evidence for this kind of attraction even at the end of the fourth century. But this is not the same as saying that such people had no awareness of the boundaries.[107]

The Parting of the Ways

Much of the debate about Jewish and Christian relationships in the ancient period has been framed around the phrase, "a parting of the ways."[108] The early debate assumed that Judaism and Christianity soon separated, although there was some disagreement as to the catalyst that propelled this development. Some scholars pointed to the Jewish War of 66–73 C.E., some to the Bar Kokhba revolt

---

[107]When boundaries are violated, it should not immediately be assumed that the boundaries must have been blurred. Usually, reports that someone has violated a boundary come from the same literature that speaks forcefully about where boundaries are located. Numerous factors could account for individuals' not respecting clear boundaries. Friendship or family connections with those on the other side might be a primary cause, particularly if individuals in the new movement were converts whose world of religious practice and social contacts was well established outside the Christian community before conversion. The case is perhaps somewhat different for those who grew up in the movement, for their history may have limited the range of social contacts and familiarity with alternative religious practices.

[108]For a review of the use of this term and some challenges to its usefulness, see Becker, *The Ways That Never Parted*, 1–33. See also Petersen, "At the End of the Road." According to Petersen, James W. Parkes was the first to use the phrase as it is currently being used in the debate (p. 45), but Petersen (47–48) attributes the prominent use of the term in today's debate to James D. G. Dunn, ed., *Jews and Christians—the Parting of the Ways, A. D. 70 to 135: The Second Durham-Tübingen Research Symposium on Earliest Christianity and Judaism, Durham, September, 1989* (WUNT 66; Tübingen: J. C. B. Mohr [Paul Siebeck], 1992).

six decades later[109]—both of which crises may have removed a substantial Jewish-Christian presence from the Christian movement.[110] Others have argued that a parting of the ways between Judaism and Christianity did not occur until the fourth century or later, and still others have questioned whether there ever was a parting of the ways.[111]

Lieu notes that the "parting of the ways" is only one of a number of possible models, and she claims that "it is not a model which would have made much sense to any of the participants or observers of the drama itself."[112] Perhaps so, but in the starkest meaning of the phrase—that is, to indicate *separation and distinction*—some early Christian authors would have found it quite acceptable. It does not matter what we call the separation of Christianity from Judaism and Christianity's coming to distinctive identity; what matters is whether Christianity came to be seen as separate and distinct from Judaism. Thus when Lieu shows that other models, such as Melito's supersessionist view, also were used to describe the separation, she makes a valid yet fairly minor point. The major point is the *awareness* of separation and distinction. So, too, Lieu contends that although Justin saw the separation as a "parting of the ways," Trypho (a Jew) and Celsus (a pagan) saw the matter as an apostasy.[113] However, the key fact is that the separation was indisputable to all observers. It hardly matters what label is used to describe the separation.

Lieu further characterizes the separation of Christianity from Judaism as a "theological construct" in contrast to a "historical reality." Yet there is no understanding of this separation that is not a theological construct. Trypho's sense of Christianity's separation as representing an apostasy (and Celsus's borrowing of this image) is as heavily theological as are Justin's or Melito's conceptions. Indeed, all terminology marking boundaries, separation, and distinctive identity, whether ancient or modern, are matters of perception and are thus constructed. No one of these constructs should have pride of place over the other as we attempt to

---

[109] For a recent review of the matter, see Murray, *Playing a Jewish Game*, 127–52; for an older review that covers some of the same material, see Steven T. Katz, "Issues in the Separation of Judaism and Christianity after 70 C.E.: A Reconsideration," *JBL* 103 (1984): 43–76.

[110] The assumption, not without foundation, is that Christian Jews who could not escape the situation either would have been killed by their fellow Jews if they did not identify with the revolt or would have been killed or enslaved by the Romans if they did. Certainly there seems to be nothing in the Jewish revolts that would have aided the growth of the Jewish-Christian group numerically overall, although in a city such as Antioch, the Jewish-Christian group may have experienced a rapid surge in membership as escaping refugees joined them. Such refugees are likely to have found increased opportunities for contact with the Gentile wing of the Christian church, compared to the contact they might have had in Palestine. See Wilson, *Related Strangers*.

[111] Fredriksen, "What 'Parting of the Ways'?" 35–64.

[112] Lieu, " 'The Parting of the Ways,' " 15.

[113] Ibid., 14–15.

understand the nature of Jewish-Christian relations in Antioch in the the late first and early second centuries.

Christianity as a Special Case

The Christian community had three characteristics that distinguished it from all other groups that made up the diversity of first- and early-second-century Judaism, and these characteristics account for the early recognition of the Christian movement as something distinctive from Judaism.[114] First, the Christian movement was perceived by the larger society as distinct from Judaism, much as Samaritans were seen as distinct from Jews.[115] What makes this kind of discrimination significant is that the Greco-Roman world seems to have shown no propensity to distinguish among other groups within the orbit of Judaism, such as the Essenes, or any of the host of other Jewish subgroups that planted their flag and chanted their distinctive chant.[116] Thus Christianity seems to have had something about it that set it apart from Judaism in a way that no other Jewish group did. With Christianity, then, we are not dealing with just one of the many Judaisms in the ancient world; we are dealing with a "Judaism" that was *uniquely* distinguishable from all other groups labeled "Jewish." Christianity reflected early on an unusual kind of identity that allowed the non-Jewish observer to distinguish it from Judaism.[117]

Second, the Christian movement, by rejecting Torah and in particular the requirement of circumcision, stood outside the boundaries of Judaism as traditionally defined.[118] It hardly changes the situation to say that Christians offered

---

[114] This does not mean that everyone knew of the distinction between Jews and Christians. In the early part of the second century, presumably many had never even heard of Christians.

[115] Or the larger society viewed Christianity as distinctive in an unusual way within Judaism. Lieu thinks Tacitus and Pliny are perhaps less clear on the boundaries between Jews and Christians than some have assumed (*Christian Identity*, 143–44). Lightfoot still offers the better read of the evidence (*S. Ignatius, S. Polycarp*, 2.1:9–11). The significant point is that Tacitus and Pliny are able to identify Christians as a distinctive group and apparently believe that it is important to do so.

[116] Feldman (*Jew and Gentile in the Ancient World*, 45–51) points this out. See also Lieu, " 'The Parting of the Ways,' " 20–21.

[117] The primary evidence for this distinction is the persecution of Christians. The name used of the suspect group ("Christian"), the questions asked by the judge ("Are you a Christian?"), and the proof that one was not guilty of the charge (cursing Christ) all point to the clarity of the matter. Jews would not be caught by the process; every Christian, whether Jew or Gentile, would be.

[118] On the issue of what constituted Judaism, see the debate about "common Judaism" (p. 60, n. 61).

a new definition of Judaism, for this is precisely the question: did the Christian movement fashion a new religious identity that was so distinct that it could not be contained within the *traditional* boundaries of Judaism? If so, such a movement is more accurately portrayed as something *different* from Judaism than as one of its many variations.

Third, having opted for the removal of uniquely Jewish elements from its qualification for membership, the Christian community became increasingly non-Jewish in a way that no other Jewish group did. The Jewishness of other Jewish groups was not threatened by the occasional proselytes who joined, for such new members were obligated to become Jewish. Further, although Judaism admitted proselytes, there is no evidence that non-Jewish converts overwhelmed the Jewish-born element in the Jewish community, making the membership of the community more non-Jewish in origin than Jewish.[119] Yet the influx of Gentiles into the Christian movement by the time of Ignatius made the Christian movement rapidly and provocatively more non-Jewish than other groups bearing the Jewish label.[120]

The possession of these three characteristics does not mean that the Christian identity was without controversy. There was vigorous debate about boundaries and essentials among Christians themselves as well as between Christians and Jews. We should not expect otherwise as the Christian movement set up significant boundaries that made it distinguishable from Judaism both in its own perception and in the perception of the larger world.

Some may object that I have described Christianity as I want it to be—a movement distinct from Judaism—for I have looked primarily at the branch of Christianity that was the most distinctive—the pro-Gentile wing of the Christian movement. Had I looked to Jewish-Christian groups, the matter would have been different. But to turn to the Jewish-Christian groups for a better window onto the developing Christian movement is to see through a window that had increasingly less to show, as Jewish-Christian groups were forced to the periphery by the pro-Gentile movement that took center stage.[121] This pro-Gentile movement drew sharp distinctions between Judaism and Christianity. This is Ignatius's world, and it is the form of Christianity that is most representative of the Christian movement in the second century. It is this movement, of which Ignatius was an important part, that merits particular focus in a study of the development of early Christianity.

---

[119] Chapter 2, above, discusses the extent of Jewish proselytization.

[120] Although it is impossible to be precise regarding the proportion of Gentiles to Jews in the Christian community at the time of Ignatius, it is highly unlikely that the Christian movement was as Jewish in its membership as the groups of Jews in Antioch—even those who may have welcomed proselytes and God-fearers.

[121] The term "pro-Gentile" is used here only because it helps to highlight the acceptance of Gentiles without the conditions of Torah. Any other term that carries this meaning may be substituted by the reader—thus avoiding an unnecessary controversy about terms.

The Burden of Historical Scholarship

The world of the early twenty-first century is heavily conditioned by profound events that have left their mark on our consciousness. We live in a post-Holocaust world and in a postcolonial era. Sensibilities shaped by both of these experiences are influencing current scholarship dealing with Jewish-Christian relations and identity in the ancient world.[122] The question of the moral burden of historical scholarship has been raised particularly by the Holocaust, and it is common to see references to the modern situation in studies of the ancient period.[123] Such linking of early Christian history and modern anti-Semitism is understandable, particularly given the harsh pronouncements against Jews and Judaism in much of the early Christian literature. Many are convinced that such literature, if not directly responsible for the Holocaust, shaped attitudes that put Jews at risk.[124]

It is not my intention here to enter the debate over early Christian anti-Semitism or to discuss the ways in which modern reconstructions of early Christianity sometimes have a post-Holocaust coloring.[125] I wish only to point

---

[122] For a brief review of the post-Holocaust change in sensibilities, see the preface in Bruce Chilton and Jacob Neusner, *Types of Authority in Formative Christianity and Judaism* (New York: Routledge, 1999), vii–xiii. See also Clark M. Williamson, *A Guest in the House of Israel: Post-Holocaust Church Theology* (Louisville: Westminster John Knox, 1993). For a specific example, Justin's comments are examined by Tessa Rajak, who notes that "readers have been remarkably unwilling to acknowledge the sheer vituperative dimension of the dialogue" ("Talking at Trypho: Christian Apologetic as Anti-Judaism in Justin's Dialogue with Trypho the Jew," in *Apologetics in the Roman Empire: Pagans, Jews, and Christians* [ed. Mark J. Edwards, Martin Goodman, Simon Price, and Christopher Rowland; Oxford: Oxford University Press, 1999], 60; see also p. 68).

[123] For a brief summary of the debate, see Becker, "Anti-Judaism and Care for the Poor," 319–21. Kraft lists some reasons the relationship between ancient Judaism and Christianity is studied: "Some of us may want to explore different solutions to old problems. If Judaism and Christianity were not always mutually exclusive by definition, perhaps some sort of contemporary rapprochement can be recreated with reference to the historical developments; history provides basic justification for trying to reset the clock to a more favorable time and situation" ("The Weighing of the Parts," 93). Petersen thinks that we need to "regain the biblical texts in a manner that gives way to the recognition of the right of Jews to remain Jews and to an acknowledgement of Judaism as a religion in its own right" ("At the End of the Road," 53). Those who make these efforts, however, seem to be forcing the past into a template of the present. We need not wait until we reshape ancient texts to fit modern sensibilities before we proceed to rectify current inequities.

[124] See John G. Gager, *The Origins of Anti-Semitism: Attitudes toward Judaism in Pagan and Christian Antiquity* (New York and Oxford: Oxford University Press, 1983).

[125] Post-Holocaust coloring in scholarship on early Christianity can be found in a variety of discussions: the discounting of the culpability of Jews in the trial of Jesus as portrayed by the Gospels; no longer viewing Jesus as a violator of Torah but rather as a Torah-observant Jew; seeing the Pharisees no longer as hypocrites but the group most similar to the early Christians; rediscovering or expanding Paul's role for Israel;

out where such sensibilities have muted ancient Jewish-Christian tensions and obscured the situation of Ignatius. My key objection is to modern scholarship's muffling of early Christian criticism of Judaism. We have already seen how some scholars have tried to redirect the sharp comments that Ignatius made about Judaism away from Judaism as a whole to a Christianized misappropriation of Judaism (the Judaizers of Ignatius's letters). Such muting of the harsh language of early Christian texts sometimes has a hidden and perhaps unconscious theological agenda. If allowed to stand in a post-Holocaust era, such harsh language seems to implicate Christianity in genocide. Further, the supersessionist view of Christianity over Judaism reflected in Ignatius appears to leave little or no place for Judaism except perhaps as a forerunner of Christianity. This position seems outdated, non-ecumenical, and arrogant in our modern age. However, if we truly want to understand early Christianity, we must first understand it *in the context of the ancient world.*

The problem with the modern redirection of the target or intensity of anti-Jewish statements in early Christian documents is that it smacks too much of a sanitizing effort.[126] This often leads to a falsification or obscuration of the kind of historical grit and grime likely to be found in group relations in the early days of any new religious movement. Granted, Ignatius's comments would generally be seen as unhelpful for contemporary Jewish-Christian relations, but his comments should not be dismissed or qualified when we attempt to understand the ancient period and Jewish and Christian relations at that time. Ignatius's comments should be set in the environment of the creative and explosive forces that come into play in the shaping of a new and distinctive identity. In that context, his comments make sense. To disallow or mute such comments is to require of all new religious movements a sensibility and a sensitivity that they, by their nature, are unlikely to have. We do not help the struggles of the present by sanitizing the past.[127] We must seek other ways to handle the problems of ancient language and attitude.

---

moving Jewish persecution of Christians from the status of reality to that of rhetoric, to list a few. I do not deny that, at least in some of these issues, the new sensibilities may have made us better historians or have at least opened up broader horizons for historical reconstructions.

[126] Todd Penner is not untypical in seeing the revisionist readings of anti-Judaism in early Christian writing as having potentially useful force in modern Jewish-Christian relationships ("Early Christian Heroes and Lukan Narrative: Stephen and the Hellenists in Ancient Historical Perspective," in *Rhetoric and Reality in Early Christianities* [ed. Willi Braun; SCJ 16; Waterloo, Ont.: Wilfrid Laurier University Press, 2005], 86).

[127] We also do not help the present by catapulting blame and responsibility from players in the present to those in the past. How the modern players employ ancient texts to carry out their contemporary agenda should not affect how these texts are treated as ancient documents.

Conclusion

Any reconstruction that pushes the point of separation between Judaism and Christianity to centuries after Ignatius must disregard the force of Ignatius's language and rhetoric. And if we disregard Ignatius's perceptive reflection, we run the risk of missing his incisive critique of his own world. It is Ignatius who grasped what the relationship between Christianity and Judaism was soon to be—indeed, if it was not already so in his day. In Ignatius's mind, the way had parted. The main path led into the Christian movement. The other path was a dead end, on which Judaism had halted. There was no way beyond this point for Judaism other than a return to the main path, which meant turning to Christ and the church. Anything that was associated with Judaism or that compromised the essence of the Christian message was thus to be rejected. His language and attitude fit well the situation we should expect as a new religious movement comes into its own distinctive identity.

The distinction drawn between Jews and Christians by authors such as Ignatius is a real one, not an imagined one. The tendency in modern scholarship to narrow the gap between Jews and early Christians sometimes causes us to overlook the simple fact that were we to put a Clement and an Ignatius together, each would have preferred the company of the other to that of the local synagogue and each would have sensed that he shared a common identity with the other that neither shared with the local Jewish community. This is the world in which Ignatius operates.

Bibliography

Alexander, Philip S. " 'The Parting of the Ways' from the Perspective of Rabbinic Judaism." Pages 1–25 in *Jews and Christians—the Parting of the Ways, A. D. 70 to 135: The Second Durham-Tübingen Research Symposium on Earliest Christianity and Judaism, Durham, September, 1989*. Edited by James D. G. Dunn. Wissenschaftliche Untersuchungen zum Neuen Testament 66. Tübingen: J. C. B. Mohr (Paul Siebeck), 1991.

Apostolic Fathers, The. Edited and translated by Kirsopp Lake. 2 vols. Loeb Classical Library. Cambridge, Mass: Harvard University Press, 1912.

Apostolic Fathers, The. Edited and translated by Bart D. Ehrman. 2 vols. Loeb Classical Library 24–25. Cambridge, Mass. : Harvard University Press, 2003.

Applebaum, S. "The Legal Status of the Jewish Communities in the Diaspora." Pages 420–63 in vol. 1 of *The Jewish People in the First Century: Historical Geography, Political History, Social, Cultural, and Religious Life and Institutions*. Edited by S. Safrai and M. Stern. 2 vols. Compendia rerum iudaicarum ad Novum Testamentum 1. Philadelphia: Fortress, 1974–1976.

———. "The Organization of the Jewish Communities in the Diaspora." Pages 464–503 in vol. 1 of *The Jewish People in the First Century: Historical Geography, Political History, Social, Cultural, and Religious Life and Institutions*. Edited by S. Safrai and M. Stern. 2 vols. Compendia rerum iudaicarum ad Novum Testamentum 1. Philadelphia: Fortress, 1974–1976.

———. "The Social and Economic Status of Jews in the Diaspora." Pages 701–27 in vol. 2 of *The Jewish People in the First Century: Historical Geography, Political History, Social, Cultural, and Religious Life and Institutions*. Edited by S. Safrai and M. Stern. 2 vols. Compendia rerum iudaicarum ad Novum Testamentum 1. Philadelphia: Fortress, 1974–1976.

Armstrong, Karen. *A History of God: The 4000-Year Quest of Judaism, Christianity, and Islam*. New York: Alfred A. Knopf, 1993.

Arnal, William E. "Definition." Pages 21–34 in *Guide to the Study of Religion*. Edited by Willi Braun and Russell T. McCutcheon. New York: Cassell, 2000.

Ascough, R. S. "Translocal Relationships among Voluntary Associations and Early Christianity." *Journal of Early Christian Studies* 5 (1997): 223–41.

———. *What Are They Saying about the Formation of Pauline Churches?* New York: Paulist, 1998.

Ashton, John. "The Identity and Function of the *Ioudaioi* in the Fourth Gospel." *Novum Testamentum* 27 (1985): 40–75.

Balch, David L., ed. *Social History of the Matthean Community.* Minneapolis: Fortress, 1991.

Ball, Warwick. *Rome in the East: The Transformation of an Empire.* New York: Routledge, 2000.

Barclay, John M. G. *Jews in the Mediterranean Diaspora: From Alexander to Trajan (323 BCE–117 CE).* Hellenistic Culture and Society 33. Berkeley: University of California Press, 1999.

Barnes, T. D. "Legislation against the Christians." *Journal of Roman Studies* 58 (1968): 32–50.

Barnett, Paul W. "Jewish Mission in the Era of the New Testament and the Apostle Paul." Pages 263–83 in *The Gospel to the Nations: Perspectives on Paul's Mission.* Edited by Peter Bolt and Mark Thompson. Downers Grove, Ill.: InterVarsity, 2000.

Baron, S. W. *A Social and Religious History of the Jews.* 2d ed. New York: Columbia University Press, 1952.

Barrett, Anthony A. *Caligula: The Corruption of Power.* London: B. T. Batsford, 1989.

Barrett, C. K. "Jews and Judaizers in the Epistles of Ignatius." Pages 220–44 in *Jews, Greeks, and Christians: Studies in Honour of W. D. Davies.* Edited by R. Hamerton-Kelly and R. Scroggs. Leiden: E. J. Brill, 1976.

————. "Paul: Councils and Controversies." Pages 42–74 in Martin Hengel and C. K. Barrett, *Conflicts and Challenges in Early Christianity.* Edited by Donald A. Hagner. Harrisburg, Pa.: Trinity Press International, 1999.

Bartlett, John R., ed. *Jews in the Hellenistic and Roman Cities.* New York: Routledge, 2002.

Bartsch, Hans-Werner. *Gnostisches Gut und Gemeindetradition bei Ignatius von Antiochien.* Gütersloh: Bertelsmann, 1940.

Bauckham, Richard, ed. *The Gospels for All Christians: Rethinking the Gospel Audiences.* Grand Rapids: Eerdmans, 1998.

Bauer, Walter. *Orthodoxy and Heresy in Earliest Christianity.* Edited by Robert A. Kraft and Gerhard Krodel. Translated by a team from the Philadelphia Seminar on Christian Origins. Philadelphia: Fortress, 1971. Translation of *Rechtgläubigkeit und Ketzerei im ältesten Christentum.* Beiträge zur historischen Theologie 10. Tübingen: MohrSiebeck, 1934.

Baumgarten, Albert I. "The Rule of the Martian as Applied to Qumran." *Israel Oriental Studies* 14 (1994): 121–42.

Becker, Adam H. "Anti-Judaism and Care for the Poor in Aphrahat's *Demonstration 20.*" *Journal of Early Christian Studies* 10 (2002): 305–27.

———— and Annette Yoshiko Reed, eds. *The Ways That Never Parted: Jews and Christians in Late Antiquity and the Early Middle Ages.* Texte und Studien zum antiken Judentum 95. Tübingen: Mohr Siebeck, 2003.

Becker, Jürgen. *Paul: Apostle to the Gentiles.* Translated by O. C. Dean Jr. Louisville: Westminster John Knox, 1993.

Beloch, J. *Die Bevölkerung der griechisch-römischen Welt.* Leipzig: Duncker & Humblot, 1886.

Bhabha, Homi K. *The Location of Culture.* London: Routledge, 1994.

Bickermann, Elias. "Les Maccabées de Malalas." *Byzantion* 21 (1951): 63–82.

————. "The Name of Christians." *Harvard Theological Review* 42 (1949): 109–24.

Boccaccini, Gabriele. *Middle Judaism: Jewish Thought, 300 B.C.E. to 200 C.E.* Minneapolis: Fortress, 1991.

————. "Middle Judaism and Its Contemporary Interpreters (1986–1992): Methodological Foundations for the Study of Judaisms, 300 BCE to 200 CE." *Henoch* 15 (1993): 207–33.

Bockmuehl, Markus N. A. *Jewish Law in Gentile Churches: Halakhah and the Beginning of Christian Public Ethics.* Edinburgh: T&T Clark, 2000.

Boer, Martinus C. de. "God-Fearers in Luke-Acts." Pages 50–71 in *Luke's Literary Achievement: Collected Essays.* Edited by C. M. Tuckett. Journal for the Study of the New Testament: Supplement Series 116. Sheffield: Sheffield Academic, 1995.

Bohak, Gideon. "Ethnic Continuity in the Jewish Diaspora in Antiquity." Pages 175–92 in *Jews in the Hellenistic and Roman Cities.* Edited by John R. Bartlett. New York: Routledge, 2002.

Bourne, F. C. "The Roman Alimentary Program and Italian Agriculture." *Transactions of the American Philological Association* 91 (1960): 47–75.

Bowersock, G. W. *Martyrdom and Rome.* Cambridge: Cambridge University Press, 1995.

Boyarin, Daniel. *Border Lines: The Partition of Judeao-Christianity.* Philadelphia: University of Pennsylvania Press, 2004.

————. *Dying for God: Martyrdom and the Making of Christianity and Judaism.* Stanford, Calif.: Stanford University Press, 1999.

————. "Judaeo-Christianity Redivivus." *Journal of Early Christian Studies* 9 (2001): 417–19.

————. "Justin Martyr Invents Judaism." *Church History* 70 (2001): 427–61.

————. "Martyrdom and the Making of Christianity and Judaism." *Journal of Early Christian Studies* 6 (1998): 577–627.

————. "Semantic Differences; or, 'Judaism'/'Christianity.'" Pages 65–85 in *The Ways That Never Parted: Jews and Christians in Late Antiquity and the Early*

Middle Ages. Edited by Adam H. Becker and Annette Yoshiko Reed. Texte und Studien zum antiken Judentum 95. Tübingen: Mohr Siebeck, 2003.

Braun, Willi, ed. *Rhetoric and Reality in Early Christianities*. Studies in Christianity and Judaism 16. Waterloo, Ont.: Wilfrid Laurier University Press, 2005.

Brent, Allen. "Ignatius and Polycarp: The Transformation of New Testament Traditions in the Context of Mystery Cults." Pages 325–49 in *Trajectories through the New Testament and the Apostolic Fathers*. Edited by Andrew F. Gregory and Christopher M. Tuckett. Oxford: Oxford University Press, 2005.

————. *Ignatius of Antioch: A Martyr Bishop and the Origin of Episcopacy*. New York: T&T Clark, 2007.

————. *Ignatius of Antioch and the Second Sophistic: A Study of an Early Christian Transformation of Pagan Culture*. Studien und Texte zu Antike und Christentum 36. Tübingen: Mohr Siebeck, 2006.

Broadhurst, Laurence. "Melito of Sardis, the Second Sophistic, and 'Israel.'" Pages 49–74 in *Rhetoric and Reality in Early Christianities*. Edited by Willi Braun. Studies in Christianity and Judaism 16. Waterloo, Ont.: Wilfrid Laurier University Press, 2005.

Brown, Charles Thomas. *The Gospel and Ignatius of Antioch*. Studies in Biblical Literature 12. New York: Peter Lang, 2000.

Brown, Raymond E. *An Introduction to the Gospel of John*. Edited by Francis J. Moloney. Anchor Bible Reference Library. New York: Doubleday, 2003.

Brown, Raymond E., and John P. Meier. *Antioch and Rome: New Testament Cradles of Catholic Christianity*. New York and Ramsey, N.J.: Paulist, 1983.

Brox, Norbert. *Zeuge und Märtyrer: Untersuchungen zur frühchristlichen Zeugnis-Terminologie*. Munich: Kösel, 1961.

Bruyn, Theodore S. de. "Naming Religious Groups in the Late Roman Empire." *Studies in Religion* 33 (2004): 147–56.

Burke, Patrick. "The Monarchical Episcopate at the End of the First Century." *Journal of Ecumenical Studies* 7 (1970): 499–518.

Carson, D. A., Peter T. O'Brien, and Mark A. Seifrid. *Justification and Variegated Nomism*. 2 vols. Grand Rapids: Baker Academic, 2001–2004.

Chadwick, Henry. *The Church in Ancient Society: From Galilee to Gregory the Great*. Oxford: Oxford University Press, 2003.

Chancey, Mark A. *The Myth of a Gentile Galilee*. Society for New Testament Studies Monograph Series 118. Cambridge: Cambridge University Press, 2002.

Chilton, Bruce. *Rabbi Paul: An Intellectual Biography*. New York: Doubleday, 2004.

Chilton, Bruce, and Jacob Neusner. *Types of Authority in Formative Christianity and Judaism*. New York: Routledge, 1999.

Clark, K. W. "The Gentile Bias in Matthew." *Journal of Biblical Literature* 66 (1947): 165–72.

Cohen, Shaye J. D. "Adolf Harnack's 'The Mission and Expansion of Judaism': Christianity Succeeds Where Judaism Fails." Pages 163–69 in *The Future of Early Christianity: Essays in Honor of Helmut Koester*. Edited by Birger Pearson. Minneapolis: Fortress, 1991.

———. *The Beginnings of Jewishness*. Berkeley: University of California Press, 1999.

———. "Crossing the Boundary and Becoming a Jew." *Harvard Theological Review* 82 (1989): 13–33.

———. "Judaism without Circumcision and 'Judaism' without 'Circumcision' in Ignatius." *Harvard Theological Review* 95 (2002): 395–415.

Collins, John J. *Between Athens and Jerusalem: Jewish Identity in the Hellenistic Diaspora*. Grand Rapids: Eerdmans, 1999.

Conzelmann, Hans. *Gentiles, Jews, Christians: Polemics and Apologetics in the Greco-Roman Era*. Translated by M. Eugene Boring. Minneapolis: Fortress, 1992.

Corwin, Virginia. *St. Ignatius and Christianity in Antioch*. New Haven: Yale University Press, 1960.

Cummins, Stephen Anthony. *Paul and the Crucified Christ in Antioch: Maccabean Martyrdom and Galatians 1 and 2*. Society for New Testament Studies Monograph Series 114. New York: Cambridge University Press, 2001.

Cunningham, Mary. "The Orthodox Church in Byzantium." Pages 66–109 in *A World History of Christianity*. Edited by Adrian Hastings. Grand Rapids: Eerdmans, 1999.

Daley, Brian E. Review of Daniel Boyarin, *Dying for God: Martyrdom and the Making of Christianity and Judaism*. *First Things* 115 (2001): 65–68.

Davids, Adelbert. "Irrtum und Häresie: 1 Clem.-Ign. von Antiochien-Justinus." *Kairos* 15 (1973): 165–87.

Davies, Stevan L. "The Predicament of Ignatius of Antioch." *Vigiliae christianae* 30 (1976): 175–80.

De Ste. Croix, Geoffery E. M. "Why Were the Early Christians Persecuted?" *Past and Present* 26 (1963): 6–38.

Dodds, E. R. *Pagan and Christian in an Age of Anxiety: Some Aspects of Religious Experience from Marcus Aurelius to Constantine*. Cambridge: Cambridge University Press, 1965.

Donahue, Paul J. "Jewish-Christian Controversy in the Second Century: A Study in the Dialogue of Justin Martyr." PhD diss., Yale University, 1973.

———. "Jewish Christianity in the Letters of Ignatius of Antioch." *Vigiliae christianae* 32 (1978): 81–93.

Donaldson, Terence L. "Jewish/Christian Relations." Pages 229–46 in *The Early Church: An Annotated Bibliography of Literature in English*. Edited by Thomas A. Robinson *et al*. Metuchen, N.J., 1993.

————. *Paul and the Gentiles: Remapping the Apostle's Convictional World*. Minneapolis: Fortress, 1997.

Downey, Glanville. *A History of Antioch in Syria from Seleucus to the Arab Conquests*. Princeton: Princeton University Press, 1961.

————. "Imperial Building Records in Malalas." *Byzantinische Zeitschrift* 38 (1938): 299–311.

————. "The Olympic Games of Antioch in the Fourth Century A.D." *Transactions of the American Philological Association* 70 (1939): 428–38.

————. "The Size of the Population of Antioch." *Transactions of the American Philological Association* 89 (1958): 84–91.

Droge, Arthur J., and James D. Tabor. *A Noble Death: Suicide and Martyrdom among Christians and Jews in Antiquity*. San Francisco: Harper, 1992.

Dunn, James D. G. *The Partings of the Ways between Christianity and Judaism and Their Significance for the Character of Christianity*. London: SCM, 1991.

————, ed. *Jews and Christians—the Parting of the Ways, A.D. 70 to 135: The Second Durham-Tübingen Research Symposium on Earliest Christianity and Judaism, Durham, September, 1989*. Wissenschaftliche Untersuchungen zum Neuen Testament 66. Tübingen: J. C. B. Mohr (Paul Siebeck), 1991.

Eckardt, Roy A. *Elder and Younger Brothers: The Encounter of Jews and Christians*. New York: Schocken Books, 1973.

Ehrman, Bart D. *Lost Christianities: The Battles for Scripture and the Faiths We Never Knew*. New York: Oxford University Press, 2003.

————. *Lost Scriptures: Books That Did Not Make It into the New Testament*. New York: Oxford University Press, 2003.

Ellis, Walter M. *Ptolemy of Egypt*. New York: Routledge, 1994.

Engels, Donald. "The Problem of Female Infanticide in the Greco-Roman World." *Classical Philology* 75 (1980): 112–20.

Esler, Philip F. *Community and Gospel in Luke-Acts: The Social and Political Motivations of Lucan Theology*. Society for New Testament Studies Monograph Series 57. Cambridge: Cambridge University Press, 1987.

————. *The First Christians in Their Social Worlds: Social-Scientific Approaches to New Testament Interpretation*. New York: Routledge, 1994.

Feldman, Louis H. *Jew and Gentile in the Ancient World: Attitudes and Interactions from Alexander to Justinian*. Princeton: Princeton University Press, 1993.

————. "The Omnipresence of the God-Fearers." *Biblical Archaeology Review* 12 (1986): 58–69.

Finn, Thomas M. "The God-Fearers Reconsidered." *Catholic Biblical Quarterly* 47 (1985): 75–84.

Fitzpatrick-McKinley, Anne. "Synagogue Communities in the Graeco-Roman Cities." Pages 55–87 in *Jews in the Hellenistic and Roman Cities*. Edited by John R. Bartlett. New York: Routledge, 2002.

Foakes-Jackson, F. J. *Josephus and the Jews: The Religion and History of the Jews as Explained by Flavius Josephus.* New York: Richard R. Smith, 1930.

Foster, Paul. "The Epistles of Ignatius of Antioch." *Expository Times* 117 (2006): 487–95; 118 (2006): 2–11.

Fox, Robin Lane. *Pagans and Christians.* New York: Alfred A. Knopf, 1987.

Frankfurter, David. "Jews or Not? Reconstructing the 'Other' in Rev. 2:9 and 3:9." *Harvard Theological Review* 94 (2001): 403–25.

Fredriksen, Paula. "What 'Parting of the Ways'? Jews, Gentiles, and the Ancient Mediterranean City." Pages 35–63 in *The Ways That Never Parted: Jews and Christians in Late Antiquity and the Early Middle Ages.* Edited by Adam H. Becker and Annette Yoshiko Reed. Texte und Studien zum antiken Judentum 95. Tübingen: Mohr Siebeck, 2003.

Frend, W. H. C. *Martyrdom and Persecution in the Early Church.* Oxford: Blackwell, 1965.

———. "Martyrdom and Political Oppression." Pages 815–39 in vol. 2 of *The Early Christian World.* Edited by Philip F. Esler. 2 vols. New York: Routledge, 2000.

———. "The Persecutions: Some Links between Judaism and the Early Church." *Journal of Ecclesiastical History* 9 (1958): 141–58.

———. *The Rise of Christianity.* Philadelphia: Fortress, 1984.

———. "Town and Countryside in Early Christianity." Pages 25–42 in *The Church in Town and Countryside: Papers read at the seventeenth summer meeting and the eighteenth winter meeting of the Ecclesiastical History Society.* Edited by Deker Baker. Studies in Church History 16. Oxford: Blackwell, 1979.

Frier, Bruce W. "Natural Fertility and Family Limitations in Roman Marriage." *Classical Philology* 89 (1994): 318–33.

Fuller, Reginald. *A Critical Introduction to the New Testament.* London: Duckworth, 1966.

Gager, John G. "Jews, Gentiles, and Synagogues in the Book of Acts." *Harvard Theological Review* 79 (1986): 91–99.

———. *Reinventing Paul.* Oxford: Oxford University Press, 2002.

———. *The Origins of Anti-Semitism: Attitudes toward Judaism in Pagan and Christian Antiquity.* New York: Oxford University Press, 1983.

Gapp, Kenneth S. "The Universal Famine under Claudius." *Harvard Theological Review* 28 (1935): 258–65.

Garnsey, Peter D. A. "Trajan's Alimenta: Some Problems." *Historia* 17 (1968): 367–81.

Gaston, Lloyd. "Judaism of the Uncircumcised in Ignatius and Related Writers." Pages 33–44 in *Separation and Polemic.* Vol. 2 of *Anti-Judaism in Early Christianity.* Edited by Stephen G. Wilson. Studies in Christianity and Judaism 2. Waterloo, Ont.: Wilfrid Laurier University Press, 1986.

Gempf, Conrad H. "The 'God-Fearers.'" Pages 444–47 in Colin J. Hemer, *The Book of Acts in the Setting of Hellenistic History*. Edited by Conrad H. Gempf. Winona Lake, Ind.: Eisenbrauns, 1990.

Georgi, Dieter. *The Opponents of Paul in Second Corinthians*. Philadelphia: Fortress, 1986.

Gilbert, Gary. "The Making of a Jew: 'God-Fearer' or Convert in the Story of Izates." *Union Seminary Quarterly Review* 44 (1991): 299–313.

Goehring, James E. "Monastic Diversity and Ideological Boundaries in Fourth-Century Christian Egypt." *Journal of Early Christian Studies* 5 (1997): 61–84.

Goodman, Martin. *Mission and Conversion: Proselytizing in the Religious History of the Roman Empire*. Oxford: Clarendon, 1994.

———. "Jewish Proselytizing in the First Century." Pages 53–78 in Judith Lieu, John A. North, and Tessa Rajak, eds., *The Jews among Pagans and Christians in the Roman Empire*. New York: Routledge, 1992.

———. "Nerva, the *fiscus judaicus*, and Jewish Identity." *Journal of Roman Studies* 79 (1989): 40–44.

———. "Proselytizing in Rabbinic Judaism." *Journal of Theological Studies* 40 (1989): 176–85.

———. *The Ruling Class of Judea: The Origins of the Jewish Revolt against Rome, A.D. 66–70*. Cambridge: Cambridge University Press, 1987.

Goulder, Michael. "Ignatius's 'Docetists.'" *Vigiliae christianae* 53 (1999): 16–30.

Grabbe, Lester L. "The Hellenistic City of Jerusalem." Pages 6–21 in *Jews in the Hellenistic and Roman Cities*. Edited by John R. Bartlett. New York: Routledge, 2002.

———. *Judaism from Cyrus to Hadrian*. 2 vols. Minneapolis: Fortress, 1992.

Grainger, John D. *The Cities of Seleukid Syria*. Oxford: Clarendon, 1990.

Grant, Robert M. "Scripture and Tradition in Ignatius of Antioch." Pages 37–54 in Robert M. Grant, *After the New Testament*. Minneapolis: Fortress: 1967.

Gray, B. E. "The Movements of the Jerusalem Church during the First Jewish War." *Journal of Ecclesiastical History* 24 (1973): 1–7.

Gray, Patrick. "Abortion, Infanticide, and the Social Rhetoric of the *Apocalypse of Peter*." *Journal of Early Christian Studies* 9 (2001): 313–37.

Green, William Scott. "Ancient Judaism: Contours and Complexity." Pages 293–310 in *Language, Theology, and the Bible: Essays in Honour of James Barr*. Edited by S. E. Balentine and J. Barton. Oxford: Oxford University Press, 1994.

Gruen, Erich S. *Diaspora: Jews amidst Greeks and Romans*. Cambridge: Harvard University Press, 2002.

Gundry, Robert H. *Matthew: A Commentary on His Handbook for a Mixed Church under Persecution*. 2d ed. Grand Rapids: Eerdmans, 1994.

———. *Matthew: A Commentary on His Literary and Theological Art*. Grand Rapids: Eerdmans, 1982.

————. "A Responsive Evaluation of the Social History of the Matthean Community in Roman Syria." Pages 62–67 in *Social History of the Matthean Community*. Edited by David L. Balch. Minneapolis: Fortress, 1991.

Gunther, J. J. *St. Paul's Opponents and Their Background*. Novum Testamentum Supplements 35. Leiden: E. J. Brill, 1973.

Haenchen, Ernst. *The Acts of the Apostles*. Philadelphia: Westminster, 1971.

Hammond Bammel, C. P. "Ignatian Problems." *Journal of Theological Studies* 33 (1982): 62–97.

Hann, Robert R. "Judaism and Jewish Christianity in Antioch: Charisma and Conflict in the First Century." *Journal of Religious History* 14 (1987): 341–60.

Hare, Douglas R. A. *The Theme of Jewish Persecution of Christians in the Gospel according to St Matthew*. Society for New Testament Studies Monograph Series 6. Cambridge: Cambridge University Press, 1967.

Harkins, Paul W., ed. and trans. *Fathers of the Church* 68. Washington, D. C.: Catholic University of America Press, 1979.

Harland, Philip A. *Associations, Synagogues, and Congregations: Claiming a Place in Ancient Mediterranean Society*. Minneapolis: Fortress, 2003.

Harris, William V. "Child-Exposure in the Roman Empire." *Journal of Roman Studies* 48 (1994): 1–22.

————. "The Theoretical Possibility of Extensive Infanticide in the Graeco-Roman World." *Classical Quarterly* 32 (1982): 114–16.

Harrison, P. N. *Polycarp's Two Epistles to the Philippians*. Cambridge: Cambridge University Press, 1936.

Hegedus, Tim. "Naming Christians in Antiquity." *Studies in Religion* 33 (2004): 173–90.

Hemer, Colin J. *The Book of Acts in the Setting of Hellenistic History*. Edited by Conrad H. Gempf. Winona Lake, Ind.: Eisenbrauns, 1990.

————. *The Letters to the Seven Churches of Asia in Their Local Setting*, Journal for the Study of the New Testament: Supplement Series 11. Sheffield: JSOT Press, 1986.

Hengel, Martin. *Acts and the History of Earliest Christianity*. Philadelphia: Fortress, 1980.

————. *Between Jesus and Paul: Studies in the Earliest History of Christianity*. London, SCM, 1983.

————. "Early Christianity as a Jewish-Messianic, Universalistic Movement." Pages 1–41 in *Conflicts and Challenges in Early Christianity*, by Martin Hengel and C. K. Barrett. Edited by Donald A. Hagner. Harrisburg, Pa.: Trinity Press International, 1999.

————. *Jews, Greeks, and Barbarians: Aspects of the Hellenization of Judaism in the Pre-Christian Period*. Translated by John Bowden. Philadelphia: Fortress, 1980.

————. *Judaism and Hellenism: Studies in Their Encounter in Palestine during the Early Hellenistic Period.* 2 vols. Philadelphia: Fortress, 1974.

————. "The Pre-Christian Paul." Pages 29–52 in *The Jews among Pagans and Christians in the Roman Empire.* Edited by Judith Lieu, John North, and Tessa Rajak. New York: Routledge, 1992.

————. "Der vorchristliche Paulus." *Theologische Beiträge* 21 (1990): 174–95.

Hengel, Martin, and Anna Maria Schwemer. *Paul between Damascus and Antioch: The Unknown Years.* Louisville: Westminster John Knox, 1997.

Henten, Jan Willem van. *The Maccabean Martyrs as Saviours of the Jewish People: A Study of 2 and 4 Maccabees.* Supplements to the Journal for the Study of Judaism 57. Leiden: E. J. Brill, 1997.

————, ed. *Die Entstehung der jüdischen Martyrologie.* Leiden: E. J. E. J. Brill, 1989.

Henten, Jan Willem van, and Friedrich Avemarie. *Martyrdom and Noble Death: Selected Texts from Graeco-Roman, Jewish, and Christian Antiquity.* New York, Routledge, 2002.

Hill, Craig C. *Hellenists and Hebrews: Reappraising Division within the Earliest Church.* Minneapolis: Fortress, 1992.

Holmberg, Bengt. "The Life in the Diaspora Synagogues: An Evaluation." Pages 219–32 in *The Ancient Synagogue from Its Origins until 200 C.E.: Papers Presented at an International Conference at Lund University, October 14–17, 2001.* Edited by Birger Olsson and Magnus Zetterholm. Coniectanea biblica: New Testament Series 39. Stockholm: Almqvist & Wiksell, 2003.

Holmes, Michael W., ed. and trans. *The Apostolic Fathers: Greek Texts and English Translations.* Grand Rapids: Baker Academic, 2007.

Hopkins, Keith. "Christian Number and Its Implications." *Journal of Early Christian Studies* 6 (1998): 185–226.

Horbury, William. "The Benediction of the *minim* and Early Jewish-Christian Controversy." *Journal of Theological Studies* 33 (1982): 19–61.

————. "Jewish-Christian Relations in Barnabas and Justin Martyr." Pages 315–45 in *Jews and Christians—the Parting of the Ways, A. D. 70 to 135: The Second Durham-Tübingen Research Symposium on Earliest Christianity and Judaism, Durham, September, 1989.* Edited by James D. G. Dunn. Wissenschaftliche Untersuchungen zum Neuen Testament 66. Tübingen: J. C. B. Mohr (Paul Siebeck), 1991.

Horst, P. W. van der. "'De waarachtige en niet met handen gemaakte God.'" *Nederlands theologisch tijdschrift* 45 (1991): 177–82.

————. "Das Neue Testament und die jüdischen Grabinschriften aus hellenistisch-römischer Zeit." *Biblische Zeitschrift* 36 (1992): 161–78.

Hvalvik, Reider. *The Struggle for Scripture and Covenant: The Purpose of the Epistle of Barnabas and Jewish-Christian Competition in the Second Century.*

Wissenschaftliche Untersuchungen zum Neuen Testament 2. Reihe, no. 82. Tübingen: J. C. B. Mohr (Paul Siebeck), 1996.

Isacson, Mikael. "Follow Your Bishop! Rhetorical Strategies in the Letters of Ignatius of Antioch." Pages 317–40 in *The Formation of the Early Church*. Edited by Jostein Ådna. Wissenschaftliche Untersuchungen zum Neuen Testament 183. Tübingen: Mohr Siebeck, 2005.

———. *To Each Their Own Letter: Structure, Themes, and Rhetorical Strategies in the Letters of Ignatius of Antioch*. Coniectanea biblica: New Testament Series 42. Stockholm: Almqvist & Wiksell, 2004.

Jackson-McCabe, Matt, ed. *Jewish Christianity Reconsidered: Rethinking Ancient Groups and Texts*. Minneapolis: Fortress, 2007.

Jacobs, Andrew S. "The Lion and the Lamb: Reconsidering Jewish-Christian Relations in Antiquity." Pages 95–108 in *The Ways That Never Parted: Jews and Christians in Late Antiquity and the Early Middle Ages*. Edited by Adam H. Becker and Annette Yoshiko Reed. Texte und Studien zum antiken Judentum 95. Tübingen: Mohr Siebeck, 2003.

Joly, Robert. *Le dossier d'Ignace d'Antioche*. Éditions de l'Université de Brussels, 1979.

Jones, A. H. M. *The Cities of the Eastern Roman Provinces*. 2d ed. Oxford: Clarendon, 1971.

———. *The Greek City from Alexander to Justinian*. Oxford: Clarendon, 1940.

Josephus. Translated by H. St. J. Thackeray et al. 10 vols. Loeb Classical Library. Cambridge, Mass.: Harvard University Press, 1926–1965.

Kasher, Aryeh. *The Jews in Hellenistic and Roman Egypt: The Struggle for Equal Rights*. Texte und Studien zum antiken Judentum 7. Tübingen: J. C. B. Mohr (Paul Siebeck), 1985.

———. "The Rights of the Jews of Antioch on the Orontes." *Proceedings of the American Academy for Jewish Research* 49 (1982): 69–85.

Katz, Steven T. "Issues in the Separation of Judaism and Christianity after 70 C.E.: A Reconsideration." *Journal of Biblical Literature* 103 (1984): 43–76.

Keresztes, Paul. "The Jews, the Christians, and Emperor Domitian." *Vigiliae christianae* 27 (1973): 1–28.

Kile, Chad. "Feeling Persuaded: Christianization as Social Formation." Pages 219–48 in *Rhetoric and Reality in Early Christianities*. Edited by Willi Braun. Studies in Christianity and Judaism 16. Waterloo, Ont.: Wilfrid Laurier University Press, 2005.

Kittel, G., and G. Friedrich, eds. *Theological Dictionary of the New Testament*. Translated by G. W. Bromiley. 10 vols.; Grand Rapids: Eerdmans, 1964–1976.

Kloppenborg, John S., and Stephen G. Wilson, eds. *Voluntary Associations in the Graeco-Roman World*. New York: Routledge, 1996.

Klutz, Todd. "Paul and the Development of Gentile Christianity." Pages 168–97 in vol. 1 of *The Early Christian World*. Edited by Philip F. Esler. 2 vols. New York: Routledge, 2000.

Koester, Craig. "The Origin and Significance of the Flight to Pella Tradition." *Catholic Biblical Quarterly* 51 (1989): 90–106.

Kolb, Frank. "Antiochia in der frühen Kaiserzeit." Pages 97–118 in vol. 2 of *Geschichte-Tradition-Reflexion: Festschrift für Martin Hengel*. Edited by H. Cancik, H. Lichtenberger, and P. Schäfer. 3 vols. Tübingen: J. C. B. Mohr (Paul Siebeck), 1996.

Kondolen, Christine. *Antioch: The Lost Ancient City*. Princeton: Princeton University Press, 2001.

Kraabel, Thomas. "The Disappearance of the 'God-Fearers.'" *Numen* 28 (1981): 113–26.

Kraeling, Carl H. "The Jewish Community in Antioch." *Journal of Biblical Literature* 51 (1932): 130–60.

Kraft, Robert A. "The Weighing of the Parts: Pivots and Pitfalls in the Study of Early Judaisms and Their Early Christian Offspring." Pages 87–94 in *The Ways That Never Parted: Jews and Christians in Late Antiquity and the Early Middle Ages*. Edited by Adam H. Becker and Annette Yoshiko Reed. Texte und Studien zum antiken Judentum 95. Tübingen: Mohr Siebeck, 2003.

Kronfeld, Chana. *On the Margins of Modernism: Decentering Literary Dynamics*. Contraversions 2. Berkeley: University of California Press, 1996.

———. "Proselytes and God-Fearers." Pages 74–96 in vol. 5 of *The Acts of the Apostles*. 5 vols. Part 1 of *The Beginnings of Christianity*. Edited by F. J. Foakes-Jackson and Kirsopp Lake. London: Macmillan, 1920–1933.

Lentz, John C., Jr. *Luke's Portrait of Paul*. Society for New Testament Studies Monograph Series 77. Cambridge: Cambridge University Press, 1993.

Leon, Harry J. *The Jews of Ancient Rome*. Philadelphia: Jewish Publication Society, 1960.

Levine, L. I. "The First-Century Synagogue: New Perspectives." *Svensk teologisk kvartalskrift* 77 (2001): 27–28.

Levinskaya, Irina. *The Book of Acts in Its Diaspora Setting*. Vol. 5 of *The Book of Acts in Its First-Century Setting*. Edited by Bruce W. Winter. Grand Rapids: Eerdmans, 1996.

———. "The Inscription from Aphrodisias and the Problem of God-Fearers." *Tyndale Bulletin* 41 (1990): 312–18.

Lewis, Naphtali and Meyer Reinhold, eds., *Roman Civilization, Volume 2: The Empire*, 3d. ed. New York: Columbia University Press, 1990.

Liebeschuetz, J. H. W. G. *Antioch: City and Imperial Administration in the Later Roman Empire*. Oxford: Clarendon, 1972.

Lieu, Judith. "Accusations of Jewish Persecution in Early Christian Sources, with Particular Reference to Justin Martyr and the Martyrdom of Polycarp." Pages 279–95 in *Tolerance and Intolerance in Early Judaism and Christianity*. Edited by Graham N. Stanton and Guy G. Stroumsa. Cambridge: Cambridge University Press, 1998.

———. "The 'Attraction of Women' in/to Early Judaism and Christianity: Gender and the Politics of Conversion." *Journal for the Study of the New Testament* 72 (1998): 8–22.

———. *Christian Identity in the Jewish and Graeco-Roman World.* Oxford: Oxford University Press, 2004.

———. "Circumcision, Women, and Salvation." *New Testament Studies* 40 (1994): 358–70.

———. "Do God-Fearers Make Good Christians?" Pages 329–45 in *Crossing the Boundaries: Essays in Biblical Interpretation in Honour of Michael D. Goulder*. Edited by S. E. Porter, P. Joyce, and D. E. Orton. Leiden: E. J. Brill, 1994. Repr. pages 31–47 in *Neither Jew nor Greek? Constructing Early Christianity*. New York: T&T Clark, 2002.

———. "History and Theology in Christian Views of Judaism." Pages 79–96 in *The Jews among Pagans and Christians in the Roman Empire*. Edited by Judith Lieu, John North, and Tessa Rajak. New York: Routledge, 1992.

———. *Image and Reality: The Jews in the World of the Christians in the Second Century.* Edinburgh: T&T Clark, 1996.

———. "'Impregnable Ramparts and Walls of Iron': Boundary and Identity in Early 'Judaism' and 'Christianity.'" *New Testament Studies* 48 (2002): 297–313.

———. *Neither Jew nor Greek? Constructing Early Christianity.* New York: T&T Clark, 2002.

———. "'The Parting of the Ways': Theological Construct or Historical Reality?" *Journal for the Study of the New Testament* 56 (1994): 101–19. Repr., pages 11–30 in *Neither Jew nor Greek? Constructing Early Christianity*. New York: T&T Clark, 2002.

———. "The Race of the God-Fearers." *Journal of Theological Studies* 46 (1995): 483–501.

Lieu, Judith, John North, and Tessa Rajak, eds., *The Jews among Pagans and Christians in the Roman Empire*. New York: Routledge, 1992.

Lifshitz, B. "L'origine du nom des chrétiens." *Vigiliae christianae* 16 (1962): 65–70.

Lightfoot, J. B. *S. Ignatius, S. Polycarp.* 2 vols. in 3. Part 2 of *The Apostolic Fathers*. 2d ed. London: Macmillan, 1889–1890.

Lindemann, Andreas. "Paul's Influence on 'Clement' and Ignatius." Pages 9–23 in *Trajectories through the New Testament and the Apostolic Fathers*. Edited by

Andrew F. Gregory and Christopher M. Tuckett. Oxford: Oxford University Press, 2005.

Lo Cascio, Elio. "The Size of the Roman Population: Beloch and the Meaning of the Augustan Census Figures." *Journal of Roman Studies* 84 (1994): 23–40.

Logan, Alastair H. B. "Gnosticism." Pages 907–28 in vol. 2 of *The Early Christian World*. Edited by Philip F. Esler. 2 vols. New York: Routledge, 2000.

Lotz, John-Paul. *Ignatius and Concord: The Background and Use of the Language of Concord in the Letters of Ignatius of Antioch*. Patristic Studies 8. New York: Peter Lang, 2007.

Lüdemann, Gerd. "The Successors of Pre-70 Jerusalem Christianity: A Critical Review of the Pella-Tradition." Pages 161–73 in *The Shaping of Christianity in the Second and Third Centuries*. Vol. 1 of *Jewish and Christian Self-Definition*. Edited by E. P. Sanders. Philadelphia: Fortress, 1980.

Lüderitz, Gert. "What Is the Politeuma?" Pages 182–225 in *Studies in Early Jewish Epigraphy*. Edited by Jan Willem van Henten and Pieter Willem van der Horst. Leiden and New York: E. J. Brill, 1994.

Lyman, Rebecca. "Hellenism and Heresy." *Journal of Early Christian Studies* 11 (2003): 209–22.

MacDonald, Dennis R. *The Legend and the Apostle: The Battle for Paul in Story and Canon*. Philadelphia: Westminster, 1983.

MacLennan, Robert S. *Early Christian Texts on Jews and Judaism*. Brown Judaic Studies 194. Atlanta: Scholars Press, 1990.

MacLennan, Robert S., and Thomas Kraabel. "The God-Fearers—a Literary and Theological Invention." *Biblical Archaeology Review* 12 (1986): 47–53.

MacMullen, Ramsay. *Christianizing the Roman Empire (A. D. 100–400)*. New Haven: Yale University Press, 1984.

———. *Paganism in the Roman Empire*. New Haven: Yale University Press, 1981.

Maier, Harry O. "The Politics and Rhetoric of Discord and Concord in Paul and Ignatius." Pages 9–23 in *Trajectories through the New Testament and the Apostolic Fathers*. Edited by Andrew F. Gregory and Christopher M. Tuckett. Oxford: Oxford University Press, 2005.

———. "The Politics of the Silent Bishop: Silence and Persuasion in Ignatius of Antioch." *Journal of Theological Studies* 55 (2004): 503–19.

———. *The Social Setting of the Ministry as Reflected in the Writings of Hermas, Clement, and Ignatius*. Dissertations SR 1. Waterloo, Ont.: Wilfrid Laurier University Press, 1991.

Malherbe, Abraham J. *The Letters to the Thessalonians: A New Translation with Introduction and Commentary*. Anchor Bible 32B. New York: Doubleday, 2000.

Malina, Bruce J. "Establishment Violence in the New Testament World." *Scriptura* 51 (1994): 51–78.

Mandell, S. "The Jewish Christians and the Temple Tax." *Second Century* (1989): 76–84.

Marguerat, Daniel. *The First Christian Historian: Writing the "Acts of the Apostles."* Translated by Ken McKinney, Gregory J. Laughery, and Richard Bauckham. Society for New Testament Studies Monograph Series 121. Cambridge: Cambridge University Press, 2002.

Marshall, John W. "The Objects of Ignatius's Wrath and Jewish Angelic Mediators. *Journal of Ecclesiastical History* 56 (2005): 1–23.

Massaux, Éduard. *The First Ecclesiastical Writers.* Vol. 1 of *The Influence of the Gospel of Saint Matthew on Christian Literature before Saint Irenaeus.* Translated by N.J. Belval and S. Hecht. New Gospel Studies 5.1. Macon, Ga.: Mercer University Press, 1990.

Matthews, Shelly. *First Converts: Rich Pagan Women and the Rhetoric of Mission in Early Judaism and Christianity.* Stanford, Calif.: Stanford University Press, 2001.

Mattingly, Harold. "The Origin of the Name *Christiani.*" *Journal of Theological Studies* 9 (1958): 26–37.

McCarthy, Carmel. "Text and Versions: The Old Testament." Pages 207–28 in vol. 1 of *The Biblical World.* Edited by John Barton. 2 vols. New York: Routledge, 2002.

McGing, Brian. "Population and Proselytism: How Many Jews Were There in the Ancient World?" Pages 88–106 in *Jews in the Hellenistic and Roman Cities.* Edited by John R. Bartlett. New York: Routledge, 2002.

McGinn, Sheila E. "Internal Renewal and Dissent in the Early Christian World." Pages 893–906 in vol. 2 of *The Early Christian World.* Edited by Philip F. Esler. 2 vols. New York: Routledge, 2000.

McKnight, Scot. *A Light among the Gentiles: Jewish Missionary Activity in the Second Temple Period.* Minneapolis: Fortress, 1991.

McLaren, James S. "Jews and the Imperial Cult: From Augustus to Domitian." *Journal for the Study of the New Testament* 27 (2005): 257–78.

Meeks, Wayne A. "Breaking Away: Three New Testament Pictures of Christianity's Separation from the Jewish Communities." Pages 93–116 in *"To See Ourselves as Others See Us": Christians, Jews, "Others" in Late Antiquity.* Edited by Jacob Neusner and Ernest S. Frerichs. Chico, Calif.: Scholars Press, 1985.

———. *The First Urban Christians.* New Haven: Yale University Press, 1983.

Meeks, Wayne A., and Robert L. Wilken. *Jews and Christians in Antioch in the First Four Centuries of the Common Era.* Society of Biblical Literature Sources for Biblical Study 13. Missoula, Mont.: Scholars Press, 1978.

Meggitt, Justin J. *Paul, Poverty, and Survival.* Edinburgh: T&T Clark, 1998.

Meyers, Eric M. "Jewish Culture in Greco-Roman Palestine." Pages 135–80 in *Cultures of the Jews.* Edited by David Biale. Westminster, Md.: Schocken Books, 1999.

Millar, Fergus. "The Jews of the Graeco-Roman Diaspora between Paganism and Christianity, AD 312–438." Pages 97–123 in *The Jews among Pagans and Christians in the Roman Empire.* Edited by Judith Lieu, John North, and Tessa Rajak. New York: Routledge, 1992.

―――. *The Roman Near East, 31 B.C.–A.D. 337.* Cambridge: Harvard University Press, 1993.

Mitchell, Stephen. *Anatolia: Land, Men, and Gods in Asia Minor.* 2 vols. Oxford: Clarendon, 1993.

Molland, Einar. "The Heretics Combatted by Ignatius of Antioch." *Journal of Ecclesiastical History* 5 (1954): 1–6.

Mouritsen, Henrik. *Plebs and Politics in the Later Roman Republic.* Cambridge: Cambridge University Press, 2004.

Murphy-O'Connor, J. "Lots of God-Fearers? *Theosebeis* in the Aphrodisias Inscription." *Revue biblique* 99 (1992): 418–24.

Murray, Alice Yang, ed. *What Did the Internment of Japanese Americans Mean?* Boston: Bedford/St. Martin's, 2000.

Murray, Michele. *Playing a Jewish Game: Gentile Christian Judaizing in the First and Second Centuries CE.* Waterloo, Ont.: Wilfrid Laurier University Press, 2004.

Myllykoski, Matti. "Wild Beasts and Rabid Dogs: The Riddle of the Heretics in the Letters of Ignatius." Pages 341–77 in *The Formation of the Early Church.* Edited by Jostein Ådna. Wissenschaftliche Untersuchungen zum Neuen Testament 183. Tübingen: Mohr Siebeck, 2005.

Nanos, M. D. *The Mystery of Romans: The Jewish Context of Paul's Letter.* Minneapolis: Fortress, 1996.

Nathan, Geoffrey S. *The Family in Late Antiquity: The Rise of Christianity and the Endurance of Tradition.* New York: Routledge, 2000.

Neusner, Jacob. "The Experience of the City in Late Antique Judaism." Pages 37–52 in *Studies in Judaism and Its Greco-Roman Context.* Vol. 5 of *Approaches to Ancient Judaism.* Edited by William Scott Green. Brown Judaic Studies 32. Atlanta: Scholars Press, 1985.

―――. *Judaism and Christianity in the Age of Constantine: History, Messiah, Israel, and the Initial Confrontation.* Chicago Studies in the History of Judaism. Chicago: University of Chicago Press, 1987.

―――. *Judaism in the Matrix of Christianity.* Repr., with new preface and introduction, South Florida Studies in the History of Judaism. Atlanta: Scholars Press, 1991.

―――. *Studying Classical Judaism: A Primer.* Louisville: Westminster, 1991.

―――. "Was Rabbinic Judaism Really 'Ethnic'?" *Catholic Biblical Quarterly* 57 (1995): 281–305.

Neusner, Jacob, William Scott Green, and Ernest S. Frerichs, eds. *Judaisms and Their Messiahs at the Turn of the Christian Era.* Cambridge: Cambridge University Press, 1987.

Neyrey, Jerome H. "Ceremonies in Luke-Acts: The Case of Meals and Table Fellowship." Pages 361–87 in *The Social World of Luke-Acts: Models of Interpretation*. Edited by Jerome H. Neyrey. Peabody, Mass.: Hendrickson, 1991.

Norris, Frederick W. "Artifacts from Antioch." Pages 248–58 in *Social History of the Matthean Community*. Edited by David L. Balch. Minneapolis: Fortress, 1991.

———. "Ignatius, Polycarp, and I Clement: Walter Bauer Reconsidered." *Vigiliae christianae* 30 (1976): 23–44.

Ó Fearghail, Fearghus. "The Jews in the Hellenistic Cities of Acts." Pages 39–54 in *Jews in the Hellenistic and Roman Cities*. Edited by John R. Bartlett. New York: Routledge, 2002.

Overman, J. A., and R. S. MacLennan, eds. *Diaspora Jews and Judaism: Essays in Honor of, and in Dialogue with, A. Thomas Kraabel*. South Florida Studies in the History of Judaism 41. Atlanta: Scholars Press, 1992.

Pagels, Elaine. *The Gnostic Gospels*. New York: Random House, 1979.

———. "The Social History of Satan, Part Three: John of Patmos and Ignatius of Antioch—Contrasting Visions of 'God's People.'" *Harvard Theological Review* 99 (2006): 487–505.

Parkes, James W. *The Conflict of the Church and the Synagogue*. London: Soncino, 1934.

Parkin, Tim G. *Demography and Roman Society*. Baltimore: Johns Hopkins University Press, 1992.

Paulsen, Henning. *Die Briefe des Ignatius von Antiochia und der Brief des Polykarp von Smyrna*. Handbuch zum Neuen Testament 18. Die Apostolischen Väter 2. Tübingen: J. C. B. Mohr (Paul Siebeck), 1985.

Penner, Todd. "Early Christian Heroes and Lukan Narrative: Stephen and the Hellenists in Ancient Historical Perspective." Pages 75–97 in *Rhetoric and Reality in Early Christianities*. Edited by Willi Braun. Studies in Christianity and Judaism 16. Waterloo, Ont.: Wilfrid Laurier University Press, 2005.

———. *In Praise of Christian Origins: Stephen and the Hellenists in Lukan Apologetic History*. Emory Studies in Early Christianity 10. New York: T&T Clark, 2004.

Perkins, Judith. *The Suffering Self: Pain and Narrative Representation in the Early Christian Era*. London: Routledge, 1995.

Petersen, Andres Klostergaard. "At the End of the Road—Reflections on a Popular Scholarly Metaphor." Pages 45–72 in *The Formation of the Early Church*. Edited by Jostein Ådna. Wissenschaftliche Untersuchungen zum Neuen Testament 183. Tübingen: Mohr Siebeck, 2005.

Rajak, Tessa. "The Jewish Community and Its Boundaries." Pages 9–28 in *The Jews among Pagans and Christians in the Roman Empire*. Edited by Judith Lieu, John North, and Tessa Rajak. New York: Routledge, 1992.

———. "Jewish Rights in the Greek Cities under Roman Rule." Pages 19–35 in *Studies in Judaism and Its Greco-Roman Context.* Vol. 5 of *Approaches to Ancient Judaism.* Edited by William Scott Green. Brown Judaic Studies 32. Atlanta: Scholars Press, 1985.

———. *Josephus: The Historian and His Society.* Philadelphia: Fortress, 1984.

———. "Synagogue and Community in the Graeco-Roman Diaspora." Pages 22–38 in *Jews in the Hellenistic and Roman Cities.* Edited by John R. Bartlett. New York: Routledge, 2002.

———. "Talking at Trypho: Christian Apologetic as Anti-Judaism in Justin's Dialogue with Trypho the Jew." Pages 59–80 in *Apologetics in the Roman Empire: Pagans, Jews, and Christians.* Edited by Mark J. Edwards, Martin Goodman, Simon Price, and Christopher Rowland. Oxford: Oxford University Press, 1999.

———. "Was There a Roman Charter for the Jews?" *Journal of Roman Studies* 74 (1984): 107–23.

Remus, Harold. "The End of 'Paganism'?" *Studies in Religion* 33 (2004): 191–208.

Renolds, Joyce, and Robert Tannenbaum. *Jews and Godfearers at Aphrodisias.* Supplementary Volume 12. Cambridge, U.K.: Cambridge Philological Society, 1987.

Rich, John, and Andrew Wallace-Hadrill, eds. *City and Country in the Ancient World.* Leicester-Nottingham Studies in Ancient Society 2. New York: Routledge, 1991.

Richardson, Cyril. *The Christianity of Ignatius of Antioch.* New York: Columbia University Press, 1935. Repr., Sunrise, Fla.: AMS, 1980.

———. "The Church in Ignatius of Antioch." *Journal of Religion* 17 (1937): 428–58.

Richardson, Peter. "Augustan-Era Synagogues in Rome." Pages 17–29 in *Judaism and Christianity in First-Century Rome.* Edited by Karl P. Donfried and Peter Richardson. Grand Rapids: Eerdmans, 1998.

———. *Building Jewish in the Roman East.* Waco, Tex.: Baylor University Press, 2004.

———. "Early Synagogues as Collegia in the Diaspora and Palestine." Pages 90–109 in *Voluntary Associations in the Greco-Roman World.* Edited by John S. Kloppenborg and Stephen G. Wilson. London: Routledge, 1996.

Riesenfeld, Harald. "Reflections on the Style and Theology of St. Ignatius of Antioch." Pages 312–22 in vol. 2 of *Papers Presented to the Third International Conference on Patristic Studies Held at Christ Church, Oxford, 1959.* Edited by F. L. Cross. 4 vols. Studia patristica 3–6. Texte und Untersuchungen zur Geschichte der altchristlichen Literatur 78–81. Berlin: Akademie, 1961–1962.

Riesner, Rainer. "Synagogues in Jerusalem." Pages 179–211 in *The Book of Acts in Its Palestinian Setting.* Edited by Richard Bauckham. Vol. 4 of *The Book of*

Acts in Its First-Century Setting. Edited by Bruce W. Winter. Grand Rapids: Eerdmans, 1995.

Rius-Camps, J. *The Four Authentic Letters of Ignatius, the Martyr.* Orientalia christiana analecta 213. Rome: Pontificium Institutum Orientalium Studiorum, 1980.

Robinson, James M., and Helmut Koester. *Trajectories Through Early Christianity.* Philadelphia: Fortress, 1971.

Robinson, Thomas A. *The Bauer Thesis Examined: The Geography of Heresy in the Early Christian Church.* Studies in the Bible and Early Christianity 11. Lewiston, N.Y.: Edwin Mellen, 1988.

———. "From the Apostolate to the Episcopate: Reflections on Development." Pages 225–50 in *Self-Definition and Self-Discovery in Early Christianity: A Study in Changing Horizons.* Edited by David Hawkin and Tom [Thomas A.] Robinson. Lewiston, N.Y.: Edwin Mellen, 1990.

Roetzel, C. J. "*Oikoumene* and the Limits of Pluralism in Alexandrian Judaism and Paul." Pages 163–82 in *Diaspora Jews and Judaism: Essays in Honor of, and in Dialogue with, A. Thomas Kraabel.* Edited by J. A. Overman and R. S. MacLennan. South Florida Studies in the History of Judaism 41. Atlanta: Scholars Press, 1992.

Rogers, Rich. *Theophilus of Antioch: The Life and Thought of a Second-Century Bishop.* Lanham, Md.: Lexington Books, 2000.

Rosenthal, Judah. "Bar Hebraeus and a Jewish Census under Claudius." *Jewish Social Studies* 16 (1954): 267–68.

Rudolph, Kurt. *Gnosis: The Nature and History of Gnosticism.* Edited and translated by Robert McLachlan Wilson. Edinburgh: T&T Clark, 1984.

Ruether, Rosemary Radford. "Judaism and Christianity: Two Fourth-Century Religions." *Studies in Religion* 2 (1972): 1–10.

Rutgers, Leonard Victor. "Roman Policy toward the Jews: Expulsions from the City of Rome during the First Century C.E." Pages 93–116 in *Judaism and Christianity in First-Century Rome.* Edited by Karl P. Donfried and Peter Richardson. Grand Rapids: Eerdmans, 1998.

Rutledge, Steven H. *Imperial Inquisitions: Prosecutors and Informants from Tiberius to Domitian.* New York: Routledge, 2001.

Safrai, S. "Relations between the Diaspora and the Land of Israel." Pages 181–215 in volume 1 of *The Jewish People in the First Century: Historical Geography, Political History, Social, Cultural, and Religious Life and Institutions.* Edited by S. Safrai and M. Stern. 2 vols. Compendia rerum iudaicarum ad Novum Testamentum 1. Philadelphia: Fortress, 1974–1976.

Sanders, E. P. *Judaism: Practice and Belief, 63 BCE–66 CE.* London: SCM; Philadelphia: Trinity Press International, 1992.

———. *Paul and Palestinian Judaism: A Comparison of Patterns of Religion.* Minneapolis: Fortress, 1977.

————. *Paul, the Law, and the Jewish People*. Philadelphia: Fortress, 1983.

Schlatter, Frederic W. "The Restoration of Peace in Ignatius's Antioch." *Journal of Theological Studies* 35 (1984): 465–69.

Schoedel, William R. "Are the Letters of Ignatius of Antioch Authentic?" *Recherches de science religieuse* 6 (1980): 116–201.

————. *Ignatius of Antioch: A Commentary on the Letters of Ignatius of Antioch*. Hermeneia. Philadelphia: Fortress, 1985.

————. "Theological Norms and Social Perspectives in Ignatius of Antioch." Pages 30–56 in *The Shaping of Christianity in the Second and Third Centuries*. Vol. 1 of *Jewish and Christian Self-Definition*. Edited by E. P. Sanders. Philadelphia: Fortress, 1980.

Segal, Alan F. *Rebecca's Children: Judaism and Christianity in the Roman World*. Cambridge: Harvard University Press, 1986.

Sherwin-White, A. N. "The Early Persecutions and Roman Law Again." *Journal of Theological Studies* 3 (1952): 199–213.

Siker, Jeffrey S. *Disinheriting the Jews: Abraham in Early Christian Controversy*. Louisville: Westminster John Knox, 1991.

Simon, Marcel. "La migration à Pella: Légende ou réalité?" *Recherches de science religieuse* 60 (1972): 40–52.

————. *Verus Israel: A Study of the Relations between Christians and Jews in the Roman Empire*. Translated by H. McKeating. Oxford: Oxford University Press, 1986.

Skarsaune, Oskar. *In the Shadow of the Temple: Jewish Influences on Early Christianity*. Downers Grove, Ill.: InterVarsity, 2002.

Slee, Michelle. *The Church in Antioch in the First Century CE: Communion and Conflict*. Journal for the Study of the New Testament: Supplement Series 244. London: Sheffield University Press, 2003.

Smallwood, E. Mary. "Domitian's Attitude toward the Jews and Judaism." *Classical Philology* 51 (1956): 1–13.

————. *The Jews under Roman Rule: From Pompey to Diocletian*. Leiden: E. J. Brill, 1976.

Smith, Jonathan Z. *Drudgery Divine: On the Comparison of Early Christianities and the Religions of Late Antiquity*. Chicago: University of Chicago Press, 1990.

————. *Map Is Not Territory: Studies in the History of Religions*. Leiden: E. J. Brill, 1978.

Smith, Robert C., and John Lounibos, eds. *Pagan and Christian Anxiety: A Response to E. R. Dodds*. Lanham, Md.: University Press of America, 1984.

Smith, Roland. *Julian's Gods: Religion and Philosophy in the Thought and Action of Julian the Apostate*. New York: Routledge, 1995.

Sprott, Duncan. *The Ptolemies*. New York: Alfred A. Knopf, 2004.

Stark, Rodney. *The Rise of Christianity*. Princeton: Princeton University Press, 1996.

Streeter, Burnett Hillman. *The Primitive Church*. New York: Macmillan, 1929.

Sumney, Jerry L. "Those Who 'Ignorantly Deny Him': The Opponents of Ignatius of Antioch." *Journal of Early Christian Studies* 4 (1993): 345–65.

Swartley, Willard M. "The Imitatio Christi in the Ignatian Letters." *Vigiliae christianae* 27 (1973): 81–103.

Taylor, Justin J. "Why Were the Disciples First Called 'Christians' at Antioch?"
Revue biblique 105 (1994): 75–94.

Taylor Miriam S. *Anti-Judaism and Early Christian Identity: A Critique of the
Scholarly Consensus.* Studia post-biblica 46. Leiden: E. J. Brill, 1995.

Taylor, Nicholas H. "Caligula, the Church of Antioch, and the Gentile Mission."
Religion and Theology 7 (2000): 1–23.

———. "Palestinian Christianity and the Caligula Crisis, Part II: The Markan
Eschatological Discourse." *Journal for the Study of the New Testament* 62
(1996): 13–41.

———. Paul, Antioch, and Jerusalem: A Study in Relationships and Authority
in Earliest Christianity. Journal for the Study of the New Testament: Supplement Series 66. Sheffield: JSOT Press, 1992.

Tcherikover, Victor. *Hellenistic Civilization and the Jews.* Translated by S. Applebaum. Philadelphia: Jewish Publication Society of America, 1959.

———, ed. *Corpus papyrorum judaicarum.* 3 vols. Cambridge: Published for
Magnes Press, Hebrew University, by Harvard University Press, 1957–1964.

Tellbe, Mikael. "The Temple Tax as a Pre-70 CE Identity Marker." Pages 19–44 in
The Formation of the Early Church. Edited by Jostein Ådna. Wissenschaftliche
Untersuchungen zum Neuen Testament 183. Tübingen: Mohr Siebeck, 2005.

Theissen, Gerd. *The Gospels in Context: Social and Political History in the Synoptic
Tradition.* Minneapolis: Fortress, 1991.

Thompson, L. A. "Domitian and the Jewish Tax." *Historia* 31 (1982): 329–42.

Thurn, Johannes, ed. *Ioannis Malalae Chronographia.* Corpus Fontium Historiae
Byzantinae 35. Berlin: Walter de Gruyter, 2000.

Tomson, Peter J. *Paul and the Jewish Law: Halakha in the Letters of the Apostle
to the Gentiles.* Compendia rerum iudaicarum ad Novum Testamentum 3.1.
Philadelphia: Fortress, 1990.

Tracy, Robin, "Syria." Pages 223–78 in *The Book of Acts in Its Graeco-Roman Set-
ting.* Edited by David W. J. Gill and Conrad Gempf. Vol. 2 of *The Book of
Acts in Its First-Century Setting.* Edited by Bruce W. Winter. Grand Rapids:
Eerdmans, 1994.

Trebilco, Paul R. *The Early Christians in Ephesus from Paul to Ignatius.* Wissenschaftliche Untersuchungen zum Neuen Testament 166. Tübingen: Mohr
Siebeck, 2004.

———. *Jewish Communities in Asia Minor.* Society for New Testament Studies
Monograph Series 69. Cambridge: Cambridge University Press, 1991.

Trevett, Christine. "Apocalypse, Ignatius, Montanism: Seeking the Seeds." *Vigiliae christianae* 43 (1989): 313–38.

————. "Approaching Matthew from the Second Century: The Under-used Ignatian Correspondence." *Journal for the Study of the New Testament* 20 (1984): 59–67.

————. "Ignatius 'To the Romans' and I Clement LIV–LVI." *Vigiliae christianae* 43 (1989): 35–52.

————. "The Much-Maligned Ignatius." *Expository Times* 93 (1982): 299–302.

————. "The Other Letters to the Churches of Asia: Apocalypse and Ignatius of Antioch." *Journal for the Study of the New Testament* 37 (1989): 117–35.

————. "Prophecy and Anti-episcopal Activity: A Third Error Combatted by Ignatius." *Journal of Ecclesiastical History* 34 (1983): 1–18.

————. *A Study of Ignatius of Antioch in Syria and Asia.* Studies in the Bible and Early Christianity 29. Lewiston, N.Y.: Edwin Mellen, 1992.

Tyson, Joseph B. "From History to Rhetoric and Back: Assessing New Trends in Acts Studies." Pages 23–42 in *Contextualizing Acts: Lukan Narrative and Greco-Roman Discourse.* Edited by Todd Penner and Caroline Vander Stichele. Society of Biblical Literature Symposium Series 20. Atlanta: Society of Biblical Literature, 2003.

————. "Jews and Judaism in Luke-Acts: Reading as a God-Fearer." *New Testament Studies* 41 (1995): 19–38.

Von Wahlde, Urban C. " 'The Jews' in the Gospel of John: Fifteen Years of Research (1983–1998)." *Ephemerides theologicae lovanienses* 76 (2000): 30–55.

Walker-Ramisch, S. "Graeco-Roman Voluntary Associations and the Damascus Document: A Sociological Analysis." Pages 128–45 in *Voluntary Associations in the Greco-Roman World.* Edited by John S. Kloppenborg and Stephen G. Wilson. London: Routledge, 1996.

Wander, Bernd. *Gottesfürchtige und Sympathisanten: Studien zum heidnischen Umfeld von Diasporasynagogen.* Wissenschaftliche Untersuchungen zum Neuen Testament 104. Tübingen: Mohr-Siebeck, 1998.

White, A. N. "The Early Persecutions and Roman Law Again." *Journal of Theological Studies* 3 (1952): 199–213.

————. *The Letters of Pliny.* Oxford: Clarendon, 1966.

Whittaker, Molly. *Jews and Christians: Graeco-Roman Views.* Cambridge Commentaries on Writings of the Jewish and Christian World, 200 BC to AD 200, no. 6. Cambridge: Cambridge University Press, 1984.

Wiedemann, Thomas. *Greek and Roman Slavery.* London: Croom Helm, 1981.

Wilken, Robert L. *The Christians as the Romans Saw Them.* New Haven: Yale, 1984.

————. "Diversity and Unity in Early Christianity." *Second Century* 1 (1981): 101–10.

————. "The Jews of Antioch." Pages 67–74 in *SBL Seminar Papers, 1976.* Missoula, Mont.: Scholars Press, 1976.

————. *John Chrysostom and the Jews: Rhetoric and Reality in the Late Fourth Century.* Berkeley: University of California Press, 1983.

Wilkins Michael J. "The Interplay of Ministry, Martyrdom, and Discipleship in Ignatius of Antioch." Pages 294–315 in *Worship, Theory, and Ministry in the Early Church.* Edited by Michael J. Wilkins and Terence Paige. Sheffield: JSOT Press, 1992.

Williams, A. Lukyn. *Adversus Judaeos: A Bird's Eye View of Christian Apologiae until the Renaissance.* Cambridge: Cambridge University Press, 1935.

Williams, M. H. "The Expulsion of the Jews from Rome in A.D. 19." *Latomus* 48 (1989): 765–84.

Williams, Michael A. *Rethinking "Gnosticism": An Argument for Dismantling a Dubious Category.* Princeton: Princeton University Press, 1996.

Williams, Rowan. *Arius: Heresy and Tradition.* 2d ed. Grand Rapids: Eerdmans, 2002.

Williamson, Clark M. *A Guest in the House of Israel: Post-Holocaust Church Theology.* Louisville: Westminster John Knox, 1993.

Wilson, Stephen G. "Gentile Judaizers." *New Testament Studies* 38 (1992) 605–16.

————. "'Jew' and Related Terms in the Ancient World." *Studies in Religion* 33 (2004): 157–71.

————. *Luke and the Law.* Society for New Testament Studies Monograph Series 50. Cambridge: Cambridge University Press. 1983.

————. *Related Strangers: Jews and Christians, 70–170 C.E.* Minneapolis: Fortress, 1995.

Winter, Paul. *The Trial of Jesus.* Berlin: de Gruyter, 1961.

Wisse, Frederik. "The Nag Hammadi Library and the Heresiologists." *Vigiliae christianae* 25 (1971): 205–23.

————. "Stalking Those Elusive Sethians." Pages 563–78 in vol. 2 of *The Rediscovery of Gnosticism.* Edited by Bentley Layton. 2 vols. Leiden: E. J. Brill 1980–1981.

Woolf, G. "Food, Poverty, and Patronage: The Significance of the Epigraphy of the Roman Alimentary Schemes in Early Imperial Italy." *Papers of the British School at Rome* 58 (1990): 197–228.

Young, Robin Darling. *In Procession before the World: Martyrdom as Public Liturgy in Early Christianity.* Père Marquette Lecture in Theology, 2001. Milwaukee: Marquette University Press, 2001.

Zahn, Theodor. *Ignatius von Antiochien.* Gotha: F. A. Perthes, 1873.

Zetterholm, Magnus. *The Formation of Christianity in Antioch: A Social-Scientific Approach to the Separation between Judaism and Christianity.* New York: Routledge, 2003.

Zuckerman, Constantine. "Hellenistic politeumata and the Jews: A Reconsideration." *Scripta classica israelica* 8–9 (1985–1989): 171–84.

Index of Modern Authors

Index of Names and Subjects

Index of Ancient Sources